RELIGION AND PUBLIC POLICY
Human Rights, Conflict, and Ethics

This book pivots around two principal concerns in the modern world: the nature and practice of human rights in relation to religion, and the role of religion in perennial issues of war and peace. Taken collectively, the chapters articulate a vision for achieving a liberal peace and a just society firmly grounded in respect for human rights, while working in tandem with the constructive roles that religious ideas, leaders, and institutions can play even amid cultural difference.

Topics covered include: the status and justification of human rights; the meaning and significance of religious liberty; whether human rights protections ought to be extended to other species; how the comparative study of religious ethics ought to proceed; the nature, limits, and future development of just war thinking; the role of religion and human rights in conflict resolution, diplomacy, and peace-building; and the tensions raised by religious involvement in public policy and state institutional practices. Featuring a group of distinguished contributors, this is a distinctive collection that shows a multifaceted and original exploration of cutting-edge issues with regards to the aforementioned themes.

Sumner B. Twiss is the Distinguished Professor of Human Rights, Ethics, and Religion at Florida State University, where he holds a joint appointment between the Department of Religion and the Center for the Advancement of Human Rights. He is also Professor Emeritus of Religious Studies at Brown University, where he served on the faculty for thirty years and as department chair for twelve years. He is the co-author and co-editor of seven books, and the author of more than seventy published articles in the areas of comparative religious ethics, biomedical ethics, philosophy of religion, global ethics, intercultural human rights, and the comparative study of just war.

Marian Gh. Simion is a political scientist and Orthodox theologian, currently appointed as Postdoctoral Fellow and Field Education Supervisor at Harvard Divinity School, and a past instructor in the areas of religion, government, and diplomacy at Harvard Extension School. He holds a Master of Theological Studies from Holy Cross Greek Orthodox School of Theology, and a PhD in Public and International Affairs from Northeastern University, where his academic advisor was Governor Michael S. Dukakis. His general research focuses on international security, comparative politics, political theology, religious phenomenology, Islamic jurisprudence, theory of religion, collective violence, and Orthodox Christianity.

Rodney L. Petersen is a social historian and Protestant theologian. Dr. Petersen served as executive director of the Boston Theological Institute (BTI), from 1990 until 2014, becoming director of Cooperative Metropolitan Ministries and of the Lord's Day Alliance in the US in 2014. He is a research associate at the Center for Global Christianity and Mission at Boston University School of Theology. Prior to coming to the BTI, he taught at Trinity Evangelical Divinity School and Webster University in Geneva, where he also worked with churches in France and Romania.

Religion and Public Policy
Human Rights, Conflict, and Ethics

Edited by
Sumner B. Twiss, Marian Gh. Simion,
and Rodney L. Petersen

A festschrift in honor of David Little

CAMBRIDGE
UNIVERSITY PRESS

32 Avenue of the Americas, New York, NY 10013-2473, USA

Cambridge University Press is part of the University of Cambridge.

It furthers the University's mission by disseminating knowledge in the pursuit of education, learning, and research at the highest international levels of excellence.

www.cambridge.org
Information on this title: www.cambridge.org/9781107090361

© Cambridge University Press 2015

This publication is in copyright. Subject to statutory exception and to the provisions of relevant collective licensing agreements, no reproduction of any part may take place without the written permission of Cambridge University Press.

First published 2015

Printed in the United States of America

A catalog record for this publication is available from the British Library.

ISBN 978-1-107-09036-1 Hardback

Cambridge University Press has no responsibility for the persistence or accuracy of URLs for external or third-party Internet Web sites referred to in this publication and does not guarantee that any content on such Web sites is, or will remain, accurate or appropriate.

Contents

Contributors   ix

Preface and Acknowledgments   xix
Editors

Foreword   xxi
Monica Duffy Toft

Introduction   xxviii
Sumner B. Twiss

PART ONE
Normative Prospects:
Human Rights Ideas and Religious Ethics   **1**

Chapter 1
David Little: A Modern Calvinist Architect of Human Rights   3
John Witte, Jr.

Chapter 2
On Reformed Christianity and Natural Human Rights   24
Gene Outka

Chapter 3
Roger Williams and Freedom of Conscience
and Religion as a Natural Right   45
Sumner B. Twiss

Chapter 4
Islam and Human Rights:
The Religious and the Secular in Conversation 77
Abdulaziz Sachedina

Chapter 5
On Grounding Human Rights:
Variations on Themes by Little 96
John P. Reeder, Jr.

Chapter 6
From Human Rights to Animal Rights? 120
Grace Y. Kao

Chapter 7
Nibbana, Dhamma, and Sinhala Buddhism:
A David Little Retrospective 138
Donald K. Swearer

Chapter 8
The Present State of the Comparative Study
of Religious Ethics: An Update 148
John Kelsay

**PART TWO
Functional Prospects:
Religion, Public Policy, and Conflict** **167**

Chapter 9
Religion, Ethics, and War: David Little and Ecumenical Ethics 169
J. Bryan Hehir

Chapter 10
War and the Right to Life: Orthodox Christian Perspectives 188
Marian Gh. Simion

Chapter 11
Swords to Ploughshares, Theory to Practice:
An Evolution of Religious Peacebuilding at USIP   207
Susan Hayward

Chapter 12
Religion and Multi-Track Diplomacy   222
Rodney L. Petersen

Chapter 13
Developing a Human Rights Lens on Religious Peacemaking   239
Scott Appleby

Chapter 14
Toward a Polycentric Approach to Conflict Transformation   252
Atalia Omer

Chapter 15
Rethinking Islamist Politics: Bringing the State Back In   280
Scott Hibbard

Chapter 16
Religion and Politics: Seeking a Reconciliation   307
Natalie Sherman & David Gergen

Chapter 17
The Core of Public Reason:
Freedom from Arbitrary Pain and Death   318
Christian Rice

Afterword   337
David Little

Index of Names   349

Index of Subjects   355

Contributors

Scott Appleby is Professor of History and the Marilyn Keough Dean of the Keough School of Global Affairs at the University of Notre Dame. His research examines the roots of religious violence and the potential of religious peacebuilding. Appleby co-chaired the Chicago Council on Global Affairs' Task Force on Religion and the Making of U.S. Foreign Policy, which released the influential report "Engaging Religious Communities Abroad: A New Imperative for U.S. Foreign Policy." He also directs Contending Modernities, a major multi-year project to examine the interaction among religious and secular forces in the modern world. Appleby is the author of *The Ambivalence of the Sacred: Religion, Violence and Reconciliation* (Rowman & Littlefield, 2000), and editor of *Spokesmen for the Despised: Fundamentalist Leaders of the Middle East* (University of Chicago Press, 1997). With Martin E. Marty, he co-edited the five-volume *Fundamentalism Project* (University of Chicago Press).

David Gergen is an American political commentator and former presidential advisor who served during the administrations of Richard Nixon, Gerald Ford, Ronald Reagan, and Bill Clinton. He is currently a professor of public service and co-director of the Center for Public Leadership at the Harvard Kennedy School, positions he has held for over a decade. In addition, he serves as a senior political analyst for CNN and works actively with a rising generation of new leaders. In the 1980s, he began a career in journalism and has been a regular commentator on public affairs for some 30 years. Twice he has been a member of election coverage teams that won Peabody awards. In the late 1980s, he was chief editor of *U.S. News & World Report*. He is an honors graduate of Yale and the Harvard Law School, a veteran of the U.S. Navy, and is active on many non-profit boards.

Susan Hayward is a Senior Program Officer specializing in the Religion and Peacebuilding Program at the U.S. Institute of Peace, where she develops conflict prevention, resolution and reconciliation projects targeting the religious sector. Since joining the Institute in 2007, her work has focused on Colombia, Iraq, Burma/Myanmar, and Sri Lanka. She also coordinates an initiative exploring the intersection of women, religion, conflict, and peacebuilding in partnership with the Berkley Center at Georgetown University and the World Faiths Development Dialogue. Her research interests are religious identity and conflict, interfaith engagement in the midst of political violence, and the role of religion in hampering and propelling women's work for peace and justice. Prior to joining the Institute, Hayward worked with the Academy of Educational Development's office in Colombo, Sri Lanka, as a fellow of the Program on Negotiation at Harvard Law School, and with the Conflict Resolution Program at the Carter Center in Atlanta. Hayward also conducted political asylum and refugee work with the United Nations High Commissioner for Refugees and the Minnesota Advocates for Human Rights. Her graduate studies were completed at Tufts, Harvard, and Georgetown Universities.

J. Bryan Hehir is the Parker Gilbert Montgomery Professor of the Practice of Religion and Public Life at Harvard Kennedy School. He is also the Secretary for Health Care and Social Services in the Archdiocese of Boston. His research and writing focus on ethics and foreign policy and the role of religion in world politics and in American society. He served on the faculty of Georgetown University (1984 to 1992) and the Harvard Divinity School (1993 to 2001). His writings include: "The Moral Measurement of War: A Tradition of Continuity and Change"; "Military Intervention and National Sovereignty"; "Catholicism and Democracy"; and "Social Values and Public Policy: A Contribution from a Religious Tradition."

Scott Hibbard is an associate professor at DePaul University, where he teaches courses on American foreign policy, Middle East politics, and international relations. He has been at DePaul since 2005 and spent the 2009–2010 academic year teaching at the American University of Cairo as part of a Fulbright Award from the U.S. Department of State. Hibbard received his Ph.D. from Johns Hopkins University and holds advanced degrees from the London School of Economics and Political Science and Georgetown University. He also worked in the U.S. government for twelve years, including five years as a program officer at the United States Institute of Peace and seven years as a legislative aide in the Congress.

Hibbard is the author of *Religious Politics and Secular States: Egypt, India and the United States* and co-author (with David Little) of *Islamic Activism and U.S. Foreign Policy*.

Grace Y. Kao is an associate professor of ethics and co-director of the Center for Sexuality, Gender, and Religion at the Claremont School of Theology. She is the author of *Grounding Human Rights in a Pluralist World* (Georgetown University Press, 2011) and co-editor, with Ilsup Ahn, of *Asian American Christian Ethics* (Baylor University Press, forthcoming). She serves on the Board of Directors of the Society of Christian Ethics (SCE) and on the steering committee of the Animals and Religion Group of the American Academy of Religion (AAR). Grace Y. Kao earned her Ph.D. (June 2003) from the Committee on the Study of Religion at Harvard University.

John Kelsay is Distinguished Research Professor in the Department of Religion at Florida State University. He is the author of numerous publications dealing with Muslim and Christian approaches to the ethics of war; these include *Islam and War: A Study in Comparative Ethics* (Westminster/John Knox, 1993) and *Arguing the Just War in Islam* (Harvard, 2007). In 2002–03, Kelsay received a Guggenheim Fellowship in connection with this work. Currently engaged in a study of fighting as an "individual duty" in Muslim discourse, Kelsay also serves as editor for *Soundings: An Interdisciplinary Journal*.

David Little is retired Professor of the Practice in Religion, Ethnicity, and International Conflict at Harvard Divinity School, and Associate at the Weatherhead Center for International Affairs at Harvard University. He is now a fellow at the Berkley Center for Religion, Peace, and International Affairs at Georgetown University. Until summer of 1999, he was Senior Scholar in Religion, Ethics and Human Rights at the United States Institute of Peace in Washington, DC. Before that, he taught at the University of Virginia and Yale Divinity School. From 1996 to 1998, he was member of the State Department Committee on Religious Freedom Abroad. Little was educated at the College of Wooster, Union Theological Seminary (New York), and holds a doctorate from Harvard Divinity School. He is co-author with Scott W. Hibbard of *Islamic Activism and U.S. Foreign Policy*

(1997), and is also author of volumes on Ukraine and Sri Lanka in the USIP series on religion, nationalism, and intolerance. In 2007 he published *Religion and Nationalism in Iraq: A Comparative Perspective* with (Donald K. Swearer), and *Peacemakers in Action: Profiles of Religion in Conflict Resolution*. In addition, he has published on the subjects of religion and law, religion and human rights, the history of rights and constitutionalism, and religion and peace. Cambridge University Press will soon publish his book, *Essays on Religion, Human Rights, and Public Policy: Ground To Stand On*.

Atalia Omer is an Associate Professor of Religion, Conflict, and Peace Studies at the Kroc Institute for International Peace Studies at the University of Notre Dame. She earned her PhD (November 2008) from the Committee on the Study of Religion at Harvard University. Her research interests include the theoretical study of the interrelation between religion and nationalism; religion, nationalism, and peacebuilding; the role of national/religious/ethnic diasporas in the dynamics of conflict transformation and peace; multiculturalism as a framework for conflict transformation and as a theory of justice; the role of subaltern narratives in reimagining questions of peace and justice; intra-group dialogue and the contestation of citizenship in ethno-religious national contexts; and the symbolic appropriation of the Palestinian–Israeli conflict in other zones of conflict. Her first book *When Peace is Not Enough: How the Israeli Peace Camp Thinks about Religion, Nationalism, and Justice* (University of Chicago Press, 2013) examines the way the Israeli peace camp addresses interrelationships between religion, ethnicity, and nationality and how it interprets justice vis-à-vis the Palestinian conflict.

Gene Outka taught in the Department of Religion at Princeton University for ten years, before joining the Yale faculty in 1975. He is the author of *Agape: An Ethical Analysis* and has co-edited and contributed to the following volumes: *Norm and Context in Christian Ethics* (with Paul Ramsey) and *Religion and Morality and Prospects for a Common Morality* (both with John P. Reeder, Jr.). His forthcoming volume, *God and the Moral Life: Conversations in the Augustinian Tradition*, will be published by Oxford University Press. He has also published "Universal Love and Impartiality" in the volume *The Love Commandments*. His articles appear in various journals and encyclopedias, including the *Journal of Religious Ethics*, *Religious Studies Review*, the *Journal* of *Religion*, the *Journal of the Society of Christian Ethics*, the *Kennedy Institute of Ethics Journal*, the *Dictionary of Christian Ethics*, the *Encyclopedia of Ethics*, *The Thomist*, the *Routledge Encyclopedia of Philosophy*, *The Companion to Philosophy of Religion*, *The Blackwell Companion to Religious Ethics*, and the *Oxford Handbook of Theological Ethics*. From 1992 to 1995, he chaired Yale's Department of Religious Studies. He was also president of the Society of Christian Ethics in 2001.

Rodney L. Petersen served as executive director of the Boston Theological Institute (BTI), from 1990 until 2014, becoming director of Cooperative Metropolitan Ministries and of the Lord's Day Alliance in the United States in 2014. He is a research associate in the Center for Global Christianity and Mission, Boston University School of Theology. Prior to coming to the BTI he taught at Trinity Evangelical Divinity School and Webster University in Geneva where he also worked with churches in France and Romania. He has taught and run workshops on track-two diplomacy in many regions of the world. He worked with the Decade to Overcome Violence of the World Council of Churches (2001–2011), teaching at United Theological College of the West Indies, a part of the International Ecumenical Peace Convocation in Jamaica (2011). He participated as faculty in the Global Ecumenical Theological Institute (GETI) attached to the 10th General Assembly of the World Council of Churches in Korea. In addition to teaching in BTI member schools and overseas, he is founding co-director (2001) of the Religion and Conflict Transformation program now housed at Boston University School of Theology, teaching in the areas of history and ethics. He serves on several local and national committees of the Presbyterian Church (USA). His publications include *Forgiveness and Reconciliation: Religion, Public Policy and Conflict Transformation* (2002); *Overcoming Violence. Religion, Conflict and Peacebuilding* (2011); and *Formation for Life: Just Peacemaking and Twenty–First Century Discipleship* (Wipf and Stock, 2013).

John P. Reeder, Jr. is Professor of Religious Studies Emeritus at Brown University. He works principally in Western ethics and Christian thought, with comparative interests in Judaic and Buddhist thought. His major areas include theories of religion and morality; the notion of a common morality; concepts of justice, love, and care; and issues about taking life. He edited and contributed to two volumes with Gene Outka, *Religion and*

Morality (Doubleday 1973) and *Prospects for a Common Morality* (Princeton 1993). He published *Source, Sanction, and Salvation: Religion and Morality in Judaic and Christian Traditions* (Prentice–Hall 1988) and *Killing and Saving: Abortion, Hunger, and War* (Penn State 1996). With Donald Swearer he taught an NEH Summer Seminar for College Teachers and he has been a visitor at Yale (Fall 1979), Amherst College (1984–5), where he was Henry Luce Professor of Comparative Religious Ethics, and Princeton (1996–7). He taught again at Amherst (2003–4) and was a Visiting Professor of Ethics at Harvard Divinity School (2006–9).

Christian Rice is the Assistant Dean for Civic Engagement and Visiting Assistant Professor of Philosophy and Religious Studies at Ursinus College. He attended Harvard Divinity School, receiving a Master of Divinity in 2001 and a Doctorate of Theology in 2008. Rice returned to Ursinus, his alma mater, in 2008, when he was hired to direct the College's civic engagement initiatives. He has overseen the expansion of the Ursinus Bonner Program and was instrumental in the creation of UCARE—the Ursinus Center for Advocacy, Responsibility, and Engagement. Rice teaches in the Philosophy and Religious Studies department, teaching courses on world religions, religious ethics, and religion's relationship to human rights. He also coordinates the College's Peace and Social Justice minor and its Peace Corps Prep Program.

Abdulaziz Sachedina is Professor and Endowed IIIT Chair in Islamic Studies at George Mason University, teaching mainly subjects associated with Islam. He has been a professor for 35 years, beginning in 1976. He annually teaches courses on Classical Islam, Islam in the Modern Age, Islam, Democracy and Human Rights, Islamic Bioethics and Muslim Theology. He was born in Tanzania, his heritage originally is from India. He has an MA/PhD from the University of Toronto and has BA degrees from Aligarh Muslim University in India and Ferdowsi University of Mashad in Iran. He was one of the students of Dr. Ali Shariati in Iran. In 1998, Grand Ayatollah Sistani issued a statement against Sachedina that advised Muslims not to listen to his talks or to ask him questions about religious matters. In addition to his work at the university, Professor Sachedina has been a consultant to the Department of Defense regarding Middle Eastern affairs and was an adviser to those drafting the Constitution of Iraq that was put into effect in 2005.

Natalie Sherman is a business reporter for the *Baltimore Sun*. She previously worked at the *Boston Herald* and the New Bedford *Standard-Times* reporting on city politics and economic development, education and crime. She was named the 2013 "Rising Star" by the New England Society of Newspaper Editors and her work has been recognized with awards from the New England Newspaper & Press Association in the areas of business, religious and investigative reporting. Prior to journalism, she worked as a researcher/writer in Argentina and Mexico for the *Let's Go* travel guides. Natalie graduated cum laude from Harvard in 2008 with a concentration in Social Studies and served as a researcher for David Gergen from 2009 to 2011.

Marian Gh. Simion is a political scientist and Orthodox theologian; currently appointed as Postdoctoral Fellow and Field Education Supervisor at Harvard Divinity School, and a past Instructor in the areas of religion, government, and diplomacy at Harvard Extension School. He holds a Master of Theological Studies from Holy Cross Greek Orthodox School of Theology, and a PhD in Public and International Affairs from Northeastern University, where his academic advisor was Governor Michael S. Dukakis. His general research focuses on international security, comparative politics, political theology, religious phenomenology, Islamic jurisprudence, theory of religion, collective violence, and Orthodox Christianity. A native of Romania, Dr. Simion studied Orthodox theology, as well as East-European philology and history for six years in Craiova and Bucharest. He possesses advanced knowledge of several European languages, and has solid expertise in post–Cold War politics, Pan–Slavism, nationalism, politics of identity, and in East European and Balkan history, culture, and religion. He is the founder of the Institute for Peace Studies in Eastern Christianity (IPSEC)—a research institute created to advance the field of peace studies in Orthodox Christianity, to function as a think tank, and to offer strategic advice to policymakers and spiritual leaders on issues of religion in the public life. Dr. Simion works as the Assistant Director of the Boston Theological Institute (where in 2001 he founded the *BTI Magazine*). He is Adjunct Assistant Professor of Religious Studies and Administrator of the Religious Studies program at Hellenic College in Brookline, MA. Dr. Simion taught Orthodox theological ethics at Boston College for six years. He serves on the scientific and editorial boards of several journals, including *The Romanian Journal of Economics* (of the Romanian Academy of Arts and Sciences), *Studii Teologice* (of the Romanian Patriarchate), and others. He is the author of several works in the area of religion and violence, including *Religion and Political Conflict: From Dialectics to Cross–Domain Charting* (Montréal: Presses internationales polytechnique, 2011, with contributions from David Little, Ambassador Mihnea Motoc, and Ecumenical Patriarch Bartholomew); *Just Peace: Orthodox Perspectives* (Geneva: WCC Publications, 2012); and others. During the past two years Dr. Simion chaired the committee on health and religion at the US Association for the Club of Rome, and contributed to its yearly think tank reports during the past three years as a member. He has a passion for music and in the early 1990s, at a very young age, he was awarded a position of professional baritone in the choir of the Romanian National Opera.

Donald K. Swearer spent a distinguished career at Swarthmore College, where, from 1992 to 2004, he was the Charles & Harriet Cox McDowell Professor of Religion. From 2004 until 2010 he was Distinguished Visiting Professor of Buddhist Studies at Harvard Divinity School and served as director of the Center for the Study of World Religions. Swearer's scholarly work has ranged widely in comparative and Asian religions. His is major fields of research include Buddhism in Southeast Asia, especially Thailand; comparative religious ethics; and Buddhist-Christian dialogue. His recent monographs include *Becoming the Buddha: The Ritual of Image Consecration in Thailand* (Princeton, 2004), *The Buddhist World of Southeast Asia* 2nd rev. ed. (SUNY, 2009).

Monica Duffy Toft is at the Blavatnk School of Government, University of Oxford, having taught previously at Harvard's Kennedy School. She was educated at the University of Chicago (MA and PhD in political science) and the University of California, Santa Barbara (BA in political science and Slavic languages and literature, summa cum laude). Prior to starting her undergraduate education, she spent four years in the United States Army as a Russian linguist. Monica is a member of the Council on Foreign Relations, the Minorities at Risk Advisory Board, the Political Instability

Task Force, and in 2008 the Carnegie Foundation of New York named her a Carnegie Scholar for her research on religion and violence. Most recently she was awarded a Fulbright Scholarship to Norway.

Sumner B. Twiss is the Distinguished Professor of Human Rights, Ethics, and Religion at Florida State University, where he holds a joint appointment between the Department of Religion and the Center for the Advancement of Human Rights, and he is also Professor Emeritus of Religious Studies at Brown University, where he served on the faculty for thirty years and as department chair for twelve years. He is the co-author or co-editor of seven books (as well as a contributor to them), and the author of over seventy published articles in the areas of comparative religious ethics, biomedical ethics, philosophy of religion, global ethics, intercultural human rights, and the comparative study of just war. He is former co-editor of the *Journal of Religious Ethics* (2001–2011) and the *Annual of the Society of Christian Ethics* (1995–2001), as well as former senior editor of the book series *Advancing Human Rights* (2003–2008). He is currently completing two additional book projects: *Chinese Just War Ethics: Origin, Development, and Dissent* (co-editor, with P.C. Lo, and co-author of three chapters; forthcoming from Routledge), and *The Practices of Global Ethics: Historical Developments, Current Issues, and Contemporary Prospects* (co-author with F. Bird et al). His recent teaching has focused on such topics as: Confucian moral and political thought; crimes against humanity and international criminal justice; the law and ethics of torture; religion, politics, and genocide; and the history and ethics of humanitarian intervention.

John Witte, Jr. is Jonas Robitscher Professor of Law, Alonzo L. McDonald Distinguished Professor, and Director of the Center for the Study of Law and Religion Center at Emory University. A specialist in legal history, marriage law, and religious liberty, he has published 220 articles, 15 journal symposia, and 27 books. Recent book titles include: *Sex, Marriage and Family Life in John Calvin's Geneva*, 2 vols. (Eerdmans, 2005, 2015); *Modern Christian Teachings on Law, Politics, and Human Nature*, 3 vols. (Columbia University Press, 2006); *God's Joust, God's Justice: Law and Religion in the Western Tradition* (Eerdmans, 2006); *The Reformation of Rights: Law, Religion, and Human Rights in Early Modern Calvinism* (Cambridge University Press, 2007); *Christianity and Law: An Introduction* (Cambridge University Press, 2008); *The Sins of the*

Fathers: The Law and Theology of Illegitimacy Reconsidered (Cambridge University Press, 2009); *Christianity and Human Rights: An Introduction* (Cambridge University Press, 2010); *Religion and the American Constitutional Experiment* (Westview, 3d ed. 2011); *Religion and Human Rights: An Introduction* (Oxford University Press, 2012); *From Sacrament to Contract: Marriage, Religion, and Law in the Western Tradition* (Westminster John Knox Press, 2d ed., 2012); *No Establishment of Religion: America's Original Contribution to Religious Liberty* (Oxford University Press, 2012); and *The Western Historical Case for Monogamy over Polygamy* (Cambridge University Press, 2015). Professor Witte's writings have appeared in 15 languages, and he has delivered more than 350 public lectures throughout North America, Europe, Japan, Israel, Hong Kong, Australia, and South Africa. With major funding from the Pew, Ford, Lilly, Luce, and McDonald foundations, he has directed 12 major international projects on democracy, human rights, and religious liberty, and on marriage, family, and children. These projects have collectively yielded more than 160 new volumes and 250 public forums around the world. He edits two major book series, "Studies in Law and Religion," and "Religion, Marriage and Family." He has been selected twelve times by the Emory law students as the Most Outstanding Professor and has won dozens of other awards and prizes for his teaching and research.

Preface and Acknowledgments

Editors

Many of the chapters of this volume are based on papers originally presented at a Conference on Religion, Ethics, and Peace, co-sponsored by Harvard Divinity School and the Kroc Institute for International Peace Studies (University of Notre Dame), and held at Harvard in November 2009. The Boston Theological Institute (BTI) provided the resources for the production of the camera-ready manuscript and is co-publisher of the volume along with Cambridge University Press.

The editors want especially to acknowledge David Little's role in prompting the schools of BTI to become more attentive to issues of religion, human rights, conflict, and ethics following the tragic events associated with 9–11.

Chapter eight, "The Present State of the Comparative Study of Religious Ethics: An Update" by John Kelsay, appeared in a slightly different version in the *Journal of Religious Ethics* 40.4 (December 2012): 583–602, and we thank Wiley Blackwell for gratis permission to use that material. In addition, we wish to acknowledge financial support from Florida State University's Center for the Advancement of Human Rights in hiring Jeffrey Gottlieb, a doctoral candidate in the Department of Religion, to provide invaluable copy-editing assistance to the editors.

The editors worked on this volume as a labor of respect and love for David Little, and they shared their editorial responsibilities equally. Marian Simion's technical expertise in producing camera-ready copy and the index is especially noted. While Sumner Twiss wrote the volume's Introduction, the other two editors concurred in its content. We would be remiss if we failed to acknowledge our deep gratitude to all the chapters' authors, to Monica Toft Duffy for her Foreword, and to David Little himself for his Afterword.

Foreword

Monica Duffy Toft

What began as a local political controversy in Denmark became a global crisis.[1] The publication of a series of twelve cartoons depicting the prophet Mohamed in the Danish newspaper *Jyllands-Posten* in 2005 resulted in mass demonstrations throughout the world, the destruction of churches and mosques, economic boycotts, and the death of scores of people in the Middle East and Asia. This "Cartoons Controversy" both highlighted critical questions about the line between freedom of expression and respect for global religious traditions, and underscored the difficulty contemporary states have had in accommodating religion in the political arena.

Be it religious minorities in Western democracies who want their traditions respected and elevated as pitted against secular majorities (e.g., France), or religious majorities in the Middle East who want a larger and freer role for religion in their public lives despite the presence of religious minorities and advocates of a more secular role for religion (e.g., Egypt, Israel, Turkey), domestic and international religious controversies have emerged as a critical issue confronting governments over the past decade. Issues like these add a sense of immediacy to the concerns of human rights, conflict, and ethics, the concerns of this book on religion and public policy.

As religious ideas, institutions, and actors move toward center stage across the globe, policy makers and academics struggle to understand why religion has become so prominent, and what the implications of this emergence may be for politics and policy. Although this resurgence began in the late 1960s and has continued well into the twenty-first century, recent events in the Arab world underscore the continued importance of religion. Islamic-based parties that won substantial majorities in Egypt and Tunisia and the Taliban seem poised for a comeback in Afghanistan, as foreign forces negotiate their own departures. This contemporary reality—in which understanding religion in all its facets has become increasingly necessary in order to understand and influence world politics—was not supposed to happen.

One of the reasons scholars and practitioners missed religion's resurgence was due to the dominance of a particular way of thinking; notably ideas about modernization and the processes of secularization, which predicted that religion would recede, not resurge.[2] Any religious sentiment would be relegated to the private sphere and certainly not impact the public square. Such ran the logic of thinking in government offices and college classrooms.

Former United States Secretary of State Madeleine Albright succumbed to such thinking, and the blind spots it engendered compelled her to write a book about it. As she explains, in the State Department of the 1990s religion as a source of motivation was ignored; it was seen as "echoes of earlier, less enlightened times, not a sign of battles to come."[3] She then admits that it was she who was stuck in an earlier time: "Like many other foreign policy professionals, I have had to adjust to the lens through which I view the world, comprehending something that seemed to be a new reality but that had actually been evident for some time." In reading the book one is left with the impression of a kind of confessional: perhaps a way to expiate her sin of allowing a secularist mind-set to blind her to important opportunities and threats in the play of events around her.

It is not just policy makers who missed the resurgence of religion. Teaching at one of the world's best schools of public policy—Harvard's Kennedy School—for also revealed a fundamental lack of respect for religion as a lens and lever of international affairs. Two episodes stand out. The first involved a student in my class on Religion in Global Politics, a course I co-taught with David Little and Bryan Hehir. As an ordained Catholic priest, Hehir showed up to class each week wearing the same thing, a priest's suit, which is a basic black suit and white collar. Well into the semester, after class one day a student asked: does Professor Hehir always wear the same? My otherwise worldly student did not know that *Professor* Hehir was also *Father* Hehir and as such he dressed as a priest. Perhaps the most remarkable thing about this comment was how unremarkable it has become in academic settings. Both ignorance of religion and theology in general, and their relevance to global politics remain widespread, *and approvingly so.*

The second involved one of my colleagues, a scholar of global politics (but not one of religion) in his own right. Shortly after September 11, 2001, and the terrible events of that day involving religiously inspired men killing innocents in the name of God, he asked me whether I thought religion really mattered. The story does not end there. A year later he heard me conversing with another colleague and he inquired again, "Does religion really matter, can it really help us to understand 9–11 and subsequent events?" My response was the same as the first time: read Mohammed Atta's letter. Atta, the chief 9–11 bomber, penned a "martyr" letter which was later found in the wreckage of the World Trade Center's twin towers. In it he explains why he did what he did (for Allah and Islam), and in line with religious teachings and, in exquisite detail, what should be done with his body (an odd request given that his body was unlikely to survive the destruction of his act). In any event, my highly esteemed colleague's inability to grasp how religion could and did motivate *rational people* to sacrifice their lives in an attack on the world's most powerful state, only served to underscore my field's general lack of understanding of how religion operates to motivate people in the world today.

The importance of Atta's letter lies not only in its emphasis on the role of his faith in shaping his and his expected audience's understanding of his actions but also in the shock and wide publicity of those actions as a watershed. For most political and social elites in the United States, 11 September is remembered as a clarion call of the rise of religion—or in this case an extreme interpretation of some precepts of Islam—as a national security issue, broadly conceived. But this is to misconstrue when and how religion came to play its increasingly important role in global politics. A report by the Chicago Council on Foreign Relations, for instance, notes that by the Fall of 2011 the trend was already two decades old. Yet even the Council's estimate understates the length of the trend: the real increase—or more accurately, resurgence—in the influence of religion began in the late 1960s, and has accelerated ever since.[4]

The 1960s saw the Catholic Church, for example, undergo a fundamental reassessment of what it means to be a Catholic, Christian, a human. Under Vatican II, no longer did the Catholic Church hold that one needed to be Catholic to be afforded basic dignity and respect. After Vatican II it was enough to be human. As a direct consequence, local actors began to challenge autocratic regimes (and, in some cases, Vatican II put local clergy into difficult circumstances because they were allies of these same regimes). Similar dynamics were at play during the 1980s when Pope John Paul II challenged communist regimes in Eastern Europe, offering local citizens an alternative set of ideas and ideals based in religion, emboldening Catholic Poles and Lutheran Germans to shake off the repressive, atheistic system that had oppressed them for four decades.

The 1979 Iranian Revolution is also revealing. The locus of resistance to the Shah was not the streets of Tehran in 1979 (where it was most visible), but earlier and within the universities and mosques. Students, teachers, and imams challenged basic understandings of what it meant to be Shī'a. The reinterpretations that began in the 1960s paved the way for revolution; a revolution that has, as with all revolutions, been forced to accommodate itself to the difficulties of interaction with the real world system of states, but one which remains central to the identity of Iran and the legitimacy of its rulers and their policies today. Some two decades after this revolution, a striking feature about the 2008 demonstrations against the government in Iran was that no one questioned whether the government in Iran should be Islamic. Iran is and will remain an Islamic Republic.

Religion is part of our landscape, yet much confusion and fear remains about what that role should or might be. Staunch secularists oppose the very idea of religion in politics because they continue to hold to the view that religion is necessarily irrational, repressive, regressive, and destructive, and that secularism is the only logical and preferred path. Such a stance is myopic at best. First, religion is not inherently irrational, repressive or regressive. In fact, the contrary is more often the case. Measurement *is* a critical issue here: we tend to recognize and remember harm related to religion, and miss and forget the good. The chapters in this book provide ample illustrations of the religious roots of human rights and ethics. Yes, religion and violence might be paired, but at least as often, if so not more, are religion and peace.

In examining efforts at democratization over the past four decades, for example, my co-authors and I discovered that religious actors were often the critical leaders in efforts to make governments more accountable and transparent to their citizenry. Who did these religious leaders go up against? In a fair number of cases, it was highly secularized regimes, from the communist states in Eastern Europe to the socialist and Baathist regimes in the Middle East. Similarly, religious actors were typically at the forefront of those who brought peace in the aftermath of civil conflict during the 1970s, 1980s and 1990s. Sudan owes the end of its second civil war between the North and the South to former Senator John Danforth, whose status as an ordained priest provided much needed trust between the two parties. In Mozambique, a lay Catholic organization, the Community of Sant'Egidio, helped to usher in peace after 15 years of civil war: their religiously inspired principles of friendship, trust and a commitment to peace persuaded both warring parties that a mediated resolution was possible.

The impact of religion in civil matters is of course not only salutary, nor is it at the heart of every political crisis, or even always a critical element; it is multifaceted, just as religious-inspired actors can bring about peace, they can foment war and terrorism. Moreover, this is not to say that religion is at the heart of every political crisis or is even the critical element, but the essays in this volume illustrate its pervasive significance.

Religion is not necessarily the sole driving force of much of the large-scale violence we see today. Since 1940 only about one-third of all civil wars have had a religious basis, and of these only about half featured religion as a central issue. Nationalism remains a powerful peer competitor, and more often than not religion is married to nationalism.[5] Sri Lanka is a case in point in which the religious tenets of the two warring parties—Buddhism and Hinduism—are intermingled with concepts of homeland and territory. Similar dynamics were at work in the troubles in Northern Ireland between the Catholics and the Protestants, as well as with the Croat Catholics, Serb Orthodox, Bosnian and Kosovar Muslims in Yugoslavia. Nationalism mixed with religion to create a volatile situation. Religion alone is rarely the sole culprit. Moreover, we need to keep in mind that it is not religion per se, but the politicization of religion, how it is interpreted and mobilized by elites and masses alike.

Again consider the 1979 Iranian Revolution, which is about as close as we get to a religiously motivated political event. A common narrative interferes with our understanding of what happened. That narrative invokes the image of religiously inspired (read: irrational), hot-headed mobs spontaneously rising to overwhelm and overturn established order (the international news media remain somewhat complicit in this: when was the last time you can remember seeing "Iranians" on television doing anything other than glowering, shouting, or threatening?). But had the Shah not previously made such a hash of Iran's economy and political system, revolution would not have succeeded. The country was ripe for revolution; whether religiously inspired or not. Ayatollah Khomeini and his followers were enterprising, and acted strategically: they returned from exile just in time to tip the already tottering apple cart (just as Vladimir Lenin did in Russia in 1917). Even in this case, religion and religious motivation were only part of the story. It is this aspect of unraveling religion, its role in violence and peace, and its implications for policy that has made research into the dynamics so complex and frustrating, and yet exciting.

I conclude by emphasizing three points. First, religious actors, like nationalist actors, are not *ipso facto* irrational actors. An excessively narrow conception of human rationality (and by extension, state rationality) has restricted the understanding of rational motivation in the West to the fear of death, and to a desire to protect tangible interests alone. Both the collapse of the Soviet Union (where nationalism and religion played primary roles) and the more recent Arab Spring (with economics, nationalism, religion, and demography all as significant motivators), were poorly anticipated by Western governments as a result of fallacious assumptions about the actors and processes involved, leading to blind spots in their officials' abilities to predict important *political* events.

Second, the interaction of faith and politics has both productive and destructive potential. The better question is not *whether*, but *under what circumstances*, religion may be either dangerous or constructive in local, regional, and global political contexts. Until religion is taken more seriously among those responsible for planning and negotiating global outcomes, we are apt to continue to be blind-sided in the future by major political shifts affecting the lives of millions.

Finally, because religion has always been in the communication business in the transmission of norms, practices, and ways of life, we should consider the interaction of media with religion. The global media communications revolution of the past three decades has empowered religion in profound and unanticipated ways. Religion in politics is here to stay, and recognizing this is the first and most important step in accommodating ourselves to the best and the worst that the interaction has to offer. This book outlines some of the implications for public policy, human rights, and ethics, as well informing us about the nature of and prospect for conflict and peace.

NOTES

[1] Jytte Klausen, *The Cartoons That Shook the World* (New Haven: Yale University Press, 2009).

[2] An excellent overview of modernization theory and secularism can be found in Pippa Norris and Ronald Inglehart, *Sacred and Secular: Religion and Politics Worldwide* (Cambridge: Cambridge University Press, 2004).

[3] Madeleine Albright, *The Mighty and the Almighty: Reflections on America, God, and World Affairs* (New York: Harper Collins Publishers, 2006), 9.

[4] Monica Duffy Toft, Daniel Philpott, and Timothy Samuel Shah, *God's Century: Resurgent Religion and Global Politics* (New York: Norton, 2011).

[5] Mark Juergensmeyer, *The New Cold War: Religious Nationalism Confronts the Secular State* (Berkeley, CA: University of California Press, 1993).

Introduction

Sumner B. Twiss

Background

Over four years ago, Harvard University hosted a conference on religion, politics, and human rights in honor of David Little's academic career and impending retirement. The conference presentations addressed various aspects of his scholarship by connecting his work to topics and issues of contemporary importance. All of the presentations were themselves original contributions to the fields representing Little's interests. In light of this fact, conference presenters were invited to submit papers based on their presentations for a festschrift that would continue to honor Little's scholarship for a broader and more public audience. In a few instances, additional or supplemental chapters were solicited. The result, long aborning, is the present volume.

Little's areas of scholarship and teaching span human rights and religious freedom; religion, war, and peacemaking; religion and politics (both international and domestic); and the theory and practice of religious ethics (including both comparative ethics and theological ethics). All of our authors are quite well-known for their previous scholarship in these areas, which, in turn, means that this volume is more than a festschrift—though it is certainly that as well—since it can stand on its own in drawing attention to and critically exploring pertinent cutting-edge issues. The book is divided into two major parts: normative prospects regarding human rights and religious ethics; and functional prospects regarding religion, conflict, and public policy. The most important thread that runs throughout the entire volume is human rights—how they are properly conceptualized; their historical, religious, and philosophical sources; their violation in various contexts; their role in helping to resolve conflict and achieve justice; how they might be supported by myriad religious and cultural traditions; and how they might be extended to protection of the environment and other species. What follows is a sketch of the contributing chapters, beginning, quite appropriately, with those relating to human rights and religion, especially religious freedom.

Human Rights Ideas and Religious Ethics

In casting Little in the role as a modern Calvinist architect of human rights thinking, John Witte draws attention to the fact that there was an ample legacy of natural or human rights development well before the Enlightenment, dating back to medieval canon law, Scholastic theology, and then Protestant Reformed thinkers. In the last regard and following upon Little's hermeneutical human rights scholarship, Witte's own considerable work on the Reformation and human rights clearly foregrounds the Calvinist contributions to the freedom of conscience and religion as the mother (or at least midwife) of many other human rights, the equality of all faiths before the law (even if sometimes only honored in the breach), the ecclesial restructuring of liberty and order in the church and its implications for a robust constitutional theory of republican government, and, in the recognition of human sinfulness, the particular need to provide safeguards against abuse of state power. In addition, the Calvinist contribution clearly coordinated human rights with human duties and responsibilities in an integrated approach that serves as a model even today.

Witte characterizes the modern human rights regime as a dynamic and progressive one that presupposes fundamental moral, social, and political values that fill the role of a *ius gentium* (common law of peoples), offering middle axioms for moral and political discourse in international and domestic settings. He also believes that this dynamic process is partly dependent on, and driven by, the transcendent principles continually being refined by religious communities in their own attempts to advance human welfare and social justice. For Witte, then, there is a constructive alliance between religious traditions of varying sorts and the regime of human rights, law, and democracy. Such is his vision for the present and the future.

Much like Witte, Gene Outka examines the Calvinist background of Little's work on human rights—especially the role of the law of love, the derivative theory of natural law, fundamental moral imperatives inscribed on the heart of humankind, and the distinction between the spiritual (religious) and civil (moral-political) spheres. In so doing, Outka is careful to highlight the trajectory in Little's scholarship that moves from John Calvin's theology and its conservative and liberal strands to an ever increasing interest in two of Calvin's heirs—John Locke and Roger Williams—who followed Calvin's more liberal strand in their more radical thinking about freedom of religion and a stricter separation of the spiritual and civil spheres of authority. After noting that Little himself embraces this more radical line of thought as a way to understand some of the roots of the Universal Declaration of Human Rights (especially Article 18 on freedom of religion), Outka is inclined to press Little on what remains, practically speaking, of his Calvinist background. In this regard, Outka poses some pointed questions which he leaves for Little to answer: Is the natural law still seen to be in some sort of intimate relation with a more inclusive theological and moral design? Is there any place left for the role of the institutional church in human rights development? What role do theological beliefs play in Little's current thought about human rights? And would Little use (and how exactly) natural human rights in appraising the comparative adequacy of Christian ethical schemes?

Sumner Twiss's chapter works within the human rights legacy forged by Little, by focusing attention on the arguments of one of Little's heroes—Roger Williams. The concern here is to interpret and accurately reconstruct Williams's defense of freedom of conscience and religion as a natural right. Twiss identifies four lines of argument in Williams's corpus: an argument from divine right and will, which takes both a theocentric form (God's conferral of such a right on humans) and a Christocentric form (Christ takes an interest in seeing this soul-right protected); an argument from natural justice, which invokes the natural moral law (embodied in the second table of the Decalogue) and then uses reason and the Golden Rule to derive equal recognition and protection of this right; an argument from the inviolability of conscience, which links conscience and personal and social moral identity in order to show what is at stake in their violation—namely, the destruction of moral personality (via soul-rape) and of religious communities (via a kind of piracy); and, finally, an argument from consensual government, whereby people use their natural power (liberty) to consent to establish a civil government in order to protect and advance their rights and interests, including most fundamentally freedom of conscience and religion, subject only to the constraint of not being used to harm or tyrannize others in the society. Twiss makes the point that the last three arguments can stand on their own apart from Williams's own theological beliefs, and he attempts to show that freedom of conscience and religion as an inalienable immunity grounded in equal dignity and people's life-conceptions—the position put forth in contemporary human rights instruments—is consonant with Williams's own conception of that right. In fact, Twiss suggests that Williams's vivid metaphors of what is at stake in respecting this right—through casting its violation as a kind of rape and piracy—are more resonant with people of conscience than the somewhat antiseptic language used by current human rights advocates.

In contrast with the preceding chapters but also complementing them as well, Abdulaziz Sachedina takes up the subject of freedom of conscience and religion from an Islamic perspective. In general terms, Sachedina holds that there is a core of fundamental principles regarding what is self-subsistingly evil and what is self-subsistently good that are broadly shared by different traditions and cultures, whether or not they have explicitly embraced the language of human rights. He then argues that it is entirely possible to build on the classical heritage of Islam an acknowledgement of universal human rights that correspond to secularly derived human rights. Sachedina claims that past Islamic human rights declarations (e.g., The Cairo Declaration) made no real, authentic, or concerted effort to develop such a linkage, but he suggests that such development is possible by connecting human rights with the bedrock Islamic idea that natural law is the divine endowment for humanity of a moral nature capable of discerning by reason what this law requires. This, says Sachedina, is the classical Sunni-Mu`tazilite position, which, though countered by the Sunni-Ash`ari position that God alone determines what is good or bad, nonetheless informed the context of classical Islam's need to make possible the peaceful co-existence of peoples with different creeds while under Islamic political rule. Sachedina further argues that the insight making this possibility a reality was the belief that—whether known by reason or revelation (or both)—God requires his people to treat Peoples of the Book (e.g., Jews and Christians) with tolerance without denying the validity of their alternative spiritual paths in the world. Thus does Islam support the freedom of conscience and religion for all within its sphere of influence and possibly more universally as well.

The remaining chapters in the first part of the volume are a bit more theoretical than the preceding four. They intend to explore the underpinnings of both human rights philosophy and comparative religious ethics through engagement with Little's work in these areas, which, in turn, inform his and others' contributions to religious human rights, animal rights, the ethics of war and peace, and the nexus of religion, nationalism, and politics.

John Reeder's chapter is cast in the form (and style) of an amicus brief that not only dissects the basic components of Little's position on human rights but also raises critical philosophical and methodological issues for its further development and defense. Thus, Reeder examines the epistemology of Little's moral intuitional grounding for human rights and in particular his fundamental principle that it is irrational and wrong deliberately to inflict pain or injury on another for purely self-interested reasons or to refuse to alleviate or mitigate another's pain or suffering at minimal cost to self. Reeder argues that, for Little, this principle is *per se nota*—knowable, indubitable, and absolute as it stands—upon which Little then develops arguments for filling out the content of human rights, taking into account features of human nature, human relationships, human vulnerability, and the human good. In developing his analysis of Little's position, Reeder is careful to compare and contrast that position with certain of its rivals—for example, neo-pragmatism, Nietzschean skepticism, and other forms of moral intuitionism. Most important in this regard, argues Reeder, are the epistemological and justificatory challenges posed by recent non-foundationalist moral pragmatisms.

By contrast with Reeder, Grace Kao takes Little's position as a given for the sake of argument in order to explore its possible limits or further implications. Her test case is that of non-human animal pain and injury, and she argues that Little's basic principle can and should be extended to non-humans at least insofar as torture, cruel treatment, and an analogue to enslavement (e.g., restricting animal freedom of movement) are concerned. Kao suggests that, with the growing recognition of the practical entanglement of human and animal interests in the environmental movement, human rights ought to be expanded to make room for and protect not only "human dignity" but also "the dignity of the creature" as well.

Donald Swearer follows a different trajectory of Little's work, by comparing and contrasting his earlier work on Theravada Buddhist ethics—informed by the typological and analytical framework of his co-authored *Comparative Religious Ethics*—with his later work on Sinhala Buddhism in the context of the Sinhala-Tamil conflict. From Swearer's point of view, Little's earlier work was ahistorical, static, and wooden to a fault. But, he suggests, Little's later work is contextually and historically sensitive and does a good job in showing how the sacred legends synthesized by Buddhist monks were used to give special authority to the Sinhala as a chosen people and encouraging in the Sinhalese a sense of entitlement to preserve and protect the preeminence of the tradition by the use of violence. From Swearer's perspective, this later work validates a more particularistic, historical approach in the field of comparative religious ethics.

John Kelsay's chapter takes up the challenge set forth by Swearer's vision, by defending the use of taxonomies and classification schemes in comparative religious ethics. For Kelsay, without such categories as laid out and deployed in *Comparative Religious Ethics*, it is difficult to say what counts as cognitive achievement (knowledge) in comparative religious ethics and what constitutes the latter as a recognizable discipline. He argues that studies of ethics are characterized in part by the way they take groups of people to respond to existential issues—for example, life, death, suffering, violence, and sex—especially the way that such groups develop formal institutions to address them. He further argues that what particularly interests ethicists—constituting their distinctive contributions to human knowledge—is describing, analyzing, and explaining procedures of argument and institutional patterns of reasoning about such existential issues. Thus, while Kelsay is open to Swearer's historical contextualization, he refuses to remain content with only edifying particularistic studies that lack the categories and conceptualizations needed to produce anything more than mere interesting curiosities from the human world of social and moral relations. If one aspires to knowledge attained by disciplined analysis and comparative exploration of reasons and arguments, then, according to Kelsay and *contra* Swearer, typologies are sorely needed.

Religion, Public Policy, and Conflict

It is fast becoming a truism that human rights and their significance are best understood and appreciated in their violation—when they are denied, not respected, or otherwise infringed. One of the principal contexts for such violation—often on a massive scale—is war, whether international or civil. In the West, at least since the time of St. Augustine, Christian thinkers have meditated on the ethics of war—when is it morally justified, who has the authority to undertake it, is it subject to constraints or limits, and so forth. All of these topics, among others, have come to be conceptualized under the broad rubrics of *ius ad bellum* (justice in going to war) and *ius in bello* (justice in the conduct of war). Bryan Hehir's chapter discusses these and other matters, but his signal contribution is the provision of clarifying chronologies and typologies, ranging from phases of development in the ethics of war (e.g., classical period, World War II, Cold War era) to types of war (classic interstate, post–Cold War intrastate ethnonational conflict, transnational terrorism by non-state actors) and their respective singular features. Of particular interest to Hehir are the problematic of state sovereignty and the principle of non-intervention in the domestic affairs of other states, the emerging trend of humanitarian intervention to rescue peoples from massive human rights abuses perpetrated by their own governments, and the apparent nexus of religion and the use of lethal force in transnational terrorism and how to interdict or otherwise deal with non-state actors who eschew the law of war, including their violation of the widely accepted norm of non-combatant immunity by directly targeting civilians. While Hehir does not resolve these issues, he is correct in emphasizing the need to address them in creative and principled ways. His chapter also has the virtue of putting peace and peacebuilding on the agenda of any future development in the ethics and law of war, thus providing the appropriate context for the other chapters in this section.

Before turning to those chapters explicitly concerned with religion and peacemaking, we need to attend briefly to Marian Simion's important contribution on Eastern Orthodox perspectives on war. Although, as Hehir says, the ethics of war is an ecumenical topic—not only within the Christian tradition but also among religious traditions the world over—very little has been written about war within Eastern Orthodoxy.

Simion attempts to remedy this lacuna in a nuanced manner. One of his main points is that, historically speaking, the Orthodox churches articulate a rather comprehensive opposition to war and violence in general. Moreover, church-state relations are conceived in such a way that the Orthodox church is to act only in an advisory capacity to the state, and, further, that it cedes to the state legal jurisdiction regarding matters of defense of the community. But these features not infrequently present a dilemma for the church—how exactly to advise the state when it is faced with internal or external aggression? Is it to endorse or not the state's use of lethal force in some cases? Simion argues that Orthodox canon law is ambivalent on this point, and later on in his chapter he makes this point especially vivid by comparing and contrasting the *Epistle of St. Athanasius* and St. Basil's *Canon 13*.

The former epistle maintains that it is not right to kill, but it also says that in war it is lawful and praiseworthy to destroy the enemy. Is this an ecclesial sanction (or permission) for war-time killing, or is it perhaps only an articulation of the state's perspective? Similarly, *Canon 13* claims that the Church Fathers did not consider killing in the course of war to be murder, properly speaking, yet at the same time it speaks of pardoning men who fight in defense of sobriety and piety, while also refusing them communion for a three-year period; so even defenders against aggression apparently have "dirty hands," to use modern parlance. Simion's discussion of this issue is further nuanced by his acknowledgment of the impact of cultural and nationalistic influences on Orthodox thinking about war, which, in turn, result in variations of Orthodox "complicity" (if that is the right word) in war. Consider, for example, the Serbian Orthodox Church's role in sanctioning (permitting) and even encouraging aggressive Serbian action against the Bosnian Muslims and the Kosovars in the Balkan conflict. It seems that while the Orthodox churches eschew the adoption of just war theory, that fact in itself helps to account for their continuing ambivalent responses to the state's use of lethal force.

In his typology of warfare, Hehir draws particular attention to post–Cold War intrastate conflicts, with battle lines drawn between (and among) ethnic, religious, and national identities. Such conflicts have resulted in massive human rights violations on the order of ethnic cleansing and other crimes against humanity, even genocide. Part of Little's later career was spent at the U.S. Institute of Peace (USIP), where, as a Senior Scholar, he headed up a program on religion, ethics, and intolerance, tracing the roles of religion, ethnic difference, and nationalistic aspirations in a number of "hot spot" conflicts in different parts of the world. This program has since grown into USIP's Program of Religion and Peacekeeping, involving not only diagnostic analyses of such cases but also efforts to address them by conflict resolution training and mediation, interfaith dialogue, support of public preaching and argument about peaceful resolution, encouraging the mining of traditions and their scriptures for norms of tolerance and rituals of reconciliation, and the promotion of appreciation for religious diversity and pluralism in stratified societies. All of this work is well described and exemplified by Susan Hayward in her "Swords to Ploughshares." Particularly provocative are her flashpoint examples of internal conflict in Sri Lanka and xenophobia in Norway, as well as her more positive and hopeful examples of ritually grounded reconciliation in Northern Uganda and the role of religious institutions is establishing early warning response systems in Nigeria.

Hayward's discussion is broadened by Rodney Petersen's analysis and typologization of different types of peace-oriented diplomacy, ranging from Track I diplomacy and intervention by nation states responding to exigent and massive human rights violations to Track III diplomacy guided by NGOs in bringing together different sectors of civil society in conflict situations to discuss how to mediate and resolve differences. The most recent concept and set of tools that has emerged is multi-track diplomacy involving the simultaneous engagement of government officials, conflict resolution professionals, business leaders, private citizens, religious leaders and representatives, and media leaders and personnel in coordinated efforts not only to resolve and prevent conflict but also to build a new community that respects the human rights of all parties (stakeholders) and that strives for a genuine and ongoing "justpeace."

Whereas Petersen's chapter traces the general contours of peacemaking (or peacebuilding), Scott Appleby chooses to focus first on the personal characteristics of religious peacebuilders and then moves on to explore a specific case. With respect to the first topic, Appleby makes it clear that he is especially interested in indigenous religious peacebuilders who have suffered with a community in conflict, and he reports that their success is very much due to their deep emotional intelligence, profound religious faith, and robust moral character (e.g., integrity, fair-mindedness), as well as their ability to engage in selective retrieval from their traditions in developing and communicating religious narratives that privilege non-violence and to further develop on that basis social practices of conflict prevention and mediation, interreligious (and interethnic) dialogue, and reconciliation. With this background in hand, Appleby then turns to a slightly different type of peacebuilder who is not indigenous but nevertheless lives in the conflicted community as a partial insider—namely, the Mennonite peacebuilder who is open to non-Mennonite cultural values, addresses immediate on-the-ground suffering, and, using culturally resonant symbols and images, elicits a fruitful mediation procedure in providing a secure space where enemies can meet. What is interesting about such peacebuilders is that they have a long-term commitment to staying within the community or society in question, with that commitment being supported by a Mennonite sub-community that accompanies them. In a sense, such peacebuilders become a part of the society they are assisting, or, perhaps more accurately put, they are third-party mediators whose strategy involves an "adoption" of sorts, and in two senses—they adopt the society in question as their own, and the society adopts them as its own. It should not go unnoticed that the Mennonite sub-community serves as a model for how the broader society could (and should) respond to a religious "other."

In her polycentric approach to conflict transformation, Atalia Omer is also interested in developing strategies that challenge the dichotomy between internal and external, between the local character of conflict dynamics and the external agencies of mediation. In her work, Omer is particularly interested in exploring the possible positive roles that diaspora communities might play in third-party mediation in their original homeland. The key here is that such communities are in some sense also part of the homeland, for their national imaginations can cut across and move beyond political and geographical boundaries such that they identify with the trials of the homeland itself but within one large imagined community of common concern. Indeed, Omer goes so far as to recommend that that such third-party mediation can be enhanced by connections with a global network of solidarity and interest groups in addition to diaspora communities: for example, non-Palestinians can use their moral imagination and rally support for the cause of a Palestinian state through their networks of influence, both national and international. Hers is a vision that comports well with current globalization processes (cultural, political, and economic), though Omer is enough of a realist to acknowledge that diasporic and other aid can have a downside if not properly managed (e.g., the past support of the IRA by many Irish American groups).

In a sense, the remaining chapters are continuous with the preceding ones, inasmuch as they are concerned with diagnosing religious conflict in the realm of politics and with strategies of mitigation and mediation. Nevertheless, these chapters strike a somewhat different note because they focus more on structural relations between religion and politics in the public sphere, involving the roles of state authority and constitutional protections (or lack thereof). Scott Hibbard's specific concern is the resurgence of Islamist politics in the post–Cold War era, utilizing the cases of Egypt and Pakistan. Such resurgence, argues Hibbard, is in part due to the state's abandoning previous commitments to secular norms and leftist political reform and turning instead to conservative forms of Islam as the basis for state authority, thereby marginalizing more liberal forms of that tradition and helping to normalize fundamentalist ones. The ironic long-term consequences of this action—seen in the cases of both Sadat and Mubarak in Egypt, for example—were that the fundamentalist forces thus unleashed turned back on the leaders in question and not only destabilized their regimes but also heightened the forces of illiberalism and intolerance. The apparent lesson here is that politics and religion can be a volatile mix when strong constitutional protections are absent.

By contrast with Hibbard, Natalie Sherman and David Gergen focus their attention on religion and politics in an avowedly liberal society—the United States. They argue that in the early republic the Founders were quite wary of religion becoming a tool for state authority and thus adopted the First Amendment (separation of church and state) precisely to avoid such a consequence. This is not to say that the Founders failed to conceive of a role for religion in public life—quite the contrary: they expected that religious values and beliefs would shape citizen discourse and debate, and institutional development within civil society. With the recent resurgence and indeed increasing prominence of religion in the public square of political debate, some think of religion and religious difference as constituting a threat to democratic politics and bemoan the fact that the Supreme Court has failed to provide clear guidance about the limits on interaction between religion and politics. Sherman and Gergen, by contrast, see this interaction much more positively, welcoming robust debate so long as it is non-violent and the religiously motivated translate their concerns into arguments and proposals that can be understood by all reasonable citizens. They conceive of American democracy as a large inclusive republic that mediates and mitigates the dangers of factional disputes through the healthy competition of ideas—in the tradition of American pragmatism—settling differences as citizens "bumble" (their term) along creating an ever more just society. Sherman and Gergen's apparent watchword here is "liberty of conscience," and they rest content that the constitutional framework, the ballot box, and good political leadership will take care of the problems posed by the mix of religion and politics.

Christian Rice's chapter on the core of public reason reiterates in more Rawlsian terms (referring to the work of John Rawls) the position argued by Sherman and Gergen—for example, discourse and debate by free and equal citizens seen as reasonable and rational, and the translatability of citizens' reasoning about public policies into terms accessible to all, and the like. However, Rice does focus greater attention on constitutional protections for minorities, and he furthermore defends these more generally as fundamental moral entitlements known as human rights. In effect, Rice argues that public reason in the American context has a conceptual kinship with international human rights instruments whereby comprehensive worldviews (often religious) must yield to non-negotiable fundamental entitlements knowable to all normal, rational, and competent human beings. Rice suggests human rights are the content of public reason globally specified and also properly normative for all societies.

Little himself has contributed an "Afterword" that not only addresses specific issues and questions raised in the volume's chapters but also helpfully identifies connecting threads among them. In the latter case, these notably include: the regulation of the use of force based on the recognition that the prohibition of arbitrary force is an absolute human (or natural) right; a two-tiered theory of the justification of human rights that distinguishes between appeals to natural reason, on the one hand, and those deriving from comprehensive moral or religious doctrines, on the other; the thesis that ethics is best pursued comparatively in relation to global moral and political issues; the thesis that a "liberal peace" is essential for proper peacemaking and conflict resolution; that just war thinking is crucial in the reconsideration of the ethics of humanitarian intervention and that *ius post bellum* concerns deserve greater attention; and, finally, that the interactions between religion and public reason need to be grounded in the recognition and acknowledgment of human rights generally.

On this note, we conclude our brief tour of the volume's contents and now invite our readers to encounter for themselves these penetrating, astute, and often morally inspiring chapters concerned with comprehending and guiding our mutual struggle with persistent ethical, religious, and intercultural issues endemic to an increasingly complex and globalized context.

Part ONE

NORMATIVE PROSPECTS:
Human Rights Ideas and Religious Ethics

1.
David Little: A Modern Calvinist Architect of Human Rights

John Witte, Jr.

I first read David Little's work nearly thirty years ago in a freshman history class at Calvin College. Among our assigned texts was his sterling 1969 *Religion, Order, and Law: A Study in Pre-Revolutionary England*.[1] In 225 pithy pages, he offered a brilliant exploration of the legal, political, and theological mind of seventeenth-century Puritans, and a respectful but critical engagement with *Überhistorian* Max Weber. This book gave me a good introduction to Little's academic style: sturdy, concise prose, trenchant criticism, close exegesis, engaging synthesis, and historical, theological, and philosophical gravitas. Here, too, was the first sustained treatment of themes that have remained at the center of his academic work: the notion that human rights are essential gifts for all persons to embrace; that religious ideas and institutions are essential allies in the struggle for human rights; and that Calvinists—yes, *Calvinists*, for all their talk of total depravity, covenantal duty, and predestination—were among the chief historical architects of our modern human rights paradigm, anticipating the Enlightenment project by two centuries and anchoring a number of its cardinal teachings on human rights, democratic government, and rule of law in a theological world view. You can imagine the excitement that Little's book stirred in my heart. As a young Calvinist, I was grateful for this blend of history, law, and Calvinist theology, well-inflected as it was with Weberian *Wissenschaft*. And I resolved then and there in 1978: "I want to be like David Little when I grow up."

In preparation for this celebration of Little, I have been reading many of his writings since that prized 1969 title—his dozen monographs, the scores of articles, reviews, and book chapters, the sundry lectures, reports, and interviews. After completing my review of his works, I have resolved anew: "I want to be like David Little." There is so much in his writings from which to learn: his insightful treatment of violence and terrorism, nationalism and foreign policy, just war and just peace-making in such places as Vietnam, Ukraine, Sri Lanka, Tibet, and Iraq;[2] his deep, constructive engagement with Islam, Buddhism, and other faiths, and his pioneering work with John Kelsay and Sumner Twiss on developing the field of comparative religious ethics;[3] his strong philosophical defense of a political liberalism that leaves ample room for private and public expressions of religion in all peaceable varieties and in all forums of public life, including notably in political and constitutional debate;[4] his devastating criticism of secularists as well as of those insensitive to human rights, such as Richard Rorty,[5] Stanley Hauerwas, and Alasdair MacIntyre.[6]

David Little on Religion and Human Rights

The theme of religion and human rights, one of Little's abiding concerns, has dominated his writings since the late 1950s. He has traced cardinal concepts like freedom of conscience and free exercise of religion from their earliest formulations in Stoic philosophy and Roman law, through the writings of Augustine and Aquinas, Luther and Calvin, and their many modern heirs.[7] He has explored the contributions of respected Calvinists to the Western understanding of human rights and religious freedom, with special focus on John Calvin,[8] John Locke,[9] Roger Williams,[10] Isaac Backus,[11] and Thomas Jefferson,[12] all of whose ideas he connects to each other and to the Calvinist tradition in fresh and inventive ways. He has written astutely on the vexed questions, for Americans, of how to interpret and apply the First Amendment's call for no government establishments of religion or prohibitions on its free exercise. And he has charted many of the religious sources and dimensions of the modern human rights paradigm, particularly the fundamental international protections of religious freedom—freedom of thought, conscience, and belief, freedom from religious hatred, incitement, and discrimination, and freedom for religious self-determination.[13]

In a moving "Personal Testament," published in 2002, Little makes clear that his devotion to the field of human rights and religious freedom is not merely a dispassionate academic pursuit.[14] For him it is a profoundly Christian commitment and calling. He was born into a Presbyterian family with roots that go back to the Puritan settlers of Massachusetts Bay in the 1640s. His father and grandfather, and five generations of Littles before them were all Presbyterian ministers well schooled in the theological arts of Geneva and Westminster. Little himself is a devout Presbyterian layman with an iron firm grip on certain "substantive necessary truths" as he calls them, echoing Hilary Putnam.[15]

Among the fundamental "necessary truths" that drive his work in the field of religion and human rights are these: that each person is equally created in God's image, and vested with reason and will and inherent and inviolable dignity and freedom;[16] that each person has a moral law written on his or her conscience that serves both as a "private monitor" to motivate, guide, and judge their pursuit of a happy and virtuous life,[17] and a public marker to signal God's sovereign claims upon their inner mind, heart, and soul which no person or institution may trespass;[18] that each person is vested with basic natural rights to discharge the dictates and duties of conscience, both in private and in public, both alone and with others in peaceable communities;[19] that our moral intuitions, shaped by these moral laws and natural rights, condemn as just plain evil (*malum in se*) the cruel logic of pain that supports grave and gratuitous assaults on the body through genocide, torture, mayhem, starvation, rape, and enslavement or on the mind through brutal coercion, pervasive mind controls, or hallucinogenic enslavement;[20] and, finally, that to protect the "rights of all humans" through both our private actions and political structures is the best way to live by the golden rule and to obey the first and greatest commandment: "to love God and to love our neighbors as ourselves."[21]

For Little, all these fundamental beliefs are foundational to a regime of human rights. As formulated, they are part and product of the Christian tradition and of his own Calvinist worldview. These beliefs, he has shown, have been only gradually uncovered and actualized in the Western tradition and only after centuries of hard and cruel experience. And these beliefs remain aspirational as we continue the work of constructing an ever sturdier human rights regime.

But these are not merely Calvinist, or Christian, or Western beliefs, Little insists. Cast more generically and generously, these beliefs are the cardinal axioms of what it takes to live together as persons and peoples.[22] Many other traditions of thought, conscience, and religion have their own way of formulating these fundamental beliefs about human nature, action, knowledge, and interaction, and have their own means of implementing them through personal habits and institutional structures. And they have and will discover them in different ways and at different times in their development. But, all that said, "it is important to remember," Little writes, "that behind or beneath all the many differences among human beings in culture, religion, outlook, and knowledge, these are indubitable and unifying features that are accessible and applicable to 'all peoples and all nations'."[23] It is on the strength of these convictions that Little calls fellow Christians and fellow peaceable believers of all persuasions to engage the regime of human rights fully, and to nurture and challenge this regime constantly to reform and improve itself.

Little calls for nothing less than a comprehensive new "hermeneutic of religion and human rights"—in the apt phrase of our mutual friend, Abdullahi An-Na'im. This is, in part, a "hermeneutic of confession."[24] Given their checkered human rights records over the centuries, religious bodies need to acknowledge their departures from the cardinal teachings of peace and love that are the heart of their sacred texts and traditions. The blood of many thousands is at the doors of our churches, temples, mosques, and synagogues, and this demands humble recognition, expiation, and restitution. This is, in part, a "hermeneutic of suspicion" (in Paul Ricoeur's phrase). Given the pronounced libertarian tone of many current human rights formulations, we must not idolize or idealize these formulations, but be open to new wisdom from our own religious traditions and those of others. This is, in part, a "hermeneutic of religious freedom"—a new way of thinking about the place of religion in public life and public law that goes beyond simple clichés of a wall of separation between church and state, that goes beyond the sterile dialectic of state secularism versus religious establishment, and that goes beyond the notion that religion is merely a private preoccupation of the peculiar and the unenlightened.[25] And, this is, in part, a "hermeneutic of history." While acknowledging the fundamental contributions of Enlightenment liberalism to the modern rights regime, we must look for the deeper genesis and genius of many modern rights norms in religious texts and traditions that antedate the Enlightenment by centuries, sometimes millennia.[26] We must return to these religious sources. In part, this is a return to ancient sacred texts freed from the casuistic accretions of generations of jurists and freed from the cultural trappings of the communities in which these traditions were born. In part, this is a return to slender streams of theological jurisprudence that have not been part of the mainstream of the religious traditions, or have become diluted by too great a commingling with it. In part, this is a return to prophetic voices of dissent, long purged from traditional religious canons, but, in retrospect, prescient of some of the rights roles that the tradition might play today.[27]

Little's own work illustrates how this four-part hermeneutic of religion and human rights works in the Western Christian tradition, particularly the Calvinist tradition. But he has also outlined comparable efforts for the Islamic,[28] Jewish, and Buddhist traditions, which others have developed more fully.[29] Let me just touch on a few of the highlights of his argument over fifty years about the Christian and other religious foundations and dimensions of human rights.

The Calvinist Roots of Rights

It takes a bit of contextualizing to appreciate the novelty and boldness of Little's argument, particularly his historical argument about the Christian foundations of human rights before the Enlightenment. Standard college textbooks—from Little's youthful days to our own—have long taught us that the history of human rights began in the later seventeenth and eighteenth centuries. Human rights, we often hear, were products of the Western Enlightenment—creations of Grotius and Pufendorf, Locke and Rousseau, Montesquieu and Bayle, Hume and Smith, Jefferson and Madison.[30] Human rights were the mighty new weapons forged by American and French revolutionaries who fought in the name of political democracy, personal autonomy, and religious freedom against outmoded Christian conceptions of absolute monarchy, aristocratic privilege, and religious establishment. Human rights were the keys that Western liberals finally forged to unchain themselves from the shackles of a millennium of Christian oppression and Constantinian hegemony. Human rights were the core ingredients of the new democratic constitutional experiments of the later eighteenth century forward. The only Christians to have much influence on this development, we are told, were a few early Church Fathers who decried pagan Roman persecution, a few brave medievalists who defied papal tyranny, and a few early modern Anabaptists who debunked Catholic and Protestant persecution.

Proponents of this conventional historiography have recognized that Western writers since classical Greek and Roman times often used the terms "right" or "rights" (*ius* and *iura* in Latin). But the conventional argument is that, before the dawn of the Enlightenment, the term "right" was usually used in an "objective" rather than a "subjective" sense. "Objective right" (or "rightness") means that something is the objectively right thing or action in the circumstances. Objective right obtains when something is rightly ordered, is just or proper, is considered to be right or appropriate when judged against some objective or external standard.[31] "Right" is being used here as an adjective, not as a noun: It is what is correct or proper—"due and meet" in Victorian English. Thus when pre-seventeenth-century writers spoke of the "natural rights" of a person they were really referring to the "natural duties" of a person—the right thing for the person to do when judged by an external standard posed by nature or by natural reason.[32] As the great University of Chicago don, Leo Strauss, put it: "Natural right in its classic form is connected with a teleological view of the universe. All natural beings have a natural end, a natural destiny, which determines what kind of operation is good for them. In the case of men, reason is required for discerning these operations: reason determines what is by nature right with regard to man's natural end."[33]

Enlightenment philosophers, beginning with Hobbes and Locke, Strauss continued, first began to use the term "natural right" in a subjective rather than an objective sense. For the first time in the later seventeenth century, the term "right" was regularly used as a noun not as an adjective. A "subjective right" was viewed as a claim, power, or freedom which nature vests in a subject, in a person. The subject can claim this right against another subject or sovereign, and can have that right vindicated before an appropriate authority when the right is threatened, violated, or disrespected. The establishment of this subjective understanding of rights is the start to the modern discourse of human rights, we are told. When early Enlightenment figures spoke of "natural rights" or the "rights of man according to natural law," they now meant what we usually mean by "rights" today—the inherent claims that the individual subject has to various natural goods like life, liberty, and property. This was "an entirely new political doctrine," writes Strauss. It was a fundamental shift "from natural duties to natural rights."[34]

Strauss's historical account of rights is much more nuanced than this, as are the later historical accounts of some of his best students. But, particularly when cast into popular secular forms, as it often is, this basic "Straussian" account of the Enlightenment origins of Western rights has persisted, with numerous variations, in many circles of discourse to this day.

One of those circles, ironically, is that of conservative Protestantism, particularly conservative Calvinism. Many conservative Calvinists and other Protestants today still view human rights with suspicion, if not derision.[35] Some view human rights as a part and product of dangerous Catholic natural law theories that Calvinists have always purportedly rejected. More view human rights as a dangerous invention of the Enlightenment, predicated on a celebration of reason over revelation, of greed over charity, of nature over Scripture, of the individual over the community, of the pretended sovereignty of humans over the absolute sovereignty of God. These critics view the occasional discussions of natural law and natural rights in Calvin and other early reformers as a scholastic hangover that a clearer-eyed reading of Scripture by later Calvinists happily expunged from the tradition. At a certain level of abstraction, this conservative Protestant critique of human rights coincides with certain streaks of "Straussian" historiography about the Enlightenment origin of rights. Various Straussians dismiss pre-modern Christian rights talk as a betrayal of the Enlightenment. Various Protestants dismiss modern Enlightenment rights talk as a betrayal of Christianity.

Whatever the philosophical and theological merits of these respective positions might be, the historical readings and narratives that support them can no longer be sustained. A whole cottage industry of important new scholarship has now emerged to demonstrate that there was ample "liberty before liberalism," and that there were many subjective human rights in place before there were modern democratic revolutions fought in their name. We now know a great deal more about classical Roman understandings of rights, liberties, capabilities, powers and related concepts, and their elaboration by medieval and early modern civilians. We can now pore over an intricate latticework of arguments about individual and group rights and liberties developed by medieval Catholic canonists, philosophers, and theologians, and the ample expansion of this medieval handiwork by neo-scholastic writers in early modern Spain and Portugal. And we now know a good deal more about the immense contribution of the Protestant reformers to the development and expansion of the Western understanding of public, private, penal, and procedural rights. The Enlightenment, it now appears, was not so much a well-spring of Western rights as a watershed in a long stream of rights thinking that began more than a millennium before. While they certainly made their own original and critical rights contributions, too, what Enlightenment philosophers contributed more than anything were new theoretical frameworks that eventually widened these traditional rights formulations into a set of universal claims that were universally applicable to all.

Little was in the vanguard of scholars in the past half century who have excavated some of these earlier historical Christian foundations of human rights and who have shown the heavy dependence of Enlightenment figures from Locke[36] to Jefferson[37] on these Christian sources. And he was one of the first American scholars to show clearly and concretely the specific contributions of Calvinists to the development of human rights.[38] He has always acknowledged the grim and cruel side of the Calvinist tradition—from the mistreatment of witches,[39] to the hanging of Quakers, to the lynching of Zulus, let alone the Calvinist tradition's ample penchant for patriarchy, paternalism, and just plain prudishness that still has not ended.[40] He has done his hermeneutic of confession. And he has also acknowledged the powerful influence of the European and American Enlightenment movements on our understanding of religious and civil rights. But, in exercising his hermeneutic of suspicion, he wants modern liberals and modern Calvinists alike to see what historical Calvinism has wrought.

One major contribution was the Calvinist theory of liberty of conscience, freedom of exercise, and equality of a plurality of faiths before the law.[41] Some of this one finds already in Calvin, Beza, and other early reformers who built on selected Roman, patristic, and medieval Catholic sources.⁴² But it was especially Roger Williams, in the seventeenth century, Little has shown, who pressed this thesis to its more radical conclusions demanding freedom of all peaceable believers to adopt, adapt, or abandon their faith, to be free from coercion or undue influence of their conscience, and where necessary to be exempt from laws that made demands contrary to the core dictates of conscience.⁴³ This view, together with Williams's own experiment with disestablishment of religion in Rhode Island, would become axiomatic for the later American constitutional experiment, espoused by Puritans, Civic Republicans, Evangelicals, and Enlightenment philosophers alike.

A second major contribution of the Calvinist tradition to the development of Western rights lay in the restructuring of the liberty and order of the church. Calvin himself contributed much to this by combining ingeniously within his ecclesiology the principles of rule of law, democracy, and liberty. Little's Puritan and Presbyterian forbearers drove home the lessons even further.⁴⁴ Calvinists urged respect for the rule of law within the church. They devised laws that defined the church's doctrines and disciplinary standards, the rights and duties of their officers and parishioners, the procedures for legislation and adjudication. The church was thereby protected from the intrusions of state law and the sinful vicissitudes of their members. Church officials were limited in their discretion. Parishioners understood their duties. When new rules were issued, they were discussed, promulgated, and well known. Issues that were ripe for review were resolved by proper tribunals. Parties that had cases to be heard exhausted their remedies at church law. Disgruntled individuals and families that departed from the church left their private pews and personal properties behind them. Dissenting congregations that seceded from the fold left their properties in the hands of the corporate body. To be sure, this principle of the rule of law within the church was an ideal that too often was breached, in Calvin's day and in succeeding generations.⁴⁵ Yet this principle helped to guarantee order, organization, and orthodoxy within the Reformed church.

Calvinists urged respect for the democratic process within the church. Pastors, elders, teachers, and deacons were to be elected to their offices by communicant members of the congregation. Congregations periodically held collective meetings to assess the performance of their church officers, to discuss new initiatives within their bodies, to debate controversies that had arisen. Delegates to church synods and councils were to be elected by their peers.[46] Council meetings were to be open to the public and to give standing to parishioners to press their claims. Implicit in this democratic process was a willingness to entertain changes in doctrine, liturgy, and polity, to accommodate new visions and insights, to spurn ideas and institutions whose utility and veracity were no longer tenable.[47] To be sure, this principle did not always insulate the church from a belligerent dogmatism in Calvin's day or in the generations to follow. Yet this principle helped to guarantee constant reflection, renewal, and reform within the church—*ecclesia reformata semper reformanda*, a reformed church dedicated to perpetual reformation.[48]

And Calvinists urged respect for liberty within the church. Christian believers were to be free to enter and leave the church, free to partake of the church's offices and services without fear of bodily coercion and persecution, free to assemble, worship, pray, and partake of the sacraments without fear of political reprisal, free to elect their ministers, elders, deacons, and teachers, free to debate and deliberate matters of faith and discipline, free to pursue discretionary matters of faith, the *adiaphora*, without undue laws and structures.[49] To be sure, this principle, too, was an ideal that Calvin and his followers compromised, particularly in their sometimes undue empowerment of the consistory and their brutality toward persistent dissenters like Michael Servetus.[50] Yet this principle helped to guarantee constant action, adherence, and agitation for reform by individual members of the church.

Calvinists integrated these three cardinal principles into a new ecclesiology. Democratic processes prevented the rule-of-law principle from promoting an ossified and outmoded orthodoxy. The rule of law prevented the democratic principle from promoting a faith swayed by fleeting fashions and public opinions. Individual liberty kept both corporate rule and democratic principles from tyrannizing ecclesiastical minorities. Together, these principles allowed the church to strike a unique perpetual balance between law and liberty, structure and spirit, order and innovation, dogma and *adiaphora*. And together they helped to render the pluriform Calvinist church remarkably resilient over the centuries in numerous countries and cultures.

This integrated theory of the church had obvious implications for the theory of the state. Calvin himself hinted broadly in his writings that a similar combination of rule of law, democratic process, and individual liberty might serve the state equally well. What Calvin adumbrated, his followers elaborated. In the course of the next two centuries, European and American Calvinists wove Calvin's core insights about the nature of corporate rule into a robust constitutional theory of republican government, which rested on the pillars of rule of law, democratic processes, and individual liberty.[51]

A third major contribution that Calvin and his followers made to the Western tradition was their healthy respect for human sinfulness, and the need to protect institutions of authority from becoming abusive. Calvinists worked particularly hard to ensure that the powerful offices of church and state were not converted into instruments of self-gain and self-promotion. They emphasized the need for popular election of ministers and magistrates, limited tenures and rotations of ecclesiastical and political office, separation of church and state, separation of powers within church and state, checks and balances between and among each of these powers, federalist layers of authority with shared and severable sovereignty, open meetings in congregations and towns, codified canons and laws, transparent proceedings and records within consistories, courts, and councils.[52] And, if none of these constitutional safeguards worked, later Calvinists called for resistance, revolt, and even regicide against tyrants.[53] Calvinists were in the vanguard of the great democratic revolutions of France, Holland, England, and America fought in the later sixteenth to later eighteenth centuries.

A fourth major contribution that Calvinists made to the Western tradition was their integrative theory of rights. Early modern Calvinists insisted that freedoms and commandments, rights and duties belong together. To speak of one without the other is ultimately destructive. Rights without duties to guide them quickly become claims of self-indulgence. Duties without rights to exercise them quickly become sources of deep guilt. Early modern Calvinists further insisted that religious rights and civil rights must go together.[54] Already in Calvin's day, the reformers discovered that proper protection of religious rights required protection of several correlative rights as well, particularly as Calvinists found themselves repressed and persecuted as minorities. The rights of the individual to religious conscience and exercise required attendant rights to assemble, speak, worship, evangelize, educate, parent, travel, and more on the basis of their beliefs. The rights of the religious group to worship and govern itself as an ecclesiastical polity required attendant rights to legal personality, corporate property, collective worship, organized charity, parochial education, freedom of press, freedom of contract, freedom of association, and more. For early modern Calvinists, religious rights and civil rights are fundamentally interdependent.

Finally, early modern Calvinists insisted that human rights are ultimately dependent on religious norms and narratives. Calvin and his early followers used the Decalogue to ground their theories of religious and civil rights; inviolable religious rights were anchored in the first table; fundamental civil rights in the second table.[55] This would remain a perennial argument in the tradition. Later Calvinists grounded their theories of rights in other familiar doctrinal heads of theology, including the doctrine of the Trinity, the creation, and the resurrection. Some human rights, they argued, are temporal expressions of what Calvin had called the "eternal rights of God." These are the rights of God the Father, who created humans in his own image and commanded them to worship him properly and to obey his law fully. They are the rights of God the Son, who embodied himself in the church and demanded the free and full exercise of this body upon earth. And they are the rights of God the Holy Spirit, who is "poured out upon all flesh" and governs the consciences of all persons in their pursuit of happiness and holiness. Human rights, Calvinists argued, are, in no small part, the right of persons to do their duties as image bearers of the Father, as prophets, priests, and kings of Christ, as agents, apostles, and ambassadors of the Holy Spirit. As image bearers of God, persons are given natural law, reason, and will to operate as responsible creatures with choices and accountability. They are given the natural duty and right to reflect God's glory and majesty in the world, to represent God's sovereign interests in church, state, and society alike. As prophets, priests, and kings of God, persons have the spiritual duty and right to speak and to prophesy, to worship and to pastor, to rule and to govern on God's behalf. As apostles and ambassadors of God, persons have the Christian duty and right to "make disciples of all nations" by word and sacrament, by instruction and example, by charity and discipline.

Why Religion and Human Rights Need Each Other

All this is not a preamble to an altar call, nor an exercise in Protestant chauvinism. It is instead one small illustration of what a rich hermeneutic of religion and human rights can offer. Comparable exercises are now afoot in other Protestant, Catholic, and Orthodox Christian communities, as well as in various Islamic, Judaic, Buddhist, Hindu, and traditional communities. A number of religious traditions have begun, of late, this process of engaging or reengaging the regime of human rights, of returning to their traditional roots and routes of nurturing and challenging the human rights regime. This process has been incremental, clumsy, controversial, and at times even fatal for its proponents. But it is now underway, and Little has been a trailblazer in showing us the way.

But just as Little found resistance to human rights in many quarters of his own Calvinist community, so modern scholars and advocates in other faith traditions have faced resistance, and sometimes violent opposition. It is one thing, many religious skeptics point out, to accept the freedom and autonomy that a human rights regime allows.[56] This at least gives them unencumbered space to pursue their divine callings. It is quite another thing for religious bodies to import human rights within their own polities and theologies. This exposes them to all manner of unseemly challenges.

Human rights norms, religious skeptics argue, unduly challenge the structure of religious bodies. While human rights norms teach liberty and equality, many religious bodies teach authority and hierarchy. While human rights norms encourage pluralism and diversity, many religious bodies require orthodoxy and uniformity. While human rights norms teach freedoms of speech and petition, several religions teach duties of silence and submission. To draw human rights norms into the structures of religion would only seem to embolden members to demand greater access to religious governance, greater freedom from religious discipline, greater latitude in the definition of religious doctrine and liturgy. So why import them?

Moreover, human rights norms challenge the spirit of religious bodies. Human rights norms, religious skeptics argue, are the creed of a secular faith born of Enlightenment liberalism, humanism, and rationalism—even if they may have earlier religious inspirations. Human rights advocates today regularly describe these norms as our new "civic faith," "our new world religion," "our new global moral language." The French jurist, Karel Vasak, has pressed these sentiments into a full and famous confession of the secular spirit of the modern human rights movement:

> The Universal Declaration of Human Rights [of 1948], like the French Declaration of the Rights of Man and Citizen in 1789, has had an immense impact throughout the world. It has been called a modern edition of the New Testament, and the Magna Charta of humanity, and has become a constant source of inspiration for governments, for judges, and for national and international legislators. . . . By recognizing the Universal Declaration as a living document . . . one can proclaim one's faith in the future of mankind.[57]

In demonstration of this new faith, Vasak converted the "old trinity" of "liberty, equality, and fraternity" taught by the French Revolution into a "new trinity" of "three generations of rights" for all humanity. The first generation of civil and political rights elaborates the meaning of liberty.[58] The second generation of social, cultural, and economic rights elaborates the meaning of equality. The third generation of solidarity rights to development, peace, health, the environment, and open communication elaborates the meaning of fraternity. Such language has become not only the *lingua franca* but also something of the *lingua sacra* of the modern human rights movement.

In the face of such an overt confession of secular liberalism, religious skeptics conclude, a religious body would do well to resist the ideas and institutions of human rights. These skeptical arguments, however, presuppose that human rights norms constitute a static belief system born of Enlightenment liberalism. But the human rights regime is not static. It is fluid, elastic, open to challenge and change. The human rights regime is not a fundamental belief system. It is a relative system of ideas and ideals that presupposes the existence of fundamental beliefs and values that will constantly shape and reshape it. The human rights regime is not the child of Enlightenment liberalism, nor a ward under its exclusive guardianship. It is the *ius gentium* of our times, the common law of nations, which a variety of ancient religious and cultural movements have historically nurtured and which today still needs the constant nurture of multiple communities.[59]

I use the antique term *ius gentium* advisedly—to signal the distinctive place of human rights as "middle axioms" in our moral and political discourse. Historically, Western writers spoke of a hierarchy of laws—from natural law (*ius naturale*), to common law (the *ius gentium*), to civil law (the *ius civile*). The natural law was the set of immutable principles of reason and conscience, which are supreme in authority and divinity and must always prevail in instances of dispute. The civil law was the set of enacted laws and procedures of local political communities, reflecting their immediate policies and procedures.

Between these two sets of norms was the *ius gentium*, the set of principles and customs common to several communities and often the basis for treaties and other diplomatic conventions. The contents of the *ius gentium* did gradually change over time and across cultures—as new interpretations of the natural law were offered, and as new formulations of the civil law became increasingly conventional. But the *ius gentium* was a relatively consistent body of principles by which a person and a people could govern themselves.

This antique typology helps us to understand the intermediate place of human rights in our hierarchy of legal norms today. Human rights are the *ius gentium* of our time, the middle axioms of our discourse. They are derived from and dependent upon the transcendent principles that religious communities (more than any other groups) continue to cultivate. And they inform, and are informed by, shifts in the customs and conventions of sundry state law systems. These human rights norms do gradually change over time: just compare the international human rights instruments of 1948 with those of today. But human rights norms are a relatively stable set of ideals by which a person and community might be guided and judged.

This antique typology also helps us to understand the place of human rights within religion. My argument that human rights must have a more prominent place within religions today is not an attempt to import libertarian ideals into their theologies and polities. It is not an attempt to herd Trojan horses into churches, synagogues, mosques, and temples in order to assail secretly their spirit and structure. My argument is, rather, that religious bodies must again assume their traditional patronage and protection of human rights, bringing to this regime their full doctrinal vigor, liturgical healing, and moral suasion. Using our antique typology, religious bodies must again nurture and challenge the middle axioms of the *ius gentium* with the transcendent principles of the *ius naturale*. This must not be an effort to monopolize the discourse, nor to establish by positive civil law a particular religious construction of human rights. Such an effort must be part of a collective discourse of competing understandings of the *ius naturale*—of competing theological views of the divine and the human, of sin and salvation, of individuality and community—that will serve constantly to inform and reform, to develop and deepen the human rights ideals now in place.

A number of distinguished commentators have recently encouraged the abandonment of the human rights paradigm altogether—as a tried and tired experiment that is no longer effective, even a fictional faith whose folly has now been fully exposed. Others have bolstered this claim with cultural critiques—that human rights are instruments of neo-colonization which the West uses to impose its values on the rest,[60] even toxic compounds that are exported abroad to breed cultural conflict, social instability, religious warfare and thus dependence on the West.[61] Others have added philosophical critiques—that rights talk is the wrong talk for meaningful debate about deep questions of justice, peace, and the common good. Still others have added theological critiques—that the secular beliefs in individualism, rationalism, and contractarianism inherent to the human rights paradigm cannot be squared with cardinal biblical beliefs in creation, redemption, and covenant.

Such criticisms properly soften the overly bright optimism of some human rights advocates. They properly curb the modern appetite for the limitless expansion and even monopolization of human rights in the quest for toleration, peace, and security. And they properly criticize the libertarian accents that still too often dominate our rights talk today. But such criticisms do not support the conclusion that we must abandon the human rights paradigm altogether—particularly when no viable alternative global forum and no viable alternative universal faith is yet at hand. Instead, these criticisms support the proposition that the religious sources and dimensions of human rights need to be more robustly engaged and extended. Human rights norms are not a transient libertarian invention, or an ornamental diplomatic convention. Human rights norms have grown out of millennium-long religious and cultural traditions. They have traditionally provided a forum and focus for subtle and sophisticated philosophical, theological, and political reflections on the common good and our common lives. And they have emerged today as part of the common law of the emerging world order. We should abandon these ancient principles and practices only with trepidation, only with explanation, only with articulation of viable alternatives. For modern academics to stand on their tenured liberties to deconstruct human rights without posing real global alternatives is to insult the genius and the sacrifice of their many creators. For now, the human rights paradigm must stand—if nothing else as the "null hypothesis." It must be constantly challenged to improve. It should be discarded, however, only on cogent proof of a better global norm and practice.

A number of other distinguished commentators have argued that religion can have no place in a modern regime of human rights. Religions might well have been the mothers of human rights in earlier eras, perhaps even the midwives of the modern human rights revolution. Religion has now, for them, outlived its utility. Indeed, the continued insistence of special roles and rights for religion is precisely what has introduced the paradoxes of religion and human rights that now befuddle us. Religion is, by its nature, too expansionistic and monopolistic, too patriarchal and hierarchical, too antithetical to the very ideals of pluralism, toleration, and equality inherent in a human rights regime. Purge religion entirely, this argument concludes, and the human rights paradigm will thrive.

This argument proves too much to be practicable. In the course of the twentieth century, religion defied the wistful assumptions of the Western academy that the spread of Enlightenment reason and science would slowly eclipse the sense of the sacred and the sensibility of the superstitious. Religion defied the evil assumptions of Nazis, Fascists, and Communists alike that gulags and death camps, iconoclasm and book burnings, propaganda and mind controls would inevitably drive religion into extinction. Yet another great awakening of religion is upon us—now global in its sweep and frightening in its power.

It is undeniable that religion has been, and still is, a formidable force for both political good and political evil, that it has fostered both benevolence and belligerence, peace and pathos of untold dimensions.

But the proper response to religious belligerence and pathos cannot be to deny that religion exists or to dismiss it to the private sphere and sanctuary. The proper response is to castigate the vices and to cultivate the virtues of religion, to confirm those religious teachings and practices that are most conducive to human rights, democracy, and rule of law.

Religion will invariably figure in legal and political life—however forcefully the community might seek to repress or deny its value or validity, however cogently the academy might logically bracket it from its political and legal calculus. Religion must be dealt with, because it exists—perennially, profoundly, pervasively—in every community. It must be drawn into a constructive alliance with a regime of law, democracy, and human rights. And there is no better way to start that exercise than to read Little's writings.

NOTES

[1] David Little, *Religion, Order, and Law: A Study in Pre-Revolutionary England* (New York and Evanston: Harper &. Row, 1969).

[2] David Little and Donald K. Swearer, eds., *Religion and Nationalism in Iraq* (Cambridge, MA: Center for the Study of World Religions, 2006); David Little, "Religion and Self-Determination," in *Self-Determination: International Perspectives*, eds. Donald Clark and Robert Williamson (London: MacMillan Press, 1996), 141–55; David Little, *Ukraine: The Legacy of Intolerance* (Washington, D.C.: United States Institute of Peace Press, 1991).

[3] David Little, "Religious Freedom and American Protestantism," in *Politics and Religion in France and the United States*, eds. Alec G. Hargreaves, John Kelsay, and Sumner B. Twiss (Lanham, MD: Lexington Books, 2007), 29–48.

[4] David Little, "In Defense of Political Liberalism," in *Toothing Stones: Rethinking the Political*, ed. Robert Meagher (Chicago: Swallow Press, 1972), 116–43.

[5] David Little, "Natural Rights and Human Rights: The International Imperative," in *Natural Rights and Natural Law: The Legacy of George Mason*, ed. Robert Davidoff (Fairfax, VA: George Mason University Press, 1986), 95–97.

[6] David Little, "The Nature and Basis of Human Rights," in *Prospects for a Common Morality*, eds. Gene Outka and John P. Reeder, Jr. (Princeton: Princeton University Press, 1993), 73–92.

[7] David Little, Abdulaziz Sachedina, and John Kelsay, "Human Rights and the World's Religions: Christianity, Islam, and Religious Liberty," in *Religious Diversity and Human Rights*, eds. Irene Bloom, J. Paul Martin, and Wayne Proudfoot (New York: Columbia University Press, 1996), 225–37.

[8] See, e.g., David Little, "The Reformed Tradition and the First Amendment," in *The First Freedom: Religion and the Bill of Rights*, ed. James E. Wood, Jr. (Waco, TX: J.M. Dawson Institute of Church-State Studies, Baylor University, 1990), 29–32; see also Little, "Religious Freedom," 29–34.

[9] See, e.g., Little, "Natural Rights."

[10] See, e.g., Little, "Reformed Tradition," 29–37; Little, "Religious Freedom," 33–38; David Little, "Roger Williams and the Separation of Church and State," in *Religion and the State: Essays in Honor of Leo Pfeffer*, ed. James E. Wood, Jr. (Waco, TX: 1985), 3–23.

[11] See, e.g., Little, "The Reformed Tradition," 21–22.

[12] See, e.g., Little, "Religious Freedom," 37–38.

[13] See, e.g., David Little, "Conscientious Individualism: A Christian Perspective on Ethical Pluralism," in *The Many and the One: Religious and Secular Perspectives on Ethical Pluralism in the Modern World*, eds. Richard Madsen and Tracy B. Strong (Princeton: Princeton University Press, 2003).

[14] David Little, "Religion and Human Rights: A Personal Testament," *The Journal of Law and Religion* 18 (2002–03): 57–58.

[15] Hilary Putnam, *Ethics Without Ontology* (Cambridge, MA: Harvard University Press, 2005), 16.

[16] Little, "Roger Williams," 8–13.

[17] Little, "Conscientious Individualism," 232–33.

[18] In "Conscientious Individualism," 237, Little speaks of the sovereignty of a different king over a different world called the "inner forum," wherein the "laws of the spirit" reigned supreme.

[19] See, e.g., Little, Sachedina, and Kelsay, "Christianity, Islam, and Religious Liberty," 224–25 for a basic discussion of Roger Williams's conception of moral duties. See more fully David Little, "Religious Liberty," in John Witte, Jr. and Frank S. Alexander, eds., *Christianity and Law: An Introduction* (Cambridge: Cambridge University Press, 2008), 249–270.

[20] See, e.g., Little, "Natural Rights and Human Rights," 96–102.

[21] See, e.g., David Little, "A Christian Perspective on Human Rights," in *Human Rights in Africa*, eds. Abdullahi Ahmend An-Naim and Francis M. Deng (Washington, D.C.: Brookings Institution, 1990), 67.

[22] Little, "Natural Rights," 68–69.

[23] Little, "Natural Rights," 70.

[24] The discussion of the three aspects of this new hermeneutic is taken from John Witte, Jr., *God's Joust, God's Justice: Law and Religion in the Western Tradition* (Grand Rapids, MI: Eerdmans, 2006), chap. 3.

[25] Little discusses the importance of Roger Williams's articulation of the freedom of the conscience, which was instrumental in development of the doctrine of the separation of the church and the state, and likely influenced Jefferson's thinking vis-à-vis Locke in Little, "Reformed Tradition," 21–27.

[26] See Little, "Christian Perspective," 59–103.

[27] See, e.g., David Little, "Does the Human Right to Freedom of Conscience, Religion, and Belief Have Special Status?" in *Brigham Young University Law Review* (2001): 603–10.

[28] Little, Sachedina, and Kelsay, "Christianity, Islam, and Religious Liberty," 225–37.

[29] See David Little, "Rethinking Human Rights: A Review Essay on Religion, Relativism, and Other Matters," in *Journal of Religious Ethics* 27 (Spring 1999): 151–177.

[30] Material in this and the following five paragraphs is drawn from my *The Reformation of Rights: Law, Religion, and Human Rights in Early Modern Calvinism* (New York: Cambridge University Press, 2007), 20–37. Parallel citations to Little's work are included.

[31] Little, "Roger Williams," 17.

[32] Little, "Human Rights," 21–22.

[33] Leo Strauss, *Natural Right and History* (Chicago: University of Chicago Press, 1953), 7.

[34] Ibid., 182.

[35] See Little, "Human Rights," 13–24.

[36] See Little, "Conscientious Individualism," 230–42.

[37] See Little, "The Reformed Tradition," 20–28.

[38] See, e.g., Little, "Roger Williams."

[39] Little, "Personal Testament," 62–63.

[40] David Little, "Roger Williams and the Puritan Background of the Establishment Clause," in *No Establishment of Religion: America's Original Contribution to Religious Liberty*, ed. T. Jeremy Gunn and John Witte, Jr. (New York/Oxford: Oxford University Press, 2013), 100–124.

[41] Much of this section is distilled from my *Reformation of Rights*, chaps. 1–5. Parallel citations to Little's work are included. Little discusses the controversial and transformative approach of Roger Williams and other Presbyterian leaders who advocated tolerance of all religions and atheism in Little, "Religious Freedom," 35–37; and more fully in Little, "Roger Williams and the Puritan Background of the Establishment Clause."

[42] See Little, "Conscientious Individualism," 230–32.

[43] Little, "Religious Freedom," 33–34.

[44] See Little, "Personal Testament," 57–68.

[45] See Little, "Personal Testament," 61–64.

[46] Little, "Personal Testament," 58–59.

[47] David Little, "Reformed Faith and Religious Liberty," *Church and Society* (May/June, 1986): 7. Calvin believed the church was to be a community guided in its direction by the community voice and that all participation was to be voluntary and consensual.

[48] Little, "A Personal Testament," 57.

[49] Little, "Reformed Faith," 22–23. An example of the Reformed Tradition's movement to separate from civil authorities is found in the appointment of a committee for reviewing "church organization, including the question of church-state relations" by the synods of New York and Philadelphia at the time Jefferson's *Statute for Religious Freedom* was being considered in Virginia.

⁵⁰ Little, "A Personal Testament," 59.

⁵¹ Ibid., 66.

⁵² Little, "Reformed Faith," 13–17. Little articulated the importance of consensual and voluntary church participation in several strains of Reformed Christianity, including Congregationalists, English Presbyterians led by Thomas Cartwright, and Puritans under Robert Browne, also in England. Cartwright emphasized a representative, self-governing hierarchy, free from interference of the civil authority. In America, John Cotton's instantiation of Calvinism in Congregationalism stressed voluntary participation by each member in church governance, evidencing a clear distinction between church and state.

⁵³ Ibid., 11–12. John Knox, leader of the Reformation in Scotland who was guided by Calvin's ideal, extended Calvin's notion of freedom of conscience to include violent resistance against secular rulers that repressed this freedom. The Huguenots in France exemplified similar ideas, advocating replacement of rulers who did not execute "God's law," thus standing against idolatry and heresy propagated through the government.

⁵⁴ Little, "Religious Freedom," 35–37.

⁵⁵ See, e.g., Little, "Reformed Tradition," 31; Little, "American Protestantism," 31; Little, "Roger Williams," 13–14.

⁵⁶ Material in this section, through the conclusion, is drawn from Witte, *God's Joust*, chap. 3. Parallel citations to Little's work are included.

⁵⁷ Karel Vasak, "A 30-Year Struggle," *UNESCO Courier*, November 1977, 29; see also Karel Vasak, "Foreword," in *The International Dimensions of Human Rights*, Karel Vasak, ed. (Westport, CT: Greenwood Press, 1982), xv; id., "*Pour une troisième génération des droits de l'homme*," in *Études et Essais sur le Droit International Humanitaire et sur les Principes de la Croix-Rouge en l'Honneur de Jean Pictet*, Christophe Swinarksi, ed. (The Hague: Martinus Nijhoff, 1984), 837–45.

⁵⁸ Vasak, "*Pour une troisième génération*," 837.

⁵⁹ See Little, "Rethinking Human Rights."

⁶⁰ See, e.g., Little, Sachedina, and Kelsay, "Christianity, Islam, and Religious Liberty," n. 1, citing Adamantia Pollis and Peter Schwab, *Human Rights: Cultural and Ideological Perspectives* (New York: Praeger, 1979), 17.

⁶¹ Little, "Rethinking Human Rights," 152.

2.
On Reformed Christianity and Natural Human Rights[1]

Gene Outka

David Little combines tenacity in normative argument with the readiness to sustain friendships in the midst of disagreements, even when the latter resist resolution. For many people these two intellectual-moral virtues can conflict, or one of them may simply dominate. Yet, impressively, he manages to hold them together over time, each retaining its integrity.

Little expounds his views energetically, enthusiastically, and with courage. Some positions he has taken in his life depart from widely held moral and political judgments, especially in the academy. On these occasions, he continues to look people in the eye, and to state his case. If you disagree, prepare to state your own position as carefully as you can. He will expressly agree and disagree, or indicate what perplexes him. He will not be unduly anxious to please. But he will listen and not simply pronounce, and will attempt to understand. On those occasions when he and I have persevered in such an argument, yet failed to agree, no damage to personal affection has resulted.

Little proceeds in a spirit of non-defensive mutual inquiry in all his work. A commitment to truth for its own sake trumps an interest in winning, or making agreement a condition for further exchanges. And normative disagreements do not ssue in accusations of personal disloyalty or betrayal. In short, Little effectively sustains a joint commitment to standing up for one's views and to friendship. To see these two virtues continuously alive and well in him is something I greatly admire and respect, and for which I have always been grateful.

One Sort of Uncertainty

Little has produced a large corpus from which I have learned much. Yet I must register here an uncertainty about one part of it: I am unsure how *he* understands his own work in Christian ethics to relate or perhaps not to relate to his own defense of natural human rights. In the short compass this chapter's restricted length affords, I propose to test my uncertainty. Because the uncertainty is mine, and not necessarily Little's, however, I do not presume to speak for him and I certainly do not try to resolve matters on his behalf. Without pronouncing for him, I aim to interpret him.[2]

On the first side of this relation, I confine my references to "religion" here to mean Christianity. I bracket parts of Little's corpus where, for example, he and Sumner B. Twiss propose comprehensive definitions of "religion" and "ethics" as "basic terms."[3] Moreover, I attend chiefly to one strand of Christianity, namely, to theological and ethical claims in the Christian Reformed tradition. This particular tradition is the ecclesial-social stratum out of which Little was "dug," and upon which he has focused in several influential writings.[4] Three of his publications in this tradition serve here to exemplify normative as well as descriptive claims—none of which have been repudiated, as far as I know.

On the second side of this relation, I consider Little's recent defense of human rights.[5] This defense is robust; it bears the marks of his seriousness, his moral passion. Yet within it, explicit mention of Christian ethics in the Reformed tradition diminishes, as he proceeds.

Reformed Christianity: Love and Law

The first side receives early articulation in a chapter on John Calvin that refers to several standard topics in Christian ethics. Little generally approves of Calvin's approach to these topics. He recognizes the complexity that the approach contains, and on occasion he uses one aspect of Calvin's thought to criticize another aspect (e.g., he favors the consensualist egalitarian themes over the hierarchical social order ones[6]), but this chapter displays general fealty to the theological and ethical affirmations it identifies. I consider two of these affirmations, love and law, and allude to several others.

Love

As Little reads Calvin, love is theologically and ethically central. The two love commandments—to love the Lord your God with all your heart, soul, and mind, and to love your neighbor as yourself (Matt. 22:31-40)—constitute the summary admonitions on which all the law and prophets depend. He locates "three substantive ethical principles" that "would appear to be suggested in Calvin's notion of love: *universalism, active benevolence,* and *voluntarism.*"[7]

"Universalism" captures the meaning of "neighbor" in that *all* persons, near and distant, are to be loved. Calvin enjoins this inclusive meaning on distinctive theological grounds. A key passage (portions of which Little quotes[8]) brings this out. Calvin allows that closer special relations may retain their appropriate exercise in God's providential design, but he commends universal scope by virtue of "contemplation in God" and Christ's own authority, saying:

> Now, since Christ has shown in the parable of the Samaritan that the term "neighbor" includes even the most remote person [Luke 10:36], we are not expected to limit the precept of love to those in close relationships. I do not deny that the more closely a man is linked to us, the more intimate obligation we have to assist him. It is the common habit of mankind that the more closely men are bound together by the ties of kinship, of acquaintanceship, or of neighborhood, the more responsibilities for one another they share. This does not offend God, for his providence, as it were, leads us to it. But I say: we ought to embrace the whole human race without exception in a single feeling of love; here there is no distinction between barbarian and Greek, worthy and unworthy, friend and enemy, since all should be contemplated in God, not in themselves. When we turn aside from such contemplation, it is no wonder we become entangled in many errors. Therefore, if we rightly direct our love, we must first turn our eyes not to man, the sight of whom

would more often engender hate than love, but to God, who bids us extend to all men that love we bear to him, that this may be an unchanging principle: whatever the character of the man, we must yet love him because we love God.[9]

Little does not oppose this strong theological warrant that Calvin offers for love's universalism. When he turns explicitly to Calvin's theory of natural law, moreover, he retains theological considerations in the midst. He holds that Calvin's theory proceeds "from the top, so to speak—from the perspective not first of all of nature, but of grace. [Calvin] … has a theory of natural law, let there be no mistake about that. But he is not interested in developing a self-contained, independent doctrine. He has what we may call a derivative theory of natural law, one that has always to be seen in relation to a more inclusive theological and moral design."[10]

Other substantive ethical principles of love—active benevolence and voluntariness (or voluntary cooperativeness)—also relate to the design. While these too are "embodied in Christian revelation," Little here proposes to "work back" from them to identify generalizations of human nature that hold as "conditions of the possibility" of making love realizable. In so doing, he appeals both to Calvin's account of the two tables of the Decalogue and to anthropological studies that locate cross-cultural "ethical universals," present in all societies.

Law

Again, the Ten Commandments elaborate the summary admonitions to love God and one's neighbor as oneself. Little follows Calvin in adhering to the traditional two-table division.

About the first table consisting of four duties to God, Little is relatively brief. He notes Calvin's claim, from which he again does not draw back, that "God, being Himself final or ultimate, wills (or purposes) what is final; therefore, what God wills is good, right, and just."[11]

In the case of the second table of six duties to human beings, Little is more detailed. Calvin holds at one and the same time that the table elaborates "the order or design of God," "the rule of God's righteousness," and that it is "the set of fundamental imperatives that are engraved upon the hearts of all men."[12] What God designs as right, and what we know in our heart of hearts to be right, do not, at the end of the day it seems, diverge. And further, what is right exceeds avoiding what is expressly prohibited. Calvin sustains part of Luther's attack on the medieval distinction between duties and works of supererogation. A spirit of uniform stringency transforms what is forbidden into "contrary duties and deeds." We should now positively practice virtue under the guidance of love.[13]

Little next introduces anthropological studies that cite culture or symbol-using, and sharing or cooperation, as distinguishing "human being" from other primate beings. He moves from these studies to identify "the character and function of the cross-cultural 'ethical' universals that are now widely recognized to exist in all societies. . . . [Clyde] Kluckhohn collects a list of six such universals: (a) prohibition against murder (wanton killing within the in-group), as distinguished from other forms of justifiable homicide; (b) prohibition against stealing within the in-group; (c) prohibition against incest, and other regulations on sexual behavior; (d) prohibition under defined circumstances against lying; (e) regulations and stipulations regarding the restitution and reciprocity of property; (f) stimulation of mutual obligations between parents and children."[14]

That these ethical universals resemble the second table of the Decalogue strikes Little as highly significant. This resemblance has to be more than accidental, as he sees it. Indeed, the items on the second table and the list of ethical universals provide "reasonably sound empirical ground" for identifying "fixed points in understanding what the term 'human' or 'humanity' means."[15]

In short, this early essay flows directly from Calvin's Christian ethics, aided and abetted by relevant social scientific studies. It includes references as well to other traditional theological topics, such as Christology, church, sin, and the distinction but never the severing of the spiritual and political realms, what he later calls the "religious-spiritual" and the "civil-moral" governments. Of course the essay hardly serves as the last word on any of these subjects. Yet I find it instructive because it displays currents then actively at work, and some of these are not so much renounced as selectively integrated into claims he makes on the second side concerning natural human rights. Consider as one example love and its relation to law. It appears both to inform these subsequent claims and yet later to cease as an explicit point of normative reference.

Let us see what he says in the early essay:

> Love informs the law in such a way as to add concern for the neighbor's welfare, or for the common good, to the negative prescriptions of the law. The natural law is not properly grasped, save in relation to active benevolence.... Love, as an essentially voluntary, self-giving activity, implies two things about human nature: in order for the human self to have the possibility for fulfilling its potentialities, its "base of operations" (the physical individual) must be regarded both as inviolable and as in need of opportunities for expressing cooperativeness. In other words, human nature possesses certain fundamental rights of existence and development. Indeed, several of the ethical constants of the Decalogue would seem to be an outline of just such a "bill of rights."[16]

I do not say that the language of rights *here* serves as the "trumpet of a prophecy" for his later work. Rather, I note key ways that love informs this bill of rights. It even supplies the corrective Little makes to Kluckhohn's specified list of ethical universals: he revises this list in one respect at a minimum. He appeals to Calvin's universalizing of the notion of love to transcend the normative limits the list reserves for the "in-group."[17] But as we saw earlier, Calvin's warrant for such universalizing requires contemplation in God and Christ's own authority. This requirement is internal to Christianity, at least some of the way, though normatively it extends outward. That is, "tradition-dependent" references remain in the mix.

Just before I turn to the second side of natural human rights, I notice briefly two later essays that attest to Little's ongoing engagement with Reformed Christianity. In "The Law of Supererogation," he considers a concept that according to David Heyd has its theological origins in Christianity.[18] Little commends Heyd's volume, though he finds it flawed in certain respects. He agrees that not all moral acts are either obligatory or forbidden. Certain acts are supererogatory when to omit them is not wrong but to perform them is morally good, and when they are done voluntarily for the sake of someone else's good. But he contends that Heyd errs in finding Calvin to offer a strict anti-supererogationism. Little defends instead in Calvin's case a reconstructed view of supererogation, where "one is bound to permissive action." I find the details of this defense laudably nuanced, but they need not detain us now. However, two things deserve mention. Little returns again to Calvin's contributions and amplifies them further. And he is prepared here to allow more generally for the historical impact that the Christian tradition can exert: "given the cultural influence of Christianity" he writes, "the sort of understanding in that tradition has profoundly affected the rules according to which the concept of supererogation appears to operate."[19]

The second essay, "Reformed Faith and Religious Liberty," addresses wider ecclesial-moral concerns. Here Little provides a brief yet highly informed history of how Reformed thinkers, from Calvin forward, variously interpret "the doctrine of the Two" in Christianity, the distinction between the "religious-spiritual" and the "civil-moral" governments.

To show how much the topic of church-state relations matters, Little cites a striking observation that George H. Sabine makes: "The rise of the Christian church, as a distinct institution entitled to govern the spiritual concerns of mankind in independence of the state, may not unreasonably be described as the most revolutionary event in the history of western Europe, in respect both to politics and to political philosophy."[20] I register as well an observation that Sabine offers several pages later: "Christianity raised a problem which the ancient world had not known—the problem of church and state—and implied a diversity of loyalties and an internality of judgment not included in the ancient idea of citizenship. It is hard to imagine that liberty could have played the part it did in European political thought, if ethical and religious institutions had not been conceived to be broadly independent of, and superior in importance to, the state and legal enforcement."[21]

The stress on ethical and religious institutions, and their independence, suggests a dynamic that seeks to preserve space beyond totalitarian ambitions, where states are after our souls. To honor the internality of judgments, and retain multiple loyalties, we should resist allowing particular communities to define for us everything that demonstrably matters in human life. So we deny that the current winners of given cultural conversations, of political contestations, can take everything there is to have.[22] Yet we should also go carefully on one matter: any claim of superiority in importance refers in the case of the church to the organized tasks of witnessing to God and love for God, not domination in the body politic. Love for God fills the space beyond, fosters internality of judgments, and engenders a sense that each of us is a *homo viator*, never *completely* at home in any earthly society.

These exceed state and legal enforcement. They form an indispensable part of what the church is to proclaim independently.

How the Reformed tradition attests in distinctive but influential ways to the timbre of Sabine's observations occupies Little in this essay. He acknowledges that the Reformed combination of ideas on the two governments never fully stabilizes, even in Calvin's case. Tensions linger, for instance, over how to relate the governments. Establishmentarians like John Knox in Scotland and John Cotton in Massachusetts vary from Independents like Robert Browne in England and Roger Williams in Rhode Island. Little prefers Williams among these later figures he considers, for notable reasons.

I offer this rude sketch.[23] Knox appeals to Calvin's Geneva ideal to resist those civil laws in Scotland he judges to be idolatrous and blasphemous. He allows the sword to be employed if necessary, administered by the civil authority, and supported by all people of "true conscience." Cotton also affirms the Establishmentarian side of Calvinism that connects true piety and civil status. To be sure, he distinguishes the religious-spiritual and the civil-moral governments and seeks to limit institutional power on both sides. Yet he demands religious qualifications for carrying out civic responsibilities. For heretics who "deal not truly with God…will not deal truly with man."[24]

On the Independent side of Calvinism, Browne, founder of separatist Congregationalism in the sixteenth century, defends an ecclesiology that is entirely consensual or covenantal. Civil magistrates lack authority over the church. They only "rule the commonwealth in all outward justice…. But to compel religion, to plant churches by power, and to force submission in ecclesiastical government by law and penalties" is always overweening.[25] Browne contends that any genuine ecclesiology should protect persons in their God-given prerogative to seek and find God in their own way. They should not be reduced by external fiat to a uniformity of belief. Sanctity attaches to the *determined conscience*. It cannot be forced.

Williams too ascribes religious importance to the determined conscience and the need within the church to honor and sanctify it. However, while he venerates unforced conscientious consideration and this inner forum, he proceeds to sever the connection that Knox and Cotton draw, between true piety and moral and civic virtue. The latter enjoys, for Williams, an independence from religiously founded beliefs and values. Little notes for instance that Williams underscores "this radical conviction by unfavorably contrasting the practices of orthodox Christians in England and America with 'the Indian wild,' whom he had come to know and appreciate in a thoroughly unconventional way. Their record in respect of 'moral virtues' was, he claimed, frequently better than that of the pious colonists."[26]

Williams leaves a complex and distinctive legacy on many matters.[27] His insistence that moral and civic virtue remains independent of religiously founded beliefs and values is one of the claims Little appropriates.[28] This insistence is a fitting point of transition.

Natural Human Rights: John Locke and the United Nations Declaration

I assume that Little presently agrees with Williams on the independence of civil and moral virtue, and that this agreement governs references to natural law and natural rights from this point forward. The assumption seems confirmed in his 2007 reply to G. Scott Davis: He writes:

> It is true that Calvin, for one, avoided taking the full consequences of his belief in natural moral knowledge by notoriously failing in practice to respect equal rights for all, regardless of religious identity or affiliation, but that was not true of other more radical, if devoted, Calvinists like Roger Williams. Williams went out of his way to affirm the equal right of conscience for all citizens, as well as other "natural civil rights and liberties," whether those rights were "understood in the context of a religious worldview or not."[29]

Little proceeds to prioritize and to limit the scope of the moral and political work he envisages for natural rights. By "natural" he means "certain basic moral directives, understood as both universal and minimal or residual"; it is these that "are known without reference to religious belief."[30] We should go first to the "basic moral directives." They flow from "both the natural-rights tradition and the more contemporary human-rights movement" that "are one in supposing that behind or beneath all the many differences among human beings in culture, religion, language, outlook, and so on, there are these indubitable and unifying features and prescriptions that are accessible and applicable to 'all peoples and all nations.'"[31] On limiting the scope, he allows elsewhere that morally speaking, "rights are not everything."[32] About what other moral considerations beyond rights are most salient, however, he recently has had less to say.

To make the account more precise, I draw further from selected articles on human rights.

John Locke

In his 1986 article "Natural Rights and Human Rights," Little initially pays tribute to George Mason's Virginia Declaration of Rights which he believes "offers the closest single approximation of any of the 'fundamental testaments' of the American Revolution to the Universal Declaration of Human Rights adopted by the United Nations on 10 December 1948."[33] Two sets of features that Mason put forward subsequently characterize how rights are depicted. One focuses on not relinquishing and not passing along: "persons may not under any circumstances give up or transfer, *for themselves or others*, certain basic natural rights."[34] The other focuses on normative standing: "fundamental human rights logically precede governments and all positive law."[35]

Later declarations and conventions, displaying similar links between the natural-rights tradition and more contemporary human rights documents, reiterate these features and specify their implications. Mason himself was a driving force for the U.S. Bill of Rights.[36] Little also duly notes the additions that contemporary human-rights instruments have advanced on behalf of economic, social, and cultural rights and rights of peoples. While these innovate in important directions, he finds they leave intact the basic rationale for rights. Finally, he acknowledges recent philosophical challenges to the very notion of human rights. The most arresting of these that he cites comes from Richard Rorty:

> [W]hen the secret police come, when the torturers violate the innocent, there is nothing to be said to them of the form "There is something within you which you are betraying. Though you embody the practices of a totalitarian society which will endure forever, there is something beyond those practices which condemns you. . . ."

> This hard saying brings out what ties Dewey and Foucault, James and Nietzsche, together—the sense that there is nothing deep down inside us except what we have put there ourselves, no criterion that we have not created in the course of creating a practice, no standard of rationality, that is not an appeal to such a criterion, no rigorous argumentation that is not obedience to our own conventions.[37]

Little emphatically opposes this hard saying. He seeks some self-evident, universally accessible "ground on which to stand,"[38] for if and when the secret police come. This search acquires momentum in the 1986 article by what, again, he finds especially in Locke.

From Egoism to Equality: He rebuts several earlier, well-entrenched readings of the natural rights tradition and the "social contract theory" associated with it. These impose settled convictions of their own for which Locke's texts offer conspicuously little support. Marxist-guided interpretations, for example, prove influential but erroneous. They posit what Marx calls "the image of *the egoistic person.*" Such a person is taken to be an "individual," *qua* "isolated monad": self-preoccupied, withdrawn from community, extolling the "rights of self-control," and by extension the rights of private property. The rights of others are admitted only grudgingly and calculatingly. They reduce to mutually self-interested bargains. Such rights end by protecting "those that have."[39]

Little allows that these sweeping verdicts contain "some grains of truth," but still they palpably distort the natural rights tradition in its Lockean form. Even Hobbes is not the unqualified "economic" or "possessive individualist" that Marxist-inspired interpreters allege.[40] But it is Locke above all who provides a non-egoistic basis for an acceptable natural rights or human rights position that Little seeks to reclaim and extend.[41]

In short, Locke is no egoist. He denies that every person's own interest is the basis for natural law. "For if the source and origin of all this law is the care and preservation of oneself, virtue would seem to be not so much man's duty as his convenience, nor will everything be good except what is useful to him; and the observance of this law would be not so much our duty and obligation, to which we are bound by nature, as a privilege and an advantage, to which we are led by expediency. And thus, whenever it pleases us to claim our right and give way to our own inclinations, we can certainly disregard and transgress this law without blame, though perhaps not without disadvantage."[42] Locke rejects such expediency. He construes the natural law as yielding rights and duties that hold for *all* members of the human family. They include negative prohibitions against offending or injuring without cause. Such prohibitions imply corresponding negative rights of potential victims against taking away or jeopardizing "the Life, the Liberty, Health, Limb, or Goods of another." They include positive injunctions as well, the "great maxims of charity" that are also mandatory.[43]

Our "Inner Flaw": The phrase lacks some Augustinian or Kierkegaardian resonances, yet is seriously meant. Locke entertains doubts about original sin, at least in its literal form of inherited fault. But he acknowledges human inclinations to use power arbitrarily, and to fail to be fair and objective. We strive to accumulate more possessions than we need, succumbing to covetousness. We twist even the moral law in our own favor, as we seek to resolve disputes with others. We defy reasonableness as we presume to be judges in our own cases. Our self-love makes us partial to ourselves and to our friends. And our passion and revenge carry us too far in the severity of punishments we mete out to others.

These tendencies so pervade human life that Locke reaches a theological judgment: "God hath certainly appointed Government to restrain the partiality and violence of Men." Little brings out what this judgment implies for our own subsequent appraisals. "[T]he primary criterion by which to assess *all* governments is the degree of success each demonstrates in excluding and preventing the arbitrary use of power, that is, action involving coercion, disfigurement, infliction of pain, or indifference to need that is performed simply at someone's pleasure, including, of course, government officials."[44]

Such assessments matter and Locke is correct to stress how governments are answerable to the rest of humankind for showing how far they succeed.

United Nations Declaration

These pressures—to be answerable to the rest—intensify in the midst of World War II and the fascism and colonialism linked to it. The Declaration emerges in response to the horrors of the war and these two deformations driving it. The international system of rights promulgated amounts to "Hitler's Epitaph," a description Little cites several times.[45] But his repetition underscores the following point. The worm at the heart of Hitler's is captured in this statement: "National Socialism takes as the starting point . . . neither the individual nor humanity . . . [but] *das Volk* . . . [and] desires to safeguard [it], even at the expense of the individual."[46] Against this, the Declaration sets its face. Little's defense of this opposition remains, I think, permanently valuable. Quite simply, we should oppose "the absolute subjection of the individual to the will of the community." Much more should be said about the importance of sociality and community as well.[47] Still, we should affirm that "each and every individual, no matter of what ethnicity, religion, culture, gender, or location, has the right to condemn, and, if possible, to resist, the sort of arbitrary injury perpetrated in the name of National Socialism. This applies especially…to the 'nonderogable rights,' the protections against genocide, ethnic cleansing, mass rape, extrajudicial killing, torture, cruel and unusual punishment, enslavement, etc., but it also entails, particularly in public life, grave respect for the 'derogable rights' as well, such as free speech, assembly, press, and participation in government, since they are assumed, among other things, to afford critical opportunities for preventing Nazi-like atrocities."[48]

To concentrate on each of the two sides as I have done so far allows me now to take stock by returning to the uncertainty with which I started.

The Uncertainty Reviewed

I confess that I remain unsure how Little understands his own work in Christian ethics to relate to or perhaps not to relate to his own defense of natural human rights. Yet I now appreciate more that these two sides need not co-exist in equal measure or with equivalent force and urgency in one's thought and writing over many years. I also appreciate more that these two sides have never exhausted or always closely contained his theoretical and practical engagements. Little's work in Christian ethics forms one part of larger inquiries into comparative and historical religious ethics, and moral and political philosophy. His work on natural human rights forms one part of national and international political and institutional studies and normative and policy engagements that have taken him to many parts of the world.

Nevertheless, I continue to respect and take seriously his work in Reformed Christianity and natural human rights. And given the shape of my study here that attends to these texts, I close by identifying four topics that address specific parts of what the prior pages explore. I do not claim to find any single red thread that runs through them all. Still, I hope the topics are apt, and that they serve to locate points at which more elucidation may be welcome.

First, the relation to Calvin

Little has said fairly recently that "Calvin avoided taking the full consequences of his belief in natural moral knowledge by notoriously failing in practice to respect equal rights for all, regardless of religious identity or affiliation." "Notoriously" seems strong to me, given Calvin's historical context, and given the account of the mixture of reason and revelation in the first essay on the prospects for natural law where Calvin has a derivative theory, and no interest in developing a self-contained, independent doctrine. Natural law, Little says, always has to be seen in relation to a more inclusive theological and moral design. Does Calvin jettison this design, or is this a break with him? Finally, the relation between love and reason is sometimes difficult to track. Does the inclusiveness in the first essay require a theological grounding to avoid the Kluckhohn "in-group" restriction? Can reason avoid this, and/or should it? What standing or force, if any, does the in-group consideration retain?

Second, individual rights and the church

The insistence that we should not subvert individual protections I take to be vital and right. Can this accommodate any ongoing place for the church? In brief, does the Sabine observation no longer instruct? Is Williams's ecclesiology as Miller describes it, where we end with a most humane and inclusive civil relationship with everyone, the one Little now professes? Or does Little want to allow some part of the institutional church to remain as a distinct institution in the spirit of Sabine? Does this stop short of Williams's radical ecclesiology, while still honoring the insistence that we should subvert no individual protections?

Third, Locke and the difference a belief in God may make

Some of Locke's affirmations about God that Little cites seem to show more attention to God in Locke than in Little on Locke. For example, "God alone owns the life," and "Men are God's property, whose Workmanship they are, made to last during his, not one another's pleasure." Are these beliefs doing some of the work on behalf of human equality, by distinguishing all of us from being one another's property? Jeremy Waldron seems to think so, especially in his last chapter. Does Little fold Locke too easily into the account of human rights that ignores the harder-to-assimilate-parts of the *Reasonableness of Christianity* that Waldron considers with a degree of sympathy?

Fourth, on connections to other current Christian ethical schemes that stress natural law

How much does Little take his defense of natural human rights to play an adjudicating role in appraising the comparative adequacy and inadequacy of Christian ethical schemes that are currently influential?

He does some adjudicating in his attacks on Alasdair MacIntyre's and Stanley Hauerwas's anti-liberalism, and their opposition to rights, for example. But I have in mind other comprehensive schemes which engage more sympathetically matters to which his own defense of natural human rights is highly relevant. Two examples must suffice. Nicholas Wolterstorff writes a Foreword to Jean Porter's volume, *Natural and Divine Law: Reclaiming the Tradition for Christian Ethics*, in which he contrasts her natural law theory with that of John Finnis and Joseph Boyle. According to him, Finnis and Boyle propose "a mode of ethical inquiry which is independent both of all comprehensive religious and philosophical perspectives, and of all concrete moral communities. In particular, they present it as independent of theology. It is from human nature as such that they propose to derive ethical principles; and it is their claim that these principles are not only knowable, but in good measure known, by every rational human being whatsoever."[49]

Porter, on the other side, as Wolterstorff interprets her, claims that "the process of moral reflection typically involves some reflection on the givens of human nature. Yet the moral significance of these givens can never just be read off from observation and experience. Christian reflection on human nature, or human experience or needs or aspirations, always involves an element of selective interpretation in the light of theological commitments. . . . Natural law theorizing is reclaimed for Christian theology. And human nature is restored to Christian ethics. Christian ethics speaks of the natural givens of human life. But in the conviction that a neutral interpretation of those givens is not possible, it offers its own scripturally based theological interpretation of those natural givens."

Were Little to attempt to adjudicate the differences in these two instances, I speculate that in relation to Finnis and Boyle, he might contrast his case for natural human rights with the specifics of their own depictions of natural law. But in his thoroughgoing anti-traditionalism, he might welcome their normative independence from all concrete moral communities, as well as their independence from theology, and their claim that moral principles are knowable by every rational adult human being whatsoever.

In relation to Porter, he might reject her scripturally based theological interpretation of natural law as too particularist. But he might welcome her commitment (in her later book[50]) to at least a weak sense of foundationalism according to which "thought is impossible without some starting points which stand in need of no justification—to put it another way, that justification is not an infinite regress"; and to her siding with Brian Tierney's history over Oliver O'Donovan's on the origins of subjective rights claims as she proceeds herself robustly to defend human rights. I at least would benefit from seeing how Little appraises works on human rights and natural law, especially among Roman Catholic moral theologians, and in that way as well to enlarge the range of those with whom he engages.

NOTES

[1] This is an expanded version of the paper I presented at the "Conference on Religion, Ethics, and Peace: Honoring the Career of Professor David Little," Harvard Divinity School, November 13–14, 2009.

[2] These interpretive efforts include taking seriously Little's ongoing engagement with Reformed Christianity. We err, I think, to ignore such engagement, though Little's later concentrated stress on natural human rights—(see, e.g., G. Scott Davis, "Comment,"

in *The Journal of Religious Ethics*, 24.2 (2006): 287–310)—makes ignoring unsurprising. I want here to take the measure of both sides. We thereby encounter added possibilities, including possible tensions, in Little's work. For instance, in his early publication on Calvin and natural law to which I turn, he refers to Calvin's proceeding from the "top-down," starting from love and "working back" to make room for the precepts of natural law. I still find this sequence congenial, but it is unclear that he does. And I prefer a more circuitous route to natural law and natural rights that I call retrospective vindication. We extend instances of natural law where we prohibit actions found to be universally destructive of the bonds of any community. Yet we proceed on two assumptions. We vindicate what is not immediately or intuitively justified. And we appeal to a sense of tradition that we find to be not simply accidentally in place. I want to distinguish between tradition-dependence and cultural contingency. See my "The Particularist Turn in Theological and Philosophical Ethics," in *Christian Ethics: Problems and Prospects*, eds. Lisa Sowle Cahill and James F. Childress (Cleveland: Pilgrim Press, 1996), 93–118. Some requisite "continuity in directedness" can characterize certain traditions, as Alasdair MacIntyre holds. For a recent brief but suggestive account of several characterizations of tradition, see Lucy Beckett, "Tradition and Traducement," [London] *Times Literary Supplement* (December 17, 2010): 12–13. Of Augustine for example, she writes: "he was a highly educated late Roman, eventually a Christian who committed himself to a tradition of life and thought which was itself already centuries old. His was both a 'tradition-constituted' and a 'tradition-constituting' achievement." He was not engaged as he saw it in what was only "accidental." For a longer and most valuable discussion of tradition, including a sense of democratic tradition he extols, see Jeffrey Stout, *Democracy and Tradition* (Princeton: Princeton University Press, 2004). It is unworkable, however, to take up this discussion here.

[3] See David Little and Sumner Twiss, *Comparative Religious Ethics* (New York: Harper & Row, 1978). Their briefer anticipatory essay appeared as "Basic Terms in the Study of Religious Ethics," in *Religion and Morality*, eds. Gene Outka and John P. Reeder, Jr. (Garden City, NY: Anchor Books/Doubleday, 1973), 35–77.

[4] See his "Calvin and the Prospects for a Christian Theory of Natural Law," in *Norm and Context in Christian Ethics*, eds. Gene H. Outka and Paul Ramsey (New York: Scribner, 1968), 175–197; "The Law of Supererogation," in *The Love Commandments: Essays in Christian Ethics and Moral Philosophy*, eds. Edmund N. Santurri and William Werpehowski (Washington, D.C.: Georgetown University Press, 1992), 157–181 (this includes an account of Calvin's "reconstructed view of supererogation"); "Reformed Faith and Religious Liberty," in *Major Themes in the Reformed Tradition*, ed. Donald K. McKim (Grand Rapids: Eerdmans, 1997), 196–213.

[5] See his "Natural Rights and Human Rights: The International Imperative," in *Natural Rights and Natural Law: The Legacy of George Mason*, ed. Robert P. Davidow (The George Mason University Press, 1986), 67–122; "The Nature and Basis of Human Rights," in *Prospects for a Common Morality*, eds. Gene Outka and John P. Reeder, Jr. (Princeton: Princeton University Press, 1993), 73–92; "On Behalf of Rights: A Critique of *Democracy and Tradition*," *Journal of Religious Ethics* 34, no. 2 (2006): 287–310; "The Author Replies," in *Journal of Religious* Ethics 35, no. 1 (2007): 171–175.

⁶ Little, "Calvin and the Prospects for a Christian Theory of Natural Law," 193.
⁷ Ibid., 191.
⁸ Ibid., 180.
⁹ John Calvin, *Institutes of the Christian Religion*, II, 8, 55, in the *Library of Christian Classics*, Vol. XX, trans. Ford Lewis Battles (Philadelphia: Westminster Press, 1960), 418–19. We find an overlapping pattern of theological appeals in a modern context when Martin Luther King, Jr., utilizes widely discussed Greek distinctions among loves to affirm the following: "Agape is more than romantic love, agape is more than friendship. Agape is understanding, creative, redemptive, good will to all men. It is an overflowing love which seeks nothing in return. . . . [W]hen one rises to love on this level, he loves men not because he likes them, not because their ways appeal to him, but he loves every man because God loves him. And he rises to the point of loving the person who does an evil deed while hating the deed that the person does. I think this is what Jesus meant when he said 'love your enemies.' I'm very happy that he didn't say like your enemies, because it is pretty difficult to like some people. Like is sentimental, and it is pretty difficult to like someone bombing your home; it is pretty difficult to like somebody threatening your children; it is difficult to like congressmen who spend all of their time trying to defeat civil rights. But Jesus says love them, and love is greater than like." Martin Luther King, Jr., "Love, Law, and Civil Disobedience," in *A Testament of Hope*, ed. James Melvin Washington (San Francisco: Harper, 1991), 46–47. The respects in which these theological appeals overlap include the insistence that too many particular neighbors too often do and say unworthy and unlovable things. That is, such things can indeed engender hate more frequently than love, and warrant disliking what is truly unappealing or threatening. Contemplation in God and Christ's authority make sense of a universalist meaning of "neighbor" that otherwise may lack sufficient sense.
¹⁰ Little, "Calvin and the Prospects," 185–86.
¹¹ Ibid., 178.
¹² Ibid., 178–79.
¹³ Consider two cases in point. The commandment, "You shall not kill," is transformed as follows. A human person "is not responsible simply to resist murder, but also . . . he must go out of his way to enhance the physical *and* spiritual well-being of his neighbor. Here we positively practice virtue under the guidance of love. And active attention to cooperation and mutuality is, Calvin argues, entailed in the structure of humanity itself." The commandment, "you shall not steal," is similarly broadened. We are indeed responsible when we defraud our neighbors by means of money, merchandise, or land. Yet here too Little presses the Calvinist interpretation as he construes it, that this commandment has "benevolence and *cooperation* as its end—that we should strive on our own initiative "to protect and promote the well-being and interests of others." Ibid., 179.
¹⁴ Ibid., 189–90.
¹⁵ Ibid., 190.
¹⁶ Ibid., 191–92.
¹⁷ Ibid., 191.

[18] David Heyd, *Supererogation: Its Status in Ethical Theory* (Cambridge: Cambridge University Press, 1982).

[19] Little, "The Law of Supererogation," 179.

[20] George H. Sabine, *A History of Political Theory*, third edition (New York: Holt Rinehart and Winston, 1962), 180 (as quoted in Little, "Reformed Faith and Religious Liberty," 196).

[21] Sabine, *A History of Political Theory*, 185–86.

[22] On two recurrent fears evident in recent debates that may cut against each other, namely, the tyranny of particular communities and epistemic hubris, see Gene Outka and John P. Reeder, Jr., "Introduction," *Prospects for a Common Morality*, esp. 24–25.

[23] For elaboration, see Little, "Reformed Faith and Religious Liberty," 200–206.

[24] Little, "Reformed Faith and Religious Liberty," 205. In the American case, we should acquire a comprehensive sense of Puritan achievements, both *pro* and *contra*. Hugh Heclo, in *Christianity and American Democracy* (Cambridge, MA: Harvard University Press, 2007) turns to Tocqueville on this subject. "But these Puritans [sic.] were also what today we would call religious extremists, and Tocqueville pulls no punches on that score. . . . [He] considered such penal codes shameful invasions of conscience and violations of human spirit. The key point, however, is that 'these ridiculous and tyrannical laws were not imposed from outside—they were voted by the free agreement of all the interested parties themselves.' Alongside the penal codes was the great host of political laws embodying the republican spirit of freedom. Local independence, broad citizen suffrage with elected officials, free voting of taxes, trial by jury, government responsiveness to social needs—this broad sphere of political freedom was undergirded rather than contradicted by the Puritans' religious convictions. Clearest of all the examples were laws for compulsory public schooling. In good Protestant fashion, enforced taxpayer support for literacy was justified as promoting a knowledge of the Bible. . . . Tocqueville answers the anti-religious sneers of France's Enlightenment *philosophes* with facts: 'In America it is religion which leads to enlightenment and the observance of divine laws which leads men to liberty.'" Heclo, *Christianity and American Democracy*, 11.

[25] Little, "Reformed Faith and Religious Liberty," 202.

[26] Ibid., 206.

[27] For a clear and perceptive account of Williams, see William Lee Miller, *The First Liberty: Religion and the American Republic* (New York: Knopf, 1986), 152–224.

[28] This appropriation does not lessen my uncertainty about the standing of certain previous claims, e.g., about love and the church. At an earlier stage Little stresses the role of love in a central, integrating way. Then, he observes: "the two realms for Calvin join and interpenetrate one another in regard to the common end they both share: love. Love is the end of the law as well as the end of grace. Consequently, while it is impossible to reduce the inner and outer worlds to each other, it is impossible completely to separate them either. The mutuality and cooperativeness demanded by the law of 'outward behavior' is certainly not alien to the love granted in Christ, which affects the 'inner mind.'" Little, "Calvin and the Prospects for a Christina Theory of Natural Law," 182. Now, apart from remarks on love and supererogation, love largely ceases to be thematized as such, though some normative overlaps between rights and earlier

claims about love may obtain. In the case of the church, nothing explicitly Reformed is familiar to me beyond "Reformed Faith and Religious Liberty." I am unaware on this ecclesial side of how he appraises Williams's own radical faith leading perpetually to separation. Miller describes the latter engaging result in this way. [Williams] "carried the effort to achieve a separated purity so far as to arrive at a paradoxical acceptance of unseparated and 'impure' inclusiveness that becomes one source, though not the only one, of his condemnation of religious persecution. Since no actual church on earth is pure enough, then give up the effort to exclude anybody in the false churches that actually exist on this earth. One might say his intense exclusiveness turned around on itself. Having pushed separation and purity so far as to remove the true church from the existing institutions of the real world, he settled in that world for a most humane and inclusive civil relationship with everyone." Miller, *The First Liberty*, 166.

[29] Little, "The Author Replies," 172. See G. Scott Davis, "Comment," in *Journal of Religious Ethics* 35 no. 1 (2007): 165–170.

[30] Little, "The Author Replies," 172.

[31] Little, "Natural Rights and Human Rights," 70.

[32] Little, "On Behalf of Rights," 308.

[33] Little, "Natural Rights and Human Rights," 67.

[34] Ibid., 68 (my italics).

[35] Ibid., 73.

[36] Ibid., 70.

[37] Richard Rorty, *Consequences of Pragmatism* (Minneapolis: University of Minnesota Press, 1982), xlii.

[38] John Reeder demonstrates—in a forthcoming article, "Little on Grounding Human Rights"—how this is a chief concern. Reeder offers a number of illuminating comparisons as he locates Little's recent claims in the midst of a range of relevant philosophical literature. My debts to this article are appreciable. I learn from the intricacies of philosophical commentary it provides about such recent claims. Still, I think we learn as well from referring to Little's earlier claims together with his more recent ones. (Regarding the recent claims, I work from Reeder's draft in typescript that is subject to revision, so I omit page numbers.) Reeder himself departs from Little in one major respect and takes a neo-pragmatist turn where justification is relative to context. See Reeder's own prior account of this turn in "Foundations without Foundationalism," *Prospects for a Common Morality*, 191–214.

[39] Little, "Natural Rights and Human Rights," 75.

[40] See, e.g., C. B. Macpherson, *The Political Theory of Possessive Individualism: Hobbes to Locke* (Oxford: Oxford University Press, 1962).

[41] Little draws on more recent studies that effectively challenge Macpherson's reading. See, e.g., James Tully, *A Discourse on Property: John Locke and his Adversaries* (Cambridge: Cambridge University Press, 1980). Tully finds alliances, as Little notes, between Locke's views on property and those of the Roman Catholic tradition. Little, "Natural Rights and Human Rights," 112.

[42] As cited in Little, "Natural Rights and Human Rights," 82.

[43] Locke writes memorably about both justice and charity. "As *justice* gives every Man a Title to the product of his honest Industry; ... *so Charity gives every Man a Title to so much out of another's Plenty, as will keep him from extream want,* where he has no means to subsist otherwise; and a Man can no more justly make use of another's necessity, to force him to become his Vassal, by with-holding that Relief, God requires him to afford to the wants of his Brother, than he that has more strength can seize upon a weaker, master him to his Obedience, and with a Dagger at his Throat offer him Death or Slavery." Little, "Natural Rights and Human Rights," 83–85. I only add now one item of controversy about Locke's views on charity that Little does not directly consider. (Its importance arguably connects for instance to modern debates about "welfare reform" that reached a pitch in the United States during President Clinton's administration.) In Locke's case, some critics claim that the closest he comes to an *uncharitable* stance occurs in his essay on the Poor Law, where for instance he criticizes the "idle poor." Yet Jeremy Waldron registers four qualifications that apply particularly to Locke. First, Locke was reputed to be notably charitable himself to all who labored as long as they could. Second, he assumed in the essay that politically the poor have a right to subsistence, that "everyone must have meat, drink, clothing, and firing." Third, he maintained that the political community can *enforce* charity, but not *radical* charity. The latter comes in two forms: (a) charity to someone who *could* work, but refuses to work; (b) charity that sells all one has and gives to the poor (a follower of Christ may practice this, but may not be forced by others to practice it). Fourth, the injunction to work, as Locke saw it, holds for *all*. "His view that the 'true and proper relief of the poor...consists in finding work for them,' is not contrary to the egalitarian premise of the doctrine of charity." Waldron, *God, Locke, and Equality: Christian Foundations in Locke's Political Thought* (Cambridge: Cambridge University Press, 2002), 186–87.

[44] Little, "Natural Rights and Human Rights," 99–101.

[45] E.g., Little, "The Nature and Basis of Human Rights," 77.

[46] As cited in Little, "On Behalf of Rights," 307.

[47] In saying more, we should reckon with complexities that a distinction between the "politics of equal dignity" and the "politics of difference" introduces. On this, see, e.g., Charles Taylor, "The Politics of Recognition," in *Multiculturalism*, ed. Amy Gutmann (Princeton: Princeton University Press, 1994), 25–73. See as well Susan Moller Okin, *Is Multiculturism Bad for Women?* (Princeton: Princeton University Press, 1999), 9–24, 117–131.

[48] Little, "On Behalf of Rights," 307. Little is also right to include not only European fascism but Japanese fascism as perpetuating atrocities before and during World War II, 297.

[49] Jean Porter, *Natural and Divine Law: Reclaiming the Tradition for Christian Ethics* (Grand Rapids: Eerdmans, 1999), 11.

[50] Jean Porter, *Nature as Reason* (Grand Rapids: Eerdmans, 2005).

3.
Roger Williams and Freedom of Conscience and Religion as a Natural Right

Sumner B. Twiss

Introduction

I recently had occasion to read some historical, philosophical, and religious materials on the foundations of human rights long on my bookshelf, works by Richard Tuck and Brian Tierney on natural rights, Jeremy Waldron on God, Locke, and equality, John Witte on rights in Reformation thought, and Morton White on the American Founders' philosophy, as well as primary source materials,[1] such as excerpts from Roger Williams's work.[2] In re-reading Tierney's essay on a historical perspective on religious rights[3] I encountered the claim that: "Roger Williams has been called an extreme proponent of natural rights because of his all-embracing argument for freedom of conscience, but this seems to be a misunderstanding of his position. I do not think Williams ever used the language of natural rights" [Williams here is strongly contrasted with William Penn and John Locke in this regard]. In his footnote to this claim, Tierney reiterates: "Williams relied on his own idiosyncratic understanding of scripture rather than any appeal to natural rights in defending religious freedom. He inveighed against the light of nature in *The Examiner Defended*."[4]

Knowing David Little as I have these many years and hearing him wax eloquent about Roger Williams's defense of the right to freedom of conscience and religion as well as Williams's possible influence on Locke's position on religious toleration, Tierney's claim took me somewhat aback. Here was the author of a definitive history of the idea of natural rights appearing to contradict Little, a reputed scholar of Roger Williams in particular, and religious tolerance generally. So I searched Little's bibliography for anything bearing on Tierney's claim. I found it in an article Little wrote over two decades ago on Williams and the separation of church and state: "As with Williams, so with Locke, 'Liberty of conscience is everyman's natural right, equally belonging to dissenters as to themselves' [quoting Locke]. In addition they would both concur that freedom of conscience is an inalienable natural right."[5] And in an endnote to the essay (referencing another section of the paper), Little wrote: "While there is no theory or doctrine of natural rights in Williams, he does mention the idea often enough in connection with religious liberty and civil organization . . . to permit the conclusion that the idea was of great moral and political significance to him. That Williams intended to apply the idea of natural rights including the idea of equal freedom to political life can be fairly inferred from his practice in Rhode Island. For example, he supported constitutional provisions for religious equality and freedom . . . in the Code of 1647." This appears to be an interpretation of Williams on the issue that is seriously at odds with Tierney's. Questions naturally occurred to me, for example: Who is right or at least has the better case? If Williams made arguments for freedom of conscience and religion as being a natural right, what were they? And what exactly might be his understanding of this natural right?

Reading the entire Williams corpus, even without a Scriptural scholar's or theologian's background, one can see relevant ethical and philosophical dimensions to his work that may inform a tentative approach to this question. Much of Williams's writing is polemical and directed to refuting ideas and practices of religious intolerance, compulsion, and persecution as being contrary to scripture properly interpreted, and it is significantly informed by Reformed, Calvinist, and Puritan thought. Williams's principal interlocutor is John Cotton, a Puritan leader of the Massachusetts Bay Colony, from which Williams was banished early on in his New World career. Many of Williams's arguments fall within the category of what we would now call "immanent critique" of Cotton's reading of New Testament passages and parables, Cotton's tendency to use Old Testament political paradigms for the then contemporary setting, and inconsistencies among Cotton's claims and between his claims and practices. Thus, I can appreciate the force of Tierney's skeptical denial of natural rights and of freedom of conscience and religion as a natural right as being a significant thread or appeal in Williams's writings. Just for one example, in his conclusion to *The Bloody Tenent Yet More Bloody*, in the person of "Truth" (conversing with "Peace"), Williams offers a summary list of his reasons against religious compulsion: blasphemy against the God of peace and order; warring against the Prince of Peace; contrary to the spirit of love; loathsomeness in the eyes of God; bar to the gracious prophecies and promises of Christ; producer of conflict, massacre, and war; undermining of the civil order; and so forth.[6] On the face of it, Williams's criticisms appear, on the one hand, principled theologically as derived from the New Testament, and, on the other, consequentialist politically and practically.

Yet, in fact, another set of appeals is sounded, though apparently more muted, here at least. Compulsion of conscience and religion involves, for example, defilement of soul and conscience, including the corruption of the civil honesty and natural conscience of a nation, and gross impartiality and denial of the principle of common justice. It remains, of course, to be seen whether any of these appeals—either of the former list or these two latter points—add up to a natural rights position of some sort, but I think it important to acknowledge at least the prima facie force of Tierney's challenge.

One might simply set out the pros and cons of both Tierney's and Little's interpretations of the contested issue between them, then draw a conclusion—suitably qualified—in favor of one or the other. But the approach that really interests me involves trying to discern those lines of argument in Williams that support Little's position against Tierney's. I am developing this approach for at least three reasons. First, I am interested in how a theologian might argue a natural rights position on the question. Second, after reading Williams, I concluded that it might be useful to provide a focused defense for regarding Williams's position on freedom of conscience and religion as one of natural right, that is, one that concentrates on the issue of natural rights and that is alert to the different lines of arguments that Williams appears to deploy on this particular issue. Third, the lines of argument I do discern are morally interesting, even to those (like me) who are not theologically inclined.

Certain results might be looked for from this methodology as well. In the first instance, even though Williams may use the language of natural rights lightly, analyzing him along these lines may provide a paradigm of sorts for seeing similar positions in other cases. In the second, one could regard my remarks as trying to develop a bit further (and thus defend) Little's interpretive position on Williams. And, in the third, I think I can show that Williams has something to offer to contemporary human rights work on freedom of conscience and religion—for example, the nature of inherent dignity and its violation and the internal complexity of the right to freedom of conscience and religion—or at least position him as a sort of participant in contemporary concern about such matters.

So far as I can determine, Williams has at least four major lines of argument for regarding freedom of conscience and religion as a natural right. I label them as: divine right and will; natural justice; inviolability of conscience; and consensual government. I will discuss the arguments in this order, simply because it appears logical to me to move from God, through morality, to politics. The order coincidently may reflect Williams's own normative priorities, as distinguished from how much he might say about each. Before I limn these arguments, I want to emphasize that in Williams's writings they are not discrete but rather overlap considerably. Williams, like many of us, is a holistic thinker, and much of his argumentation is jumbled together, not only because of his holism but also because he wrote with passion and "on the fly" so to speak without apparently editing his work prior to publication. Nonetheless, I think it is analytically more useful to distinguish his lines of argument, because each appears to be an integral thread in the fabric of his position. Prior to reconstructing each argument, I will cite illustrative passages from his writings bearing on the argument. Perforce I will need to be selective from many other similar passages. I might also add one further point or disclaimer. I am well aware that many of Williams's ideas—not all, but many—can be found in Reformed thought generally, as is signaled by the fact that he not un-occasionally refers to Luther, Calvin, and Beza, among others, and also by the fact he was personally acquainted with, for example, John Milton. Tracking and noting such historical influences are not, however, my concern; nor, for that matter, would doing so be within my competence. I am concerned solely with Williams's lines of arguments as he appears to invoke and lay them out. I leave it to others to deal with the historical dimensions of his arguments.[7]

Before turning to Williams's specific lines of argument, I want to say a few words about the terminology of rights and natural rights. There is an important distinction to be drawn between the idea of objective right, on the one hand, and the notion of subjective rights, on the other. Objective right, in my view, is simply a way of referring to what is the case, morally speaking: for example, it is morally right to assist people in need when the cost to oneself of doing so is minimal. This is a matter of right principle, entirely apart from a recipient's claiming a right to my assistance; in many moral systems there is no personal (or subjective) right to such assistance, though in those same systems it would be morally right or correct for an agent to render assistance to people in need. A subjective right, by contrast, is a power or entitlement that one holds in one's personal capacity as a subject: for example, I have a subjective right to express my opinions freely so long as I am not infringing the important subjective rights of others or breaking important moral rules such as non-maleficence. I mention this distinction because, when examining the writings of older thinkers working within the natural law tradition, it may not always be clear whether they are using "right" to refer to an objective moral principle (or rule) or, alternatively, a subjective right held by a person. The lack of clarity arises from the fact that beginning in the twelfth century, certain natural law theorists (of objective right) began to use the language and conceptuality of natural subjective rights—often deriving and justifying these on the basis of objectively right natural moral principles—and so it is sometimes not always clear whether in using the term "right" in its singular form, they meant objective right or a subjective right. Determining which meaning was (or is) operative depends on contextual considerations that weigh in one direction or the other in settling the question.

With respect to subjective rights in particular, it is also important to be aware of how they function. Generally speaking, such rights identify individual or subjective entitlements to demand certain actions or forbearances from others such that their non-compliance justifies sanctions—whether moral or legal or both. Such entitlements may be interpreted as requiring a social guarantee for others' compliance, and the rights are typically invoked as strong reasons for justifying why others must comply on threat of sanction. These reasons can relate to personal status or role within a normative social order (as in parental rights) or important personal interests defined by the normative social order (as in free expression). The status or interest at issue both explains and justifies the right. Regarding natural subjective rights in particular, the entitlements at issue are rooted in the way we are—that is, the status or interests we have as human beings—within the natural moral order, however that order might have been originally established, for example, by divine decree or creative act, or by reasonable discernment of implicitly operative principles in the human condition. There are additional things to be noted about subjective rights, but I will allow these to emerge from Williams's own arguments, to which I now turn.

Divine Right and Will

The first argument from divine right and will actually has two interconnected components, one generally theocentric and the other specifically Christological. I begin with the first component. The following excerpts illustrate the broader theocentric line of reasoning:[8]

> *I plead the conscience of all men to be at liberty . . . only let not Caesar (or Constantine) rob the God of Heaven of his Right, the conscience of his subjects, their heavenly rights and liberties.* [HM, 179]

> *I affirm that the cutting off by the sword other consciences and religions is contrarily most provoking to God, expressly against his Will.* [BT, 284]

> *Over souls God will not suffer any man to rule: only he himself will rule there. Wherever whosoever doth undertake to give laws unto the soul and conscience of man, he ursurpeth that government himself which appertains unto God.* [BT, 36]

> *At last . . . proclaim a true and absolute soul-freedom to all people of the land impartially, so that no person be forced to pray or pay otherwise than his soul believes and consents. This act . . . I believe . . . to be the absolute will of God as to this and all . . . nations of the world.* [MB, 135]

> *I desire not that liberty to myself which I would not freely and impartially weigh out to all consciences of the world beside. And therefore I do humbly conceive that it is the will of the Most High and the express and absolute duty of the civil powers to proclaim an absolute freedom in . . . all the world . . . that each . . .*

division of people, Yea, and persons, may freely enjoy [whatever] worship, ministry, [and] maintenance to afford them [that their soul desire]. [HM, 174]

Passages such as these (and there are many others) appear to project the following line of argument:

1) God is the author of creation and as such has rights over it.

2) Exercising these rights, God wills through his creation that his subjects (humankind) have rights and liberties.

3) God further wills that civil powers respect the rights and liberties that he has granted to his subjects.

4) Among these rights and liberties is soul-freedom, that is, freedom of conscience and religion.

5) With respect to the right of soul-freedom in particular, civil powers have the absolute duty to respect, proclaim, and defend it.

Williams is clearly conceiving of soul-freedom as a right conferred by God, according to his own right, to all people the world over and claiming, I believe, that they were created this way. Thus, it appears to me that that soul-freedom is a natural right deriving from God's own right and will, even though the specific language of natural rights is not used here by Williams. Moreover, it cannot go unnoticed that correlative with God's right and humankind's right of soul-freedom is an absolute duty laid by God on all civil powers to respect and protect this right. The parallel between Williams's latter claim and the contemporary conception of human rights as being claimable against and imposed on governments such that they have duties to respect and guarantee them should not go unnoticed.

The second component of the divine right and will argument is Christological and equally clear in its import. Here again are some illustrative passages:

By the word of Christ no man should be molested with the civil sword [for religious reasons] . . . this foundation [thus] laid is the Magna Charta of highest liberties. [BT, 220]

Christ's interest in the commonweal is the freedom of souls of the people. . . . It is the design and decree of heaven to break to pieces yokes and chains upon souls and the conscience of men. . . . The interest of the Son of God is soul-freedom against the tyranny and persecution of any conscience. [ED, 204]

> *Christ had no intent to save souls by destroying of bodies—but to save soul and body and that for soul's sake, for religion's sake, for his sake, the bodies of [all] should be permitted to enjoy a temporal being which might prove a means of their eternal life and salvation.* [BTM, 256]

> *If the civil officers judge and punish in spiritual causes . . . he acts without a commission and warrant from Christ and so stands guilty at the bar of Christ as a Transcendent Delinquent.* [BT, 228]

This phase of the argument speaks of the interest of Christ in soul-freedom and links that interest (and the reasons for it) to Christ's word and the design and decree of heaven. So we appear to have an argument of this form:

1) Christ's interest, and the rationale for his presence in the world, is to save the souls of all persons.

2) The possibility of salvation requires that persons have the opportunity in their temporal existence to respond freely to Christ's message and presence.

3) This possibility, in turn, requires the civil recognition of what has been previously established—that the soul must be free in religious matters within civil jurisdictions.

4) Thus, it is Christ's word that this freedom be the Magna Charta of liberties respected by all civil authority.

5) If any civil authority breaches this word, then he is a transcendent delinquent before Christ.

Though Christological, it appears to me that this argument operates as a reaffirmation of the theocentric argument by using the language of Magna Charta for soul-freedom as a right and by holding civil authorities accountable for any breaches regarding its violation.[9] Thus, I am inclined to regard this argument as a continuation of the preceding one and still linked to the defense of soul-freedom as a natural right. As Williams writes in another place, religious compulsion and persecution in "hunting the life of the Savior is fighting against God" (BTM, 515). That is, the transcendently delinquent civil authority who disobeys the word of Christ contravenes the will of God regarding the exercising of God's right in conferring on humankind the right of liberty of conscience and religion. Aside from the metaphors of Magna Charta and Transcendent Delinquent, which seem to me especially powerful (e.g., regarding right and its correlativity with duty), this second phase of Williams's argument is particularly interesting for another reason, namely, its attempt to link Christ's interest to God's will and right. This linkage calls to mind two alternative contemporary theories about the meaning and function of rights generally: the will theory and the interest theory.[10] Will theories hold that a right makes its holder sovereign with respect to power exercisable over another's duty. Interest theories hold that a right functions to protect the holder's important or fundamental interests. With respect to God and Christ, it is fascinating that Williams seems to shift from something like an implicit will theory (for God) to an implicit interest theory (for Christ). The shift—if it is a shift—raises the provocative question of whether in the case of God and Christ at least, these theories are significantly related, such that God's will and Christ's interest are really the same, which, in turn, raises the question as to whether in the case of fundamentally defining interests—such as Christ's in soul salvation and freedom—these interests confer sovereignty, or put alternatively, whether sovereignty is most properly explicated and applied with respect to fundamental interests. The distinction and especially its possible collapse in Williams's argument here raises the further question as to how Williams may have conceived of the natural right to freedom of conscience and religion—under the aegis of a small-scale sovereignty on the part of human being, or within the frame of people's fundamentally important interest in soul-freedom, or both, with respect at least to this particular right.[11] We at least need to be alert to this matter in considering Williams's other arguments.

Natural Justice

The second line of argument in Williams for freedom of conscience and religion is related to the first—since it derives from similar premises—and, as will be seen later also functions significantly in his other two arguments as well. It is an argument from natural law, natural reason, natural justice, or equity. Whether or not this argument can stand by itself as an argument for a natural right is open to question. I am frankly not utterly sure, but I think the argument is worth exploring from that point of view. The illustrative passages from Williams include these:

> *What is the light of Nature in man but that order which the most glorious Former of all things has set (like wheels in clocks) a going in all his creatures.* [GF, 359]
>
> *Natural wisdom is two-fold. First, what is common to all mankind in general. Second, that which is more noble, refined, and elevated by education, study, and experience.* [These two are clearly distinguished by Williams from any salvific knowledge brought by Christ, which cannot be attained by natural wisdom, common or refined.] [HM, 241]
>
> *All mankind having the law are persuaded that some actions are naught . . . as to steal, to murder, etc.* [GF, 364–5]
>
> *[According to Tertullian], it agreeth both with human reason and natural equity that every man worship God uncompelled and believe what he will.* [BT, 35]
>
> *[There is a] difference between state necessity of freedom to different consciences and the equity . . . of such freedom. . . . This [the second] comes nearer to the life of the business. . . . There is no true reason of policy or piety what that man that will subscribe to civil engagement . . . his conscience should be deprived and robbed of the liberty of it in spiritual and religious matters.* [BTM, 6–8]
>
> *A tenent whose gross partiality denies the principles of common justice, while men weigh out to the consciences of all others, that which they judge not . . . right to be weighed out to their own: since the persecutor's rule is, to take and persecute all consciences, only, himself not be touched.* [BTM, 498]
>
> *Framing a safe communication of freedom of conscience in worship . . . to them to whom it is due as to any other conscience.* [BTM, 11]
>
> *Freedom of all consciences in matters of worship . . . [is] no more than their due and Right.* [BTM, 47]
>
> *[T]here is a moral virtue, fidelity, ability, and honesty which other men (besides church members) are, by good nature and education, by good laws and good examples, nourished and trained up in—[so] that civil places of trust and credit need not be monopolized into the hands of church members . . . and all*

others deprived and despoiled of their natural and civil rights and liberties. [BTM, 365]

From passages such as these, it appears possible to reconstruct the following argument:

1) God's creation imbeds a moral natural law that can be accessed as natural wisdom by all people and by some it can be developed and refined by reason in the light of experience.

2) This natural law includes at a minimum prohibitions on actions such as stealing, murder, and bearing false witness (roughly the second table of the Decalogue).

3) By reason or natural equity, including significantly the Golden Rule or the principle of reciprocity, the natural law can be extended to include the prohibition of religious compulsion for all impartially, or put alternatively, the equal protection of freedom of conscience and religion.

4) This freedom of conscience and religion is not only a matter of due justice (or equity) but also one of subjective right, that is, a natural right.

Given Williams's many references to historical contemporary experience in connection with this natural law and justice argument, it may very well be argued that his cited cases of religious compulsion and persecution and their negative effects function as part of this line of argumentation—as a sort of demonstrative outworking of natural equity with respect to freedom of conscience and religion. But allowing this expansion does not, in my view at least, get to the heart of the argument for such freedom as a natural right. That is to say, it appears to me possible for a natural law argument to be deployed to support a prohibition on religious compulsion without at the same time claiming a natural right. Thus, while, for example, I have interpreted Williams, in the above cited passage about people's freedom of conscience being their due and right, as claiming a subjective right in addition to saying that such freedom ought, according to equity and reciprocity, be recognized for all impartially, some might respond that Williams is speaking only of "objective right" as what justice requires and no more. My evidence for the additional claim of a subjective right is the explicit passage I cited where Williams appears to derive natural rights and liberties generally from a refined interpretation of what moral virtue, fidelity, ability, and honesty entail. Just in case this derivation may not be utterly convincing, I believe that it may also be the case that Williams's other arguments (e.g., inviolability of conscience and consensual government), aspects of which also include references to natural law and natural rights, can give us even more confidence in thinking that natural law and natural rights are related in his thinking and that freedom of conscience and religion is regarded by him as a subjective natural right. In fact, I believe that the two additional lines of arguments that Williams deploys weigh in favor of such an interpretation, or so I wish to suggest.

Inviolability of Conscience

I think that Williams's third line of argument regarding the normative inviolability of conscience is his most powerful one for the natural right of freedom of conscience and religion, even though he does not use the language of natural rights in developing it. As will be seen, this argument is largely about what violation of conscience entails, and though at first blush it may seem simply consequentialist in citing and characterizing the harms of religious compulsion and persecution, his reasoning about and his images of violation appear to point toward a stronger and more deontological argument that I believe is associated with the denial of a crucially important natural right. Consider, for example, the following passages:

> *The natural truth or light is received internally by a natural or moral understanding—civil and moral light sorts and agrees with those moral and civil convictions of natural light . . . [they are received] by an internal faculty . . . a receptive faculty within willing to receive but only with regard to natural and moral understandings.* [GF, 370–1]

> *Remember that that thing which we call conscience is of such a nature . . . that . . . although it be groundless, false, and deluded [with respect to religious matters], yet it is not by any arguments or torments easily removed. . . . I speak of conscience, a persuasion fixed in the mind and heart of a man, which forces him to judge . . . and to do so and so, with respect to God [and] his worship. This conscience is found in all mankind, more or less.* [BTM, 508–9]

[The] light of nature leads men to hear that only which nature conceives good for it, and therefore not to hear a messenger . . . whom conscience persuades is a false messenger or deceiver . . . as millions of men and women in their several respective religions and consciences are so persuaded, conceiving their own to be true. [BT, 287]

In matters of religion and conscience the violent motion must break . . . the tenderest part of man, his conscience. [BTM, 13]

The best religion is a torment to the soul and conscience that is forced against its own free love and choice to embrace and observe it. And therefore there ought to be no forcing, but the soul and mind and conscience of man—that is, indeed, the man—ought to be left free. [BTM, 439–40]

Persecution in proper and ordinary speech signifies penal and corporeal punishment and affliction . . . corporeal violence inflicted for some spiritual or religious matter. [BTM, 105]

A chaste wife will not abhor to be restrained from her husband's bed as adulterous and polluted but also abhor (if not more) to be constrained to the bed of a stranger. And what is abominable in corporeal is much more loathsome in spiritual whoredom and defilement. [BT, 63]

[In] practices of persecution . . . fathers are forced to accuse and betray their children, the children their fathers, husbands their wives . . . for fear of horrible death on the one side or else of running on the rocks of perjury on the other. [BTM, 177]

Straining of men's conscience by civil power . . . cause men to play the hypocrite and dissemble in their religion. . . . [It] so weakens and defiles it [the conscience] that it loses its strength and the very nature of a common honest conscience. [BTM, 209]

Soul oppression [involves] yokes where [people are] forced to receive a doctrine and pray . . . wracking their souls, bodies, and purses. . . . [A] great load may be made up by parcels and particulars, as well as by in mass or bulk . . . and the backs of some men . . . may be broke, by a withdrawing from them some civil privileges and rights (which are their due) as well as afflicting them in their purses, or flesh upon their backs. [BTM, 527]

Forcing of a woman that is a violent act of uncleanness upon her body against her will we count as a rape: by proportion that is spiritual or soul rape a forcing of the conscience of any person to acts of worship. [BTM, 325]

Conscience ought not to be violated or forced . . . indeed a soul or spiritual rape is more abominable . . . than to force and ravish the bodies of all the women in the world. [BT, 182]

The bloody tenent of persecution for cause of conscience [is] a notorious and common pirate that takes and robs, that fires and sinks the spiritual ships, the consciences of men. [BTM, 5]

The fact that I have quoted for this third line of argument so many passages from Williams is a reflection of the facts that not only does he write more about it but also that it appears to have a number of subtle and nuanced components. It was apparently very important to him and appeared to dominate his thinking about freedom of conscience and religion, and so it is equally important to get it right. I think, in outline, his argument goes something like this:

1) All people are created with a conscience conceived as a natural internal faculty with access to moral knowledge essential to the formation of personal moral identity, which, in turn, may involve significant religious convictions of diverse sorts—it is not only the tenderest part of a person but also "the man," the essential core of every moral personality that defines who he is for both himself and others.

2) This identity, personality, or core involves not only defining moral and religious convictions, epistemically speaking, but also manifestation of these convictions in both pertinent behavior and social relationships within a social setting.

3) This identity, personality, or core is in principle open to change that, however, can only by effected by means of evidence, argument, and personal experience and that as a matter of fact is resistant to compulsion by means of coercion and force imposed by others: at best such latter means can only result in changes of behavior, whether by restraint from behavior manifesting a person's core convictions or by constraint to new modes of behavior that are cognitively dissonant with the person's original core convictions.

4) Compelled behavior against a person's core convictions can damage the conscience in the sense that such compulsion uses the natural instinct of self-preservation in the face of bodily affliction to cause the person to betray those convictions (self-betrayal) and to betray conviction-related and equally defining intimate and social relationships (betrayal of others); over time such betrayals not only will erode the person's moral identity but also can destroy it.

5) Religious compulsion of any sort—which can be arrayed along a spectrum of severity ranging across taxation, loss of civil standing, loss of livelihood, imprisonment, torture, and death whether threatened or actually imposed—entails using bodily affliction in the service of restraining from or constraining to certain religious practices in the false belief that such compulsion itself can change a person's core convictions without damaging the person.

6) Involving as it does such compelled self-betrayal, religious compulsion is so serious as to amount to a heinous crime begging comparison with rape and piracy, with rape being understood as an intrinsic violation of a person's bodily integrity, and piracy being understood as an intrinsic violation of a group's fundamental security in the world. If, therefore, one regards the latter as serious crimes, so too must religious compulsion be a crime of equal seriousness—indeed, suggests Williams, even greater seriousness.

Now, one might fairly ask, why regard this argument as a natural rights argument, since after all the language of natural rights is nowhere used by Williams in deploying it. I have two broad suggestions here, which I will attempt to deepen subsequently as I further examine its features. First, Williams's argument seems to involve a notion of the normative inviolability of conscience in the way that it was created and operates. Second, by invoking the parallel with the crimes he cites, Williams appears to be presuming that all persons—by the light of nature—can and do recognize these crimes as being beyond the pale of any civilized human behavior, thereby constituting *ius cogens* prohibitions or preemptory norms (to adapt a phrase from international law), and within the orbit of such crimes he includes religious compulsion and persecution. In broad sweep, these two observations support the idea that Williams subscribed to a notion of normative violability of a person's conscience and moral personality, and

I think that such a notion provides a strong basis or ground for ascribing a human or natural right to persons in matters of religious conscience. That is to say, Williams is pivoting his argument on a certain feature or attribute that human beings have by nature or in virtue of their humanity, and he is claiming that this attribute ought to have a presumptive normative inviolability. This claim is more than simply one of intrinsic value, and I suggest that this "more" is captured by the language of a natural right to freedom of conscience and religion.

Even at the risk of repeating what I have just said, I would like to say a bit more about the character of Williams's argument. In light of the images of soul-rape and piracy, along with others that he uses (e.g., slavery), I think it is worth asking just what it is about religious compulsion that is so bad, why Williams might employ these violative terms, and what they might imply. I take it that Williams thinks of corporeal rape as heinous because such an act constitutes a particularly egregious attack on a person's body that is central to her physical existence as a person. That is, one's body is an aspect of one's being as a person and to intentionally invade it is to deny the victim's very personhood and agency as (dare I say it?) an autonomous and integral being. In effect, it assaults the victim's embodied personhood and agency and makes her into a mere object or slave to be manipulated by another in such a way that the victim experiences total subjugation and loss of control of her body.[12] That this is Williams's conception of physical rape can be fairly inferred from his conception of soul-rape—even though this might seem like circular reasoning of sorts—for it is utterly clear that he sees soul-rape as a radical dehumanization of the person in that it assaults the very core of a person—"the man" and the natural God-given conscience as the basis of moral personality. Soul-rape inflicts pain (of one sort or another) on the body precisely in order to try to manipulate a moral and religious identity. According to Williams, it hunts for conscience and seeks to force it to betray itself (or oneself) as well to betray others who are intimately connected with its (or one's) identity. Religious compulsion seeks, for its own reasons, to make its victim into a slave to alien convictions and practices with the inherent feature of dehumanizing the victim and turning him into an object to be manipulated for another's reasons and commitments. This focus—Williams's focus—on the meaning of soul violation comes very close to saying that a person qua person has or ought to have an immunity to being thus coerced and that others, because of that immunity, not only lack the normative authority to so coerce but also have the duty to respect that immunity. Since the basis for this immunity is a natural one—by virtue of creation as well as natural justice inherent in that creation—this line of reasoning appears to imply that a person has a natural right qua immunity to not being thus coerced.

Now, in addition to rape, Williams uses the image of piracy for religious compulsion and persecution. This metaphor is interestingly different from rape inasmuch as, though the ordinary pirate may rape one or another of his victims, piracy appears to be an attack on an entire collectivity—a ship and its company, including officers and passengers, not to mention an attempt to steal their goods aboard the ship. So, from Williams's point of view, by analogy, religious compulsion can have—usually has—a collective or social dimension that involves plunder of goods, violence on bodies, and even the entire "sinking" or destruction of a religious group. So, from his perspective, religious compulsion is a piratical assault on an entire community, and by parity of reasoning with what I said about soul-rape, such an assault appears to violate a group's collective moral and religious identity. And, again, by parity of reasoning, analogous to individual persons or souls, religious communities have, normatively speaking, a natural immunity or right not to be compelled against their collective religious convictions and practices. Indeed, Williams comes close to saying something like this, without using the language of rights, when he writes: "[The bloody tenent] corrupts and spoils the very civil honesty and natural conscience of a nation" [i.e., a collectivity] (BTM, 498). And he abides by this view in his own practice, even amid his passionate arguments against and condemnation of the Foxians (Quakers) as treasonous, rebellious, abominable, hypocritical, pharisaical, atheistical, and "more obstructive and destructive [to the true conversion and salvation of souls] than most of the religions that are at this day extant in the world" (GF, 257–58). Williams does not even entertain compelling the Foxians as a group in their convictions and practices so long as they abide by civil laws and even though he himself thinks their convictions might themselves have a potential (short of an actuality) toward religious persecution of others.

One small issue about Williams's metaphor of piracy should be noted. Although in his time, a distinction was drawn between piracy and privateering—wherein the former was a crime and the latter an authorized role (similar to contracting with mercenaries to act on a state's behalf)—I seriously doubt that Williams would have acknowledged the distinction in the metaphor's application.[13] I say this because no civil magistrate, according to Williams, has the legitimate authority to compel religious individuals or groups to believe and act according to religious lights other than their own, that is, to compel religious belief and its exercise from or to any religion other than the individual's and group's own conscience.

So far I have attempted to argue—whether successfully or not you be the judge—that for Williams the freedom of conscience and religion is a subjective natural right created by God and inhering in the person by virtue of his conscience, moral personality, and moral–religious identity. I have also suggested that for Williams this right functions as a type of immunity right in his argument, and furthermore that this immunity has both an individual and collective dimension. Can anything more be discerned from Williams's third argument about this right and its features? I think so, though for some my additional observations may seem obvious or even banal. For example, it seems utterly clear that from Williams's perspective, this right is both epistemic—in the sense that people are entitled to hold their conscientious beliefs as they see fit—and behavioral—in the sense that they are entitled to express or manifest these convictions in action, subject only to not interfering with (or tyrannizing) the similar right of others within the civil society (I will return to this limitation in Williams's fourth argument).

It appears that for Williams the epistemic dimension is due to the very nature of belief-formation itself, since it is an intellectual process, which the will follows, controlled solely by reason, evidence, argument, experience, and persuasion. But it also appears to me that this process can be deformed by the dynamics of self-betrayal described earlier and involving affliction and threat of affliction, even to the point of "dulling" or side-tracking the "honest conscience."[14] In the latter instance, according to Williams, compelling behavior through self-betrayal of one's core convictions involves hypocrisy (a strong dissonance between what one believes and what one does in speech and action), which, in turn, has the effect of undermining the moral conscience and its capacity to reason according to natural wisdom and basic moral norms. The behavioral dimension of the right to freedom of conscience and religion seems clear enough in Williams's argument, and I am not sure I can say much more than for him beliefs naturally manifest themselves in and govern associated behavior. Thus, from his point of view, the immunity involved in the right to freedom of conscience and religion extends to both the internal or private sphere of beliefs held and the public sphere where these beliefs are expressed and manifested.

Immunities, of course, are passively held, and so I might note that Williams's conception of this right has not only this passive aspect but an active one as well: namely, a fundamental liberty to express religious beliefs imposing on others the duty of non-interference. Similar to the first of Williams's arguments—invoking both God's will and Christ's interest—it seems to me that Williams regards the right to freedom of conscience and religion as having the dual function of projecting for the person a small sphere of sovereignty over the world in respect of liberty of belief and action (within the limits to be discussed later) and also appealing to a person's fundamental interest in having and maintaining an integral moral and religious identity. The former function appears to follow from the active aspect of the right as I have just identified, while the latter appears to make sense of what is at stake in Williams's entire argument about the normative inviolability of conscience and personality. It relies on and aims to protect a fundamental human interest shared by all people.

It perhaps remains to be said that Williams's third argument appears to be formally characterizable as a status theory of justification for the right to freedom of conscience and religion. That is, Williams is here offering a justification based on a human being's fundamental attribute—that he or she is a person with a moral conscience and personality that makes him what he is—and that this attribute in itself makes it fitting (for want of a better term) that he or she be recognized and respected in this regard.[15] This attribute is, according to Williams, inherent to all human beings because they were created that way, and, although it may ultimately refer to God's right and will, it is nonetheless deployed by Williams as a distinctive line of argument. It does, in fact, contrast strongly with Williams's other more instrumental and consequentialist arguments that freedom of conscience and religion promotes the peace and welfare of humankind and that its denial has led and continues to lead to considerable suffering and death for the peoples of the world. I am far from denying that these latter sorts of appeals are important in Williams's thinking and writing, but they do seem to me distinct from the arguments that I am discussing in this chapter.

I also do not wish to be seen as denying that consequentialist arguments can be used to support religious rights, but I do not think that such arguments extend to supporting freedom of conscience and religion as a distinctively natural right, which, of course, is my focus here.

One final point, though it is a more speculative one that connects the inviolability argument to the preceding one from natural justice. If Williams is in fact construing freedom of conscience and religion as projecting a sphere of sovereignty for all persons with respect to religious convictions and behavior, then one might argue—in combination with that preceding argument—that he is thinking of natural law as defining a permissive area of autonomy and free choice in religious matters. This comports well with Brian Tierney's suggestion in a more recent article—Roger Williams aside—that a number of natural law positions since the twelfth century invoke "the idea of permissive natural law . . . as a ground of natural right," and further that "the permissions of the law of nature were bounded by the commands and prohibitions of that same law," for example, not to violate the similar rights of others.[16] Although Tierney's own examples relate to property (and property rights), I can think of no good reason why the natural right to freedom of conscience and religion could not be similarly construed. The irony here, of course, is that I am invoking the scholarship of Tierney generally on natural law and natural rights to deepen our comprehension of Williams's own position, which Tierney himself does not think operative in Williams. I will return to this point in Williams's argument from consensual government.

Consensual Government

The fourth argument for freedom of conscience and religion as a natural right involves Williams's conception of consensual government and the elements that it appears to entail. While it is certainly the case that Williams did not develop a full theory of government, he nonetheless projects a view of civil government that is broadly democratic in orientation and that rests clearly on the natural rights of people, which I interpret to include freedom of conscience and religion and which limits government intrusion in this regard. Here are some representative passages that appear to suggest this line of argument, though one also cannot help but notice that they occasionally refer to and even further develop elements of the previous arguments I have tried to adduce:

> *That the civil power may erect and establish what form of civil government may seem in wisdom most meet. . . . I acknowledge as an ordinance of God to conserve the civil peace of the people so far as concerns their bodies and goods. But from this I infer that the sovereign, original, and foundation of civil power lies in the people (civil power distinct from the government set up). And, if so, that a people may erect and establish what form of government is to them most meet for their civil condition: it is evident that such governments as are by them established have no more power, nor for longer a time, than the civil power in people, consenting and agreeing shall betrust them with. This is clear not only in reason but in experience . . . where the people are not deprived of their natural freedoms by . . . tyrants.* [BT, 249–50]

> *It is civil justice to preserve the civil rights, and the Rights of a civil society ought justly to be preserved by a civil state: and yet if a company of men combine themselves into a civil society by voluntary agreement and voluntarily dissolve it, it is not justice to force them to continue together.* [BTM, 74]

> *The rise and fountain whence [a civil magistrate] springs [is] the people's choice and free consent. . . . The object of it—the commonweal or safety of people in their bodies and goods . . . as object the duties of the Second Table. . . . Since civil magistrates . . . can receive no more in justice than what the people give, and are therefore but the eyes and hands and instruments of the people . . . it must follow that magistrates have received their power from the people.* [BT, 355]

> *The Ship of the Commonwealth . . . must share her weals and woes in common. . . . Now in a ship there is the whole, and there is each private cabin. A private good engageth our desires for the public, and raiseth cares and fears for the due prevention of common evils. Hence is it, that in a ship all agree (in their commanding orders, and obeying stations) to give and take the word, to stand to the helm and compass, to the sails and tacking, to the guns and artillery. This is, this must be done . . . in each civil ship and commonweal. Hence . . . not to endeavor the common good, and to exempt our selves from the sense of common evil, is a treacherous baseness, a selfish monopoly, a kind of tyranny, and tendeth to the destruction both of cabin and ship, that is, of private and public safety.* [ED, 203]

> *I ask whether the office [of magistrates] be not (in the ship of all commonweals in the world) merely and essentially civil, just as the office of a captain or master of a ship at sea, who ought of all his passengers to be . . . respected, paid and rewarded for his service: But as to the consciences of the passengers, whether Jews, Turks, Persians, Pagans, Papists, Protestants, etc. whom he transports from port to port upon a civil account of payment and recompense; I ask whether he go not beyond the sphere of activity, if he act by any authoritative restraining them from their own worship, or constraining them to his?* [ED, 209]
>
> *I ask whether . . . have the nations and peoples of the world, in their mere natural . . . capacities, any one jot of spiritual and divine power, with which to betrust their magistrates. And if . . . it be found that they not, is not this challenging of spiritual power to judge and determine what is soul-food or soul-poison (I mean in a coercive binding of souls of them that sent them, and who neither did nor could commit such power to them) Is not this, I say, a soul-rape, and tyranny? . . . I ask whether the magistrate being the civil officer of the people, hath any might, authority, or power, but what the people commit unto him? And whether any people will or can betrust such a power to the civil magistrate, to compel their souls and consciences?* [ED, 210]
>
> *I readily acknowledge, that in these cases [of religiously motivated cruelty and murder, e.g., human sacrifice] and in all other cases wherein civility is wronged, in the bodies or goods of any, the civil sword as God's sword as well as man's for the suppressing of such practices.* [ED, 243]
>
> *In such cases it may be truly said [that] the magistrate bears not the sword in vain for either the punishing or the preventing of such sins, whether uncleanness, theft, cruelty, or persecution. And therefore such consciences as are so hardened . . . as to smite their fellow servants, under the pretense of zeal and conscience . . . they ought to be suppressed and punished, to be restrained and presented. And hence is seasonable the . . . security by wholesome laws and other ways . . . each state is to provide for itself against the delusions of hardened consciences, in any attempt which merely concerns the civil state and commonwealth.* [BTM, 90–1]

While it is clear that some of these passages refer to previous lines of argument in Williams—signaled, for example, by the mention of the injustice of religious compulsion and the reiteration of the image of soul-rape—I think that we discern another distinctive thread or argument at work, to wit:

1) On the basis of their natural freedoms (or rights), people have the natural power to agree among themselves and mutually consent to establish a civil government and entrust it with the authority to protect their bodies and goods and to preserve their rights and liberties through the exercise of legislative, executive, and judicial means.

2) The people's natural freedoms and rights entitle them to withdraw their consent and trust to the government that they established and to voluntarily dissolve that government if it fails to exercise its authority properly and to their satisfaction in the protection of their bodies, goods, and rights; this is most especially the case when the government in effect tyrannizes its citizens.

3) The people's natural freedoms and rights include the freedom of conscience and religion, which is regarded as inalienable, except in those cases where a conscience is so deluded as either to break criminal laws (based on the second table of the Decalogue) or to tyrannize others through the non-fulfillment of voluntarily assumed important obligations to pursue the common good in cooperation with others.

4) Thus, exercising this inalienable right is not absolute in the strict sense: while the conscience cannot in principle be alienated at least with respect to its epistemic dimension, a person's exercise of this right can be restrained if and only if such exercise harms others or significantly tyrannizes them by actions of omission or commission that either break criminal laws or significantly tend to the destruction of the common good that every citizen has previously consented to uphold and pursue.

Now, I do not wish to over-interpret Williams's argument from consensual government as a democratic theory of society and government, for two reasons. First, he does not develop a full-blown theory—that is not his concern. Second, Williams appears to think that his argument holds for various types of government, ranging from monarchies to democracies—that is, peoples can with their power establish any number of forms of government. On the other hand, the logic of what he does say, not to mention his language of "natural rights" and the power of people collectively appear to me to support this reconstruction of his claims. I also do not wish to claim that Williams is entirely sophisticated in this line of argument. He does not, for example, lay out specific criteria for assessing the threshold of tyranny justifying the people's withdrawal of agreement and consent to a government and their voluntary dissolution of a government, nor do I think that he is entirely clear about the criteria for when religious people themselves in exercising their freedom of conscience and religion might cross the threshold of tending to undermine the common good beyond, of course, a degree of clarity about the contravention of socio-moral norms embodied in criminal laws. With respect to undermining the common good, Williams does appear to argue in one place that conscientious objections leading to refusal of military service in defense of the civil society might be punishable for lack of service because this constitutes an important obligation assumed by all the people collectively in forming a civil society and government (L, 278–79).[17] To shirk this duty—for religious reasons—tends to the destruction of the common good and thus in a sense tyrannizes others for selfish concerns.

But I do want to suggest that Williams appears to project a reasonably recognizable natural rights position with respect to the government's general responsibility to protect the bodies, goods, and rights of citizens, including their freedom of conscience and religion, so long as the latter is not exercised to harm or tyrannize others. The point about the inalienability of the latter right, subject to this limitation, adds a component to the inviolability argument that I addressed only indirectly in my previous discussion, so Williams's argument from consensual government contributes a new point to his third argument, which was earlier gestured at but now developed with respect to the inalienability of a conscientious conviction at least in its epistemic aspect. Clearly, from Williams's point of view, people lack the power to alienate their religious beliefs by turning them over to civil magistrates. This point is somewhat analogous to the position that because of their prior duty and right of self-preservation, including their moral-religious identities, people cannot consent to being enslaved. Though Williams himself does not explicitly argue this analogy, it is I think implicit in his metaphor of soul-rape, soul-oppression, soul-tyranny, and soul-slavery.

The really interesting question is whether Williams is caught in some sort of internal inconsistency by arguing that (1) the right to freedom of conscience and religion is normatively inviolable and inalienable, and (2) at the same time subject to limitation in egregious cases where its exercise itself involves significantly harming and tyrannizing others within a society, thus calling for by intervention by civil magistrates. I frankly do not think that Williams is being inconsistent here, for he appears to argue that in the case of such harmful and tyrannizing exercise, a person is acting from a morally deluded conscience that manifestly falls short of being governed by crucial moral norms—in effect, this behavior indicates that the person has a significantly corrupted moral-religious identity and personality for some reason or other. If this point does not satisfy a critic of Williams's position, then one might well argue that in cases of egregious harm to the natural and civil rights of others the scale of the violation of others' rights outweighs the violation of the right of one person or even a group when it comes to free exercise of religious beliefs. This second line of reasoning also appears implicit in Williams's argument, and it seems characterizable as a rights-oriented balancing argument on this point as a way to handle and resolve a conflict of rights.

Little has suggested that Williams's thinking about government and civil organization in connection with freedom of conscience and religion is reflected in his practice within the colony of Rhode Island. I agree but I have to admit that I could not find either in his letters describing Rhode Island or in the Acts and Ordinances of 1647 any explicit mention of natural rights generally or freedom of conscience and as a natural right in particular. In his letters, for example, Williams writes:

> *I say liberty and equality both in land and government. [And] Blessed be God for his wonderful Providences, by which this town and colony and that grand cause of Truth and Freedom of conscience hath been upheld.* [L, 263–4]

> *We have long drunk of the cup of as great liberties as any people that can hear under the whole . . . not felt the chains of tyrants, not known what an excise means, almost forgotten what tithes are.* [L, 268]

Now, as I said, there is no mention of natural rights here, but it is somewhat interesting to note that the 1647 Acts and Ordinances appear to reflect aspects of the argument from consensual government, even though within the frame of the original charter granted to Rhode Islanders by the English Parliament:

> *We do jointly agree to incorporate ourselves and so remain a Body Politick . . . and do declare to our ownselves and one another to be members of the same Body and to have Right to the freedom and privileges thereof. . . . And . . .*

> the power to govern ourselves . . . by such a form of Civil Government as by Voluntary Consent. . . . It is by this present Assembly . . . and by this present act declared that the form of Government established is Democratical; that is to say, A Government held by ye free and voluntary consent of all or the greater part. . . . And now to the end that we may give each to other (notwithstanding our different consciences) as good and hopeful assurance . . . touching each one's peaceable and quiet enjoyment of his lawful right and liberty, we do agree unto and enact, establish, and confirm these orders [i.e., a set of criminal laws roughly conforming to the second table of the Decalogue, a court system (both trials and appeals), a set of legislative procedures based on majority vote, and an elected executive system].[18]

Again, so far as I can tell the rights and liberties mentioned are civil, but it is abundantly clear that this Act details an understanding of government established by voluntary agreement among the people who have the prior power to do so and whose government is conceived by them as a democracy. I speculate but cannot prove from these texts that this prior power is based on natural rights and freedoms; this speculation is based on the similarity between this Act and Williams's argument from consensual government that I outlined earlier. My general point in distinguishing the fourth line of argument in Williams is to suggest that he appears to view people as having natural rights and liberties, including the freedom of conscience and religion (within the limits adumbrated), which are subsequently transmuted by common agreement and consent into civil rights and liberties, which, in turn, the civil authorities established by the people are duty-bound to respect.[19] When this line of argument is considered in the light of the preceding three—divine will, natural justice, and inviolability of conscience—and what they say or otherwise imply—Williams appears to be articulating a position that, more or less robustly, conceives and defends the freedom of conscience and religion as a natural right.

A final observation seems in order, once again returning to the issue of the connection between natural law and natural rights. In Williams's argument from consensual government, it appears to me—and this is in line with my earlier comment about Tierney's general notion of permissive natural law—that Williams is arguing generally that natural law is the ground of consensual government in at least two ways: as the source of people's prior power in the form of their natural rights, and as the source of limitations on the exercise of their rights vis-à-vis others in the civil society that they establish.[20] That is, natural rights derived from natural law explain and justify the people's licit power to come together to forge common agreements about government, its form, its purposes, and its limits. And, simultaneously, within the frame of that same natural law, people have the obligations not to infringe on the similar rights and freedoms of others in their society—to not do to others what they would not have others do to them, that is, socio-moral obligations to abide by the rule of law and to further the common good. It seems to me that Williams employs precisely this line of reasoning with respect to the freedom of conscience and religion and its exercise.

Conclusion

At the risk of appearing otiose, I would like to suggest that seventeenth-century Roger Williams's theologically based natural rights argument for freedom of conscience appears to anticipate or at least encapsulate many aspects of contemporary understandings of the nature, significance, and justification of this human right. My principal reference points here are the 1966 *International Covenant on Civil and Political Rights* (coming into force in 1976), Article 18 and reference to its non-derogation in Article 4, and the 1981 *Declaration on the Elimination of All Forms of Intolerance and Discrimination Based on Religion and Belief.* Both of the documents advance the idea that the right to freedom of conscience and religion has both passive and active dimensions, for example, in holding conscientious convictions and being free to change or modify them as one sees fit, and in being free to express or manifest these convictions (within limits) in worship, assembly, publication, teaching, and all the rest. Moreover, this right appears to be conceived of as an inalienable immunity (an inference I make from its non-derogability) from the coercive interference by others, and most especially a state government, imposing on the latter affirmative duties to protect this right and its exercise and to take effective measures to prevent and eliminate all discrimination based on religious identity as well as to combat intolerance, subject only to possible limitations on behavioral manifestations of religious beliefs that are necessary to protect, for example, public order or infringement on the fundamental rights and freedoms of others within a democratic society and prescribed by law.

Moreover, the contemporary understanding appears to ground this right in the equal dignity inherent in all human beings generally and in the nature of religious or conscientious belief as being "one of the fundamental elements in the person's conception of life" (preamble to the declaration), which I interpret as being another way to refer to a person's moral-religious identity. The preamble to the declaration also develops—as does Williams himself, though I did not explore the theme in detail—the consequentialist line of argument that the disregard and infringement of this right results, directly or indirectly, in wars and great suffering to humankind and that its protection should contribute to the attainment of world peace and social justice.

While Williams's arguments are clearly in line with this contemporary vision of the human right to freedom of conscience and religion, I think that they probe more deeply the precise nature of what violation of conscience and religion entails for both individuals and groups—soul rape and piracy—thus providing an explication and justification of that aspect of inherent human dignity rooted in the nature of conscience and moral-religious identity. I will not here repeat Williams's explication of the normative inviolability of conscience and identity that is entailed by their violation and the dynamics of betrayal, but I do wish to reiterate that his justification clearly involves the status of human beings as well as their fundamental interest in being the persons that they are. Although I am fully aware that Williams's theological (and Christological) beliefs constitute the ultimate grounds of his justificatory appeals, I think that his three mediate arguments—natural justice, inviolability of conscience, consensual government—nonetheless stand independent of those beliefs inasmuch as they involve an understanding of human nature per se as rational, self-aware, and morally responsible. That is to say, his natural justice argument clearly relies on natural moral reason and its entailments. His inviolability argument specifies a normative attribute of all human beings in virtue of their humanity. And his consensual government argument relies exclusively on considerations that are natural, human, and civil with respect to the basis of legitimate political authority. As a consequence of these naturalistic and rational appeals, the rights derived from them by Williams are quite properly construed as natural rights.

The fact that Williams further imbeds these three arguments in a broader scheme of explicitly religious beliefs does not vitiate this latter point, and I believe it is no accident that Williams expects his mediate arguments to be persuasive for persons and peoples of varying sorts, ranging across Christians, Muslims, pagans, and atheists. In a significant sense, therefore, we might say that Williams's first theological–Christological argument encapsulates his own background religious beliefs and premises that for him ultimately vindicate and license the development of more mediate natural rights arguments which themselves foreground the human and in principle permit others to have their own different background beliefs as appropriate to their consciences in their own identity-forming circumstances.[21] This is not to say that Williams would regard these other ultimate beliefs as true—in fact he thinks them quite false—but so long as they permit conformity with the natural light of reason and respect the natural rights of others, tolerance of religious difference is the rule for Williams, precisely because it respects the right to freedom of conscience and religion, is naturally reasonable, and is in keeping with the natural power and rights of people underlying legitimate political authority.

I do think that an interesting philosophical question is raised by Williams's three mediate arguments. For apart from his theological beliefs, they appear to imbed a metaphysical or ontological view of human nature and its epistemic powers that beg comparison with both the recent resurgence of interest in the inherence doctrine of human rights and the not infrequent appeals by international human rights lawyers to a naturalistic moral basis for significant human rights norms (e.g., *ius cogens* prohibitions).[22] That is to say, Williams's more mediate arguments point to a metaphysical or ontological dimension to human rights discourse generally and to the right to freedom of conscience and religion in particular that resonates (I wager) with many, if not all, of us regardless of whether we are religious believers or not. In the latter regard, I do think that Williams's violative images of soul rape and piracy are utterly compelling, whatever worldview to which one might subscribe, and that means there is something equally compelling about his notion of normative inviolability of conscience as either a fundamental status or fundamental interest shared by all of us in virtue of our humanity.

NOTES

[1] Richard Tuck, *Natural Rights Theories: Their Origin and Development* (Cambridge University Press, 1979); Brian Tierney, *The Idea of Natural Rights* (Scholars Press, 1997; Jeremy Waldron, *God, Locke, and Equality: Christian Foundations in Locke's Political Thought* (Cambridge University Press, 2002); John Witte, Jr., *The Reformation of Rights: Law, Religion, and Human Rights in Early Modern Calvinism* (Cambridge University Press, 2007); Morton White, *The Philosophy of the American Revolution* (Oxford University Press, 1978).

[2] Excerpts from James Calvin Davis, *On Religious Liberty: Selections from the Works of Roger Williams* (Harvard University Press, 2008); hereinafter, however, when I cite passages from Roger Williams's corpus, I will be using the facsimile version republished as *The Complete Writings of Roger Williams in Seven Volumes*, reprinted by The Baptist Standard Bearer, 2005, and Wipf and Stock Publishers, 2007.

[3] Brian Tierney, "Religious Rights: An Historical Perspective," in eds., John Witte, Jr. and Johan D. van der Vyver, *Religious Human Rights in Global Perspective: Religious Perspectives* (Martinus Nijhoff Publishers, 1996), 17–45; the following quotations from this essay are from page 42.

[4] Tierney's interpretation of Williams on natural rights is not far from that of Alan Simpson, "How Democratic Was Roger Williams?" in *William and Mary Quarterly* 13 no.1 (January 1956): 53–67; esp. 60, 64.

[5] David Little, "Roger Williams and the Separation of Church and State," in ed. James E. Wood, Jr., *Religion and State: Essays in Honor of Leo Pfeffer* (Baylor University Press, 1985), 3–23; the following quotations are from pages 10 and 23, respectively.

[6] Williams, *The Complete Writings*, Vol. IV, 493–501.

[7] Two excellent discussions of Williams's thought are found in: Timothy L. Hall, *Separating Church and State: Roger Williams and Religious Liberty* (University of Illinois Press, 1998), and James Calvin Davis, *The Moral Theology of Roger Williams: Christian Conviction and Public Ethics* (Westminster John Knox Press, 2004).

[8] After each quote here and throughout the remainder of the paper, I cite the source from Williams's *Complete Writings* in abbreviated form, followed by page number: HM=*The Hireling Ministry None of Christs*; BT=*The Bloudy Tenent of Persecution*; BTM=*The Bloody Tenent Yet More Bloody*; GF=*George Fox Digg'd Out of His Burrowes*; ED=*The Examiner Defended*; L=*Letters of Roger Williams*; and MB=*Fourth Paper Presented by Major Butler*.

[9] The first article of 1215 *Magna Charta* deals with the inviolable rights of freedom of the English Church (as contrasted with Williams's concern with the subjective right of individual persons), as well as the (subjective) liberties of all freemen of the kingdom (note the constraint). Nonetheless, Williams's metaphorical use of *Magna Charta* of the highest liberties seems to me not entirely inapt for the time in which he was writing.

[10] See, for example, Leif Wenar, "Rights" (revised July 9, 2007) in the open-access *Stanford Encyclopedia of Philosophy* (http://plato.stanford.edu/enries/rights/, Last accessed: September 14, 2009.)

[11] The question is whether Williams primarily conceives of the right as conferring a small-scale sovereignty, or as representing a fundamental human interest. Perhaps he

conceives of the right as a fundamental interest which *for that reason* confers a small-scale sovereignty *qua* defensive shield.

[12] Williams uses considerable slave and enslavement imagery for compulsion and persecution of conscience and religion; see, for example, ED, 235–36, BT, 401, and GF, 17. A useful article on rape generally is Rebecca Whisnant, "Feminist Perspectives on Rape" (first published May 13, 2009) in the open-access *Stanford Encyclopedia of Philosophy*, (http://plato.stanford.edu/entries/feminism-rape/ Last accessed: September 15, 2009.) Also useful for thinking about Williams on persecution and bodily affliction is Anne G, Myles, "Arguments in Milk, Arguments in Blood: Roger Williams, Persecution, and the Discourse of Witness," *Modern Philology* 91 no. 1 (November 1993): 133–160; see esp. 145–47.

[13] See Eugene Kontorovich, "The Piracy Analogy: Modern Universal Jurisdiction's Hollow Foundation," in *Harvard International Law Journal* 45 no. 1 (Winter 2004): 183–237.

[14] Compare Williams on the dynamics of self-betrayal to the account of how torture works (via "betrayal" by the victim's bodily responses) in David Sussman, "What's Wrong with Torture?" in *Philosophy and Public Affairs* 33/1 (2005): 1–33.

[15] On this point, see Warren Quinn, *Morality and Action* (Cambridge University Press, 1993), 173: "It is also true, of course, that we think it good [in a consequentialist sense] if people actually respect each other's rights. But this value depends on the goodness of the moral design that assigns these rights. It is not that we think it fitting to ascribe rights because it is a good thing that rights be respected. Rather we think respect for rights a good thing precisely because we think people actually have them—and . . . that they have them because it is fitting that they should." I am indebted to Wenar, "Rights," previously cited, in drawing my attention to this source and the language of "fittingness" that I adapt here to clarify Williams's position.

[16] Brian Tierney, "Natural Law and Natural Rights: Old Problems and Recent Approaches," in *Review of Politics* 64 no. 3 (Summer 2002): 389–406.

[17] This possible position is a construction from a comment such as this by Williams: "I further add . . . that withstanding this [religious liberty] the commander of this ship [society] ought to command that justice, peace and sobriety, be kept and practiced. . . . If any of the seamen refuse to perform their services, or passengers to pay their freight; if any refuse to help, in person or purse, towards the common charges or defence; if any refuse to obey the common laws and order of the ship, concerning their common peace or preservation . . . in such cases, whatever is pretended, the commander or commanders may judge, resist, compel and punish such transgressors, according to their deserts and merits" (L, 278–79). Furthermore, in the Acts and Orders of 1647, the shirking of public duties is subject to the penalty of a fine or forfeiture of wages, and it is explicitly stated "in the case of eminent danger, no man shall refuse." *Acts and Orders* (http://oll.libertyfund.org/index.php?option=com_content&task=view& Last accessed September 7, 2009.) See also Clinton Rossiter, "Roger Williams on the Anvil of Experience," in *American Quarterly* 3 no. 1 (Spring 1951): 14–21; esp., 18–19, dealing with Williams on the necessity of authority and the reciprocity of rights and duties.

[18] This text is also available in Donald S. Lutz, ed., *Colonial Origins of the American Constitution: A Documentary History* (Liberty Fund, Inc. 1998). The 1647 Act and Orders was replaced by the 1663 Royal Charter for Rhode Island and Providence Plantations, granted by King Charles II and in force until a new constitution was adopted in 1842. (The text of this charter is available at http://www.usgennet.org/usa/ri/state/richarter.html; last accessed: September 8, 2009.)

[19] The logic of this argument begs some interesting comparisons with that of Thomas Paine in Part One of his *Rights of Man*. See Eric Foner, ed., *Thomas Paine: Collected Writings* (Library of America, 1995).

[20] For a more general exposition of this point, see Philip A. Hamburger, "Natural Rights, Natural Law, and American Constitutions," in *The Yale Law Journal* 102 no. 4 (January 1993): 907–960; see esp. 922–30.

[21] For a discussion of vindication and vindicatory reasoning, see David Little and Sumner B. Twiss, *Comparative Religious Ethics: A New Method* (Harper & Row, 1978), ch. 5. I am indebted to David Little for encouraging me to make this point explicit.

[22] See, for example, Johannes Morsink, *Inherent Human Rights: Philosophical Roots of the Universal Declaration* (University of Pennsylvania Press, 2009).

4.
Islam and Human Rights:
The Religious and the Secular in Conversation

Abdulaziz Sachedina

Introduction

David Little has inspired my work on human rights ever since we co-authored the volume *Human Rights and the Conflict of Cultures: Western and Islamic Perspectives on Religious Liberty* (1988).[1] He noted the Qur'anic reference to freedom of religion and its implications for the article on liberty of religion in the Universal Declaration of Human Rights (UDHR). His unique reading of Qur'anic verses on the Prophet's role as the deliverer of God's message to humanity without compelling the people to believe in God and that human beings were free to negotiate their spiritual destiny took me on the journey that has now culminated in my study *Islam and the Challenge of Human Rights* (2009).[2]

In this journey Little has functioned as my mentor and I have, to the best of my ability, and in keeping with my reading of the classical Islamic tradition, followed his lead. The present chapter underscores my indebtedness to him for having opened a fresh avenue in my legal and ethical studies of Islam. Our conversations and exchanges at the University of Virginia shaped my interest in comparative ethics as one of the most important methodological breakthroughs in the derivation of universal language. This recognition undergirds both the international secular documentary and Islamic revelatory sources with reference to the principle of inherency in deriving human moral agency as well as dignity. This accrues to humans qua human, without any reference to external qualifications like race, creed, or gender. This chapter, then, is the summation of much of what Little and I have discussed, agreed, and disagreed, about how religion can function as a promoter of human rights rather than as its violator.

Religion in the Islamic Public Square

The present chapter proposes to examine theological, philosophical, and juridical-ethical resources in Islam to demonstrate to Muslim as well as non-Muslim human rights theoreticians that it is possible to construct an internal and universal paradigm of human rights discourse that can actually provide cultural legitimacy to the international bill of human rights in the Muslim world. The human rights discourse in the Muslim world is faced with an internal crisis generated by the refusal of the Muslim traditionalists to recognize the religious validity of the secular document of the UDHR.[3] The universal claim of this document is rejected in a number of areas where it is seen as an affront to the religiously derived claim to independent universality.[4] Hence, the universality founded on the rationally derived concept of the equality of all human beings endowed with an inherent dignity and the freedom of religion has been intensely debated and opposed by the traditionalist Muslim scholars as a Western hegemonic imposition on Muslim peoples.[5] However, if this position were an honest academic review of the UDHR, then it would have led these scholars to the inevitable search for authentic Islamic notions of, at least, religiously promulgated immunities and entitlements for human beings regardless of their religious affiliation.[6]

Much of the scholarship on human rights and Islam that has emerged in the last fifty years has failed to provide a critical redefinition of the purposes for which God has created humanity.[7] This is a subject that has occupied Muslim jurists in the past when they had to define the scope of the sacred norms and their application in society.[8] The concept of human rights in Islam needs to be explored in the light of this crucial redefinition of divine purposes and their attainment in the context of the contemporary reality of the nation-state in which non-discriminatory membership determines human rights and obligations.[9] The situation is further aggravated by the refusal of traditional scholars, the *ulema*, to undertake a critically needed review of the historical Islam preserved in its juridical corpus to provide informed disagreement between the secular human rights and Muslim apologists. The direction Muslims need to follow in order to respond positively and constructively to one of the most formidable moral challenges today is how to develop religious-moral and political commitments to human rights.

With thirteen centuries behind its historical engagement with social and political forces, Islam has shaped much of the Muslim experience in dealing with the change of power structures and political realities of the post-colonial Muslim world. In the twenty-first century, Muslims are faced with autocratic governments which have for the most part denied the human rights of their citizens, whether Muslim or non-Muslim. Ordinary people continue to suffer under these corrupt governments that have even resorted to justify their immoral behavior in God's name and religion. Systematic undermining and devaluing of human dignity and disregard for some basic rights of people to freedom of worship and expression are daily occurrences in some parts of the Muslim world where the government and traditional religious leadership have joined hands in curbing dissenting voices and the rights of religious minorities.

In the growing manifestation of religious militancy in the Muslim world in the post-9–11 period, extremist religious leadership has demonstrated little ability to deal with modern, liberal notions of democracy or human rights. At the global level there is a need for a cautious and yet constructive evaluation of the role that a religion like Islam can play in affirming at least some universal rights that accrue to all humans qua human. They are inalienable rights to freedom and security without which any existence would be considered less than human. The relation of religion to rights is open to many possible interpretations. One of the most challenging interpretations deals with the application of the universal rights within the domain of religiously conceived legitimacy.

Religious diversity in the public square presents problems to proponents of liberal thought. In a liberal society, the separation of public from private, while difficult to maintain at all levels of human existence, is regarded as necessary in order to enable individuals to practice their faith in the private domain without any interference by the state. The state must be neutral regarding the choices of its citizens as to how they want to live their lives. Liberal thought, as a matter of pragmatism, bypasses any consideration about the neutrality of the state in determining the public good. The state does maintain a particular vision of a good society and therefore it cannot be regarded as neutral in its conception of the good. It does project purposefulness in what it deems beneficial for its citizens. Accordingly, it takes it upon itself to make choices for individuals and for future generations within its boundaries with a view to defend political and civil, social and economic human rights under the rubric of fundamental freedom to choose how its citizens live. However, if a state is to be liberal, it has to actively promote a political system that upholds liberty and security based on the rights of the individual at the cost of other values. It is at this stage that liberal political systems disregard the practical dimensions of religious teachings and values as one of the sources of political decision-making. The assumption is that when comprehensive beliefs supported by religious systems enter political space they give rise to intolerant attitudes, which lead to violence and religious oppression.

When it comes to specifically dealing with fundamental freedoms, liberal secularists have always maintained an incompatibility between relatively conceived religious traditions and the universal, secular notion of inalienable rights and individual freedoms. This secular notion of universal rights transcends the exclusionary boundaries of religiously constructed visions of human community. In addition, the secularists regard absolute truth-claims and the universality of religiously promoted moral values as major obstacles to world peace and sources for the violations of minority rights in countries where religious tradition dominates public institutions. In other words, as the secularists contend, religion is not capable of defending the moral worth and the inalienable rights of the individual.

We need to raise a critical question here: Is there a neutral way of supporting the priority of human rights without garnering the support of other value systems in domestic societies, including religiously derived values? To expect a society to provide legitimacy to imported claims of universality requires rigorous homework in domestic systems that may provide basic elements for furthering the primacy of rights. There is no reason to ignore the arguments of some Muslim nations that the recognition of liberal, secular notions of universal rights has turned into an authoritarian discourse leading to the same kind of exclusionary intolerance that non-liberal systems are being criticized for perpetrating.

At the international level, authoritarian definitions of authentic rights create a commotion because the focus shifts from people to the states engaged in curtailing the freedoms of their people and the inability of the international order to interfere within the boundaries of states. To be sure, the international order is not made up of liberal states in which a human person is prior to the community and to authority. This is not to say that there is no government to protect the rights of the people from the possible transgressions by others. But it might choose to define itself in a way that is compatible with its own sense of authenticity and yet be completely antithetical to human rights principles and to the human rights of its individual members, or a group within its territorial boundary. Here is the source of commotion: How to reconcile universal human rights with the principle of toleration in those societies where human rights violations are endemic?

The Challenge of Cultural Relativism

A number of Muslim states have used the argument based on Islam being the source of their citizens' primary identity and that there are enough guarantees within Islamic values that reject gross abuses of human rights in principle. Hence, there is no need for them to adopt universal human rights principles within their cultural boundaries. Moreover, they have resorted to cultural relativism by arguing that since values are relative to the circumstances that define a culture, Muslims cannot be expected to adopt the rights that Western culture has defined in relation to its own circumstances. This argument also expects that the principles of toleration will be applied to Muslim societies whose actions cannot be judged by outsiders simply because there is no universal moral standard against which Western countries can judge the Muslim world. Undoubtedly, the argument about cultural relativism has been a reaction to the colonial and imperialist past of the Muslim world that has also treated liberalism with much suspicion. In the context of human rights, those who entertain the thesis about cultural relativism need to keep in mind that if morality were to be defined by circumstance and history, and therefore regarded relative to cultures, then the urgently needed dialogue between Muslim and non-

Muslim nations to discover universal moral concerns and principles would cease.

Historically religions have divided rather than united people on a common, universal moral ground. Their universal and absolute claims have ignored the relativity of human experience and its impact upon relational ethics. In fact, there is much evidence to show that the more absolute a religious tradition claims itself to be, the less tolerant it becomes in recognizing the principle of coexistence with harmony and peace. And yet it is imperative to seriously engage the human rights debates in the context of religious traditions and their legitimating resources for the religiously advanced notion of rights to become part of the international discourse. Thus far, in the Muslim world the human rights debate has been circumscribed and tainted by its particular association with Western powers. In fact, the frequent call to implement the core values of respect for individual freedoms and human rights is viewed by some prominent Muslim religious leaders as a Western hegemonic strategy to undermine Islamic social and moral values.

A core set of fundamental principles is widely shared in countries that have not yet adopted rights instruments and in cultures that have not embraced the language of rights. There is little doubt that basic human rights rest on common convictions or common moral terrain as I have demonstrated in my earlier study on *The Islamic Roots of Democratic Pluralism* (2001), even though those convictions are stated in terms of different philosophical principles and on the background of divergent political and economic systems. Even people who seem far apart in theory can agree that certain things are self-subsistingly evil in practice and no one will publicly approve them, and certain things are self-evidently good in practice and no one will publicly oppose them.

Hence, my basic working assumption that there is a universal character to human rights that can be embraced by all peoples globally cannot be denied. At the same time, cultural values and resources that could promote these rights are born locally and adhered to differently in the context of a set of communal beliefs and societal relations. This is the source of tension: a universal claim that seeks implementation in the relative cultural and religious environment with its own self-proclaimed universalism. How to bridge this conceptual and ideological gap in the Muslim world is the thrust of my research on the relationship between

Islamic tradition and human rights in my book *Islam and the Challenge of Human Rights*.

The Theological, Philosophical, and Juridical-Ethical Resources of Islam

The main objective of this study is to build upon the classical heritage of Islam to convey the theology, metaphysics, and natural law that facilitate the acknowledgment of universal human rights without neglecting to point out the duties that Islamic legal-ethical sources emphasize in regulating human relationships. Human relationships, outside the natural bonds, are based on contractual agreements that require a logical connection between duties and rights. The inclusion of duties along with rights is the framework of religious life, and therefore, within the framework of the assumption about a just society. Accordingly, a detailed legitimating and rational, legal justification is necessary to encourage Muslim participation in the global implementation of human rights. The burden of this study has been to identify and articulate foundational Islamic sources that could establish a legitimate correspondence with secularly derived human rights. Both the advocacy and regulation of human rights are essentially matters of religion and ethics. It is religion that teaches universally recognized principles of conduct, which have a basis in elementary truths about human beings and the purpose for which they have been created. Religious teachings about humanity as endowed with ends anticipate a teleological notion of nature that stems from a common morality shared by two dichotomous universal claims, one founded upon secularism and the other on scriptural sources. Even the Qur'an insists upon the interdependence between universal claims and religious duties.

The language of inalienable human rights is modern, in which accruing responsibilities that come with the claims to entitlements are under emphasized. This is the source of tension between universal, secular claims of the UDHR and the religious-cultural specificity that demands a responsive voice in fulfilling duties that are imposed on humanity by the simple fact of being God's creatures. This does not, however, mean that religious language limits itself to the performance of duties at the exclusion of rights. Rather, a religion like Islam is interested in striking a balance between claims and duties to establish a viable ethical order on earth. Diverse world communities are engaged in searching for this balance.

To put forward an adequate paradigm that suits the needs of the faith community without losing sight about its relation to other communities in the international order, it is imperative that Islamic discourse receives an independent, detailed treatment in the context of the Western dominated discourse on human rights. The real issues connected with the dichotomous relationship between secular and spiritual, universal and relative aspects of moral norms that seek application in specific cultural contexts with a view to a search for an overlapping consensus over values that touch all others outside the specific community should assume a critical spot in this discourse. At the international level, two apparently dichotomous universalisms—secular and religious—are in competition for cultural legitimacy by appealing to two sets of normative sources: reason and revelation. Islam, with its world-embracing ideology and historical standing as a highly successful civilization, more than any other religious tradition, claims to present an alternative universal paradigm of religio-political civilization. As such, we need to engage Islam on its own terms, without imposing categories of discourse on the debate between Islam and human rights externally. To begin with, Muslims need to abandon the between-the-lines reading of the colonizer-colonized relationship between the West and the Muslim world that has led to a negative evaluation of the UDHR as a hegemonic ploy to impose Western domination on the rest of the world.

A number of Islamic documents have appeared that purport to offer an ideal alternative to the UDHR. A careful examination of these documents reveals that they do very little in terms of responding to the hard questions like the universality of moral values or the status of those who do not accept the authority of the divinely ordained Shari`a as the sole guarantor of justice. More importantly, if the community-oriented Shari`a becomes the universal legal system for the Muslim community, what interpretive mechanisms would be in place to overcome the intrinsic plurality and divisiveness of the various schools of Shari`a? The fact is that the language of these documents does not offer an alternative or an addendum to boost the ethics of relationship that the secularly inspired UDHR neglects to emphasize. The apologetics conveyed in these documents have led to misleading and intellectually impoverished assessments of normative Islamic sources for Muslim adherence to the application of human rights in those areas in which there have been serious violations of women's and religious minorities' human rights.

To be sure, the Islamic legal-ethical tradition puts forward a framework for human claims that are comprehensive and not oblivious of the responsibilities. The real challenge for any faith community lies in the way religious traditions, when politically empowered, become steeped in claims of absolute exclusiveness and total disregard for the rights of those outside their own faith communities. In *The Islamic Roots of Democratic Pluralism*, I identified and analyzed primary religious sources to overcome politically volatile claims of exclusionary theology, and accept religious pluralism supported by Islamic scripture as a self-evident reality of human societies. As a sequel to that study, this research undertook the groundbreaking work of demonstrating the compatibility of at least some of the universal rights connected with freedom of conscience and religion in the competing world of religions trying to win the soul of humanity with the Islamic tradition. I mention freedom of religion because the majority of the cases of human rights violations, usually underreported and less publicly debated, occur in this particular area. My academic goal is to undermine the exclusionary discourse perpetrated by the extremist elements in the international community and to demonstrate the logical inconsistencies in this violence-prone theology in the light of the universal, tolerant language of the Qur'an and the classical tradition. Both of these highly valued sources among Muslims draw logical connections between human rights and human obligations— not only to fellow humans, regardless of their religion, race, or color, but also to nature as a whole.

The Dialogue between Universal Human Rights and Obligations

The universal elements of an Islamic human rights discourse can hardly benefit from the hermeneutical move to bring the normative tradition in line with some of the rights that are derived by reference to the geopolitical context rather than some abstract notion of justice without a serious assessment of the situation on the ground. The real test for any document of rights remains its practical implementation in the community of nations. Many Muslim countries are ruled by autocratic regimes, mostly supported by the Western countries that have suspended their people's basic rights to freedom of conscience and expression under flimsy excuses of the non-applicability of the human rights principles or that democratization will threaten the region's political stability. Ironically, it is this kind of support of these autocratic regimes by some Western powers that has done more harm to the credibility of the UDHR than all the arguments based on the inconsistencies between religiously and secularly derived rights or moral relativism.

There is a need for a dialogue between the advocates of the UDHR and the advocates of religiously derived human rights and obligations. Undeniably, Islam provides legitimacy for much of the interpersonal relationships in Muslim societies, including Shari`a-based claims and duties. The liberal, secular antagonism toward religion is not very conducive to this dialogue because, by its very definition, dialogue assumes conversation between equals, and religion is not valued by the secularists as an equal partner in resolving the legitimacy of universal human rights documents across cultures.

The call for secularization and the disestablishment of Islam through its privatization has not found much support among traditional Muslim leaders who refuse to deny Islam its public role in shaping the Muslim polity. The secular solution of the separation of "church" and "state" to allow the state to assume its neutral stance in the matters of religious belief and a defense of the human rights of all its citizens has only some resonance in Islam, pointedly as it endorses some form of secularity to meet the demands of separate jurisdictions for matters that are strictly between God and humanity (i.e., spiritual dimension of human activity) from those that are between human beings (i.e., "secular" aspect of social life). Without the cooperation of religious leadership in extracting and upholding an inclusive religious doctrine that takes human dignity as the sole criterion for treating all humans, regardless of any differences (religion included), as equal, it is hard to see how a majority of the Muslim peoples would endorse a secular international document on human rights.

The world community of nations is faced with the danger of endless violence provoked by the violation of basic human rights in various regions of the world. Without responding to the injustices and humiliations suffered by innocent peoples caught in the crossfire of political conflicts that remain unresolved, there will be hardly any credibility to the efforts of an international organization like the UN. Human rights will be hard to defend across cultures until the religious and secular leadership comes to terms with human suffering that demands our unabated attention. Any claim to entitlement requires a reciprocal responsibility, and that is where religion meets ethics in forging responsible relationships with implications for upholding fundamental human rights.

The Foundationless Argument for Human Rights

This is an important issue because I believe that the conversation between the religious and secular theorists of the UDHR must be resolved. The failure to do so impairs the document's legitimacy in the Muslim world. In deriving human rights principles many human rights theorists have argued for a foundationless model of human rights. The basic assumptions underlying this model are twofold: on the one hand, a foundational model, in particular a religious one, appears to be limited to its faith community, hardly suitable for generating international consensus on human rights principles across traditions. This assumption is also responsible for the secularization of the international document. On the other hand, since there is a sharp distinction between liberal Western and other non-liberal cultures, especially Muslim cultures, the foundationless model will achieve better results by focusing on practical issues that arise when these states do not provide instruments of human rights to defend their citizens' rights. Such practical considerations have also led these secular theorists to avoid focusing on philosophical or religious foundations of human rights principles. The problem is that without due consideration of religious or philosophical sources it would be difficult to garner the support of Muslim communities to work toward improving human rights instruments to effect the necessary implementation of the UDHR.

An emphasis upon the secular-religious dichotomy will necessarily lead to the foundationless model, which actually stifles the critical dialogue between the secular and traditionalist theorists. In addition, Western-Islamic polarization in terms of liberal-non-liberal societies is also detrimental to the need for international consensus on protecting freedom of conscience and religion. An Islamic model for democratic pluralism, as I have argued, for instance, is not inherently antithetical to a central concept of human dignity and an individual's inalienable right to determine her spiritual destiny without interference. I am convinced that enforcement of human rights will be taken even more seriously in Muslim societies if, using the foundational model, one can derive the inherent worth of the individual and argue for the freedom of religion. The issue of human rights is originally a Western concept that needs to become an Islamic one with all of its ramifications. With this in mind, let me very briefly demonstrate a revelation-based foundation for a foundational model that is not oblivious of the concerns raised by the supporters of foundationless theories, and yet able to derive comparable, and even an equitable, conception of human worth.

A Revelation-Based Foundation for Human Rights

First, let us try to understand again the outlines of a foundationless model of human rights. Human beings are endowed with reason and possess natural rights, which the state in the social contract between the individual and political authority ought to protect. This is the foundation of secular rationalism and its emphasis on individual entitlements independent of obligation, undefined by a socially assigned role, and unconditional on status or circumstance. Human reason, liberated from its religious or metaphysical antecedents, is free to negotiate its potential and creativity without any restrictions. The human being is the ultimate locus of knowledge, and empowered to determine the relationship between knowledge and moral truth. There is no need for revelation to provide any guidance in constructing the moral foundation of human society, because reason is a self-subsistent source of moral cognition as it interacts with the human experience of living in a society. Such a notion of human knowledge about moral truth is also the source of moral relativism governed by culture and determined by time and place.

Ironically, this moral empowerment of the individual and its relation to the culture of the region has become a major source for the defeat of the claim of universality of human rights when it comes to their application in diverse cultures. How did this contradiction with its pernicious effect occur?

In order to make human reason the sole criterion for moral cognition, it had to be separated from its divine origin. Reason was also severed from its bedrock in natural law, which provided all the necessary guidance to achieve the divinely ordained purposes for human life on earth. The secularization of reason, coupled with economic and social development, led to the depreciation of the role of natural law and its religious and metaphysical foundations. This undermining of the revelation has been gradual and almost concealed until more recently, when questions about fundamental agreement on values and the demands of reason between peoples and across cultures have flared up between Western powers and Muslim nations regarding the enforcement of human rights.

In Islam, as in other Abrahamic traditions, natural law is the divine endowment for humanity through the very creation of human nature (*fitra*), the receptacle for reason. Moral cognition is innate to this nature and because of it human beings are capable of discerning moral law. This law is universal and can be discovered by all due to the simple fact of sharing a common humanity. Reason, as described in the Qur'an, is the "light of God." This divine light can guide humans in all matters, spiritual and temporal, private and public. Who creates morality?

There are two theses about morality among Muslim theologians: The first thesis reaches to the majority Sunni-Ash`ari thinkers who did not allow the concept of the autonomous individual, freely exercising his rights and determining the course of his life, to evolve. Human beings were born to obey God, who alone determined what was good or bad. In fact, without God's intervention there was no way for a person to know the moral worth of his actions. God's commands and prohibitions establish what is good and evil, respectively. This is the traditional position on human worth which denies any independent source other than God for the knowledge of moral truth. The second thesis, which recognized reason as God's gift to humanity to develop moral knowledge, was propounded by the Sunni-Mu`tazilite theologians. Their doctrine about God's justice upheld a logical necessity on God's part to endow humanity with an autonomous moral cognition through creation (*fitra*). Accordingly, moral knowledge was part of human nature and prior to the revelation, which elaborated in detail what was already known in general. Mu'tazilites did not develop a theory of natural law as such; but their doctrine of the autonomous moral agency of human beings clearly made humans the locus of reason and morality by the act of God's creation.

Although the Mu`tazilite-Sunni thesis was defeated by the Ash`ari traditionalism, their rationalistic natural theology continued to influence Muslim thinkers at all times, and it found, in fact, a home among the Shi'ite theologians. The tension between the two schools can be described as the debate between those who think that human beings need religious authority to inform them about moral truth, and, therefore must submit to it for moral guidance; and those who hold that morality is part of human nature and human beings autonomously determine the rules of its application in their lives. The two positions as they stand are ultimately contradictory and could hardly be suggested to form the essential part of a foundational theory for human rights. What is clear, however, is that, without reducing the two positions to the common denominator needed for a vibrant theory, it would be difficult to maintain liberal, secular freedom with a religiously negotiated understanding of the moral worth of the human person qua human person. Yet to dismiss the theological enterprise as non-functional simply because it cannot resolve its internal contradiction is to overlook the fact that both positions were possible on the basis of two different readings of Islamic revelation.

It is not farfetched to suggest that Muslim theologians were responding to the specific political climate of the society in which the hold of religious law, the Shari`a, was necessary to make the peaceful coexistence of people with different creeds possible. Hence, the belief in the omnipotent God who required people to obey the divine commands also included the command about treating the Peoples of the Book with tolerance without denying the validity of their spiritual paths. Historical reality alone was insufficient to generate tolerance without any reference to freedom with human moral worth in the foundational text of the Qur'an. The absolute values of the Qur'an, in large measure, were responsible for disciplining and regulating the natural tendency of denigrating the minorities and providing sanctions for trampling on the rights of others. Indeed, the notion of claims by any group was founded upon the religiously declared sanctity of all "children of Adam" equally honored and provided for by God.

The rationalist-traditionalist divide among theologians did not lead to a drastic conclusion about God's plan for humanity. According to them, religion established the connection between private and public, individual and society, spiritual and mundane. Human progression was guaranteed if they could manage to balance contradicting demands of various spheres of human existence. Two positions on morality did not in any significant way undermine the ability of ordinary people to understand this balance between demands of reason and revelation. Revelation depended on reason for its validity; and reason sought to validate its conclusions by showing their correlation to revelation.

Conclusion

The secular liberal thesis that liberty can survive only outside religion and through secularization of a religious tradition was founded upon the historical experience of Christianity. There the solution was clearly to separate the public and the private in order to guarantee that the public square would remain inclusive and tolerant of differences. The value of freedom had to be raised over that of Christian religious exclusivity. Secularization helped in reducing the hold of religious law and the institutional church over society, thus making pluralism in the public square possible. Evidently, the experience of religious practice rendered people less tolerant of other faith communities and of various denominations within the Christian faith.

The religious experience of those who argue for foundationless theories of human rights is worth keeping in mind, particularly when such an evaluation of religion is extended to the different historical experience of Muslim societies. The foundationless theories give witness to a critical concern, to be a guarantor of basic human rights. Or we might put this as a question, how to reconcile basic freedoms with the moral worth of all human persons as human persons? To be sure, in the light of the tragic unfolding of the exclusivity of human religiosity and moral absolutism that concern was and remains real even today.

Was the Muslim historical experience any different than that of the West? Evidently it was and this is what seems to be the source of the alternative human rights paradigm presented by Muslim apologists. What is missing in this alternative paradigm is the discussion of any foundational capacity in the Islamic tradition to sit in dialogue with the secular human rights theorists to make a case for the inclusive notions of human entitlements tempered with human responsibilities in maintaining the overall well-being of humanity in all its areas and spheres of existence.

In my study I initiate a substantial theoretical discussion of an inclusive foundational conception of human rights that would appeal to the suspicious traditional authorities in the Muslim world, apparently threatened by secular ideologies that they believe are determined to destroy the spiritual and moral foundations of a global community to make room for liberal secular ideas of inalienable human rights. The point of departure for my research is to argue for a foundational theory of human rights based on some of the pluralistic features of Islam and its culture, totally ignored by Muslim traditionalist and fundamentalist discourse. True to its internal plurality, Islam's concern with the preservation of freedom against an authoritative theology, especially in view of its refusal to afford any human institution like the "church" the right to represent the divine interests on earth, was less of a problem in preserving peaceful coexistence among peoples of diverse faiths and cultures. The functional separation of the spiritual from the temporal was institutionalized to guarantee fundamental agreement on public values and to meet the demands of the multifaith and multicultural societies of the Islamic world to regulate human relationships between peoples of different faiths and cultures. Hence, the Western experience of religion by default remained alien to Muslim experience.

It is this difference in the historical experience of the West from that of Muslim societies that makes my project a viable proposition in the ongoing debate over whether a foundationless secular model can on its own provide the universal standards that can be applied across cultures, or whether it needs to look to a foundational religious model with its own universal claim to offer a more comprehensive understanding of what it means to be a defender of human rights today. Religion cannot and will not confine itself to a private domain where it will eventually lose its influence in nurturing the human conscience. It needs a public space in the development of an international sense of a world community with a vision of creating an ideal society that cares and shares.

NOTES

[1] Cf. David Little, John Kelsay, Abdulaziz Sachedina, *Human Rights and the Conflict of Cultures: Western and Islamic Perspectives on Religious Liberty*. (University of South Carolina Press: Columbia, 1988).

[2] See, Abdulaziz Sachedina, *Islam and the Challenge of Human Rights*. (Oxford University Press: New York, 2009).

[3] In his book on human rights, the prominent traditionalist scholar of Egypt, Muhammad al-Ghazāli lends a qualified support to the international document that must be respected by Muslims because, some of its "foundations" are also enunciated in the Qur'an. For Ghazāli, like other traditionalist scholars in the Muslim world, Islam provides the norms that are culturally legitimate and applicable within the Islamic world. As such, an alternative declaration of Islamic human rights is appended to the translation and discussion of the international document. See *Huqūq al-insān: Bayn ta'ālīm al-islām wa i'lān al-umam al muttahida* [*Human Rights: Between the Teachings of Islam and the Declaration of the United Nations*] (Alexandria, Egypt: Dār al-Da'wa, 1422/2002). This trend in traditional human rights scholarship has undermined the legitimacy of the universal declaration in the Muslim eyes. The only way to lessen the negative influence of this trend is to engage the traditional scholars in exploring the metaphysical foundations of the human rights declaration and demonstrate the common moral ground that is shared by world religions in upholding the norms that under gird the international document. By denying any normative foundations for the human rights declaration and insisting upon its secular thrust, the opportunity to stimulate conversation with the actual representatives of Islamic tradition is lost.

[4] Several studies in the relationship between Islam and human rights have, understandably, concentrated on the legal component of the rights and their compatibility with the international standards provided in the Declaration. See, for instance, studies by Abdullahi Ahmed An-Na'im, Ann Elizabeth Mayer, and others. However, there is a need to shift the debate about the compatibility to investigation about the possibility of seeking legitimacy for the Declaration through theological-ethical doctrines that could dispel the sinister attitude that prevails among Muslim religious thinkers about the document's European pedigree. This negative attitude has also served as a powerful weapon for Muslim political authorities to deny the human rights of their own citizens, especially women and minorities. See Ann Elizabeth Mayer, "Citizenship and Human Rights in Some Muslim States," in *Islam, Modernism and the West: Cultural and Political Relations at the End of the Millennium*, ed. Gema Martin Munoz (London: I. B. Tauris Publishers, 1999), 109–121.

[5] Muhammad 'Amāra, *al-Islām wa huqūq al-isān: Darūrāt . . . lā huqūq* [*Islam and Human Rights: Necessities . . . not Rights*] (Kuwait: 'Alam al-Ma'rifa, 1405/1985), 9–10, criticizes both Muslim fundamentalist and Muslim secular scholarship for having failed to demonstrate human rights within the parameters of Islamic comprehensive doctrines. The secularist scholarship—which was produced under the Orientalist masters, and which followed the Western cultural and civilizational domination of Muslim minds—was guilty of not examining Islamic sources carefully before agreeing with the Western

thesis about the inadequacy of Islam and its juridical tradition to issue anything similar to the international declaration of human rights. The Muslim secularists' prescription that one must derive the human rights from Western civilization instead of searching for these in Islamic sources, according to 'Amāra, must be totally rejected because it smacks of new Western hegemony over Muslim societies.

[6] Roger Ruston, in the introduction of his work, *Human Rights and the Image of God* (London: SCM Press, 2004), traces the development of Christian-Catholic critic of the liberal paradigm of human rights since the Universal Declaration in 1948. While there are some common themes that unite Muslim critics with their Christian counterparts, for Muslims the major problem with the liberal paradigm has been its hostile attitude to religion per se, and its enormous confidence in secularism which has failed time and again in delivering justice in Muslim countries that adopted its presuppositions for their reconstruction of modern Muslim societies. It is not only Turkey that institutionalized secularism through constitutional politics and is faced with internal challenges posed by Islamic cultural revival; Algeria also stands out as another unmistakable example of enforced from the top secularism of the colonial power that failed to deliver democratic political system and justice and fair distribution of national wealth to its citizens.

[7] In my work, *The Islamic Roots of Democratic Pluralism* (New York: Oxford University Press, 2000), I have examined Islamic ethical and theological notions to demonstrate the Qur'anic principles of social coexistence as well as the civil cooperation founded on common morality that touches all humans, independent of one's faith affiliation.

[8] Khaled Abou El Fadl touches upon "the moral trajectory" of the Qur'an which he develops to derive relevant understanding of, for instance, sanctity of life in human rights discourse. Cf. Khaled Abou El Fadl "A Distinctly Islamic View of Human Rights: Does it exist and is it compatible with the Universal Declaration of Human Rights?" in *Islam and Human Rights: Advancing a US-Muslim Dialogue*, ed. Shirin T. Hunter with Huma Malik (Washington, DC: The CSIS Press, 2005), 27–42. In another scholarly chapter, "Islam and the Challenge of Democratic Commitment," in *Does Human Rights Need God?*, ed. by Elizabeth M. Bucar and Barbara Barnett (Grand Rapids, MI: Wm B. Eerdmans Publishing Co., 2005), 58–103, El Fadl has detailed what I consider to be part of the "political theology," as outlined in this chapter. El Fadl's thesis that Islam itself is compatible with democratic politics is built upon his meticulous analysis of the legal writings of the classical jurists and their aversion to unrestrained authoritarianism and preference for a government bound by religious law "where human beings do not have unfettered authority over other human beings, and there are limits on the reach to power" (Ibid., 59). This characteristic is certainly compatible with ethical limits on the exercise of unrestrained power which must finally submit to public scrutiny.

[9] Such a view of religion and its problematic for the establishment of democracy and implementation of human rights has had a long history in the West. Two centuries ago, Alexis de Tocqueville, in his assessment of American republic, pointed out that the "great problem of our time is the organization and the establishment of democracy in Christian lands." Cf. Alexis de Tocqueville, *Democracy in America* (New York: Harper Collins, 1988), 311. During the nineteenth century it was Christianity that was seen as incompatible with democracy; and today it is Islam which is regarded as the "greatest

problem of our time." The extension of the nineteenth century view about Christianity to the twenty-first-century Islam is not merely a coincidence. In the wake of September 11, 2001 events, the Western views about religion's relationship to democracy have hardened to the extent that a number of prominent American social scientists now share Francis Fukuyama's opinion that Islam is resistant to modernity. As Fukuyama wrote, "[t]here seems to be something about Islam or at least fundamentalist versions of Islam that have been dominant in recent years, that makes Muslim societies particularly resistant to modernity." (Francis Fukuyama, "History is Still Going Our Way," in *Wall Street Journal* (October, 5 2001).

5.
On Grounding Human Rights: Variations on Themes by Little

John P. Reeder, Jr.

Finding "ground to stand on" is one of David Little's central concerns. When the secret police come to the door, one needs to be able to say that there is something within them that condemns their actions, something that is universal and necessary, not a local and contingent "social construction"; something discovered, not invented.[1] This is what animates his recent disputes with some "neo-pragmatists."[2] I am not going to analyze these exchanges or interpret his views in detail. Instead I will offer, if you will, some "variations on themes" by Little. I will first lay out eight issues and then discuss how one could move forward. This is an amicus brief, so to speak, presented with gratitude and affection.

The Self-Evident Ground

Schopenhauer quotes a Latin saying: "*Neminem laede, imo omnes quantum potes, juva*" (hurt no one but, so far as you are able, help all). He argues this is "the *principle*, the *fundamental proposition*, concerning whose purport all teachers of ethics are in agreement, however much they may clothe it in different forms."[3] It seems that Little also agrees that, suitably understood, this is the basic principle of morality: "it is irrational or unnatural and thus wrong deliberately to inflict pain or injury upon another person for the pleasure of doing it, or for other purely self-regarding purposes . . . or [to]refuse . . . aid at minimal cost to ourselves."[4]

Why would it be irrational to deny this principle? What is its status? It does not seem *a priori*, at least in the sense of a category of thought we must assume in any conception of experience that we could make intelligible to ourselves.[5] Is it *per se nota*, in the sense of a proposition we could not deny once we had understood it?[6] Is it self-evident or self-justifying in the sense that it does not require other backing?[7]

Little took his bearings from Locke in his own classic 1986 essay "Natural Rights and Human Rights: The International Imperative." Basic rights are "inherent" in human nature; they are accessible across cultures.[8] Little stood against Richard Rorty's denial that "there is something within" which the secret police betray.[9] It is not enough for Little that one "happens to believe" in human rights.[10] "Reason" imposes an obligation which is the basis of negative and positive rights.[11]

Thus Little calls the principle—don't hurt and help—a "*primary normative principle*." One is "bound to believe it"; it is a "fundamental" truth, on "which a great many others rest." The principle is not "innate" but is "always available to reason" and can be "discovered . . . by a process of active cogitation and reflection." Little quotes a point made about Leibniz to capture Locke's view of the nature of "bottom" truths: "the intellectual necessity we find ourselves under to accept them as soon as they are perceived and the intellectual impossibility of supposing their contraries."[12]

A type of neo-pragmatist critic claims, however, that a universally self-evident ground or justification is not available; basic moral beliefs are "justified relative to context," that is, in relation to webs of belief in particular historical contexts.[13] This neo-pragmatist will typically deny that any appeals to rational agency as such have been successful.[14] The idea that justification is relative to context means specifically for Jeffrey Stout, for example, that one's beliefs are justified so long as one has not been epistemologically negligent or failed to respond to defeaters.[15] One is required to respond to defeaters when they arise—to engage in the activity of justifying—if one is able to.[16] One responds in light of one's beliefs in a particular place and time. This sense of "holism" does not require that one appeal to the coherence of an entire web of belief or claim that cultures are "self-contained" wholes.[17] The idea that justification is relative to context is compatible with the realization that cultures are contested within and permeable without.[18]

Thus Little's fundamental principle would be regarded on the critic's view as one which has been articulated in particular traditions in particular historical contexts; its justification—whatever that is—ultimately rests as well on a set of contingent beliefs.[19]

One might, however, also explain the principle as an expression of a psychological disposition which is a product of our evolutionary history. As Frans de Waal puts it, the "moral domain of action is Helping or (not) Hurting."[20] The principle may not be self-evident, but neither is it, as Little would rightly insist, merely a contingent social construction in some times and places.[21]

An explanation, of course, is not a justification. Even if we are hard-wired for this or that disposition, the question remains, as Christine Korsgaard argues, whether we let our conduct be determined by a particular disposition, whether we endorse the disposition as justified.[22]

Whatever evolutionary story we tell, and however we think Little's principle has normative authority over us, the principle still needs specification. But the fact that the principle needs specification does not entail that it is merely a summary, generalization, or "abridgement" of particular judgments.[23] The principle has a foundational role, normatively speaking, even if it needs filling in. The fundamental principle is a substantive presupposition of more specific principles and judgments. It is not yet human rights, but it is the framework.

All of us, I presume, agree with Little, moreover, that we should not hurt or fail to help for "obviously mistaken reasons."[24] Rationality itself does seem to require that so far as we are able we should not act out of mistaken beliefs. In particular, we should not try to cover up wrongdoing with "manifestly unfounded" reasons.

A Normative Base-Line

The first question of specification has to do with what the principle rules out and what it permits. If it only rules out hurting or not helping for "purely" self-interested reasons, then by implication it permits hurting or not helping for self-interested reasons so long as one aims to benefit others as well. But Little clearly reads the principle to rule out some self-interested reasons altogether—for example, torturing babies for pleasure—whatever other-regarding motives one might also have.[25]

The principle, moreover, does not imply, as Little specifies it, that I am justified in hurting or not helping *merely* because I do so for the sake of others. To fill out the principle, one needs to specify who the others are and for what reasons one is justified in hurting or not helping someone. As we will see, one can incorporate these specifications, for example, into a notion of the right not to be killed.

Scope

The principle could be read to apply only to the in-group. The phrase "another person" could refer in context only to members of group X: Let us not hurt and not fail to help an X solely for our own self-regarding gain, for we are members of community X. Outsiders would not fall under the protection of the principle. Little, however, extends the principle regarding both agents and recipients to any human person (or perhaps even any rational agent): no one should hurt or fail to help anyone at reasonable cost for a purely self-regarding reason.

How does one extend the scope of the principle to human persons as such? Little handles this problem by making a Thomas Nagel-like move.[26] If we grant that we are all persons, then my headache is as much something for you to alleviate as it is for me. If a headache is a reason for action, then it is a reason no matter whose head it is in: *anyone's* headache is a *reason* for *anyone* to act.[27]

The critic makes an immediate objection, however: It would indeed be inconsistent if I insisted that my headache is a reason for me, but then denied your headache is a reason for you. Headaches are headaches, and in this sense the proposition that a headache is a reason is "agent-neutral." But this modest sense of an agent-neutral reason, so the critic argues, does not imply the stronger claim that my headache is a reason for you and vice-versa. I will return to this objection.

Inviolability

Let us assume that we do have some reason in our web of belief to make your headache, whoever you are, our concern. When one makes the extension to anyone—anyone's headache is a reason for anyone—this amounts to saying that anyone's headache is as morally significant as anyone else's. We could then go on to specify the extended principle in a utilitarian way. The principle so far does not rule out hurting or failing to help some if that promotes the greatest good overall—for example, the reduction of headaches—so long as all who are affected are considered (counted) without bias.

What one needs at this point is a Rawlsian insistence on the "inviolability" of the individual person who should not be sacrificed for the collective good. We need other concepts and beliefs to add the inviolability qualification to the principle. Unless we have inviolability, we would not violate the principle if we harmed or did not help, not for personal gain, or at least not solely for personal gain, but for the good of all affected. I violate the principle if I torture only for some self-interested goal, but I would not violate it if I torture for the greater good. Inviolability closes this door.

Rights

With the scope expanded and inviolability in hand, one can further specify that one has claims or rights that correspond to the duties of others. Not only do others have duties or obligations toward us, and in that sense we have a claim on them, but we also have the normative capacity to *make* claims on them. We can say to the oppressor, you violated our *rights*. If we are not competent agents, others can make claims on our behalf.

I think this specification is substantive, and not merely an analytical truth. It is an analytical truth, let us assume, that if you have a duty to me then I have a claim against you. This is so whether or not my duty is in virtue, say, of my status before God or in virtue of human nature alone. But it is another question whether I have the moral capacity to *make* that claim. Masters, for example, may have duties to servants, duties which imply claims, but servants may still not have a moral *right* to make claims. In some traditions, others have duties toward us, but we are not assigned the task of standing up for ourselves; that is the task of spirits, elders, prophets, social superiors, or gods. To give individuals this normative capacity—to assert claims as rights—is a further step.[28]

Self-Determination

Little also adds the idea that our rights are not just rightful claims we can make on others, but a matter of our sovereignty over ourselves. The normative reins to my freedom and wellbeing are in my hands. I can either insist on the fulfillment of your duty to me—don't hurt me, bind up my wounds—or I can yield or waive my right. No one else holds the reins. The idea that I can yield or waive is a further substantive specification of the meaning of rights.[29]

Basic Rights

It is an additional step, moreover, to specify what sorts of negative rights (don't injure or coerce) and positive rights (help if you can at a certain cost) we want to specify. We have to consider whether there are circumstances, that is, conditions, under which it is justifiable to hurt others or to fail to help. If so, then the content of these rights will include these exemptions, for instance, cases of self-defense or cases in which we legitimately prefer the near neighbor to the far. Little also distinguishes between *basic* human rights we are prepared to acknowledge universally, and other *secondary* rights which are devised in one tradition or another in order to protect and promote basic rights.[30]

For Little, these basic rights are "legally enforceable" in the primary sense that they ought to be enforced, that is, one is entitled to have them enforced.[31] It is another question whether they are legally enforceable in the sense that they in fact are part of some legal system. And it is still yet another question whether they are actually enforced in a particular jurisdiction.[32]

Moral Absolutes

Even if we can hope for much agreement in the specification of basic rights, there is a further question: Are these basic rights derogable (i.e., overridable), or do they consist of a set of moral absolutes—never harm, coerce, or fail to help. The rights themselves, as I noted, will specify certain circumstances in which it is justified to hurt or fail to help (in these cases the rights are not violated). But now the question is whether the rights *as specified* are prima facie or absolute. I argue as others have for a moral absolute, the immunity of innocents from direct, intentional harm, but some think that both negative and positive basic rights are prima facie.[33] Even if torture, for example, cannot be justified simply on utilitarian grounds, the question remains whether the right not to be tortured based on the inviolability of the individual can be overridden. The point to emphasize, says the neo-pragmatist, is that the answer to this question does not lie in reason as such, but in a wider web of belief.

How might we go forward?

Little very cogently replied to the "communitarian" objection: His basic principle itself is a matter of a normative *relationship* between members of the human "family."[34] Just as we provide for making claims and for self-determination within families, so Little can insist that rights function within the family of humankind.

He also can reply to the objection that his view makes ends and emotions, aims and attachments, merely the raw material constrained and directed by moral reason. He thinks that one must presuppose a fairly thick view of *human good*. Like Martha Nussbaum, he thinks we are creatures who value freedom and wellbeing but are vulnerable in certain characteristic ways.[35] He also assumes, I believe, a basic *attachment* to others: one's regard for the other is not only respect; one loves the neighbor as part of the human family.

He presumably would want to defend the basic principle as *self-evident*. Against the neo-pragmatist, he would argue that there is at least one substantive moral truth which is self-evident and hence it is held (i.e., believed) non-inferentially.³⁶ There are "'propositions which the soul . . . may . . . come certainly to know the truth of.'"³⁷ For Little, fundamental norms cannot rest on "contingent and hypothetical" injunctions.³⁸ If one could only appeal to the "empirical," then a Nietzschean could just as well cite inclinations to "appropriation, injury, overpowering what is alien and weaker."³⁹ The contrast ultimately is between rationality understood in Hobbesian terms—the "pursuit of self-advantage"—and a Lockean notion of reason which requires consideration of the good of others.⁴⁰

Our neo-pragmatist, however, will argue there are no basic deliverances of moral reason, no self-evident bottom truths, on which we could build and by which we could test the body of our moral beliefs.⁴¹ To counter the neo-pragmatist, perhaps one could employ Jean Porter's account of *per se nota* principles:⁴²

a) Such principles, she argues, in part with Alasdair MacIntyre, "need no justification": "the predicate is in some way implied by the meaning of the subject; however, such principles are not necessarily self-evident to us, because the meaning of the relevant terms may only be apparent after extensive reflection."⁴³ The first principles are a "result, not a starting point for investigation."⁴⁴ The meaning of the predicates (e.g., good is to be *sought and done*) is not analytically included in the subject (e.g., *good*) but are "known through themselves" in the sense that "knowledge of these principles presupposes an informed grasp of the *ratio* of their relevant subjects—and this may well require reflective deliberation, such as can only be expected of the 'wise.'"⁴⁵ "Good is to be done," however, is "grasped by everyone."⁴⁶

b) Porter posits several first principles: "good is to be sought and done, and evil is to be avoided"; "Do no harm"; "Observe one's particular obligations"; and the imperative to love God and neighbor.⁴⁷

c) For Porter first principles reflect metaphysical truths. "Good is to be done" is the "reflection in the human intellect of a universal tendency to seek the good in accordance with the creature's own specific good of perfection, a tendency which in the case of the human creature is expressed through the universal desire for happiness." The principle of love for God reflects "the universal tendency which Aquinas explicitly describes as natural to every created existence, to love God more than self, in the sense of in some way desiring the universal good more than one's own." Love of neighbor, do no harm, and respect particular obligations do not reflect "general" metaphysical truths, but rather our specific "nature as animals, and more specifically as social animals." In sum, first principles "reflect exigencies of operation stemming from the person's character as a creature, an animal, and an animal of a specific kind." To deny first principles is to be "guilty of self-contradiction," not in the sense of using words inconsistently, but of denying "norms [which] spontaneously present themselves as reasonable because they reflect basic aspects of our nature…moreover, the patterns of individual and social lives are structured by these norms before it ever occurs to us to reflect on them."[48]

How does Little's view compare?

a) Little like Porter insists that his first principle is not innate, but learned.[49] But Porter also says that "the role first principles play is logical or conceptual, not epistemic."[50] Little, in contrast, sees his principle to as the epistemic foundation on the basis of which negative and positive human rights are erected.

b) Little posits one first principle whereas Porter with Aquinas posits several.[51] I think this is a family quarrel, however. Little might argue that his principle, when specified, with the exception of love for God, encompasses the moral content of Porter's series.[52]

c) Little, in contrast to Porter, would not want, I believe, to characterize his first principle as the normative expression of a metaphysical truth. He is "Kantian" in the sense that " moral reasoning takes its starting point from principles which do not in themselves depend on factual or metaphysical truths" about human nature or final end.[53]

But Little goes some of the way with Porter. Although he would insist that basic norms are accessible and justifiable to all competent agents, and hence do not depend on a religious or quasi-religious view of human nature and a final end, he would welcome in his own voice a theological interpretation of creature and Creator.[54] Little and Porter also agree that *per se nota* principles need specification. For instance, "do not kill without substantial justification" has to be filled out in particular communities with judgments about which killings, if any, are justified.[55] In addition, they agree that *per se nota* principles issue in a notion of moral or human rights which the law should protect.[56]

There is an alternative to both Little and Porter that a neo-pragmatist might offer. They give the status of *per se nota* principles to certain valued patterns of conduct and character, that is, to the norms which constitute certain moral practices, for example, come to the aid of the neighbor. The neo-pragmatist might think, however, that different moralities are contingent ways of valuing and ranking various natural inclinations to which we are genetically predisposed. Little and Porter argue that reason (properly understood) commands us to do no harm and to help, but the neo-pragmatist sees no demand of this sort in reason as such.[57]

The neo-pragmatist suggestion—which I only sketch here—is that *per se nota* principles are better described and explained as valued patterns of conduct and character to which we are disposed. But there are other such dispositions—apparently also selected by evolution—manifest in tendencies to aggression and conquest in which the strong kill or dominate the weak.[58] Moral traditions are best seen as selections of what evolution has selected. In other words, moral traditions rest on valuing and relating sets of actions and traits to which we are disposed by evolution.

Thus the question why we should go in one direction or another cannot be addressed by an appeal to what is *per se nota*. General norms (e.g., aid the neighbor) are norms which are constitutive of patterns of social activity or practices. To cite the norm is operationally sufficient as a penultimate justification to participants within the practice (who at least tacitly endorse it). In this sense the norm is self-evident or self-justifying. But from a wider perspective, it is our valuation of the pattern that grounds it. For the justification of our practices we have only what the neo-pragmatist offers us, namely, the support of our contingent webs of belief.[59]

In addition to the question of the epistemic status of the primary principle, there is the question of *scope*. One could perhaps defend the extension of the scope of the principle—from the in-group to all persons—by taking a leaf from the neo-Kantian argument Korsgaard makes. The very structure of consciousness in human animals requires that they reflect on and endorse particular desires by formulating a law-like rule for their actions (e.g., do such and such under such and such circumstances).[60] She argues, moreover, that as a purposive agent—one who reflects on and endorses desires—I must value my capacity to do this, my "humanity."[61] And if I value my capacity as a self-determining agent, I must by the canon of consistency value the same capacity in others.[62] Thus we must come to respect ourselves and others as "ends in themselves": "if you believe my argument," you will see that "it is just a non-contingent *fact* . . . that my essential identity is that of a citizen of the Kingdom of Ends and that this identity trumps all my contingent identities."[63]

But as Korsgaard herself recognizes, there is the familiar objection to this line of argument mentioned earlier. In her words, "Consistency can force me to grant that your humanity is normative for you just as mine is normative for me. It can force me to acknowledge that your desires have the status of reasons for you, in exactly the same way that mine do for me. But it does not force me to share in your reasons or make *your* humanity normative for me."[64]

Korsgaard has a reply to this objection, however. If the objection were true, then "We each act on our own private reasons, and we need some special reason, like friendship or contract, for taking the reasons of others into account. . . . If reasons *were* essentially private, consistency would not force me to take your reasons into account. . . . The solution …must be to show that reasons are not private, but public in their very essence."[65] Thus reasons "must be inherently shareable. . . . What both enables and forces us to share our reasons is . . . our *social nature*."[66] "It is not just that we go in for friendship or prefer to live in swarms or packs. The space of linguistic consciousness—the space in which meanings and reasons exist—is a space we occupy together."[67] Thus "the myth of egoism"—in the sense that we act for private reasons—"will die with the myth of the privacy of consciousness."[68]

My response to this reply is as follows: I agree that we live in a public world of "linguistic consciousness," but I think we still need a "special reason, like friendship or contract" to identify normatively with the interests of others. The fact that we understand each other and give reasons to each other, reasons which are public and shared, the fact that we live in an intersubjective world, does not entail that I must take your headache as a reason for me to act, that I must acknowledge you along with myself as an equal member of the Kingdom of Ends. I necessarily share your reasons in one sense—the public character of language and consciousness—but I need not take your headache as a reason for me. The moral question is about what we should do in response to reasons we commonly recognize.

The basic objection, then, to theories which rest normativity on our social nature is that even if there are basic intersubjective features of human existence that we share, these features do not require us to treat others as ourselves. I don't think that the recognition of others as persons like ourselves, or even of the contribution each makes to the "constitution" of the other, is sufficient as the "ground of ethics" as Frederick Olafson claims.[69] The ontology of *Mitsein* does not entail that our actions must be acceptable to all affected, or that we necessarily stand in a relation of caring about others as we care about ourselves.[70]

But I think Korsgaard is right to note that there are a number of notions of our equal humanity.[71] Each of these is embedded in wider webs of belief in which we assign a morally normative role and status to persons as such. For example, a theist will think that we are all equally children of God. The theist's justification for affirming this status may be relative to context, but the judgment is universal in application: All humans are children of God. Thus, as Raymond Geuss remarks, to "take account of others" [in a morally normative sense] requires a web of "further reasons": "What one would be left with would be a highly context-dependent, non-Kantian form of reflective endorsement."[72]

The extension of Little's basic principle then requires a specific web of belief; it does not rest on the nature of reasons alone. Nor does it rest on the nature of pain as a special sort of reason. Even if pain is not merely a sensation, but something we identify in a public way, it only follows that pain is something we all can recognize as a reason; it does not follow that I should be concerned about your pain just as I am about my own. The question is not whether pain is a shareable reason, but whether I take your pain as something to inflict or to relieve.[73]

With the scope of the principle extended, Little argues, as I would, that *inviolability* can be defended without theological grounds, Jeremy Waldron and Nicholas Wolterstorff to the contrary.[74] The inviolability of the individual is a central tenet for many secular humanists as well as theists. Both give justifications; the arguments for and against utilitarianism or other notions of a collective good are ongoing.

Little would argue, moreover, that the right to life, for example, is not "alienable," while admitting that our *self-determination* or sovereignty over life is nonetheless limited by duties to others.[75] Our right to life, including our moral capacity to yield the right, is not something that can be taken from us or we can divest ourselves of, but it should be defined in relation to our duties to others. Little then would not need to deny that we have sovereignty over ourselves, as some theologians may, in order to argue that our moral capacity for self-determination must be qualified in light of responsibilities to others.

One must also argue for *absolutes*. First, one may argue that some norms are not prima facie; they are not overridable by another moral duty; they are *always overriding* and absolute in this sense. Second, one may even argue that the absolute *cannot be in conflict* with another putative moral duty. The person who believes in absolutes (in this second sense) argues that where an absolute duty is concerned one simply does not *have* any duty which conflicts with it. I don't have a duty to save a greater number of innocents if the only way I can do that is to attack some innocents directly. If one believes, however, that moral duties can conflict, and that in some cases *none* is overriding, then one is prepared to have "dirty hands." There can be a morally motivated violation of one duty for the sake of another.[76]

The Secret Police

Before concluding, I want to return to the secret police at the door. Little argues that if we want to hold competent agents morally responsible, we must presuppose universal justifiability.[77] In other words, to hold the secret police blameworthy, we must presuppose that they know or should know that what they do is wrong.[78] It is not enough that they simply "happen" to share our convictions, for they might not share them. They must grasp as self-evident—or they would grasp were it not for culpable ignorance—that those they take away for torture or death have basic rights.[79]

The neo-pragmatist who believes that justification is relative to context could perhaps point to resources in the police's own tradition of which they could and should have been aware.[80] But if there are no such resources, then hypothetically their beliefs would be justified relative to context (assuming they have not been negligent in how they formed these beliefs). The neo-pragmatist seems to be committed, as Little rightly argues, to the view that the agent in this hypothetical situation could not be held morally responsible and hence blameworthy any more than a noncompetent agent could. I think the neo-pragmatist has to bite this bullet. Since some evildoers (evil in our eyes) are not epistemically culpable, they are not morally blameworthy.

But what about intervention? I think one could say that even when we do not hold an evildoer blameworthy—morally wrong in our eyes, but supposedly justified in theirs—restraint by force is sometimes legitimate. We make a moral judgment within our web of belief about evil and our responsibility to overcome it. We can still resist the secret police whose beliefs are justified in their own context, just we can resist the noncompetent aggressor (e.g., the deranged tyrant); both take something, as Little would say, they have no right to take.[81]

Thus so far as I can see one does not need to insist on a self-evident norm in order to justify intervention. Of course, in the hypothetical case where the evildoers' beliefs are justified in their own context, one is prepared to be a strong parentalist: One is prepared not only to disregard the judgment of the noncompetent (weak parentalism); one is prepared to intervene against competent agents whose moral judgments (even if justified in their context) one regards as gravely mistaken (strong parentalism).

I think Little would be correct to say, then, that the neo-pragmatist is stuck with strong parentalism. The neo-pragmatist cannot affirm what Little wants us to: except in cases of noncompetence, evildoers can grasp or should grasp the self-evident wrongness of their actions; when we stop the unjust aggressor, we are not *imposing* our moral views, but acting on behalf of rights the aggressor recognizes, or should recognize were it not for culpable ignorance.[82] For the neo-pragmatist, in contrast, strong parentalism is not avoidable, unless one gives up on intervention.[83]

But can Little himself avoid parentalism? What if Little insists that he has good reason to hold that his epistemology is correct for all human beings, even for ones who deny it?[84] On the one hand, he can correctly say that he does not impose his own *moral* views, for the wrongdoer has or should have the same views; the competent wrongdoer knows or should know better. But on the other hand, he has to impose, as it were, his own *epistemology*. In order to claim that the wrongdoer either knows or should have known better, one has to *presuppose* that the wrongdoer grasps or should have grasped self-evident moral truths. Thus if a person denies, as our neo-pragmatist would, that there are self-evident moral truths in Little's sense, one must say that the person has the wrong epistemology. Little then must be a strong parentalist in an epistemological even if not in a moral sense; that is, he is prepared to intervene against competent agents whose actions he condemns and whose epistemological views he regards as gravely mistaken.[85]

Conclusion

Little begins with a self-evident principle which forbids injury or failure to aid (at reasonable cost) for purely self-interested or unfounded reasons. While our formulation of the principle may be correctable in minor detail, and while we may give it additional support, its basic content is not only self-evident, but "inalterable."[86] Are we still faced with the basic disagreement between Little and Rorty? Do we have a noncontingent starting-point, or are we the creatures of our contingent webs of belief and value? Even if there is a non-contingent moral order (in God or reason) can we relate to it epistemologically and morally only through our historically conditioned and fallible capacities?[87] The discussion continues![88]

NOTES

[1] David Little, "Natural Rights and Human Rights: The International Imperative," in *Natural Rights and Natural Law: The International Imperative*, ed. Robert P. Davidow (Fairfax, VA: The George Mason Press, 1986), 73–74.

[2] See David Little, "On Behalf of Rights: A Critique of Democracy and Tradition," in *Journal of Religious Ethics* 34.2 (June 2006): 287–310; David Little, "The Author Replies," in *Journal of Religious Ethics* 35.1 (March 2007): 171–75.

[3] Arthur Schopenhauer, *On The Basis Of Morality*, trans. E. F. J. Payne, 1841 (Indianapolis, IN: The Library of Liberal Arts, Bobbs-Merrill Educational Publishing, 1965), 69.

[4] Little, "Natural Rights and Human Rights," 91, 93–94; see also 90, 98, 100–1, 102, 103, 108; David Little, "The Nature and Basis of Human Rights," in *Prospects for a Common Morality*, ed. Gene Outka and John P. Reeder, Jr. (Princeton, NJ: Princeton University Press, 1993), 73–92. Little is referring to self-regard or self-interest here in the sense of self-advantage, not in the sense of the "interests of a self" which could be self-regarding or other-regarding, or in the wider sense of a type of self-love which includes the good of others. Cf. Diana Fritz Cates, *Choosing to Feel: Virtue, Friendship, and Compassion for Friends* (Notre Dame, IN: The Notre Dame University Press, 1997).

[5] Peter Strawson, *The Bounds of Sense: An Essay on Kant's Critique of Pure Reason* (London: Methuen, 1966).

⁶ Jean Porter, *Nature as Reason: A Thomistic Theory of the Natural Law* (Grand Rapids, MI: William B. Eerdmans, 2005).

⁷ Joseph Boyle argues that a Thomistic view of natural law can grant that inquiry is dependent on languages and cultures and that it develops as a tradition ["Natural Law and the Ethics of Traditions," in *Natural Law Theory: Contemporary Essays*, ed. Robert P. George (Oxford: Clarendon Press, 1992), 5–9]; but it cannot grant that a "lived experience of values in a community" is a necessary condition of moral knowledge itself (ibid., 9–16.) Thus natural law posits a "set of universal prescriptions whose presumptive force is a function of the rationality which all human beings share in virtue of their common humanity" (ibid., 4). These principles are self-evident or *per se nota*; they cannot be "deduced from more basic truths" but they can be "defended dialectically" against those who deny them in the name of moral diversity (ibid., 23–24.)

⁸ Little, "Natural Rights and Human Rights," 69, 70.

⁹ Ibid., 73–74, 95–96; Richard Rorty, *Consequences of Pragmatism: Essays 1972–1980* (Minneapolis, MN: University of Minnesota Press, 1982), xlii–xliii; Bernard Reginster, *The Affirmation of Life: Nietzsche On Overcoming Nihilism* (Cambridge, MA: Harvard University Press, 2006), 83.

¹⁰ Little, "Natural Rights and Human Rights," 79; see Bernard Williams, "History, Morality, and the Test of Reflection," in *The Sources of Normativity*, Christine M. Korsgaard with G. A. Cohen, Raymond Geuss, Thomas Nagel, Bernard Williams, ed. Onora O'Neill (Cambridge: Cambridge University Press, 1996), 214–15.

¹¹ Little, "Natural Rights and Human Rights," 83, 89–90.

¹² Ibid., 91, 92, 92–92, 94, 116–17 n. 87.

¹³ There are, of course, different versions of the pragmatist tradition.

¹⁴ Jeffrey Stout, "On Having a Morality in Common," in *Prospects for a Common Morality*, ed. Gene Outka and John P. Reeder, Jr. (Princeton, NJ: Princeton University Press, 1993); Jeffrey Stout, *Ethics After Babel: The Languages of Morals and Their Discontents* (Princeton, NJ: Princeton University Press, 2001).

¹⁵ See David Copp, "Moral Knowledge in Society–Centered Moral Theory," in *Moral Knowledge?: New Readings in Moral Epistemology*, ed. Walter Sinnott-Armstrong and Mark Timmons (New York: Oxford University Press, 1996), 262–63. One is justified in one's beliefs (assuming no faults in how they are acquired) so long as there is no reason to doubt or if doubts do arise one dismisses the doubts "in a way that is reasonable according to epistemic standards" one "justifiably accepts."

¹⁶ Stout, "On Having a Morality in Common"; Jeffrey Stout, *Democracy and Tradition* (Princeton, NJ: Princeton University Press, 2004), chap. 10.

¹⁷ See Jeffrey Stout, *The Flight From Authority: Religion, Morality, and the Quest for Autonomy* (Notre Dame, IN: Notre Dame Press, 1981), 274 n. 9; Stout, *Democracy and Tradition*, chaps. 8, 12; Robert Audi distinguishes between "conceptual coherentism" as regards the "acquisition and function of concepts" and "epistemological coherentism . . . the view that the justifiedness of beliefs and other cognitions is grounded in the mutual coherence of the relevant items." See *The Good in the Right: A Theory of Intuition and Intrinsic Value* (Princeton, NJ: Princeton University Press, 2004), 73. Mark Timmons suggests that Stout may hold to a version of "structural contextualism" ("Outline of a

Contextualist Moral Epistemology," in *Moral Knowledge?: New Essays in Moral Epistemology*, ed. Walter Sinnott-Armstrong and Mark Timmons (New York: Oxford University Press, 1996), 323 n. 43; *Morality Without Foundations: A Defense of Ethical Contextualism* (New York: Oxford University Press, 1999), 213 n. 43). The structural contextualist thinks that "certain beliefs, in certain contexts at least, do not need to have . . . positive evidential support (either inherently or from other beliefs and experiences) in order to play a redress-stopping role in the structure of justified belief" (cf., Timmons, *Morality Without Foundations*, 187 n. 14).

[18] Michele M. Moody-Adams, "Culture, Responsibility, and Affected Ignorance," *Ethics* 104 (January 1994): 291–309; Kathryn Tanner, *Theories of Culture: A New Agenda for Theology* (Minneapolis, MN: Fortress Press, 1997); Timmons distinguishes his own "structural contextualism" not only from coherentism, but from "normative contextualism," the view that one is justified in believing a proposition only if one's holding it conforms to the " relevant set of epistemic practices and norms operative" in the context. However, his own view requires that one conform to "the epistemic norms and practices characteristic of (an) epistemically responsible agent." One is responsible for "recognizing and checking any relevant counterpossibilities"; these in turn depend on background beliefs and "information widely shared by a relevant community" (*Morality Without Foundations*, 186–87, 236–43, 185, 205, 198–201, 211, 212).

[19] See Wolterstorff for instance versus Locke: "In forming beliefs in response to experience, I do not and cannot operate as a generic human being. I operate as a person with such-and-such a contour of beliefs, such-and-such a contour of affections, such-and-such a contour of habits and skills of attention—and so forth. . . . We live *inside* our traditions, not *alongside*," Nicholas Wolterstorff and Robert Audi, *Religion in the Public Square: The Place of Religious Convictions in Political Debate* (Lanham, MD: Rowman and Littlefield Publishers, Inc., 1997), 89; Nicholas Wolterstorff, *John Locke and the Ethics of Belief* (Cambridge: Cambridge University Press, 1996), 89, 118–48. Thus, for Wolterstorff, "Something about the belief, the person, and the situation brings it about that the person is entitled to the belief. But that need not be another belief whose propositional content functions as a reason," ibid., 87. Cf. Audi and Wolterstorff: "For me judging that an action is morally wrong counts as a reason to oppose it; one need not have a further reason—roughly a premise—for this judgment. . . . To require that would beg the question against even a minimal foundationalism," *Religion in the Public Square*, 173–74.

[20] Frans de Waal, *Good Natured: The Origins of Right and Wrong in Humans and Other Animals* (Cambridge, MA: Harvard University Press, 1996), 162–64; Frans de Waal, *Primates and Philosophers: How Morality Evolved*, ed. Stephen Macedo and Josiah Ober (Princeton, NJ: Princeton University Press, 2006). For one statement of the explanation, see Barbara Hannan, *The Riddle of the World: A Reconsideration of Schopenhauer's Philosophy* (New York: Oxford University Press, 2009), 92: The "moral intuitions of justice and benevolence" are "psychological tendencies, appearing in the population due to random genetic variations" which "proved conducive to strong social groups, thereby enabling individuals within those groups to survive and pass on their genes."

[21] Marc Hauser argues that "an unconscious and universal grammar" underlies our judgments of right and wrong, that this knowledge is independent of religion, and is filled out by "parameters" in specific moral languages (*Moral Minds: How Nature Designed Our Universal Sense of Right and Wrong* (New York: HarperCollins Publishers, 2006), xviii, xx, 66, 72, 74, 83, 129–30, 138, 154–59, 165, 214, 260, 262–63, 290, 295, 298–303, 331, 419–26). Hauser's notion of a toolkit of categories with which are genetically equipped still leaves substantive content to specific cultures and traditions. Thus a neo-pragmatist could argue that even if the evolutionary biologist is right, the patterns are so extremely general that cultural specification does the final work.

[22] Korsgaard, *The Sources of Normativity*, 9–10, 12–13, 14–16. To claim that a moral disposition is motivationally ineluctable would still not answer the question of justification. As Korsgaard puts it, "Perhaps the pain of ignoring this disposition breaks you down, like the pains of torture or extreme starvation. Then you might be moved by the instinct even though you *don't* upon reflection endorse its claims. In that case the evolutionary theory would still explain your action. But it would not *justify* it from your point of view," ibid., 15.

[23] If Alan Donagan grants, argues Stout, that any purportedly self-evident principle must rely for its specification on other beliefs, then in effect it is a process of reflective equilibrium against a background of presuppositions, e.g., Western views of the self as Donagan grants in his own case, that does all the work. The basic principle should not be regarded then as self-evident, but only as an "abridgement" of more specific judgments. Alan Donagan, *The Theory of Morality* (Chicago: The University of Chicago Press, 1977); Stout, *Ethics After Babel*, chap. 6.

[24] David Little, "Ground to Stand On: A Philosophical Reappraisal of Human Rights Language" (Harvard Divinity School, 2009).

[25] Little's view is close to Judith Jarvis Thomson's: "One ought not to torture babies to death for fun" is a necessary truth which has no "other things being equal" qualification (*The Realm of Rights* (Cambridge, MA: Harvard University Press, 1990), 17–18).

[26] See Little, "Natural Rights and Human Rights," 97; Thomas Nagel, "The Limits of Objectivity," in *Tanner Lectures on Human Values*, ed. Sterling M. McMurrin (Salt Lake, UT: University of Utah Press, 1980).

[27] This point is also made in Little, "Ground to Stand On."

[28] On the emergence of the idea of "subjective rights," see Brian Tierney, *The Idea of Natural Rights: Studies on Natural Rights, Natural Law, and Church Law 1150–1625* (Grand Rapids, MI: William B. Eerdmans Publishing Company, 1997). As a matter of terminology, one could say that duties analytically imply rights, but that the normative capacity to assert rights is another matter. I think it is simpler to say that duties and claims imply one another, and that claims become rights when we have the capacity as individuals to assert them.

[29] To yield a right is not to divest oneself of the right, but to forego, to waive, its protection in a particular case. One does not forfeit the right to life, moreover, in the strong sense of lose completely, even if one becomes an unjust aggressor.

[30] Little, "The Nature and Basis of Human Rights," 84, 92 n. 32.

[31] Ibid.

[32] Basic rights for Locke are not alienable (capable of being annulled, surrendered, or transferred). Nor can they be forfeited; the person who is justly punished, for example, is coerced or injured for the sake of "reparation and restraint" which benefits self and other. The exceptions (specified, I think, in the rights themselves) for punishment, restraint, and therapy are worked out by communities and usually assigned to special officials and procedures (Little, "Natural Rights and Human Rights," 104, 120–21 n. 101, 98–99). (In "Ground to Stand On," Little lists overall relief of pain, survival, and restraint. To inflict pain on one innocent for the sake of another can be at most an excuse, but one is justified in resisting the wrongdoer.) Given our temptation to hurt others for personal advantage, God has "appointed Government." Constitutionalism and human rights law, Little argues, specify and enforce the basic principle and the negative and positive rights which express it (Little, "Natural Rights and Human Rights," 99–100, 112–14).

[33] See John P. Reeder, Jr., "Terrorism, Secularism, and the Deaths of Innocents," *Journal for Peace and Justice Studies* 21.2 (2011): 70–94.

[34] See Little, "Natural Rights and Human Rights."

[35] See Martha C. Nussbaum, *Frontiers of Justice: Disability, Nationality, and Species Membership* (Cambridge, MA: Belknap Press, 2006).

[36] See Little, "Ground to Stand On." See Timmons, *Morality Without Foundations*, 179–80, on the distinction between "propositional justification" and "doxastic justification," i.e., the justification of propositional content as such in contrast to the justification of believing that proposition.

[37] Little, "Natural Rights and Human Rights," 116–17 n. 87. See Little on the tension in Locke between theological voluntarism and rationalism (ibid., 115–16 n. 77). See also Wolterstorff who, like Little, cites John Colman, *John Locke's Moral Philosophy* (Edinburgh: Edinburgh University Press, 1983): "Locke's theory of moral obligation may be summed up thus: God's will is necessary and sufficient to put men under an obligation; the facts of human nature are necessary and sufficient to delimit the obligations men are placed under" (Wolterstorff, *John Locke and the Ethics of Belief*, 140–48, 143 n. 141). Locke may also have held that the will of God is the justificatory ground of the moral law (God as legitimate lawgiver establishes obligations or moral laws); but God makes it the case that human beings through Reason (aided by Revelation) grasp the basic principle of the moral law. Thus Locke would be a "voluntarist" as regards the ultimate justificatory basis of the moral law, but a "rationalist" as regards the epistemic status of the moral law in human experience. Little agrees with Wolterstorff that for Locke the "law of nature" means "a law of moral obligation which can in principle be known by Reason" (ibid., 140). See G. A. Cohen, "Reason, Humanity, and the Moral Law," in *The Sources of Normativity*, Christine M. Korsgaard, 167–88, on the sovereign as the lawgiver who is a law unto himself.

[38] Little, "Natural Rights and Human Rights," 94.

[39] Ibid., 94, 94, 117–18 n. 90.

[40] Ibid., 118 n. 92.

[41] See Wolterstorff, *John Locke And The Ethics Of Belief*, on Locke.

[42] Porter, *Nature as Reason*.

⁴³ See Alasdair MacIntyre, *First Principles, Final Ends, and Contemporary Philosophical Issues* (Milwaukee, WI: Marquette University Press, 1990); Porter, *Nature as Reason*, 109, 109 n. 77.

⁴⁴ Porter, *Nature as Reason*, 110 n. 80.

⁴⁵ Ibid., 263.

⁴⁶ Ibid., 264. For MacIntyre, first principles are "evident *per se*, but their evidentness is intelligible only in the context of the relevant body of perfected theory within which they function as first principles." The "analytic antifoundationalist and the deconstructive critique of first principles" ends in an epistemological impasse: "Where rationalists and empiricists appealed to epistemological first principles, their contemporary heirs identify socially established forms of life or paradigms or epistemes" (*First Principles*, 30–31, 32–34, 22, 62–63).

⁴⁷ Porter, *Nature as Reason*, 263.

⁴⁸ Ibid., 264, 264–65, 263–64 n. 52, 272. What is good for human beings is the actualization of the potential embodied in their form or functional arrangement. As Korsgaard puts it, "The form of a thing is its perfection, but it is also what enables the thing to be what it is. So the endeavor to realize perfection is just the endeavor to be what you are—to be *good at being what you are*" (*The Sources of Normativity*, 3, 2–5).

⁴⁹ Little, "Natural Rights and Human Rights."

⁵⁰ Porter, *Nature as Reason*, 210.

⁵¹ Little, "Natural Rights and Human Rights."

⁵² Porter takes particular obligations and love of neighbor as implied in do no harm. See her analysis of how do no harm is related to duties to protect the innocent (ibid., 271–73, 272–82).

⁵³ Ibid., 263. Porter disagrees with Martin Rhonheimer about the moral status of inclinations. For Aquinas and for herself Porter argues that "the scope of morality is not limited to an ordering generated by reason itself"; "prerational nature "already has "moral significance" which reason does not bestow, but discovers; cf., "Natural Law and Practical Reason," review of Martin Rhonheimer, *A Thomist View of Moral Autonomy* in *Theological Studies* 62.4 (December, 2001): 1–2. Another point of disagreement is Rhonheimer's view that reason recognizes goods without reference to a "speculative "account of human nature or final end; cf. Porter, "A Response to Martin Rhonhimer," *Studies in Christian Ethics* 19.3 (2006): 381. In contrast for Porter, reason's grasp—at least a fully rational grasp—of goods presupposes "judgments . . . about the final end of human life, the individual's path to this end, and the way in which the desideratum at hand relates to the final end" (ibid., 382–85). I take Little's view of inclinations to be closer to Rhonheimer's. Little also is like Rhonheimer in thinking that reason can do its moral work independent of visions of the *final* end. Little argues that the basic principle and human rights are not dependent on "comprehensive" beliefs about the "ultimate ground and nature of the moral life" ("Ground to Stand On").

⁵⁴ David Little, "Calvin and the Prospects for a Christian Theory of Natural Law," in *Norm and Context in Christian Ethics*, eds. Gene H. Outka and Paul Ramsey (New York: Charles Scribner's Sons, 1968), 175–97.

⁵⁵ Porter, *Nature as Reason*, 272–82, 309, 338–42; Porter, "A Response to Martin Rhonheimer," 387–88.

⁵⁶ Porter, *Nature as Reason*, 342–78.

⁵⁷ See John P. Reeder, Jr., "Hearing and Obeying: Nussbaum, Kierkegaard, and Nietzsche," (unpublished manuscript).

⁵⁸ On aggression vs. cooperation, see Hannan, *The Riddle of the World*, 95, 92. See also Martha C. Nussbaum, "Pity and Mercy: Nietzsche's Stoicism," in *Nietzsche, Genealogy, Morality: Essays on Nietzsche's* On the Genealogy of Morals, ed. Richard Schacht (Berkeley, CA: University of California Press, 1994), 140, 154, 166 n. 44, who argues that the hardness Nietzsche advocates is that of a "disciplined dancer," not the cruelty of the master or conqueror. See also Reginster who argues that the will to power is not so much control and domination, but a second-order desire for the "overcoming of resistance" to the satisfaction of first-order desires. Since I value the overcoming of resistance, I value suffering as the "experience of such resistance." Thus "increased control and domination" is a consequence of overcoming resistance, but not the essence of the will to power (*The Affirmation of Life*, 34–35, 37, 39, 45, 41). However we interpret Nietzsche, it seems to me that we have inherited dispositions to kill and dominate.

⁵⁹ Timmons argues that some beliefs if held responsibly can serve in ordinary contexts to justify other beliefs. But he grants that this holds only within an "engaged context"; when one looks from a "detached context," then the relevant group is not those who share the outlook but sceptics and one is not permitted to "take one's core beliefs and assumptions as basic" (*Morality Without Foundations*, 220–21). MacIntyre, however, insists that a virtue such as "just generosity" requires no "further reason." While all the virtues contribute to human good, and one can represent this in a chain of reasoning, the virtuous "will be unable to conceive of such a reason as requiring or being open to further justification. To offer and even to request such a justification is itself a sign of defective virtue," Alasdair MacIntyre, *Dependent Rational Animals: Why Human Beings Need the Virtues* (Chicago: Open Court, 1999), 158–59. My sense, however, is that MacIntyre is talking about the engaged context; he himself offers the sceptic the chain of reasoning.

⁶⁰ A rule can be universalizable even if it only pertains to certain agents and recipients: all privates must salute officers, so anyone who is a private must do so. In contrast a rule which pertains to persons as such—as agents and recipients—is not only universalizable but universal. Thus Korsgaard distinguishes between a rule or law as such, and the moral law which pertains to members of the Kingdom of Ends who value their own and their neighbor's humanity.

⁶¹ Korsgaard, *The Sources of Normativity*, 143–45, 277–78.

⁶² Ibid., 196; see also Raymond Geuss, "Morality and Identity," in *Creating the Kingdom of Ends*, Christine M. Korsgaard (Cambridge: Cambridge University Press, 1996), 192.

⁶³ Korsgaard, *The Sources of Normativity*, 196. Korsgaard puts her argument in the vocabulary of identity. Human animals need practical identities. These identities are normative and a source of reasons. One must recognize this as a fundamental truth

about human beings (ibid., 118–23, 119, 123, 129). See Geuss, "Morality and Identity," 196–97.

[64] Korsgaard, *The Sources of Normativity*, 134; see Adina Schwartz, "Review of *Reason and Morality* by Alan Gewirth," *The Philosophical Review* 88 (1979): 654–56; Alan Gewirth, *Reason and Morality* (Chicago: University of Chicago Press, 1978); Geuss, "Morality and Identity," 197; see Alasdair MacIntyre, *After Virtue: A Study in Moral Theory* (Notre Dame, IN: University of Notre Dame Press, 2007), 66–68; see Mathias Risse on Korsgaard and Nietzsche, on the standard objection, and on the broader opposition between a Kantian model of rational agency overagainst desires and the Nietzschean picture of the self as an effecter of desires ("Nietzchean 'Animal Psychology' versus Kantian Ethics," in *Nietzsche and Morality*, eds. Brian Leiter and Neil Sinhababu (Oxford: Clarendon Press, 2007), 61–62, 68–70, 69 n. 18, 73–74, 70–4); see also Joshua Knobe and Brian Leiter, "The Case for Nietzschean Moral Psychology," in *Nietzsche and Morality*, eds. Brian Leiter and Neil Sinhababu (Oxford: Clarendon Press, 2007), 82–109.

[65] Ibid., 134–5; see also ibid., 140–41, 144–45. See Thomas Nagel, "Universality and the Reflective Self," in *The Sources of Normativity*, Christine M. Korsgaard with G. A. Cohen, Raymond Geuss, Thomas Nagel, Bernard Williams, ed. Onora O'Neill (Cambridge: Cambridge University Press, 1996), 207–8; Korsgaard, *The Sources of Normativity*, 245–47.

[66] Ibid., 135.

[67] Korsgaard, *The Sources of Normativity*, 145.

[68] Ibid., 144. See also Ronald M. Green, "What Does it Mean to Use Someone as 'A Means Only': Rereading Kant," *Kennedy Institute of Ethics Journal* 11.3 (2001): 255, "basic moral reasoning takes place for Kant from within an impartial standpoint." The question is whether the impartial standpoint is a requirement *of* reason, or whether it is a normative construction *for* reason. I favor the latter view.

[69] Frederick A. Olafson, *Heidegger And The Ground Of Ethics: A Study Of Mitsein* (Cambridge: Cambridge University Press, 1998), 10–12, 48–49, 48 n. 16, 68.

[70] Ibid., 52–59. Neera Kapur Badwahr argues that the sense of common humanity which moved Holocaust rescuers may be explained by Nagel's notion of oneself as "merely one person among others equally real" which disposes one to be motivated by the interests of others ("Altruism Versus Self-Interest: Sometimes a False Dichotomy," in *Altruism*, eds. Ellen Frankel Paul, Fred D. Miller, Jr., and Jeffrey Paul (Cambridge: Cambridge University Press, 1993), 98. My view, in contrast, is that the notion of others as equally real is not sufficient to ground common humanity as a normative status.

[71] Korsgaard, *The Sources of Normativity*, 118.

[72] Geuss, "Morality and Identity," 198–99, 199.

[73] Ibid., 197–98. See Korsgaard, *The Sources of Normativity*, 145–50; Little, "Ground to Stand On." Thomson, *The Realm of Rights*, 13–16, argues that some statements of fact—you will cause pain if you do something—entail a moral conclusion—you should not do it. She says that the "conjunction" of a general principle—you should not other things being equal cause pain—with the factual premise above entails the moral conclusion, whether the general principle is a necessary truth or not; but if the general principle is a necessary truth, then the factual statement "by itself" entails the moral

conclusion. I assume that pain is bad in a nonmoral evaluative sense (even when pain is necessary as a means or as a side-effect or as an inherent part of a valuable experience as Nietzsche argued), but that from its badness nothing is entailed as regards the moral wrongness of inflicting or not relieving it.

[74] See Jeremy Waldron, *God, Locke, and Equality: Christian Foundations of John Locke's Political Thought* (Cambridge: Cambridge University Press, 2002); Nicholas Wolterstorff, *Justice: Rights and Wrongs* (Princeton, NJ: Princeton University Press, 2008).

[75] Rights cannot be alienated for Locke because "humans do not possess these rights over themselves in the first place. . . . One is never free to commit suicide because God owns the life of any human being. It is his right and not the right of any human being's" (Little, "Natural Rights and Human Rights," 105). See Waldron, *God, Locke, and Equality*.

[76] On absolutes, see Paul Lauritzen, "Torture Warrants and Democratic States: Dirty Hands in an Age of Terror," *Journal of Religious Ethics* 38.1(March 2010): 93–112; Reeder, "Terrorism, Secularism, and the Deaths of Innocents"; Edmund N. Santurri, "Philosophical Ambiguities in Ostensibly Unambigous Times," *The Journal for Peace and Justice Studies* 12.2 (2002): 137–161; Sumner B. Twiss, "Torture, Justification, and Human Rights: Toward An Absolute Prescription," *Human Rights Quarterly* 29 (2007): 246–67.

[77] Little, "On Behalf of Rights," 297, 299 n. 15, 302–4.

[78] Blame-*capable* competent, that is, responsible, agents can be blame-*deserving*.

[79] See Moody-Adams, "Culture, Responsibility, and Affected Ignorance," on "affected ignorance" which includes culpable ignorance of facts or of their moral significance, as well as other forms of epistemic avoidance.

[80] Stout, *Democracy and Tradition*; Little, "On Behalf of Rights."

[81] As Stout remarks, other practices can condemn totalitarian ones even without a universal ground (*Ethics After Babel*, 259, 256–60).

[82] Ignoring what you really at some level know is one sort of epistemic fault, but there is also the case where someone is simply ignorant, but culpably so. I will refer to both sorts of ignorance under the heading of "should know better." Thus in my terminology evil persons either straightforwardly know that what they do is wrong, or they should have known better, either in the sense that at some suppressed level they do know, or that they are simply, yet culpably, ignorant.

[83] Little also makes the point that even noncompetent agents, say, by reason of mental defect, may be *legally* liable, although the charge and the sentence may be adjusted. The neo-pragmatist also grants this; the mad bomber can be imprisoned. (In some cases one might even be culpable for one's incompetence.) The neo-pragmatist can also allow that competent although gravely mistaken agents can be held legally liable: We need to restrain and deter terrorists even if their beliefs are contextually justified. Here as well the nature of the charge and the sentence might be adjusted. In the neo-pragmatist's view, these are normative legal issues to be addressed just as we do in all cases, namely, in light of our contingent webs of belief.

[84] Alvin Plantinga argued, "We do not think that any normal human being could honestly arrive at the view that . . . if inflicting severe pain on someone else affords a certain mild pleasure, then there can be no real objections to so doing. We do not believe

anyone of good will could honestly come to the conclusion that, say, an entire racial group could rightly be eliminated to avoid the possibility of racial contamination." Thus Plantinga straightforwardly appeals to the "makeup of human beings," the "normal human condition." This is not only a psychological point, but an epistemological one: "we can simply see that heinous actions are indeed heinous. . . . If we think a person really *lacks* this inclination to see some actions as morally wrong, then we do not hold him responsible." We regard the person as "defective," as legally "insane." But if we do not think the person is deeply defective, then we will believe he or she "*knows better*," that they have "ignored or suppressed the promptings and leadings of nature" in order perhaps to justify "a desire for self" ("Reason and Belief in God," in *Faith and Rationality: Reason and Belief in God*, eds. Alvin Plantinga and Nicholas Wolterstorff (Notre Dame, IN: University of Notre Dame Press, 1983), 35–37).

[85] One might argue that if one knows or should know a self-evident truth, one knows or should know it *as* self-evident. But see Audi, *The Good in the Right*, 42–43, 60: Ross did not distinguish, as he should have, between "apprehending the truth of a proposition that is self-evident and . . . apprehending its self-evidence." To apprehend its self-evidence, I assume, is to accept a theory of its epistemological status.

[86] See Little, "The Nature and Basis of Rights," 81, 87.

[87] See Gene Outka, "The Particularist Turn in Theological and Philosophical Ethics," in *Christian Ethics: Problems and Prospects*, eds. Lisa Sowle Cahill and James F. Childress (Cleveland, OH: The Pilgrim Press, 1996), 93–118, on "socially" going "all the way down."

[88] Thanks first to David Little for all our conversations and for all his communications. Thanks also to Diana Cates, Gene Outka, Bharat Ranganathan, Jonathan Schofer, and James Swan Tuite.

6.
From Human Rights to Animal Rights?

Grace Y. Kao

Despite the extensive body of laws and literature on human rights, questions remain about their philosophical bases. There is the longstanding suspicion that human rights are ethnocentrically Western in origin or content and thus may not be universally applicable. Among those who accept their universal legitimacy, a growing number insist upon their unavoidably religious theoretical foundations, while another camp retorts with equal confidence that human rights can be justified without any necessary recourse to religious or metaphysical ideas. There are, of course, still others who support their global promotion, but hold that a conceptual rationale for them is no longer necessary given their massive popular appeal, widespread institutionalization, and various enforcement mechanisms at the national, regional, and international levels.

Amidst that chorus of familiar concerns and positions lies yet another question—one that is widely perceived by those who move primarily in the field of human rights to be ancillary at best, and at worst displacing the "real" work that needs to be done. That question is the following: what is the relationship between human rights and animal rights? More specifically, might normative justifications for the former be extended in the direction of the latter? Some theorists best known for their advocacy on behalf of animals unambiguously connect their theoretical grounding of the rights that all humans possess by virtue of their humanity alone to cover the rights of other creatures. A still smaller number of thinkers support both human and animal rights, though for heterogeneous reasons.[1] But the vast majority of human rights proponents explicitly or implicitly affirm some account of our morally relevant differences from other animals in such a way as to grant human beings superior, if not unique, moral standing, and accordingly dismiss the idea of animal rights as categorically mistaken.

Now there is a fourth type of response that is arguably distinct from the other three: those who have defended the universal validity of human rights in such a manner that is prima facie anthropocentric, though could be adapted to the case of animals without impairing the integrity of the basic argument. It is this fourth category that I wish to explore here, particularly with reference to the work of well-known Christian ethicist and human rights scholar, David Little.

Why the question of animal rights when discussing human rights?

Before extending a recently proposed philosophical justification for human rights to cover the case of animal rights, it is worth pausing to consider why we should even raise the animal question in conjunction with the human one. While there are several good reasons for doing so, two deserve mention here: a widespread desire in the academy and the public-at-large to rethink our treatment of animals, and the practical entanglement of human and animal interests, thereby making the question unavoidable.

In the first case, there is a growing understanding both within and outside of the academy that animals "count." Animal studies is a burgeoning field of study, wherein scholars examine human-animal relations in the past and present, and in numerous fictional forms from a variety of disciplinary perspectives. In the fields of philosophical and religious ethics in particular, the bracketing of "the animal question" has increasingly become untenable, as our interactions with nonhuman animals and the ethics of consumption have become respectable topics of analysis. There are now a handful of reputable academic journals that are expressly devoted to animal ethics, and Peter Singer's seminal *Animal Liberation* (1975), a book widely recognized as having spearheaded the contemporary animal movement, regularly appears in applied ethics anthologies and in philosophy PhD qualifying exam reading lists. His view that the interests of nonhuman animals should be counted equally alongside of those of humans admittedly remains a minority position—even among scholars and activists dedicated to improving animal welfare. Nevertheless, most ethicists today, regardless of their own proclivities toward encompassing nonhuman animals in their sphere of moral concern, are increasingly being pressed to give a reasoned response to the claims of animal protectionists.

This increasing consciousness about the use and treatment of animals has not surprisingly made a noticeable impact in the law. Since the late 1990s, the U.S. Congress now considers approximately fifty to sixty bills each year related to animal welfare, with even more at the state level.[2] In California, for example, Proposition 2 in the November 2008 General Election entitled "Standards for Confining Farm Animals" passed by almost a 2-1 margin, and it requires calves raised for veal, egg-laying hens, and pregnant pigs to be "confined only in ways that allow these animals to lie down, stand up, fully extend their limbs and turn around freely."[3] There are also several respectable law review journals that publish the latest scholarship on animal law and public policy, at least forty law schools in the United States now routinely offer courses in animal law,[4] and some schools even award students academic credit for work on actual cases involving animal issues. In the summer of 2009, Bolivia enacted the world's first ban on the use of all animals in circuses, whether wild or domestic, and the European Union (EU) is scheduled to abolish the use of battery cages for egg-laying hens.[5]

Of course, the cutting edge of animal law goes beyond calls for more or better regulation of industry through attempts to change their legal status. In 1992, Switzerland became the first nation in the world to enshrine the concept of the "dignity of the creature" in its federal constitution,[6] and later declared in Article 641a in a revision to its Civil Code in 2003 that "Tiere sind keine Sachen" (animals are not things). In 2002, Germany became the first EU nation to protect animals in its national constitution when German legislators, after a ten-year battle, voted to add the words "and animals" to a clause obligating the state to respect and protect the dignity of humans.[7] In 2008, for a first anywhere in the world, a national legislature voted to extend a limited set of legal rights to some nonhuman animals—the Great Apes. The nonbinding resolution, passed by the Spanish Parliament's environmental committee, commits Spain to (1) promote the Great Apes Project internationally and ensure the protection of apes from abuse, torture, and death, (2) outlaw harmful experiments on great apes, and (3) criminalize the keeping of great apes for circuses, TV commercials, or filming (n.b., the keeping of apes in zoos will remain legal, but conditions for the several hundred apes in Spanish zoos will have to improve). Most recently, the European Court of Human Rights has agreed to hear a case involving a petition to declare a 28 year-old ape named Matthew Hisal Pann a "person" and accordingly recognize his legal standing.

The second reason why the "animal question" would be appropriate to entertain when discussing human rights is that the latter framework has arguably been moving in an ecological direction in ways that would encourage radical changes in our conventional treatment and usage of animals. A 2006 report by the United Nations Food and Agriculture Organization (UNFAO) found that the global production of meat is one of the major causes of the world's most urgent environmental problems, including climate change, air and water pollution, land degradation, and a loss of biodiversity. In assessing the environmental impact of the entire commodity chain, the UNFAO found that the global livestock sector contributes an even higher percentage of greenhouse gas emissions, and thus anthropogenic global warming, than does the worldwide transportation sector.[8] The connection to human rights is then made by the growing recognition since the 1972 Declaration of the United Nations Conference on the Human Environment ("The Stockholm Declaration") that environmental degradation leads to human rights violations and *vice versa*. In the words of the 1994 UN Draft Declaration of Principles on Human Rights and the Environment, everyone has the right to a "secure, healthy, and ecologically sound environment," which is why we all have a "special responsibility" to prevent environmental harm in light of the "potential irreversibl[e]" damage that we are causing. While the aforementioned UN resolutions and reports stress the adverse consequences of environmental ruin only for humans and their future generations, it is not difficult to see why nonhuman animals would also stand to gain if we were to heed their various calls for reform. For a reduction in the global demand for meat would mean that fewer animals would be forcibly bred into existence under intensive farming conditions, only to be later slaughtered for human consumption (n.b., according to 2003 UNFAO statistics, the world consumes 53 billion land animals for food annually).

More importantly, as this example about the environmental and human rights impact of global meat production should reveal, the manner in which we in the world community will seek to implement human rights will itself disclose whether we also believe that animals have rights of their own, and if they do, whether the rights of humans should in all (or only some) cases trump theirs. As Article 11 of the International Covenant on Economic, Social, and Cultural Rights (ICESCR) provides for the right of everyone to have "adequate food, clothing, and housing," fulfillment of the terms of the treaty will require us to answer the prior questions of whether we will deem the use of animals for food or clothing morally acceptable and whether disruption to or even destruction of animal habitats should play any role in our deliberations about where to build or expand shelter for human needs. Since the question of the moral status of animals is thus inescapable for, and in many cases already unreflectively answered by, all defenders of human rights when they seek to actualize many of their provisions, more serious and focused attention to the animal question would be apropos.

Retrieving David Little's Work on Human Rights to Cover the Case of Animals

While Little's professional and scholarly contributions to the field of human rights are extensive, he has neither worked in animal advocacy, nor published anything directly in animal ethics. Although we must accordingly apply a hermeneutics of retrieval and even immanent critique to flesh out the animal-friendly implications of his philosophical grounding of human rights, it is important to underscore that there is nothing blatant or obvious in his account that would undermine its application beyond humans. That is, unlike many fellow Christian ethicists who ground our inherent moral worth, and thus our inherent rights, biblically or otherwise theologically, Little's defense is neither premised upon the notion that only humans have been created in the image of God and have divinely mandated dominion over the other creatures (Gen 1:26–28), nor upon any account of universal divine love, much less Divine existence.[9] What is more, unlike many Kantian-inspired accounts of human rights which locate the source of our dignity and moral standing on our rational capacities for autonomous legislation, Little's justification for the rights we all have as human beings does not turn on our species' apparently unique ability to evaluate the reasons for our actions.

To be sure, rationality-based justifications for human rights have been faulted for their inability to withstand what has been called, awkwardly in my view, the "argument from marginal cases" (hereafter AMC). The AMC holds that there is no morally relevant property or capacity that could successfully distinguish *all* human beings from *all* other animals. For example, the ability to use language, form beliefs, or govern oneself morally will not do, since there are "marginal" human beings who are cognitively under-developed, profoundly mentally retarded, irreversibly comatose, or otherwise severely brain-damaged and thus lack these capabilities, just as there are highly intelligent animals such as dolphins, whales, and the great apes who lead complex psychological lives. One way that some philosophers have gotten around the AMC is to have bitten the proverbial bullet, by redefining the "human" in human rights to apply only to the smaller class of persons or "functioning . . . human normative agents" and not all members of *homo sapiens*, so as to exclude both animals and "marginal" humans from the class of rights-bearers.[10] But as we shall soon see, the narrowing from all "humans" to all "persons" is a move that Little does not make, for the torture of infants and young children (both of whom can hardly be counted as fully rational) serves as one of his paradigmatic examples of what a gross human rights violation even *is*.

Little's defense of human rights can be further differentiated from other reputable alternatives in ways that could also prove hospitable to animal interests. His understanding of human rights does not ultimately depend on the extensive network of domestic, regional, and international laws that have been promulgated to protect them, or the equally impressive "overlapping consensus" on human rights standards that has arguably been accepted by the vast majority of the world's societies, cultures, and religious traditions, or any real or hypothetical "social contract" that we humans have made to respect individual rights as a way of augmenting mutual self-interest. If Little had argued otherwise, the extension of his arguments beyond the human community would prove more difficult, since the vast majority of the world's extant laws clearly privilege human interests over animal ones, the reigning consensus among a wide diversity of cultures and religions is for human superiority, not cross-species equality, and it is doubtful given the power differential that we humans would be willing to conceptualize nonhuman animals as co-equal parties in any Rawlsian "original position" or other contractualist framework of deliberation.

A Moral Intuitionist Defense of Human Rights

What then is Little's philosophical grounding of human rights, and how might it be broadened in an animal-friendly direction? His account of the rights we all have as human beings rests on what he calls an admittedly "unfashionable" view of moral intuitionism.[11] It is one that he presents in a "tradition-independent" manner, involves what John Rawls would label as a "comprehensive" epistemological view and some implied metaphysical ones,[12] but otherwise takes no position on "philosophical or theological controversies regarding the ultimate grounds and nature of moral life and responsibility."[13] Following the work of Johannes Morsink, Little interprets the drafters of the Universal Declaration of Human Rights (UDHR) as having based the rights they came to enumerate on a "feeling of shared moral revulsion" against the Holocaust and "other consequences of midtwentieth-century fascism."[14] To be clear, their argument is not that the post-WWII community "came for the first time to believe that genocide . . . was wrong and ought to be condemned and resisted," but that they "came to see dramatized before their eyes the full pathological implications of certain discriminatory beliefs" and practices.[15]

The intuitionism that Little shares with Morsink involves at least three distinct claims. First, every "morally competent" human being, regardless of his or her particular beliefs or social location, has the epistemic capacity to "comprehend immediately certain basic moral truths," so long as no "impeding or debilitating circumstances . . . derail the prescribed recognition."[16] Second, the moral truths that everyone knows by intuition are self-justifying. This is to say, with G. E. Moore to whom Little refers, that they are "incapable of proof," and also to assert, with William Gass from whom he borrows for illustrative purposes the "Case of the Obliging Stranger," that the wrongness of baking the stranger one has assaulted and kidnapped under false pretenses is not so much "inexplicable" as it is or should be totally "transparent."[17] Third, anyone who systematically denies the truth of the "universal and absolute wrongness" of practices such as baking that unfortunate stranger or torturing a young child in order to coerce his parents to retract their criticism of the government should be regarded as morally unhealthy, handicapped, and quite possibly pathological.[18]

Now the animal advocacy implications of Little's account of human rights become most evident when we bundle his intuitionist approach with the principal argument of his unpublished 2009 essay entitled "Ground to Stand On." Without that text, the prospect of bridging human rights to animal rights in his work would remain opaque, since there has been no historical event involving animals like the Holocaust that has shocked the world to act in their defense,[19] and since most people do not experience any "moral revulsion" about baking animals (as per Gass's unfortunately obliging stranger), as the popularity of oven-roasted meats suggests.

To continue, then, to make the case that there are certain moral truths that all rationally competent humans should be able to know noninferentially (i.e., the first two of the aforementioned claims), Little directs our attention to the relation of "reason-giving to the experience of severe physical pain."[20] He defines pain as a "strongly unpleasant bodily sensation," such as a "stick in the eye, a needle under the fingernail, or a metal drill penetrating the root of a tooth," and then reminds us, as Hume famously did, that it would be "senseless to ask for reasons why human beings seek to avoid (or relieve) pain."[21] The normative conclusion to be drawn is that anyone engaged in either inflicting pain upon others or depriving them of relief from it would bear a "very heavy burden of proof."[22] At a minimum, reasons that were obviously *mistaken*, defined as manifestly untrue or self-contradictory, would have to fail. So, too, would wholly *self-serving* reasons, where pain would be caused for the pleasure, self-gratification, or interests of only the *perpetrator* and/or others but not the *recipient*, since pain, if it must be delivered at all, must be discretionary, self-giving, or otherwise beneficial for the one who is to bear it.[23]

It is thus the "moral condemnability" of the infliction of pain for plainly mistaken or purely self-serving reasons that ultimately accounts for our enforcement of its prohibition in the law and through other non-legal measures (e.g., verbal censure). In turn, once we connect the concept of a right *simpliciter*, an "individual or subjective entitlement to demand a certain performance or forbearance under threat of sanction for noncompliance," with Little's interpretation of the nonderogable rights in the International Covenant on Civil and Political Rights (ICCPR) as "fundamental protections against violations of the logic of pain," we will see clearly how the relationship of reason to pain and the role pain plays in the "justification of action" serve as his moral intuitionist justification for universal human rights.[24]

Extending the Argument to Animal Rights

Having directly connected the "logic of pain" to the task of justifying human rights, the implications for animals should now be obvious. Those intent on advancing animal rights would only have to establish that animals, too, are capable of pain in order to compel us to recognize their rights-bearing status. Admittedly, as voluminously discussed in the literature and connected to the philosophical "problem of other minds," pain is obvious in the first person but can neither be directly experienced nor observed in others, which is why one must ascribe to others the subjective phenomenon of being in pain by analogy. Still, whether we are talking about my hand, your foot, a raccoon's paw, a seal's flipper, or an alligator's leg, if someone were to forcibly place our neurologically undamaged limbs over an open flame and if we were all to flinch, draw back, writhe, moan, yelp, scream, contort our faces, attempt to avoid the source, and so forth, it would be totally unreasonable to conclude that only *I* was in pain but you and the other animals were not, or that only you and I were in pain but the nonhuman animals were not.

Indeed, when we consider the evolutionary usefulness of pain (i.e., the role that the perception of pain plays in the avoidance of serious injury or death), the physiological structures common to many animal species that are generally considered the indicia of sentience (e.g., central nervous systems, nociceptors), and observable behavioral and physiological responses to noxious stimuli in animals that are similar to humans who self-report that they are in pain, the Cartesian hypothesis that animals are automatons who are only feigning consciousness is simply not credible.[25]

Thus, if we were to apply the normative implications of Little's "logic of pain" to nonhuman animals, we would have to delegitimize all of the "mistaken" and "self-serving" reasons we humans continue to use animals merely as means to our own ends. Of course, as both animal welfarists and animal rightists fully acknowledge, we may have to "draw the line" somewhere in advance of the evidence concerning *which* animals truly are sentient and *whether* to extend the benefit of doubt in questionable cases (e.g., early fetuses, crustaceans). But the point to underscore is that reasonable uncertainty about the pain capabilities of, say, shrimp should not give us license to ignore the legitimate welfare interests of, say, pigs or other livestock. All things being equal, then, we could no longer slaughter animals for food simply because we like their taste or believe (falsely) that we must consume meat to satisfy our nutritional needs, since the consumption of animal protein is not necessary for good health. Nor could we breed, confine, trap, and kill animals because we want to wear their skins or fur or make other useful animal-based products, such as soaps and natural adhesives. Nor could we conduct scientific experiments upon them to test the safety of consumer products, develop new pharmaceutical drugs, or find other ways to improve or extend our lives.

To be sure, there is disagreement among proponents of animal rights themselves about whether some uses of animals for human benefit might still pass muster. Christine Korsgaard, herself a defender of treating animals as ends-in-themselves, has suggested that we might still be able to use animals as companions or aides or even as providers of wool, milk, and eggs if we could reasonably imagine them giving consent to these interactions and if the arrangements were genuinely mutually beneficial and fair (i.e., if the animals were provided with comfortable living conditions and were able to live "something reasonably like their own sort of life").[26] Legal scholar Gary Francione, in contrast, has taken an abolitionist stance in his advocacy of the right of all sentient creatures to not be legally treated as property—a position which would preclude *any* kind of ownership by humans, however benign or seemingly reciprocally advantageous.[27] This internal debate notwithstanding, an extension of Little's "logic of pain" beyond the human community would require radical changes in the *status quo*—an upending of every industry and human-animal relationship that was premised upon the treatment of animals as merely our resources or commodities.

While I have attempted to show that the logical structure of Little's grounding of human rights practically invites its further application to the case of animal rights, I would be remiss if I did not include some discussion about the few explicit remarks he makes about the latter. We might understand him as having developed a latent, but still hesitant, concession about the injustice of treating animals merely in service to our own projects. The beginnings of Little's acknowledgment that (some) animals might have (some) rights can be clearly seen if we compare two passages, written in 2007 and 2009, respectively:

> [A] highly condensed version of my defense [of human rights] goes like this. The use of force, namely, the infliction of death, impairment, severe pain/injury, or confinement *on other human beings*, requires an extremely strong justification, wherever it occurs, for two principal reasons: the obvious adverse consequences that result from using force, and the strong temptation in human affairs to use force arbitrarily.[28]

> While it is obviously incorrect . . . to hold that human rights apply only to individuals who are fully competent rationally, it is not incorrect to apply them to beings who *ideally may be expected* to exhibit rational competence, namely beings born of *homo sapiens*. . . . Some human rights, of course, continue to apply to infants and incompetent people (*and conceivably by extension to higher animals as well*), such as nonderogable rights prohibiting discrimination, arbitrary life-taking, torture, cruel treatment, and medical experimentation, enslavement, and the suspension of certain legal protections.[29]

Despite his tentative, parenthetical inclusion of some animals into the class of legitimate rights-bearers, the question remains why he should have characterized the relationship between higher cognition and the "logic of pain" accordingly. Little is right that that we should only hold moral agents (i.e., those with "rational competence") accountable to moral standards, just as he correctly ascertains that moral patients would have a comparatively reduced schedule of provisions (i.e., not because moral patients would have less inherent value or dignity, but because some rights would simply fail to be relevant to them, such as the right of free elementary education to someone who was born so mentally or physically incapable as to be unable to benefit from formal schooling). But Little appears to have taken an erroneous turn in having combined those two ideas accordingly, so as to imply that only "higher animals"—not any sentient one—could be moral patients, legitimate bearers of rights, and thus capable of being either directly wronged or treated justly by others.[30] The correct conclusion should have been the following: the provisions of the International Bill of Human Rights which would be irrelevant to, or even nonsensical for, nonhuman animals need not apply to them (e.g., the rights to form trade unions, to enter into marriages freely, to enjoy various belief-related rights). But since all sentient creatures would have interests in Little's aforementioned nonderogable rights, not to mention some derogable ones (e.g., the freedom of movement and association), this smaller subset of rights should apply equally to higher and lower animals alike.[31]

Concluding Remarks and Lingering Questions

If I am right about the implications and immanent critique of Little's work on human rights, then we should regard him as having unwittingly laid the groundwork for one of the most powerful defenses of animal rights today. His account's theoretical independence from, but arguable compatibility with, many religious ideas and assumptions would have the potential of attracting a wider audience than, say, the "theos rights" approach taken by the world's foremost animal theologian, Andrew Linzey, since Linzey ultimately grounds the rights of all Spirit-filled creatures upon God's right to have the created order treated with appropriate respect.[32] He would also have offered an even greater expansion of the community of rights-bearers than either the aforementioned Declaration on Great Apes or the work of the best known philosophical advocate of animal rights, Tom Regan; the former because the rights to life, the protection of individual liberty, and freedom from torture are to apply only to those creatures who are most genetically and behaviorally similar to us to justify their inclusion in the "community of equals,"[33] the latter because Regan's "subject of a life" criterion recognizes the equal inherent value, and thus inherent rights, of only sentient beings who also possess a complex mental life (i.e., creatures that have perceptions, desires, beliefs, memories, intentions, a sense of the future; in short, awareness of the world and what happens to themselves in it).[34] In short, Little's understanding of human rights should lead us to conclude that human rights are not human after all—that species membership in *homo sapiens* is not in the final analysis morally relevant to the question what kinds of creatures possess rights.[35] What is more, if we were to marshal the whole apparatus of Little's intuitionist approach to the case of animals, we would have to conclude that all rationally competent human beings should be able to immediately apprehend the wrongness of inflicting severe pain on them for mistaken or self-serving reasons, that we would need no further justification for this view than the observation that animals can indeed suffer greatly by our own doing, and that anyone who refused to assent to these conclusions should themselves be treated with suspicion.

Still, I have neither established the validity of Little's philosophical defense of human rights, nor affirmatively made the case that animals, too, have rights. Instead, I have simply taken my point of departure from the former, and then worked out what is logically entailed by those arguments with respect to the latter. A critic might accordingly be tempted to retort that even a successful demonstration of the moral relevance of pain would at best ground calls for more humane treatment of animals, not the total abolition of most of our contemporary practices involving them. Under such a view, we would only be obligated to change *how*, but not *whether*, we could justifiably continue to use animals as commodities or resources for human purposes. While such an objection deserves a longer response than can be provided here, two quick rejoinders should suffice. First, Little is explicit about wanting to extend what he is calling the "logic of pain" to other types of morally condemnable behavior, the argument being that it would be similarly impossible for one to fully understand what confinement, impairment, deprivation, torture, or the infliction of death *is* and not understand either its rational structure (i.e., that we need not press others for reasons why they would seek to avoid being so confined, killed, etc.) or its role in the justification of action (i.e., in grounding our rights not to be treated by others accordingly).[36] Second, Little's account of pain places all sentient creatures in a structurally parallel position, so if the "logic of pain" cannot adequately ground the case for *animal* rights, it must be understood as failing to ground *human* rights as well.

While the moral principle of treating similar cases similarly has largely prompted me to compel Little to recognize the need to analogize from humans to animals and regard both as ends-in-themselves, a case could nevertheless be made about legitimately treating humans and animals differently with respect to the question of positive rights. Little has argued that "willfully inflicting or permitting starvation, malnutrition, and disabling sickness are as much a violation of the logic of pain as are resort to torture or to cruel and unusual treatment or punishment."³⁷ Assuming *arguendo* that he is correct, here is a case where the wisest and presumably most justifiable course of action would not be to extend exact parity to all sentient creatures, but perhaps make some distinctions between them—say, between wild animals and domesticated ones. For it would be one thing to argue that we humans could not justifiably kill or inflict pain upon animals for our food or pleasure; it would be another matter to suggest that we would be equally morally culpable if we failed to *prevent* them from being killed for food or pleasure by all others. This is not to deny that an animal would presumably feel the same or even a greater amount of pain if it were torn apart by its predators than if it were captured and slaughtered by humans, or if it were suffering from malnutrition or sickness in the wild as opposed to in a Concentrated Animal Feeding Operation (CAFO) or "factory farm." But it is to be reminded that if animals have rights, they would only have them against *us*: they would have a right not to be tortured or mutilated or sickened, but not necessarily have the right of rescue if they were to suffer ostensibly the same or similar fate, though not by our doing. Still, once the long reach and effects of human activity make us at least partially responsible for many current conditions even in the wild, how much we should intervene in nature remains subject to considerable debate, particularly in light of concerns that we may end up doing more harm than good.

As should be clear, the transcendental form of argumentation that I have pursued here leaves a number of important questions unresolved, as even a successful demonstration that philosophical justifications for human rights can be logically be extended to cover the case of animal rights will say nothing on their own about *which* animals have rights, *what* rights they have, and *how* real conflicts among various rights-bearers are to be adjudicated. Recall that I have tangentially addressed the first of these two questions, though not attempted to engage this last one. These outstanding questions notwithstanding, the point to underscore is that those who wish to make the case for animal rights have more options than either attempting to conjure novel arguments, or providing heterogeneous reasons to that end. In addition, as my hermeneutics of retrieval and immanent critique of Little's work has hopefully shown, they might also mine productive lines of argumentation in human rights theory by extending them beyond the human community.

NOTES

[1] Examples of the first type include the work of leading animal rights scholar-activist, Tom Regan (see *infra*, n. 24), and Italian philosopher Paola Cavalieri, the latter of whom is coeditor and contributor to *The Great Ape Project: Equality Beyond Humanity* (New York: St. Martin's Press, 1993). Examples of the second type include moral philosopher Christine M. Korsgaard, *Self-Constitution: Agency, Identity, and Integrity* (New York: Oxford University Press, 2009), 33 n. 3; Christine M. Korsgaard, "Interacting with Animals: A Kantian Account," in *Oxford Handbook on Ethics and Animals*, eds. Tom Beauchamp and R. G. Frey (Oxford: Oxford University Press, 2010), 91–118.

[2] See Bernard Rollin's Foreword to the *Animal Ethics Reader*, 2nd edition, eds. Susan J. Armstrong and Richard G. Botzler (New York: Routledge, 2008).

[3] See "Proposition 2: Standards for Confining Farm Animals," State of California, http://www.smartvoter.org/2008/11/04/ca/state/prop/2/ (Last accessed: June 5, 2014.)

[4] Douglas Belkin, "Animal Rights Gains Foothold as Law Career," March 6, 2005, http://www.boston.com/news/local/massachusetts/articles/2005/03/06/animal_rights_gains_foothold_as_law_career/ (Last accessed: June 5, 2014.)

[5] "Bolivia Bans All Circus Animals," *Associated Press*, July 31, 2009, http://www.guardian.co.uk/world/2009/jul/31/bolivia-bans-circus-animals (Last accessed: June 5, 2014.)

[6] In 1992, the Zurich canton in Switzerland also required a lawyer to be appointed to represent animals in cases alleging abuse or mistreatment. On March 7, 2010, the Swiss soundly rejected a referendum that would have required each of the nation's twenty-six cantons to do the same.

[7] Article 20a of the German Basic Law now reads as follows: "The state takes responsibility for protecting the natural foundations of life and animals in the interest of future generations."

[8] The full report is available at "Livestock's Long Shadow: Environmental Issues and Options," Food and Agriculture Organization of the United Nations, Rome 2006, http://www.fao.org/docrep/010/a0701e/a0701e00.HTM (Last accessed: June 5, 2014.)

[9] For a sampling of these views, see Max Stackhouse, "Why Human Rights Needs God: A Christian Perspective," in *Does Human Rights Need God?*, eds. Elizabeth M. Bucar and Barbra Barnett (Grand Rapids, MI: Wm. Eerdmans Publishing, 2005), 25–40; Michael Perry, *Toward a Theory of Human Rights: Religion, Law, Courts* (Cambridge: Cambridge University Press, 2006); Nicholas Wolterstorff, *Justice: Rights and Wrongs* (Princeton, NJ: Princeton University Press, 2008).

[10] See, e.g., James Griffin, *On Human Rights* (Oxford: Oxford University Press, 2008), 34, 50.

[11] For a representative sampling of David Little's work of the theoretical foundations of human rights, see, David Little, "The Nature and Basis of Human Rights," in *Prospects for a Common Morality*, ed. Gene Outka and John P. Reeder, Jr. (Princeton, NJ: Princeton University Press, 1993), 73–92; David Little, "Rethinking Human Rights: A

Review Essay on Religion, Relativism, and Other Matters," in *Journal of Religious Ethics* 27 (Spring 1999): 151–77; David Little, "On Behalf of Rights: A Critique of Democracy and Tradition," in *Journal of Religious Ethics* 34.2 (June 2006): 287–310; David Little, "The Author Replies," in *Journal of Religious Ethics* 35.1 (March 2007): 171–75; David Little, "Ground to Stand On: A Philosophical Reappraisal of Human Rights Language" (Harvard Divinity School, 2009). Little delivered a version of this last article the 2009 annual meeting of the Society of Christian Ethics and he understands it to be his most considered reflections of previous arguments made in his 1993, 2006, and 2007 essays.

[12] In *Political Liberalism* (New York: Columbia University Press, 1993), John Rawls distinguishes a "comprehensive view" from the narrower scope of a political conception of justice for in that the former applies to all subjects and includes "what is of value in human life, ideals of personal character, friendship, familial and associational relationship, and much else that informs our conduct," while the latter is concerned only with the justice of the basic structure of a society; cf., Rawls, *Political Liberalism*, 13, 59. In *Justice as Fairness: A Restatement* (Cambridge, MA: Belknap Press of Harvard University Press, 2001), Rawls specifically cites intuitionism as an example of a philosophical-moral doctrine that is comprehensive; cf., Rawls, *Justice as Fairness*, 14. In *The Law of Peoples* (Cambridge, MA: Harvard University Press, 1999), he contrasts his politically liberal approach to human rights to various comprehensive ones, including those that are premised upon a "philosophical doctrine of human nature," where our "moral and intellectual powers . . . entitle [us] to these rights"; cf., Rawls, *The Law of Peoples*, 68, 81.

[13] Little, "Ground to Stand On," 7.

[14] Little, "On Behalf of Rights," 296; Johannes Morsink, *The Universal Declaration of Human Rights: Origins, Drafting, and Intent* (Philadelphia, PA: University of Pennsylvania Press, 2000); Johannes Morsink, *Inherent Human Rights: Philosophical Roots of the Universal Declaration* (Philadelphia, PA: University of Pennsylvania Press, 2009).

[15] Little, "The Nature and Basis of Human Rights," 86.

[16] Consider Little's earlier remarks ("Rethinking Human Rights," 166) on the issue of epistemological inclusivity: "Human beings are held to have access to human rights and to be accountable and obligated to live up to them, *not* because they are Muslim, or Christian, or Buddhist, or Jewish, or Hindu, or a member of any particular religious or philosophical tradition. On the contrary, they are assumed 'without distinction' to have a common capacity for moral competence and moral responsibility that does not depend on particular cultural membership. In that sense, it *must* be possible to conceive of a neutrally formulated normative regime, or the whole idea of human rights disappears."

[17] William H. Gass, "The Case of the Obliging Stranger," *The Philosophical Review* 66 (1957), reprinted in Gass, *Fiction and the Figures of Life* (New York: Vintage, 1958), 225–41. Little's reference to this case appears in "Religion and Human Rights: A Personal Testament," *The Journal of Law and Religion* 18 (2002–03), 57–77; Little, "The Nature and Basis of Human Rights," 91 n. 27, 79.

[18] Little, "Ground to Stand On," 11; Little, "On Behalf of Rights," 297; Little, "The Nature and Basis of Human Rights," 80, 84.

[19] This point notwithstanding, several writers and animal protection groups have directly compared our treatment of animals, especially in scientific experimentation and

intensive animal agriculture ("factory farms"), to the Nazi treatment of Jews in the Holocaust. A non-exhaustive list of those who have done so includes Nobel laureate J. M. Coetzee, Jewish Nobel laureate Isaac Bashevis Singer, and People for the Ethical Treatment of Animals (PETA).

[20] Little, "Ground to Stand On," 14.

[21] Ibid., 14 n. 42.

[22] Ibid., 15.

[23] Ibid., 14–16. To be clear, Little does consider the "necessity excuse" that contravenes the aforementioned principle, where one deliberately inflicts pain on another person to save the life of a third person (e.g., one "painfully knock[s] an individual unconscious who might otherwise unintentionally divulge the whereabouts, and thereby occasion the death, of an innocent fugitive"). He emphasizes that even if such an excuse were acceptable, it would only cover a very narrow set of conditions and mitigate the "responsibility of the inflictor of pain" without itself overriding the "fact that a violation has occurred" in ibid., 16.

[24] Ibid., 6, 20. Little suggests that so-called secondary rights, such as the "rights of legal due process, political participation, freedom of expression, movement, and association," are helpful for preventing "the arbitrary infliction of severe suffering like torture" and thus for protecting our primary rights, though he is also willing to entertain that their value may not be purely instrumental in ibid., 24; Little, "The Nature and Basis of Rights," 84.

[25] For an extended discussion of these points, see Bernard E. Rollin, *Animal Rights and Human Morality*, 3rd ed. (Amherst, New York: Prometheus Books, 2006), 76–95.

[26] Christine M. Korsgaard, "Exploiting Animals: A Philosophical Protest," *AV Magazine* (Fall 2009): 14–15. See also Christine M. Korsgaard, "Fellow Creatures: Kantian Ethics and Our Duties to Animals," in *The Tanner Lectures on Human Values*, vol. 25/26, ed. Grethe B. Peterson (Salt Lake City: Utah University Press, 2004); Christine M. Korsgaard, "Facing the Animal You See in the Mirror," in *The Harvard Review of Philosophy* 16 (2009), 2–7.

[27] See, e.g., Gary L. Francione, *Animals as Persons: Essays on the Abolition of Animal Exploitation* (New York: Columbia University Press, 2008); Gary L. Francione and Robert Garner, *The Animal Rights Debate: Abolition or Regulation* (Columbia University Press, 2010).

[28] Little, "The Author Replies," 172–73; emphasis added.

[29] Little, "Ground to Stand On," 12; italics in original, underlining mine.

[30] It is, of course, possible that the pain of a "higher" animal being tortured, cruelly treated, experimented upon medically, and so forth, might be greater than that of a "lower" animal placed in an identical position—perhaps because the "higher" animals would be experiencing a larger share of psychological suffering (e.g., anticipatory dread, existential malaise) in addition to the pain itself. Still, it is not clear why the *qualia* of one's pain or suffering would affect one's ability to even have moral standing, so long as a minimum threshold of sentience were present.

[31] We might subject another curious, though this time more ambiguous, element in Little's "Ground to Stand On" to immanent critique. Put in the form of a question,

what is the *normative* force of his observation that "prohibitions against torture of and cruelty to higher animals have wide moral appeal, while prohibitions against arbitrary life-taking, medical experimentation, and 'enslavement' (coercive confinement in zoos or as pets) are much more controversial" (Little, "Ground to Stand On," 12 n. 38)? Assuming for the sake of argument that his description is accurate, it should still be morally problematic under the "logic of pain" to make these animals suffer for "self-serving" reasons, however widely supported or popular these practices might be.

[32] For a development of this concept, see Andrew Linzey, *Christianity and the Rights of Animals* (New York: Crossroad, 1987), chap. 5; Andrew Linzey, *Animal Theology* (Champaign, IL: University of Illinois, 1995), chap. 1; Andrew Linzey, *Animal Gospel* (Louisville, KY: Westminster John Knox Press, 1998), chaps. 4–5.

[33] See "A Declaration on Great Apes" in *The Great Ape Project: Equality Beyond Humanity*, eds. Peter Singer and Paola Cavalieri (New York: St. Martin's Griffin, 1994), 4–7. To be sure, the editors of the book hope to *extend* the class of rights-bearers beyond the great apes, and thus only began with other primates because they understood this to be the easiest case.

[34] For Tom Regan's defense of animal rights, see Tom Regan, *The Case for Animal Rights* (Berkeley, CA: University of California Press, 2004); Tom Regan, *Defending Animal Rights* (Champaign, IL: University of Illinois Press, 2001). While Regan's own line-drawing includes all mentally all normal mammals aged one or older, he has repeatedly emphasized that he is not certain how "far down the phylogenetic scale" we should go and in recent work has included birds, some fish, and possibly many other vertebrates.

[35] According to Paola Cavalieri, the AMC and extension of rights to non-paradigmatic human beings reveals that "the characteristics appealed to in order to justify the ascription of such rights . . . lie at a cognitive-emotive level accessible to a larger number of nonhuman animals" in *The Animal Question: Why Non-Human Animals Deserve Human Rights* (New York: Oxford University Press, 2001), 139.

[36] Little, "Ground to Stand On," 14.

[37] Ibid., 27.

7.
Nibbana, Dhamma, and Sinhala Buddhism: A David Little Retrospective

Donald K. Swearer

In addition to David Little's significant contributions to the literature on peace and human rights, at several junctures in his distinguished academic and professional career he engaged topics central to Buddhist ethics. In this chapter I propose to superimpose a trajectory on this engagement that begins with his chapter on Theravada ethics in *Comparative Religious Ethics: A New Method*, which he co-authored with Sumner B. Twiss;[1] his debate with Frank E. Reynolds in *Ethics, Wealth, and Salvation: A Study in Buddhist Social Ethics*;[2] and his several publications on Buddhism, nationalism, and ethnicity in Sri Lanka.[3] I shall argue that Little's account works best when contextualized in terms of Sri Lanka, and is least successful in *Comparative Religious Ethics: A New Method*. At each of the three junctures in this trajectory, Weberian-like perspectives loom large: in broad terms they are the interdependence between belief and behavior; and a typological construction of religious systems of thought and action.

I have chosen these three junctures in Little's work that engage Buddhist ethics, in part because they mark three moments in my personal and academic relationship with him beginning with my review of *Comparative Religious Ethics* in *Religious Studies Review*;[4] the Harvard-Berkeley-Chicago conferences in comparative religious ethics in which we participated;[5] and the conferences that we co-led at the Center for the Study of World Religions at Harvard Divinity School on Religion and Nationalism in 2005, and Visions of Peace and Reconciliation in 2007.[6]

Comparative Religious Ethics: A New Method

The three case studies that Little and Twiss take up in the Application section of *Comparative Religious Ethics: A New Method*—Religion and Morality of the Navajo, the book of Matthew, and Theravada Buddhism—first address the issue of the relationship between moral and religious action guides, and then examine the structure of the practical reasoning or the way in which the tradition justifies action. In the case of Theravada Buddhism they argue that "properly understood, all action-guides have as their object nirvanic attainment."[7] Given the preeminence of the basic religious claim, that is, Nibbana/Nirvana as sacred authority, the Theravada practical system must necessarily be a thoroughgoing religious system; and, that as a religious system it ultimately transcends morality follows from the fact that Nibbana obviates the concepts of self and other. All prescribed and proscribed acts are ultimately defined in reference to self-conquest.[8] Even though Little and Twiss find that Theravada Buddhism encourages the cultivation of attitudes and acts that reflect a regard for the material welfare of others and that a central role is assigned to the virtues of sympathy and generosity, they contend that

> there can be no doubt that the content of the action-guides, when systematically analyzed, is, in the last analysis, religious in character. ... All moral attitudes and acts are consistently modified by a belief in a sacred authority (nirvana) that not only drastically subordinates the material welfare of others in favor of their spiritual enlightenment, but also, and even more importantly, disallows the ultimate reality of selves and others.[9]

The validational patterns—the character of an act, rules, principles of validation, and considerations to persuade—of Theravada practical teaching leads to a similar conclusion. The first, a qualified intrapersonal teleology, aims at the realization of one's highest happiness, that is, Nibbana, without directly benefiting others; the second, a qualified extrapersonal teleology, aims at the realization of Nibbana for oneself and for all sentient beings; and the third, a pattern of unqualified intrapersonal teleology, aims at maximizing one's happiness according to the calculus of karmic consequences. The last pattern is seen as secondary or subsidiary, while the first two contain the premise of a fundamental belief in the ultimate unreality of human persons.

The key concept in the content and structure of Theravada practical teaching is the notion of *dhamma/dharma*, ontologically understood as reducing reality, including human existence, to basic elements or constituents and, hence, the concept of *dhamma* becomes another way of perceiving the "unreality of the concept 'self,' by reducing all putative selves to their more basic elementary constituents."[10] Thus, while there is a moral dimension to the Theravada action guide (value concepts, action-guiding concepts, dispositional concepts), it is provisional and subsidiary, qualified by a belief in a sacred authority, Nibbana, according to which the concept of the self and the other is dissolved.

In addition to the Nibbanic and the Dhammic deconstruction of reality into elements, much is made of the Theravada concept of not-self (*anatta*), especially in regard to Little and Twiss's assessment of the tradition as a thoroughgoing religious system in which other-regarding concerns are subsidiary and provisional. Morality is by definition interrelational, that is, it involves relations among persons; and one of the special conditions of the legitimacy of a moral action guide is that it is other-regarding.[11] Logically, for a religious tradition which has as one of its cardinal teachings the concept of not-self and in which the character of all prescribed and proscribed acts is ultimately deemed in reference to "self-conquest," a moral action guide, as defined in *Comparative Religious Ethics*, will have a secondary place at best. Furthermore, at the vindication level of the structure of the practical teachings of the Theravada, the "radical depersonalization of humanity" entailed by the analysis of the self into dhammic components re-enforces Little and Twiss's claim: "In the ultimate sense…discussion of morality is inappropriate because the notion of morality presupposes persons, or at least intentions normally associated with persons, and these are not found in Nirvana."[12]

In brief, Little and Twiss's description of religion and morality in Theravada Buddhism utilizes a typological strategy (a transpersonal teleological action guide) in which the major justificatory terms—Nibbana, not-self, and reality/human existence as constituted by evanescent dhammic particulars—at the very least, problematize an ethic of other-regard.

It is perhaps an understatement to say that *Comparative Religious Ethics* raised a storm of controversy, especially among historians of religion who argued that the formal model of appellate reasoning which informed the interpretation of Theravada ethics sacrificed the complexity and historical realities of the Theravada tradition to a logical reductionism determined primarily by Nibbana as the overriding "sacred authority." Little recalls a contentious incident that took place at the Harvard comparative religious ethics discussions when the late Wilfred Cantwell Smith, then director of the Center of the Study of World Religions, "delivered a furious denunciation of the approach [Twiss] and I took . . . [and argued] that the book represented an enormous setback in the comparative study of religious ethics, bringing to it unwelcome Western analytical techniques whose only effect is to distort severely the materials under consideration."[13] Little himself has reevaluated the Little/Twiss approach to *Comparative Religious Ethics* and, "had I [to] do it over again," he observes, I "would approach the subject quite differently."[14]

Ethics, Wealth, and Salvation: A Study in Buddhist Social Ethics

The lively debate sparked by *Comparative Religious Ethics* in the formative days of the development of the field of comparative religious ethics, was a measure of its significance, especially around issues of theory and history. At the time, Buddhologists *cum* historians of religion, especially Frank E. Reynolds, took aim at two major monographs in the field of comparative religious ethics published in 1978: *Comparative Religious Ethics: A New Method* and Ronald M. Green's *Religious Reason: The Rational and Moral Basis of Religions*.[15] Reynolds opined that when historians of religion take up the task of comparative religious ethics they place the study of ethics of a religious tradition within the context of a holistic understanding of that tradition including a diversity of texts and ritual practices, and that they "do not become so enmeshed in abstract theoretical discussions that they are distracted from their empirical research."[16]

In his essay in the conference volume, *Ethics, Wealth, and Salvation: A Study of Buddhist Social Ethics,* Reynolds proposes a multivalent interpretation of *dhamma* that challenges Nibbana as the foundational "sacred authority" for religion and morality in Theravada Buddhism. Furthermore, Reynolds critiques Little's singular interpretation of the concept of *dhamma* as the constitutive elements of reality and human existence that, in conjunction with the concept of not-self, undermine an ethic of other-regard. Reynolds contends that *dhamma*, broadly conceived, is a complex and dynamic reality and, as such, stands as the Theravadin religio-ethical center of gravity and normative truth that establishes *guidelines for all forms of action*. Dhammic norms do, indeed, have soteriological significance in that they express and cultivate non-attachment, however, at the same time adherence to dhammic norms is conducive to the production of goods such as wealth and the general well-being of individuals and communities. Although dhammic norms are the basis of the monastic code of discipline (*vinaya*), they are equally the foundation of lay ethics. Adherence to dhammic norms by rulers is of particular importance for the well-being of the entire community. Righteous kings (*dhammraja*) ensure peace, prosperity, and justice in their realms by embodying a set of ten virtues, the *dasarajadharma*—generosity, high moral character, self-sacrifice, integrity, gentleness, non-indulgence, non-anger, non-oppression, tolerance—and adherence to the *dhamma* is understood in this instance as a universal moral law. "In addition to the dhammic activities of kings," observes Reynolds, "the dhammic actions of other laymen and laywomen are recognized as contributing to social harmony, to a supportive natural environment, and to the economic prosperity that is associated with a properly ordered natural and social world."[17]

Little offers three responses to Reynolds. First, Little defends his typological construction of Theravada religion and morality as fundamentally teleological, dominated by the concept of Nibbana. Although Little admits that Reynold's shift from Nibbana to the category of *dhamma* as the over-arching concept informing Theravada religion and morality "suggests a need for some modification and further elaboration and clarification of the Little-Twiss interpretation,"[18] he insists that it does not contradict that interpretation. Although strictly speaking I would agree, Little's characterization of Theravada as a system "according to which dhammic activity, if properly performed leads ultimately to the highest goal of Nibbana and its achievement signifies the condition of complete non-attachment" does not take sufficient account of Reynolds's expansive, multiplex interpretation of *dhamma*. Reynolds intends his shift from Nibbana to *dhamma* as Theravada's sacred authority to be not merely an "extension" of the concept of "sacred authority," as Little opines, but as a substantive "revision."[19]

Second, Little challenges historians of religion like Reynolds to translate their tradition-embedded description into ethical categories amenable to cross-cultural comparison such as the structure of practical justification advocated in *Comparative Religious Ethics: A New Method*. He proposes that an "ethical translation" of historians' "data" into "conventional categories for the study of practical reasoning," makes Theravada reflections on issues such as wealth and poverty more adaptive to cross-cultural comparison and difference; for example, contrasting understandings of distributive justice, or contrasts between the Theravadin and Puritan economic ethic.[20] Little's point is perennially relevant, and both provocative and problematic when it comes to comparative work as Jeffrey Stout brilliantly pointed out in his critical review of *Comparative Religious Ethics*.[21]

Third, Little agrees with Reynolds's challenge to ethicists to broaden their scope of investigation to include non-normative texts and doctrines, but, in his consistently gentlemanly manner, he contends that Reynolds's "holism" really does not live up to its billing. He critiques holism for its high level of generality and lack of historical, contextual, and empirical detail that the informed historian of religion might bring to the enterprise of comparative religious ethics. Although Little's teleological-Nibbanic driven model overrides Reynolds's more complex and nuanced interpretation of *dhamma*, his critique of historians of religions' holism for being insufficiently historical is well taken and has served to advance the on-going comparative religious ethics debates between ethicists and historians of religion. Furthermore, in his work on Sri Lanka, Little moves beyond his Nibbanic preoccupations to become more empirical, contextual, and historical.

Theravada Buddhism and Sri Lanka

In his more recent work on Sri Lanka, one of the countries included in the U.S. Institute of Peace Religion, Nationalism, and Intolerance project, Little moves from the meta-ethical project represented by *Comparative Religious Ethics: A New Method*, and his subsequent dhammic dialogue with history of religion "holism," to a specific historical context in which Buddhism has played a significant role in the discourse and practice of chauvinistic Sinhala nationalism. In his *Sri Lanka: The Invention of Enmity* and related essays, Weberian interests are also evident, but now woven into a more historically and contextually complex tapestry.[22] Reflecting Weber's view regarding the close entanglement of religion and ethnicity, Little challenges assessments of the Sinhala-Tamil conflict in Sri Lanka that focus primarily on nationalism, or privilege ethnicity to the near exclusion of religion. He points out that ethnic groups elevate their status above their neighbors by invoking a sacred warrant; hence, "religious shaded ethnic tensions appear to be latent in the very process of ethnic classification."[23] In support of his view, Little quotes the Sri Lankan historian, K. M. deSilva: "In the Sinhala language, the words for nation, race and people are practically synonymous, and a multiethnic or multicommunal nation or state is incomprehensible to the popular mind. The emphasis on Sri Lanka as the land of the Sinhala Buddhists carried an emotional popular appeal, compared with which the concept of a multiethnic polity was a meaningless abstraction."[24]

In the construction of the Buddhist warrant for an ideology of Sinhala nationalism, Little points to the legitimating power of the authoritative Sinhala Buddhist chronicle, the *Mahavamsa*, and its valorization of King Duttagamaani's defeat of the Tamils, the rise of Sinhala nationalistic sentiment in response to British colonialism, and ever increasing anti-Tamil attitudes and policies after the 1956 election of S. W. R. D. Bandaranike culminating in the internecine armed conflict that began in 1983. Little concludes, "[t]here can be little doubt that religious belief has, for several reasons, functioned in an important way as a warrant for intolerance so far as the Sinhala Buddhists are concerned. There is also evidence, though it is more controversial and perhaps less pronounced, that the same is true for Tamils."[25]

Little sees religion as being one of the factors, along with ethnicity, language, cultural habits, and historical dynamics contributing to one group declaring superiority and preeminence over another. He notes that social scientists tend to claim "that nationalist conflicts are either not about ethnicity and religion at all, but rather about economic and political matters, or that they are at bottom more about ethnic than religious issues."[26] In the case of Sri Lanka, however, "it was the religious factor—the sacred legends synthesized by Buddhist monks into the *Mahavamsa* and the other chronicles—that gave special authority to the Sinhala as a 'chosen people' and thereby entitled them . . . to preserve and protect the preeminence of the Sinhala Buddhist tradition in Sri Lankan life."[27]

In "Belief, Ethnicity, and Nationalism," Little frames the Sri Lanka case typologically in terms of two types of modern nationalism: liberal and illiberal, civic versus ethnic, non-aggressive versus aggressive. Citing Weber's characterization of nationalism as, at bottom, both a homogenizing and a differentiation mode of discourse that drives toward cultural standardization, Sri Lanka exemplifies illiberal, ethnic, aggressive nationalism sanctified by the Buddhist *sangha* (monastic order). Little is not claiming that Buddhist belief, as such, legitimates a virulent, chauvinistic Sinhala nationalism. Indeed, as he points out, the basic tenets and doctrines of Buddhism would not seem to support ethnic favoritism. Such attitudes, rather, resulted from a combination of historical pressures on the Theravada *sangha* in the fifth and sixth centuries CE, and colonial and post-colonial experiences in the nineteenth and early twentieth centuries, including attitudes of racism and anti-Buddhist intolerance fostered by Christian missionaries and British colonial authorities.

In conclusion I choose to highlight one of several issues that Little's engagement with Theravada Buddhist ethics raises within the on-going debates in the field of comparative religious ethics, namely, the relationship—might we say the dialectical relationship—between theory and history broadly construed. *Comparative Religious Ethics* was criticized for being overly theoretical and insufficiently historical. Stout, for example, observed, "What would a more genuinely historical approach to religion and morality look like? Probably rather like some of the work Little and Twiss find lacking in rigor. What seems like insufficient dedication to rigor on the part of historians may well be an altogether healthy willingness to make contact with all the messy details of historical change."[28] Little acknowledges that he would now approach Theravada ethics quite differently than he did in *Comparative Religious Ethics*. Putting the shoe on the other foot, he criticizes historians of religion for their generalized holism which, he argues, is insufficiently historical. In contrast, Little's work on Buddhism and nationalism in Sri Lanka is quite attentive to historical detail within the dual typology of liberal and illiberal nationalism: "We must be as attentive to the conditioning effects of politics, economics, historical accidents and so on, on religion and culture, as we are to the contribution of religion and culture to the formation of nationalism."[29]

Finally, of the Weberian perspectives that inform the examples of Little's work I have cited in this brief chapter, a Nibbanized Theravada that limits an ethic of other-regard, and a politicized Theravada that warrants ethnic nationalism—it is the latter that engages the "complexity and historical realities of the Theravada tradition" and in doing so might be seen as Little's answer to his critique of holism for not taking sufficient account of changing social, political, and historical contexts.[30]

NOTES

[1] David Little and Sumner B. Twiss, *Comparative Religious Ethics: A New Method* (New York: Harper & Row, 1978).

[2] Russell F. Sizemore and Donald K. Swearer, eds., *Ethics, Wealth, and Salvation: A Study in Buddhist Social Ethics* (Columbia, S.C.: University of South Carolina Press, 1990).

[3] David Little, *Sri Lanka: The Invention of Enmity* (Washington, D.C.: United States Institute of Peace Press, 1994); David Little, "Belief, Ethnicity, and Nationalism," in *Nationalism and Ethnic Politics* 1.2 (Summer 1995): 284–301; David Little, "Religion and Ethnicity in the Sri Lankan Civil War," in *Creating Peace in Sri Lanka: Civil War and Reconciliation*, ed. Robert I. Rotberg (Washington D.C.: Brookings Institution Press, 1999), 41–55.

[4] Donald K. Swearer, "Nirvana, No-Self, and Comparative Religious Ethics," in *Religious Studies Review* 6.4 (October 1980): 301–6.

[5] The three conferences led to the publication of Sizemore and Swearer, *Ethics, Wealth, and Salvation: A Study in Buddhist Social Ethics*; John S. Hawley, ed., *Saints and Virtues* (Berkeley, CA: University of California Press, 1987); Robin W. Lovin and Frank E. Reynolds, eds., *Cosmogony and Ethical Order: New Studies in Comparative Ethics* (Chicago: University of Chicago Press, 1986).

[6] See the conference volume, David Little and Donald K. Swearer, eds., *Religion and Nationalism in Iraq: A Comparative Perspective* (Cambridge, MA: Harvard University Press, 2006).

[7] Little and Twiss, *Comparative Religious Ethics*, 215.

[8] Ibid.

[9] Ibid., 235.

[10] Ibid., 246.

[11] Ibid., 27–29.

[12] Ibid., 247.

[13] E-mail communication to the author from David Little. November 6, 2009.

[14] Ibid.

[15] Ronald M. Green, *Religious Reason: The Rational and Moral Basis of Religious Belief* (New York: Oxford University Press, 1978).

[16] Sizemore and Swearer, *Ethics, Wealth, and Salvation*, 60.

[17] Ibid.

[18] Ibid., 77.

[19] Ibid., 81.

[20] Ibid., 82–85.

[21] Jeffrey Stout, "Weber's Progeny, Once Removed," *Religious Studies Review* 6.4 (October 1980): 289–95.

[22] Series on Religion, Nationalism, and Intolerance. Washington, D.C. United State Institute of Peace Press; David Little, "Religion and Ethnicity in the Sri Lankan Civil War," in *Creating Peace in Sri Lanka: Civil War and Reconciliation*, ed., Robert I. Rothberg (Washington, D.C.: Brookings Institution Press), 41–55; David Little, "Belief, Ethnicity, and Nationalism," in *Nationalism and Ethnic Politics* 1.2 (Summer 1995): 284–301.

[23] Little, "Religion and Ethnicity in Sri Lankan Civil War," 42.

[24] Ibid., 42–43.

[25] Little, *Sri Lanka: The Invention of Enmity*, 104.

[26] Little and Swearer, *Religion and Nationalism in Iraq*, 5.

[27] Ibid.

[28] Stout, "Weber's Progeny, Once Removed," 294.

[29] Ibid.

[30] Sizemore and Swearer, *Ethics, Wealth, and Salvation*, 86.

8.
The Present State of the Comparative Study of Religious Ethics: An Update

John Kelsay

Introduction

I want to begin by acknowledging my debt to David Little—really, for just one of many things I owe to him. For purposes of this chapter, the debt I owe has to do with a way of analyzing arguments. From Little, I learned the value of paying close attention to the ways people relate a variety of normative interests. Human beings mix and mingle religious, moral, political, legal, and strategic directives. And it is often in the interplay between these that one ascertains the distinctive patterns of order by which groups identify themselves, and according to which conceptions of the good life obtain shape.

When I arrived at the University of Virginia in the Fall of 1980, Little was beginning to think about the variety of criticisms made of his and Sumner Twiss's attempt to outline a program of research consistent with such close attention to normative discourse. And in the Fall 1981 issue of the *Journal of Religious Ethics*, he published the article to which my own title alludes.[1] I shall return to that article momentarily. For now, though, I can summarize the general point of my chapter in this way. In his introduction to a posthumously published collection of essays by Evans-Pritchard, Ernst Gellner comments that as the great anthropologist approached retirement, he expressed satisfaction at the way ethnography had turned away from a focus on universal structures, and toward social-historical accounts of particular groups. At the same time (Gellner writes), Evans-Pritchard worried that the pendulum had swung too far. For without some agreement regarding terminology or conceptions that would enable classification and comparison—in short, without some form of taxonomy—no one would be able to say what counted as knowledge in the field of anthropology. The notion of progress in an area of study would be inapplicable to ethnography, which would thereby become a series of edifying discourses. As such, the contributions of anthropologists would be pushed to the side in the competition for resources in the academy. And this would not be entirely unjust, since no anthropologist would be able to provide an account of the kind of contribution his or her discipline makes.[2]

I think Evans-Pritchard's worries apply to the comparative study of religious ethics. Over the last thirty years, scholars ready to identify their work with this rubric have produced a number of interesting studies, characterized by great sensitivity to context and also to their own social location—that is, to the "stance" of the interpreter. But we have little sense of a vocabulary or classification scheme by which the disparate analyses of behavior produced in these studies may be brought together. Without such a vocabulary and the sense of purpose that goes with it, we produce edifying discourses—good analyses, interesting accounts, with some of them useful to people working in fields like politics or law. We do not have a discipline, however. So long as this description holds, the contribution to knowledge made by scholars of comparative religious ethics will remain marginal, at least as compared with those of historians, philosophers, linguists, or people working in any of the natural sciences.

Comparative Religious Ethics, 1970–1983

Following such an introduction, the first order of business is to acknowledge that many readers will respond with a shrug and ask "so what"? I hope ultimately to answer that question. I shall proceed by giving an account of how we came to the current point, followed by a discussion of some of the work produced by scholars identifying with the rubric "comparative religious ethics" over these last decades. I shall conclude with an indication of why my thesis matters, and how scholars might proceed.

First, then: How did we come to this point?

It is possible to tell a story about comparative religious ethics that begins in the late nineteenth and early twentieth centuries. For our purposes, though, the modern discussion begins in the early 1970s, and Little was a major player. In 1970, the Ramsey–Wilson volume *The Study of Religion in Colleges and Universities* included Little's short essay on the topic. And in 1973, Little and Twiss published an outline of the position they would develop in *Comparative Religious Ethics: A New Method*.[3]

These early articles were important. More basic, however, was a long essay Little published in one of the first issues of the *Journal of Religious Ethics*. "Max Weber and the Comparative Study of Religious Ethics" identified the roots of a particular approach to comparative study, in which scholars would combine an interest in the development of particular institutional and communal arrangements with analyses of the patterns of reasoning by which participants spoke about the normative quality of behavior. Weber's sociology of rationality provided an excellent model for comparative study, Little argued. One could identify important weaknesses in Weber's approach. But of these, the most important—a failure to attend sufficiently to the details of practical reasoning—was precisely the sort of thing an ethicist could address. Schooled in the practice of analytic philosophy, scholars could draw on a body of critical historical studies in order to refine Weber's vocabulary. The analysis of early Christian materials provided a fine example, as Little indicated that Weber's overreliance on the notion of charismatic authority hid from view the ways these materials mixed appeals to divine commands and to natural law.[4]

The 1978 publication of *Comparative Religious Ethics* took the point further. This emerging field would benefit from a consensus regarding basic terms like "religion," "morality," and "law." So Little and Twiss argued; as well, they proposed a model for the analysis of diverse patterns of practical reasoning, complete with a schema distinguishing "situational judgment," "validation," and "verification" as "levels" designed to sort the distinctive appeals people make in order to justify patterns of action. Case studies illustrated the approach, and invited further debate.

We need not go further into the details of the proposal at this point. For my purposes, the important thing is that *Comparative Religious Ethics* offered a classificatory scheme for scholarly work. As the authors made clear, the project was intended to facilitate comparison. After all, one can compare anything with anything, albeit in terms that are highly idiosyncratic. Assuming the point of scholarly conversation is to build or produce knowledge, however, such variety—let us call it a relativism in the use of terms—will not do. A field of study needs some agreement in such matters, so that specific proposals may be evaluated through peer review.

It did not take long for objections to emerge. Ronald Green argued that *Comparative Religious Ethics* ignored the "deep structure" of practical reason. Donald Swearer and others with expertise in Theravada Buddhism opined that Little and Twiss were insufficiently sensitive to the variety of arguments and approaches developed in that tradition. And Jeffrey Stout characterized the project as reliant on an outmoded philosophical vocabulary, in which a formalistic outline of "levels" of practical justification could be correlated with a pretense to professional objectivity. As Stout had it, *Comparative Religious Ethics* obscured the issue of purpose. Why, he asked, did Little and Twiss think comparative study important? Definitions of terms, interpretive schemes, and the like relate to this issue, and no claim to impartiality or objectivity can escape this point.[5]

This brings us to Little's 1981 article entitled "The Present State of the Comparative Study of Religious Ethics." Much of this essay responds to the aforementioned criticisms, which Little parsed in terms of a distinction between advocates of "grand theories" and of various kinds of "holism." Green represented the former, and Little's response suggests that the kind of approach advocated by Green in *Religious Reason* proves insufficiently sensitive to context.[6] Of course, that had been the criticism of *Comparative Religious Ethics* offered by Swearer and others; Little turned to this under the category of holism, and suggested that the dispute regarding patterns of reasoning in Theravada Buddhism be adjudicated through a conversation about the evidence—in other words, as a typical scholarly debate about the interpretation of a body of material (in this case, the Pali canon).

Of the various criticisms, those advanced by Stout would prove most significant. To the points already mentioned, Little responded by admitting that the presentation in *Comparative Religious Ethics* did not make clear that the "levels" of practical justification should be construed as interactive—for example, that situational judgments might be altered in view of appeals to norms (at the level of validation) or of worldview (what Little and Twiss termed "vindication"). And with respect to the purposes of comparative study, Little returned to Weber (and to Ernst Troeltsch), arguing for the priority of "conceptual self-clarification" as an impetus for academic work. Scholars work as "cultural individuals," driven to comparison by their social-historical location. The vocabulary in which they work (for example, a normative discourse in which religion, morality, and law may be distinguished) is a function of this location, and thus guides interpretation. In saying this, Little suggested, one need not deny the possibility of a scholarly account which concludes by acknowledging that a particular vocabulary does not fit the case at hand, or with a confession that an alternative vocabulary seems more compelling than one's own. What is important is the identification of a starting place, a perspective. To these points, Stout responded that his version of holism required a more consistent focus on changes in moral vocabularies, and thus a selection of larger units for purposes of comparison.[7] For example, one would want more than an analysis of patterns of practical reason in the Gospel according to Matthew, or in the Theravada Buddhist canon (to take two of the cases in *Comparative Religious Ethics*). One would want to know about the subsequent history of interpretation or about the place of such scriptural texts in the long course of centuries by which Christian and Buddhist communities adjudicated questions of virtuous living. Aside from these issues, Stout wondered whether he and Little actually had any significant disagreements, given the latter's reflections on conceptual self-clarification.

Comparative Religious Ethics, 1983–2006

As anyone interested in religion and ethics knows, there were and are important differences between Stout and Little. But most of these have to do with the status of truth claims in moral discourse.[8] They do not go to the question of method and approach in comparative study, though some points may affect a scholar's sense of what he or she is describing, or of the ultimate goal of scholarship—on this I think there is some ambiguity.

What *is* clear, I think, is the way this exchange of view played out in the subsequent development of comparative religious ethics. Whether scholars followed Little or Stout—more often, the latter, or so I think—the move toward perspectival studies, and away from a classificatory scheme is plain. For example, my own dissertation began with a discussion of the controversies addressed by Little in 1981, and defended a more or less modified version of the approach developed in *Comparative Religious Ethics*. In conversation with Little, I determined to characterize this as a perspectival approach, which allowed me to discuss the development of a divine command theory of ethics in early Muslim writings, and to compare the ways this theory functioned in the politics of eighth- and ninth-century Islamicate culture with analogous approaches in Christian ethics.[9]

I defended this dissertation in the summer of 1985. In December of that year, Frank Reynolds and Robin Lovin's edited collection *Cosmogony and Ethical Order* appeared, arguing that a perspectival approach rooted in the empiricism of Hume would mitigate the most prominent weaknesses of Little and Twiss's approach.[10] Subsequent work by William Schweiker (characterizing comparative study in terms of "The Drama of Interpretation"), by Twiss and Bruce Grelle (connecting comparative ethics and the practice of interreligious dialogue), by Lee Yearley and Aaron Stalnaker (on virtues and spiritual exercises), by James Turner Johnson and myself (on cultural traditions and the regulation of armed force), and by Little himself (on religion, nationalism, and intolerance) further illustrated the turn to perspectival approaches.[11] All these studies were driven by an interest in a particular issue. All emphasized the importance of cultural location and of self-criticism, along with the need for sensitivity to the internal complexities of religious-moral traditions. While the types of work mentioned in this list varied considerably with respect to problems addressed, materials to be studied, and the adoption of a longer or shorter historical expanse, all avoided proposing or even developing a classificatory scheme that might serve as a model for a discipline. To borrow a phrase from Thomas Kuhn, "normal science" for scholars working in the comparative study of religious ethics involved (1) stating a problem; (2) explaining why this problem might be thought important, in terms reflective of the cultural location of the author; (3) offering an interpretive or explanatory account of materials deemed relevant to the problem selected; and (4) expressing the hope that readers might find the results illuminating, based on an assumption that the cultural location of the author would not be singular, but shared by others. Looking now at this list of procedures, one might well wonder whether it qualifies as a description of normal "science"—normal *practice* might serve better, since there is no indication of a consensus regarding the type of knowledge at which the various studies aim.

Reflections on Davis's
"Two Neglected Classics of Comparative Ethics" (2008)

There is no sign that this state of affairs will change any time soon. Indeed, the best recent article on the methods and purposes of comparative ethics epitomizes the move of the field toward perspectival studies. G. Scott Davis's brilliant essay deals, as the title suggests, with "Two Neglected Classics of Comparative Ethics"—namely, Mary Douglas's *Purity and Danger* and Herbert Fingarette's *Confucius: The Secular as Sacred*. As even a casual reader will ascertain, however, the essay deals with much more than these noteworthy books.[12] On Davis's account, Douglas and Fingarette deserve attention because they model an approach. The short way of summarizing this would be to say that it makes comparative ethics look a lot like other kinds of historical and ethnographic studies. A more suggestive way of putting the point would, in my view, draw an analogy between comparative study and travel literature. This seems particularly apt when we read Davis's account of the virtues and vices of recent contributions to the field. Of these, Davis most admires William Lafleur's *Liquid Life*, largely because he (Davis) judges that the book follows in the path of Douglas and Fingarette.[13]

Lafleur begins with a story—an American, whose identity as a cultural individual disposes him to think and feel about issues of life and death in certain ways, learns Japanese and tries to study Japanese Buddhism with a combination of empathy and critical distance. During a visit to Japan, he is struck by the odd juxtaposition between Buddhist ideals of non-maleficence and the ubiquitous statuary devoted to Jizo, whose special place as a bodhisattva has to do with guarding small children. Through and with Lafleur, we learn that the statuary points to a highly particular way of addressing the prominence of abortion in Japanese life. On Lafleur's account, the Jizo-ritual is rooted in several centuries of Japanese (Buddhist) practice, and indicates a means by which contemporary Japanese may express, and perhaps resolve the conflicting emotions associated with aborting a child for which they are not ready or for other reasons do not want to bring into the world.

As Davis has it, *Liquid Life* provides the best recent expression of the inheritance of Douglas and Fingarette, which stresses three points:

> (1) Comparative religious ethics must be willing to erase any disciplinary boundary that blocks the road of inquiry. Whatever comparison we are likely to attempt, it will try to connect two or more figures or phenomena that are thoroughly embedded in time and place. It is essential to incorporate as much history and anthropology into our comparisons as possible.
>
> (2) When we get into the details of other peoples, times, and places, we should not be surprised that we are most struck by the ways that those peoples interpret and respond to issues of life, death, sex, and sustenance. Taken separately, those are the components of our religious and moral worlds. Taken together, they make up our political life.
>
> (3) When we can make what another people does go from bizarre and maybe even horrifying to a compelling option, then by juxtaposing that option to another, perhaps more comfortable, way of addressing similar issues, we may want to revise where we draw the distinction between the horrifying and the compelling.[14]

Or, as Davis concludes, in a brief discourse on (really, against) method: "There is, in short, no substitute for history and ethnography. If the pursuit of method short circuits the history and ethnography, by providing categories and cubbyholes in which to file and dismiss the counterintuitive, it is a positive danger to good work."[15]

Many, perhaps most, would agree with Davis. And as he puts the point, it is hard to argue against him. Of course it is true that comparative study should avoid circumventing or disguising the distinctive characteristics of human societies! But what is it that makes the study a contribution to *comparative ethics*? There are, after all, fields of study that stake out territory under rubrics like "comparative politics," "comparative literature," "ethnomusicology," and "cultural anthropology." There are divisions in departments of religion, as at the American Academy of Religion, whereby scholars offer their work as a contribution to comparative theology, ritual studies, or the history of religions. What is distinctive about the contributions of scholars of ethics to the study of religion? What sort of knowledge are we after, and how do we distinguish good work from work that is less so? In this, the most compelling aspect of Davis's approach, as of perspectival studies generally, is that it lowers the bar for comparative ethics as a discipline. People claiming to "do" comparative ethics simply go out and "get to know" other people, and the groups in which those others participate. Work that counts as interesting will be of the type that sensitive journalists or writers in the genre of travel literature produce—guided less by a rigorous training in or acquaintance with a particular scholarly discipline, and more by a kind of intuition through which the author serves his or her audience "back home" by entering vicariously into the experience of others. In this way, Davis reminds us of a point stressed by J. Z. Smith: faced with the choice between treating others as exotic species and treating them as "folks like us," we do well to tack in the direction of the latter. The point is not, or at least not simply to marvel "how odd!" but rather to explain how beings like ourselves could be attracted and sustained by practices different from our own.[16]

It is good to be reminded of this. Nevertheless, it is not enough to build a conversation or discipline called "comparative religious ethics." For that, we need something like the interest in taxonomy developed by Little and Twiss. Otherwise, we will simply produce a series of more and less edifying discourses. Some may be useful to people in other fields. For example, Lafleur's work is clearly a significant, though controversial contribution to Asian or Japanese Studies.[17] Little's studies of Ukraine and Sri Lanka in the U.S. Institute of Peace series on Religion, Nationalism, and Intolerance are useful to scholars working in peace studies, international relations, and studies of human rights. Some of the work produced by Johnson and myself draws interest from professional military and public policy types. And so on. But what do we talk about among ourselves? And how do we characterize the contributions of "religious ethics" or "comparative religious ethics" when we talk with our colleagues in departments of religion, or make arguments with administrators about the allocation of positions and funds? The interest of our projects may seem clear to us. But how do we explain it to others? And how do we explain why some work seems good, and other work less so?

How, then, should we proceed? Actually, I think Davis gestures in the right direction in the second of his three "lessons": "When we get into the details of other peoples, times, and places, we should not be surprised that we are most struck by the ways that those peoples interpret and respond to issues of life, death, sex, and sustenance. Taken separately, those are the components of our religious and moral worlds. Taken together, they make up our political life."[18] Without being overly precious (I hope!), one might say that Davis presumes much in the use of the reference "we." While interpretations of and responses to "issues of life, death, sex, and sustenance" are certainly of broad interest, one does not need to spend much time to realize that many scholars are actually interested in other things. For example, the focus of Mircea Eliade's *oeuvre* came to be hierophany—the various ways in which people claimed to experience "the sacred" as distinct from "the profane." Antonio Guistozzi's recent work on political leadership in Afghanistan focuses on the varieties of "warlordism" in that and other societies, and makes a comparative argument regarding the role of this phenomenon in the formation of the political units we call "states." In each case, there is much from which scholars interested in ethics can learn. But I do not think anyone, least of all Eliade or Guistozzi, would argue that their works fit into the category of ethics.[19]

In a sense, Davis's "we should not be surprised" makes the point too lightly. Studies of ethics are distinguished, in part, by the fact that they take the ways groups of people "interpret and respond to issues of life, death, sex, and sustenance" to be at least as, if not more revealing than the ways such people appropriate "the sacred" or the processes by which they form states. To put it another way, studies of ethics select the more and less formal institutions by which groups organize interpretation and response to life, death, sex, and sustenance as an entry point by which one may understand other aspects of communal existence. To put it yet another way, the comparative study of ethics involves collating and explaining the various systems of proprieties by which groups instantiate and extend a vocabulary that parses the diverse aspects of their environment in terms of a hierarchy of values.[20]

This set of interests is, I say, the entry point for studies of ethics. It is distinct from the entry point for scholars in political science, literature, history, and ethnography. As well, the approach by which scholars of ethics proceed to analyze their data is distinct from these other disciplines. For what interests ethicists is argument. It is one thing to note that a group consistently treats corpses in a certain way—say, though rapid and unadorned burial—and that those who act in some way different than the norm are sanctioned in various ways. It is another to try to ascertain what happens when curious youngsters ask "why do we bury our dead so quickly?" or when new circumstances suggest another mode of dealing with the dead, or even render previously established procedures inoperable. In those kinds of cases, an ethicist is interested in the ways discourse "makes explicit" norms that previously operated implicitly. Observing and attempting to describe or explain the procedures of argument by which behaviors are judged legitimate or not—this, I say, is the identifying feature of studies of ethics.

In fact, this is precisely what Davis, along with his heroes, does. It is true that Douglas and Fingarette suggest the importance of ethnographic and historical study. One might add that good descriptions of human behavior can also benefit from a good acquaintance with demography, geography, and linguistics. Nevertheless, ethicists make their contribution in terms of an analysis of institutionalized patterns of reasoning about the legitimacy of practice. It is this that sets their work apart, and which serves as the starting point in an argument for their existence in the academy.

A Way Forward?

The focus on institutionalized patterns of argument in relation to legitimation also provides a starting point for the development of the kind of taxonomy or classification scheme required for comparative study. It provides a starting point—all I have done thus far is to propose a theme or distinctive characteristic of the type of work associated with "ethics." One might well pile up examples of communities whose discourse demonstrates the phenomenon of institutionalized reasoning—all one will have is a kind of series of ethnographic studies or, if one chooses to arrange the account in a certain way, an encyclopedia. For serious comparison, one needs something more—a typology, a notion of universal development (along the lines of certain notions of evolution), or something else that qualifies as a "classification scheme."

As noted previously, developing such a scheme was in part the goal of Little and Twiss's 1978 volume. The portion of their model most apt for what I have in mind is the distinction between teleological and deontological systems. Recall their case studies: the Gospel according to Matthew suggests a model of reasoning oriented toward duty; accounts of the Navajo point toward a this-worldly teleology; the Pali canon suggests an intra- or perhaps trans-personal teleology, in which the development a certain kind of disposition serves to orient and qualify other aspects of practical reasoning. I have already recounted the ways critics characterized these presentations as insufficiently attentive to the internal dynamics or different strands in these cases.

But is that really so? Personally, I have always thought that Little and Twiss's case studies presented remarkably complex accounts of the materials discussed. This is particularly so when one consider the brevity of their presentations. The problem with the studies did not, and still does not seem to be, that Little and Twiss fail to recognize diversity or complexity. Rather, it is that the presentation lacks dynamism, in the sense of helping readers to understand how the materials relate to living communities of human beings.

In some sense, this relates to one of Stout's criticisms of *Comparative Religious Ethics*. When Stout averred that his holistic approach would favor descriptions of larger historical units, he was onto something. The Gospel of Matthew, for example, makes little sense unless one is interested in the emergence of Christian communities, and particularly in their relation to a context world dominated by the culture of Greece and the power of Rome. As well, the emergence of those communities makes little sense without reference to the bits and pieces we know regarding the relative position of Jews in the Greco-Roman world. Little and Twiss's discussion needed some account of those factors, so that one could have some sense of the difference it made for certain groups of people to stress duty rather than *eudaimonia*, and to construe duty in terms of norms thought to cohere both with God's directives and with the "true nature" of human beings.

Now, it is certainly difficult to construct a rich picture of the community "behind" or served by the editor(s) of Matthew, though one would expect an ethicist to make use of the best accounts developed by those who specialize in the study of Judaism and Christianity in the Greco-Roman environment. Here again, it is worth stressing the importance of Davis's discussion of the embedded nature of normative discourse, and thus of considerable ethnographic and historical learning in descriptions of ethics. All this suggests, again, that Little and Twiss's case studies lacked richness.

That does not mean their typology was wrong or lacked utility, however. So far as the distinction between teleological and deontological trajectories goes, they were on to a generally useful classification, which has served in studies of ethics for at least two centuries, and can serve us still.

What of other aspects of their scheme—the distinction between levels of justification, for example? Here I think the idea of listening in or discerning the ways norms become explicit provides a better way of making the point than *Comparative Religious Ethics*. As Little noted in his response to Stout, the latter's point is correct—the distinction between situational judgment, validation, and vindication was overly rigid. It may be that, in a given case, there is a point to distinguishing types of reasons given regarding a certain matter. On some accounts, for example, the conduct of practical reasoning in the United States may be described in such a way that some appeals are "central," because more widely supported by consensus, while others are "private," in the sense that they explain why a certain person or group takes a stand, but do not help in describing the ways such a person or group may collaborate with others. Think, for example, of the debate over John Rawls's characterizations of public reason. While one need not accept the late philosopher's more rigidly normative judgments about the public/private distinction in these matters, one could imagine a contribution to the comparative study of ethics in which something like it makes sense.[21] Or again, think of the ways that certain kinds of intellectuals—I am thinking in particular of the type of person whose writing is characterized by the attempt to systematize the normative discourse of his or her community—clearly consider judgments about the proper way to speak about politics is related to views, say, of God's attributes. The Muslim theologian al-Ash`ari provides a good example. He clearly thinks that "getting it right" in one of these matters requires proper discourse in the other—even though the most direct appeals he makes regarding political judgment do not involve citations of the divine *sifat*.[22]

The point here is that it is sometimes worth noting that practical reason can involve more and less direct appeals. Stout was right to say that this interest is not well served by a distinction between validation and vindication. That does not mean that we can treat all the reason-giving that a particular person or group brings to bear on practical issues as of one type.

Concluding Remarks

I could go on with respect to these points. For example, I think that Little and Twiss's interest in distinguishing religious from non-religious approaches to normative discourse remains useful, even if one acknowledges the current trend to see the related project of defining religion as problematic. As I take it, the most evident use to which ethicists can put the offerings of Talal Asad, Tomoko Masuzawa, Russell McCutcheon, and others on this matter would be to say that the terms "religion" and "religious" serve to make a distinction, and that it is important to consider the purposes for which the distinction is made in a particular case.[23] To invoke Little's response to Stout again, it is important to recognize that this distinction may be made in relation to the institutional arrangements of our own cultural location. For us, it is important to ask whether the invocation of particular notions of deity "make a difference" in the ways people and groups judge and argue about matters of legitimation. And it is certainly not wrong to ask whether people in other places and times, speaking a different language and considering that the world is rather differently constructed than we, nevertheless might have considered such a distinction important.

This brings me to a final point. I have been arguing that the comparative study of religious ethics developed in ways that rejected Little and Twiss's proposal of a classification scheme. Since 1978, the history of this type of study has been dominated by the kind of approach I call perspectival, in the sense that good work proceeds with careful attention to context with respect to the interpreter, as well as to the material presented through interpretation. While there is a sense in which this has been a good thing, we are now at a point when something more is needed. If we are to make progress in the comparative study of ethics, some agreement regarding the overarching purposes and vocabulary—in short, on the type of knowledge we wish to produce—is necessary.

To this end, I am suggesting that we can still learn from the example of *Comparative Religious Ethics*. In some cases, the distinctions proposed in that book remain useful. As examples, I have mentioned the distinction between teleological and deontological appeals, as well as that between religious and non-religious arguments. In other cases, the distinctions Little and Twiss made do not stand—with respect to validation and vindication, which Little gave up fairly quickly, there is no need to attempt rehabilitation.

I am not yet ready to propose a full classificatory scheme myself. But I do think the general outline of my proposal is clear. It seems to me that one could usefully begin with a focus on groups or communities in the manner of social theorists or even sociobiologists, and place this in a creative relationship with Robert Brandom's proposals about the ways a group's norms become explicit. If one thinks further about the ways Brandom's studies in the history of philosophy distinguish between varieties of rationality, the argument being that "historical" rationality may in the end be construed as inclusive of others, one may well have project that enables the sort of conversation I advocate.[24]

In the future, I hope to offer more than these cursory remarks. For now, let me conclude that the study of groups in connection with an interest in rationality is not particularly new. In a nutshell, it is the program of Weber. In the 1974 article mentioned at the outset of this chapter, Little argued for the utility (within limits) of Weber's project for the development of comparative studies of ethics. By 1978, Little and Twiss were more strictly focused on the sort of discourse analysis characteristic of analytic philosophers, and the sociological portions of Weber's legacy fell largely into the background. Little's 1981 response to Stout and others brought Weber back in, but only piecemeal.

Now I wish to bring Weber back in, specifically in the sense of a notion of comparative ethics as a kind of sociology of rationality. Which makes one wonder: why did ethicists drift away from Weber in the first place?[25]

NOTES

[1] David Little, "The Present State of the Comparative Study of Religious Ethics," in *The Journal of Religious Ethics* 9.2 (Fall 1981): 210–27.

[2] Ernst Gellner, "Introduction," to E. E. Evans-Pritchard, *A History of Anthropological Thought*, ed. Andre Singer (New York: Basic Books, 1981).

[3] Paul Ramsey and John F. Wilson, eds., *The Study of Religion in Colleges and Universities* (Princeton, NJ: Princeton University Press, 1970), 216–45; David Little and Sumer B. Twiss, *Comparative Religious Ethics: A New Method* (San Francisco: Harper & Row, 1978); the article to which I refer is "Basic Terms in the Study of Religious Ethics," in *Religion*

and Morality, eds. Gene Outka and John P. Reeder, Jr. (Garden City, NY: Anchor Press, 1973), 35–77.

[4] David Little, "Max Weber and the Comparative Study of Religious Ethics," in *The Journal of Religious Ethics* 2.2 (Fall 1974): 5–40.

[5] Ronald M. Green, Review of *Comparative Religious Ethics*, *Journal of Religion* 61.1 (January 1981): 111–13; Donald K. Swearer, "Nirvana, No-Self, and Comparative Religious Ethics," in *Religious Studies Review* 6 (October 1980): 301–6; Jeffrey Stout, "Weber's Progeny, Once Removed," *Religious Studies Review* 6 (October 1980): 289–95.

[6] Ronald M. Green, *Religious Reason* (New York: Oxford University Press, 1978).

[7] See Jeffrey Stout, "Holism and Comparative Ethics: A Response to Little," in *The Journal of Religious Ethics* 11.2 (Fall 1983): 301–16.

[8] See, for example, the more recent offering of Little: "On Behalf of Rights: A Critique of *Democracy and Tradition*," in *The Journal of Religious Ethics* 34.2 (June 2006): 287–310.

[9] John Kelsay, "Religion and Morality in Islam: A Proposal Concerning Ethics in the Formative Period," Ph.D. Dissertation, University of Virginia, 1985.

[10] Robin Lovin and Frank Reynolds, eds., *Cosmogony and Ethical Order: New Studies in Comparative Ethics* (Chicago: University of Chicago Press, 1985); see also "Focus on Cosmogony and Religious Ethics," in *The Journal of Religious Ethics* 14.1 (Spring 1986): 48–156.

[11] William Schweiker, "The Drama of Interpretation and the Philosophy of Religions: An Essay on Understanding in Comparative Religious Ethics," in *Discourse and Practice*, eds. Frank Reynolds and David Tracy (Albany, NY: State University of New York Press, 1992), 263–94; Sumner B. Twiss and Bruce Grelle, eds., *Explorations in Global Ethics: Comparative Religious Ethics and Interreligious Dialogue* (Boulder, CO: Westview Press, 1998); Lee Yearley, *Mencius and Aquinas: Theories of Virtue and Conceptions of Courage* (Albany, NY: State University of New York Press, 1990); Aaron Stalnaker, *Overcoming Our Evil: Human Nature and Spiritual Exercises in Xunzi and Augustine* (Washington, D.C.: Georgetown University Press, 2006); James Turner Johnson and John Kelsay, eds., *Cross, Crescent, and Sword* (Westport, CT: Greenwood Press, 1990); John Kelsay and James Turner Johnson, eds., *Just War and Jihad* (Westport, CT: Greenwood Press, 1991); David Little, *Sri Lanka: The Invention of Enmity* (Washington, D.C.: United States Institute of Peace, 1993); David Little, *Ukraine: The Legacy of Intolerance* (Washington, D.C.: United States Institute of Peace, 1991).

[12] G. Scott Davis, "Two Neglected Classics of Comparative Ethics," in *The Journal of Religious Ethics* 36.3 (September 2008): 375–424.

[13] William R. LaFleur, *Liquid Life: Abortion and Buddhism in Japan* (Princeton, NJ: Princeton University Press, 1992).

[14] Davis, "Two Neglected Classics," 394.

[15] Ibid., 398.

[16] Jonathan Z. Smith, *Imagining Religion: From Babylon to Jonestown* (Chicago: University of Chicago Press, 1988).

[17] See the essays by Underwood, Harrison, LaFleur, and Green in *Journal of the American Academy of Religion* 67.3 (September 1999).

[18] Davis, "Two Neglected Classics," 394.

[19] See Mircea Eliade, *The Sacred and the Profane: The Nature of Religion*, trans. Willard R. Trask (New York: Harcourt Brace Jovanovich, 1987); Antonio Guistozzi, *Empires of Mud: Wars and Warlords in Afghanistan* (New York: Columbia University Press, 2009).

[20] In this and following paragraphs, readers will recognize the allusions to Robert Brandom, *Making It Explicit* (Cambridge, MA: Harvard University Press, 1998).

[21] For a recent and insightful account of Rawls's position on these matters, see Elizabeth A. Barre, "Reconciled to Liberty: Catholics, Muslims, and the Possibility of Overlapping Consensus," Ph.D. Dissertation, Florida State University, 2009.

[22] I explore al-Ash`ari's reasoning in an (as yet) unpublished paper, "Predestination and Theological Ethics: Abu'l Hasan al-Ash`ari and the Divine Decree."

[23] Talal Asad, *Genealogies of Religion: Discipline and Reasons of Power in Christianity and Islam* (Baltimore, MD: Johns Hopkins University Press, 1993); Tomoko Masuzawa, *The Invention of World Religions* (Chicago: University of Chicago Press, 2005); Russell T. McCutcheon, *Studying Religion* (New York: Equinox Publishing, 2007). Thanks to my Florida State University colleague Matthew Day for conversations on this point.

[24] Robert B. Brandom, *Tales of the Mighty Dead: Historical Essays in the Metaphysics of Intentionality* (Cambridge, MA: Harvard University Press, 2002).

[25] At this point, let me comment on two matters not discussed in the body of my essay. First, insofar as my argument rests on the need for comparative ethics to establish a "place" in the academy, it is useful to recall that a portion of Stout's commentary on *Comparative Religious Ethics* suggested that Little and Twiss were interested in "professionalism." I am not sure what was at stake for Stout in this, but judging from Little's (and others') responses, it was taken to be a negative. It is easy to see why: if one takes the charge to indicate a desire for status, position, and control with little or no attention to the quality of studies produced, then "professionalism" is something to be avoided. It may be, however, that in responding to the charge of "professionalism" Little and others missed the opportunity to talk about what it means to "have a profession," which would imply gathering a community of scholars defined by agreement on the importance of certain subject matter, and on the desirability of a common approach by which hypotheses may be advanced, tested, and results evaluated. This seems benign, at least; it may even be a desideratum in the development of an academic field. The creation and publication of *The Journal of Religious Ethics*, with its first issue produced in 1973, was certainly a signal that such a sense of "having a profession" was in the works.

Putting my comments in this context, I think one might say that the turn to perspectival studies has delayed this development, and thereby limited the impact of religious ethics as an approach within the academy, specifically within the study of religion. I have no scientific evidence or survey in support of this opinion, though I think anyone who has participated in meetings of faculty whose tenure rests in departments of religion will recognize the point. It is difficult, to say the least, to maintain space for ethics, as for studies of religious thought and philosophy of religion, except in connection with those posts designated as "theory of religion." And in that connection, if one turns to a journal like *Method and Theory in the Study of Religion* or to its institutional base in the North American Society for the Study of Religion, one will find a strongly held view that the aforementioned fields are "crypto-theology," meaning that the study is really designed to provide a means of self-expression for people whose normative commitments are strongly felt, but who cannot fit into the more obviously suitable frame of a theological faculty or seminary. As well, the "self-expressive" aspect of such studies is held to delimit the possibility of effective peer review.

Without granting all these points, I think it is useful to follow Twiss and Grelle in noting that religious ethics is a "hermeneutical and applied" discipline, particularly if one stresses the first term in the pair. In the study of religion, "ethics" stands for an approach focused on the ways groups of human beings are organized in terms of proprieties, and the ways these become explicit in argument about the legitimacy of behaviors.

So much for the importance of "having a profession." I also want to comment on the most obvious movement by which some scholars might be said to "aim beyond" the perspectivalism described in this essay, and thus to move in the direction of a consensus about knowledge—a research project, if you will. Here, I have in mind the projects associated with the group of scholars described by Elizabeth M. Bucar as a "third wave" in the comparative study of religious ethics. (See Elizabeth M. Bucar, "Methodological Invention as a Constructive Project: Exploring the Production of Ethical Knowledge through the Interaction of Discursive Logics," in *The Journal of Religious Ethics* 36.3 (September 2008): 355–74.) I will not try to name all those who fit into Bucar's category, but a good indication of the group and its direction would be the "Focus on Anthropos and Ethics" in *The Journal of Religious Ethics* 33.2 (June 2005), which included essays by Thomas A. Lewis, Jonathan Wyn Schofer, Aaron Stalnaker, and Mark A. Berkson. In this and other works, most recently essays collected for publication in *The Journal of Religious Ethics* 38.3 (September 2010), the project is defined as a series of studies of the ways communities develop notions of selfhood and instantiate techniques by which virtuous persons may be formed. In a response to the essays in *The Journal of Religious Ethics* 38.3 (September 2010), I offer a number of criticisms of this project, notably (1) that much of the work produced seems (strangely) to ignore or otherwise play down the role of more and less formal institutions in the production of virtue, and (2) almost all of the work ignores or plays down the role of argument, in the sense of procedures of deliberation and justification, in the life of the groups studied. Here, I should like to add that while these shortcomings can in principle be addressed, another requires some different kinds of work than the scholars of the "third wave" are as yet inclined to undertake: that is, the development of a vocabulary or classification scheme that would enable comparisons at some level other than at the level of observation. If one thinks of J. Z. Smith's various "approaches" to comparison (outlined in *Imagining Religion*, see n. 16 for publication information), the project is at present inclined toward either "ethnography" (individual and more or less idiosyncratic comparisons of the type associated with travel literature) or "encyclopedic" (topical arrangements of material that is sorted but still presented in the "so many of this, so many of that" genre). If the comparative study of ethics remains at this, perspectival level, it will produce studies that are ideographic, but not explanatory. Some of these will, as I have said, be useful; but they will not identify a discipline or create a profession.

Part TWO

FUNCTIONAL PROSPECTS:
Religion, Public Policy, and Conflict

9.
Religion, Ethics, and War: David Little and Ecumenical Ethics

J. Bryan Hehir

The tragic tale of war runs like a red thread through secular history and religious history. The project of restraining war is also part of both; wars are not only fought, won and lost, they are measured in moral terms. Those who have engaged the difficult task of measuring war include theologians, philosophers, lawyers (canon and civil), historians, and political scientists. David Little's lifetime work on the boundaries of theology, ethics, and politics has located him squarely in this long secular-religious narrative. My purpose in this chapter is to describe this intersection and locate (in broad terms) his work on these boundaries. As this volume indicates, his theological-ethical work on war has been only one piece of his ongoing contribution, but it has been a substantial piece. This chapter opens by locating Little's work in the arena of ecumenical ethics. It moves then to an assessment of the changing nature of war over this past century. Finally, it closes with a commentary on changes in the field of religion and ethics in addressing the issues of war and peace today.

The Ethics of War: An Ecumenical Topic

The discussion of ecumenical ethics is sometimes defined solely in terms of Protestant–Catholic relationships. This omits the Protestant ecumenical movement, often dated from the World Missionary Conference in 1910.

The more recent meaning of ecumenical, the Protestant-Catholic dimension, dates from the Second Vatican Council (1962–65) which opened Catholicism to serious ecumenical engagement, a major shift from the previous four centuries.[1]

For most of those four hundred years, theology (in all its various dimensions) had been done principally in confessional isolation. The exceptions to this statement were usually the work of individual theologians who crossed lines that were often carefully guarded.

Interestingly enough, one topic which sustained an ecumenical history in spite of divisions of religious communities and the counterpart separations of church and state was the subject of war and peace. In the Christian tradition, the standard synthetic narrative of ethics and war began with the Jewish and Christian scriptures, moved to Augustine (✝430), then to the Middle Ages, and on to the work of the Spanish Scholastics and Hugo Grotius (✝1645), before it came to the twentieth-century authors. Inevitably, the compressed character of the story eliminates historical and textual complexity. James Turner Johnson's work on the Middle Ages illustrates how historians render the synthesis a more complex and richer narrative.[2]

Nonetheless, the convergence of the Scholastics (Francisco de Vitoria [✝1546] and Francisco Suárez [✝1617]) with the later work of Grotius shows that religious differences did not entirely eliminate the possibility of analysis that had common objectives and invoked some common principles and methods. The era in which they worked, covering two hundred years, could hardly be called ecumenical, but their witness of seeking limits, restraint, and a sense of our common humanity in spite of religious and political conflicts, is a rare and refreshing theme in our often conflicted history.

The time from Grotius to the twentieth century has its own complexity that can be acknowledged here but not retraced. Locating Little's work requires a focus on the last century and this one. Indeed the relevant framework is the period between the Second World War and 2010. The baseline of World War II is significant not only because of the nature of the conflict, its methods and means, but also because religious-moral argument had only marginal impact on war and politics. It is the case that the voices of Reinhold Niebuhr and John Bennett were crucial in the Protestant community in persuading a heavily pacifist community to support U.S. participation in the war.[3] Likewise the voice of John Ford,

S.J., during the war, condemning the policy of obliteration bombing (along with Niebuhr), testified to the ability of Christian theology to confront and address modern warfare.[4] But post-war judgment on the role of religious-moral influence during the war was rendered accurately by John Courtney Murray, S.J., speaking to the Catholic community: "I think it is true to say that the traditional doctrine was disregarded during World War II. This is no argument against the traditional doctrine. The Ten Commandments do not lose their imperative relevance by reason of the fact that they are violated. But there is a place for an indictment of all of us who failed to make the tradition relevant."[5]

The indictment is not my focus here; by the time Murray wrote these words the Cold War and, more importantly, the nuclear age, were in progress. The indictment of which Murray spoke led in the 1950s and 1960s to a review and renewal of the Christian ethic of the use of force. To locate Little's work it is useful to distinguish in the post-war era two generations of ecumenical ethics focused on war and peace. The first generation was led by Niebuhr, Murray, and Paul Ramsey.[6] Ramsey's work continued well into the second generation, but functionally his leadership can be paired with Niebuhr and Murray, both of whose work was completed in the 1960s. Taken together, their work on war and peace constituted a powerful renewal of what Murray called "the traditional doctrine," even though it is impossible to collapse their substance and style into a single method or theory. Murray was solidly rooted in both the Natural Law and Just War traditions; Ramsey had an affinity to the first but resisted being identified with it, while he was thoroughly immersed in Just War Reasoning. Niebuhr was critical of both Natural Law and Just War, but developed his own distinctive method of addressing the standard categories of ends, means, consequences, and motives in war.[7] The cumulative effect of their engagement with war and politics had a two-fold significance: all three were exquisite craftsmen in rendering an ancient tradition relevant for a very new age, and they inspired the next generation to keep alive and relevant for policy and personal conscience principles, rules, and categories which had been marginalized in political discourse for the first two-thirds of the twentieth-century.

Little fits into the second generation of ecumenical work on war and peace. He fits into the company of Ramsey, James Turner Johnson, Le Roy Walters, James Childress, David Hollenbach, Frank Winters, and others, whose work spans from the final quarter of last century to today. In comparison to the first generation, denominational lines and distinctive differences of Protestant–Catholic styles of analysis matter less. There was a broad legacy of thought and argument which had acquired a status of a common possession and was used—with differences—across the second generation. There were quite clear differences (to which I will return) between the second generation and others, in both Protestant and Catholic communities, who found "the traditional doctrine" quite inadequate. The work of John Howard Yoder, Stanley Hauerwas, Paul Peachey, Gordon Zahn, and Jim Douglass found ecumenical common ground in witness to the tradition of nonviolence and pacifism.[8]

Little fit securely into the broader framework of ecumenical ethics, and into the specific tradition of Just War ethics. Emerging from Harvard Divinity School in 1965 with a ThD in ethics, he was by conviction, background and training a mainline representative of the Protestant tradition. But his interests and his scholarship extended across ecumenical lines. A scholar in the Reformed Tradition and an interpreter of John Calvin, Little has had long-term interests in Natural Law and in the pursuit of common morality in public discourse. These interests established a foundation for his work on human rights which in turn is crucial for assessing both the ends and means of the use of force. In all of these areas he had colleagues across the Christian spectrum.

On the specific questions of war and peace, Little's interest surfaced early, and while its scope and focus have shifted in response to the changing character of modern war and world politics from the 1960s into this century, his grounding in Just War thought is consistent. To trace his evolution as a reflection of the broader changes in the ethics of war and peace, it is helpful to sketch the developments in war and peace questions since World War II.

War and Politics: Post-War Era to Post-9–11

In the years between 1945 and 2010 the international system has generated and confronted three types of warfare: interstate war, intrastate war, and transnational war. While they can be discussed in chronological or linear fashion, these various forms of war overlapped across sixty-five years.[9]

The Cold War and the two World Wars exhibited both continuity and discontinuity of character. World Wars I and II were classic interstate conflicts, and the Cold War, viewed through the lens of the United States and the Soviet Union, can be classified in the same way (although some would prefer a designation of two empires in conflict). Viewed in this way, the traditional elements of interstate conflict are evident: national boundaries, definitions of aggression, alliances, military forces as the predominant measurement of power, and zero-sum calculations of outcomes. Given the size, scope of influence, and global reach of the superpowers, there was more than enough in the traditional categories to establish the distinctive interstate status of the Cold War. But the complicating factor of discontinuity was nuclear weapons. These instruments of mass destruction transformed this interstate conflict into a threat and policy problems unlike anything in the annals of warfare. Henry Kissinger, a key actor and interpreter of the Cold War era, captured one dimension of the uniqueness of this conflict:

> Throughout human history, humanity has suffered from a shortage of power and has concentrated immense effort on developing new sources and special applications of it. It would have seemed unbelievable even fifty years ago that there could ever be an excess of power, and that everything would depend on the ability to use it subtly and with discrimination. . . . [Kissinger went on to conclude his analysis] Yet this is precisely the challenge of the nuclear age.[10]

Concentrating only on the destructive power of the new technology does not convey the full range of the challenges of the Cold War. The threat of mutual destruction did not eliminate or erode the competition for territory, influence, and control on the part of the two Great Powers. The competition continued but in new ways; strategy and policy were shaped by deterrence; new weapons and new attempts at arms control coexisted. Other states were swept into the conflict, often serving as proxies of the superpowers. There is a vast literature on the politics and strategy of the Cold War, much of it rendered purely of historical value with the collapse of the conflict.

The unique problems posed for diplomats and strategists were matched by questions posed for the traditional ethic by the Cold War. An ethic specifically designed to set limits on force faced an era of massive destructive power. The strategist's creation of deterrence raised intractable issues about threatening civilians versus the consequences of stability and maintaining a quasi-peace. The proxy wars of the superpowers in Vietnam, Central America, and Afghanistan subordinated the fate of others to the interests of the major powers. A divided Europe remained a political-military threat. Little was never absent from the ethics of war debates, but the extended arguments about deterrence theory, targeting and arms control did not often claim his attention.

The end of the Cold War was followed by a decade of intense conflict within states, focused upon issues of nationalism, ethnicity, and religion, joined with traditional struggles of power, politics, and economics. The evidence is not at all clear that the end of the Cold War was a causal factor in these conflicts; one might make that case in the fracturing of Yugoslavia, but surely not in Rwanda, Sierra Leone, Sri Lanka, or Haiti. Little wisely argued that many of these conflicts were taking their toll during the Cold War, but the wider world simply did not pay attention.[11] These internal conflicts of the 1990s posed a double problem. First, defining the causes in each case; there was no ideal type for these conflicts—save the general elements cited above. The analytical challenge of causation was only a preface to the question of what resources societies had—military, social, economic, or legal—to address these conflicts. Issues of preventive diplomacy, peacemaking or peacekeeping, the role of purely internal action by states and civil society versus the need to engage regional actors or international security and development institutions were raised in almost every case.[12]

Second, the scale of violence, human rights violations, and creation of refugees and internally displaced persons did raise the issue of humanitarian intervention (diplomatically or militarily) for the wider community of states and for the United Nations. The Cold War had experienced multiple interventions but none of them were humanitarian; they were usually part of the global strategy of both East and West. Those interventions subordinated states and peoples to Great Power interests. The 1990s raised the need to "rescue" populations caught in chaos.[13] Internal conflicts which produced violence, large scale human suffering, and refugees struck directly at the fragile intersection of world politics where the UN Declaration of Human Rights meets the basic concept of state sovereignty. The first commits states to responsibilities to monitor and address human rights; the second affirms the role of sovereignty and domestic jurisdiction as a baseline of international order, ruling out coercive intervention by other states, or by the United Nations.[14] The call for military intervention in Bosnia, Rwanda, Sierra Leone, and Kosovo raised a political–juridical problem (and a political–military challenge) for individual states, regional organizations, and the United Nations.

The 1990s produced a series of ad hoc responses to internal conflict, leading to Kofi Annan's 1999 address to the UN General Assembly in which he acknowledged that the organization had a serious policy vacuum on humanitarian intervention.[15] An international panel (The International Commission on Intervention and State Sovereignty), formed under the initiative of the Canadian government, produced a significant response to the vacuum—*The Responsibility to Protect*—a report that redefined the meaning of state sovereignty in terms of the responsibility to protect the human rights of citizens, and argued that default on this question meant that responsibility to protect devolved to other institutions in the international community. The report has generated strong support, including endorsement at the UN Millennium Summit (2000), but it is not settled law yet, and the traditional claims of sovereignty are very much still the accepted basis of international politics.

The shift from the Cold War conflicts to the internal conflicts of the 1990s was substantial for politics and strategy, and for religion and ethics. During the Cold War most moral arguments were about preventing, containing, and limiting resort to force. In the 1990s at least some moralists were invoking arguments about why states and others were *obliged* to resort to force to prevent humanitarian catastrophes up to and including genocide. This change in policy discourse was not the only one. The nature of internal conflict in the 1990s pushed the normative debate beyond ethics, to the role of religion within societies and within a globalized world. The analysis of the role of religion recognized both its capacity to contribute to peacemaking and its capacity to catalyze or intensify conflicts.

Little's range of scholarly interests, and his position as Senior Scholar at the U.S. Institute for Peace in Washington, D.C. (1989–1999) prepared him well to engage the changed agenda about war and peace. His interest in both religious ethics and common morality were resources for analysis within religious traditions and for discussion in global civil society and in the United Nations. His long-term interest in the philosophy of human rights as well as in the policy implications of human rights claims engaged him in internal and transnational policies about those rights. His interest in the resurgent post–Cold War attention to nationalism fit the analysis of cases from the Balkans, the post–Soviet Union and the Middle East. His decades of participation in interreligious dialogue prepared him for intense debates about Islam, following 9–11.

The internal conflicts of the 1990s have continued into the new century, but they have been eclipsed in many ways by the 9–11 terrorist attacks on the United States, and the wars in Iraq and Afghanistan which followed. The terrorist attacks were a transnational war, a war across international borders by a nonstate actors.[16] Two characteristics signified the changing landscape of war. First, while terrorism was a well known phenomenon in domestic politics, transnational terrorism raised new challenges for strategy and politics. Second, while transnational actors had been an increasingly important dimension of world politics since the 1970s, military capabilities of the kind exhibited by al-Qaeda had not been part of the standard understanding of transnationality. As with the Cold War and internal war, these changes in the political-strategic arena posed accompanying normative challenges and questions. A transnational threat, by definition, required an assessment within states where it originated, and across state lines where it was executed. Moreover, the 9–11 attacks posed normative challenges that cut across religion, ethics, law, and culture. The specific form of the post-9–11 threat was the way it joined a certain version of Islam with a political-military agenda. Ancient issues took on new meaning: the nexus of religion and war had been a destructive one in European history; the status of a nonstate actor carrying out military actions on a global basis posed questions for international law and the ethics of war; the narrative of Islam and the West reached back centuries, incorporating memories of the crusades, the Ottoman Empire, Western colonialism, Arab nationalism, and the central place of Middle East politics in world politics.

These issues have been joined from all sides since 9–11. Little's work in the 1990s had engaged some of these themes, but 9–11 expanded his field of activity substantially. Returning to Harvard Divinity School in 1999 as the T. J. Dermot Dunphy Professor of the Practice in Religion, Ethnicity and International Conflict, and bringing with him his multiple relationships from the Institute for Peace, Little addressed the Iraq war, the role of religion in global conflict, and the religious and secular roots of human rights.

Religion, Ethics, and War

The path from 1945 to 2010 not only changed the understanding of war, it also changed the elements of the normative evaluation of war and peace. Little's academic career, research and writing has engaged and reflected this pattern of change and continuity in religious-moral discourse. My purpose in this closing section is to capture the framework of analysis, understanding and debate in the evaluation of war and the search for peace one decade into a new century, and to close with Little's place in those debates.

The Classical Debate

In the Christian tradition, as noted earlier, the debate about war and peace has been constant. War, in its methods, motivation and consequences, contradicts the Christian vision of life, of relationships, and of conduct. Yet, it has been a constant in human history, so the "realist dimension" of Christian moral reflection has been compelled to engage war and peace rather than simply ignore it. The consequence of engaging it has produced, "hardly more than a *Grenzmoral*, an effort to establish on a minimal basis of reason a form of human action, the making of war, that remains fundamentally irrational."[17] That effort, a realist effort from Augustine to Niebuhr, has never gone uncontested. The classical debate in the tradition, therefore, has been about fundamentals: which premises guide the moral enterprise, what participation is possible for Christians, what contribution can Christian thought and witness provide to secular history? The pacifist, nonviolent tradition, with its own logic and working from its distinct premises, has never seen Augustine's move to the idea of "just war" as a *development* of doctrine, but as a *corruption* of the tradition.

Some contemporary commentators regard the classical debate as either exhausted in content, or stale in its repetition. A sounder view, I believe, is to recognize that the classical debate should not absorb all contemporary normative thinking, but retains its fundamental importance.

That is to say, all participants in the war and peace discussion should be explicit and clear about their premises and principles, and *then* proceed to as much common ground and new insight as possible from distinct starting points. In brief we should not be consumed by rehearsing the classical debate, but we should not forget its fundamental importance.

The Rise of Religion

This topic is broader than the analysis of war and peace, but it stands as the overarching framework for it and for other themes. Religious convictions and religious communities have been at least as much constants in world politics as has warfare. But their presence and power of influence have not always received the attention warfare has. The narrative of religion and world politics is long and complex, and there have been varying interpretations of it. Since the formal study of international relations has a Western pedigree, the West's version of religion and politics often is overemphasized but necessary to understand. Synthetically stated, the transition from ancient to medieval history saw the rise of Christianity as a religious and political institution; the rise of sovereign states and the divisions of Christianity, followed by war in Christendom, led to the modern era of international relations. At the heart of the modern era was a process of secularization of world politics. Religious convictions and communities continued, but their role in the world of diplomacy and the academy (where politics were taught and practiced) was not acknowledged. In a phrase used by many, religion was a "black box" for international relations.

For much of the Cold War this model of politics without religion was sustained, but the post Cold War and post-9–11 worlds had to confront the role of religion in its potentially positive and negative dimensions. Beginning in the 1970s and carrying through the 1990s, the role of religion as a social catalyst from Latin America to Eastern Europe and from Seoul to South Africa could not be ignored. Its results were both positive and negative but its presence was indisputable. At times it stood for social justice and human rights; at times it could solidify and deepen internal conflicts rooted in other factors. Its role could be primarily local or national or transnational, or some mix of the three. By the 1990s, scholarship had begun to analyze and integrate the religious factor into its lens on world politics.[18] Statecraft and diplomacy were more cautious, but the recognition of the role of religion at the UN Millennium Summit (2000) established a foundation for more explicit attention to religion in all its dimensions.

The events of 9–11 produced different reactions; to some they confirmed the conviction that religion will inevitably provide more conflict than peace; for others they confirmed the conviction that religion must be addressed explicitly by scholars and leaders of states. The inevitable focus on Islam after 9–11 was too narrow a lens to capture the role of religion; but the debates about the full meaning of Islam served to illustrate the complexity of any religious tradition.

By themselves the post-9–11 debates were too constricted to address religion and world politics. But combined with the previous thirty years, and under the pressure of a globalized world order, the full range of religion and its impact are now open for analysis.

Ethics and War Again

The full range of religious influence extends substantially beyond issues of war and peace. It must address the religious potential to expand moral imagination, to respond to suffering and need in different ways, to open paths of understanding, *and* the religious potential to consolidate divisions, foster exclusion and make political compromise more difficult if not impossible. The full range of influence extends to culture as well as politics, to family life and education, to economics, human rights and standards of political legitimacy (the right to rule). These broader themes are rich in potential but none of them eliminate the imperative for religious traditions to address war and peace. This topic, and how skillfully it is managed practically, is to some degree the precondition for achieving the broader goals of religion in world politics.

Two broad characteristics mark the contemporary debates about the ethics of war and peace. First, the "traditional doctrine," the Just War ethic as it has been developed, expanded and applied has become the common property of the world of politics, war and law. A symbolic statement of this development is Michael Walzer's essay "The Triumph of Just War Theory (and the Dangers of Success)." Walzer's essay reflects how the basic categories of the traditional ethic have established a framework for analysis and argument about war and peace.[19] The framework involves criticism of the theory as well as support of it. An example of how the categories of the traditional doctrine have been adopted (and adapted) is the use of them in the "Responsibility to Protect" initiative which translates the moral arguments of Just War into the legal and political standards of the United Nations and sovereign states. The danger here is that carefully constructed theological and philosophical categories can be captured and eroded of essential content; they can become rationalizations of policies rather than restraints on them. The positive potential, however, is to move the normative arguments (on religion, ethics, and law) closer to the center of policy discourse and decision-making. Walzer's essay makes the point that those who hold the theory must be guardians of its use.

Second, in somewhat paradoxical but interesting fashion, the expansion of Just War theory in the secular debate has been matched within some religious communities by an effort to limit its role in religious discourse. The word "limit" here is not intended to dismiss or reject the traditional doctrine. It is, rather, to propose that the focus of the traditional doctrine—to legitimize and to restrain the use of force—should not be *all* that religious traditions bring to issues of war and peace. Particularly in the Christian context, the primary home of the traditional doctrine, the religious discussions today use an old distinction between negative and positive conceptions of peace to expand the parameters of the religious analysis, ministry and witness in the quest for peace.[20] Negative peace focuses upon preventing, containing and limiting the resort to war while retaining the understanding that some are "just"; this has been the primary focus of Just War theory. Positive peace focuses upon the component elements of peace—the idea that peace must be "built" through the protection of human rights and the promotion of social justice, within states and among states. The Second Vatican Council, in its document *Gaudium et Spes*, both affirmed the traditional ethic of war and provided its own affirmation of a positive conception of peace:

> Peace is not merely the absence of war. Nor can it be reduced solely to the maintenance of a balance of power between enemies. . . . Instead it is rightly and appropriately called "an enterprise of justice" (Isa. 32:7). Peace results from that harmony built into human society by its divine Founder, and actualized by men as they thirst after ever greater justice.[21]

The Vatican text appeared at the very height of the Cold War and to some degree was overshadowed by its discussion of deterrence and protection of civilians in war. But the post–Cold War conflicts within states have focused attention on the possibilities of prevention of conflict, and the need for rebuilding states and civil societies after conflict. This focus, now recognized in both religious and secular circles, comprises distinct elements of "peace-building."[22] Michael Walzer, in *Arguing about War*, called early for a "post ius bellum" addition to the Just War theory. Secular institutions, at the international and state level, were convinced by the experience of the 1990s that coercive intervention, however necessary in some cases, was insufficient in most unless followed by stabilizing initiatives like peace-building. Within the religious community, discussion of peacebuilding and just peace policies arose through reflection on the potential to complement and supplement the traditional ethics of war with a theology of peace. The resources of the religious communities involve a multidimensional presence in a globalized world, traditions of ethical and theological analysis, experience of specific communities and individuals in conflict situations and a history of relationships with issues of war and peace. The call for peace-building and just peacemaking arises from a desire to fill out the framework of analysis of war and peace. There are different conceptions of how to relate the traditional ethic of Just War to the recent reflections on positive conceptions of peace. My own view is they are distinct efforts, can and should be complementary and are both necessary. Neither is sufficient by itself. The world is too dangerous and too prone to unauthorized violence to deny appropriate authorities the right and responsibility to use limited force. The wars of the same world are too destructive to ignore either preventative diplomacy or peacebuilding.

The final consideration of this chapter is to return to Little's work in light of what has been examined here in the world of politics, and the world of religion and ethics. The survey of both has been necessarily described in broad strokes and that characteristic will continue.

First, it is clear that Little has consistently held a version of Just War ethics. Attention to the problem of the use of force has marked his writings from the late 1960s through 2014. It is fair to say that this has not been his primary academic interest; human rights, for example, appear more frequently in his bibliography than the ethic of war, but Little's work has mirrored change in warfare. In the 1960s and 1970s he addressed the dominant and divisive issue of U.S. policy in Vietnam. In a fascinating lecture Little gave at St. Olaf's College in 2007,[23] he traced his own changing judgments in Vietnam, adopting his own version of a critique of U.S. policy based, it would seem, on the "moral possibility of success" criteria of Just War thought. What is striking about his retrospective analysis is his attention to the functional role of moral arguments in policy debate and the way in which Just War principles can serve to discipline the interaction of empirical data and moral principles. Little's abiding concern as a moralist about method, clarification of concepts and critique of moral argument came through in the St. Olaf lecture and provided more important insight than his specific positions on the Vietnam case. The same attention to the structure and role of Just War theory is manifested over twenty years later when Little addressed humanitarian intervention.[24]

Second, as noted above, while the ethics of war has never been absent from Little's work, his bibliography does not indicate virtually any attention to the complexities of the nuclear age, either in terms of the viability of Just War theory in the face of this new kind of force, or the questions Ramsey and others pursued about the details of the strategic debate on nuclear targeting and noncombatant immunity. At the time those issues dominated moral argument (1960s through 1980s), Little's work took him in different directions.

Third, when the end of the Cold War shifted predominant attention from nuclear weapons to the very different problems of intrastate warfare, the issues, like human rights, which had come to be central for him, suited him for these questions of internal warfare. His role at the U.S. Institute of Peace required attention to these issues and his interests in interreligious dialogue, religious and philosophical ethics and the rising significance of nationalism were at the heart of the *internal* causes of the wars of the 1990s. When he addresses the *external* dimension of these cases, and thus the permissibility or necessity of armed humanitarian intervention, Little supports the moral legitimacy of the idea, but does so with much inner tension in his argument. The tension arises from Little's strong general support for the role of the UN Charter, and for the tradition of international law. As Catherine Guicherd examined in detail, within the UN system there is political-legal tension between the perspective of the UN Charter, and the content of the UN Declaration of Human Rights.[25] The UN Charter, rooted in the Westphalian tradition, protects the twin concepts of state sovereignty and the rule of nonintervention. The two are treated as complementary. Little is conscious of the strength of these ideas: "Forceful intervention in the internal affairs of a sovereign state without Security Council authorization, whether for humanitarian or any other reasons, is clearly outlawed by the charter."[26] Both the Guicherd and Little articles (as well as Kofi Annan, whom Little cites) point to the need for a revision of the UN Charter to address problems of intrastate war, and to bring coherence to the normative content of the UN system. I find their position exactly right, but I have some difference with Little's statement of his case. In his article, "Humanitarian Intervention: A Theoretical Approach," Little lays stress on the inability of the Just War ethic to provide clear guidance on humanitarian intervention. I would argue that the gap lies principally between the moral argument of Just War and the legal doctrine of the UN Charter. It is, it seems to me, a classical case of international jurisprudence and the way forward lies in using an adaptation of the Just War ethic to call for a revision of the Charter's position. The UN Charter is clear on the permissibility of the use of force to resist aggression by one state against others; the memories of the 1930s and the causes of World War II exercised decisive influence on the UN Charter. As Little observes, extending legitimation to humanitarian intervention would represent "a revolution in international understanding that will hardly be welcome in many quarters."[27] Resistance to the idea there is, but the ravages of the 1990s have produced a chorus of moral-legal support for UN Charter revision.

Here is where I believe the Just War ethic provides a structured argument for revision. Essentially (I have tried to argue) it is possible to recast the Just War legitimation for (limited) war at the interstate level into an argument for morally justifiable humanitarian intervention.[28] Without rehearsing the case here, it amounts to respecting the value of the nonintervention norm as a prima facie duty, then defining a quite limited list of exceptions to the duty, then establishing three levels of authorization: Security Council first, regional authorization if the Council deadlocks (e.g., Kosovo) and single state interventions only in the most extreme cases (e.g., Rwanda). The transposition of the moral argument into black-letter law is a formidable challenge. But the tensions are greater at the legal level than they are, I believe, within the moral doctrine.

Finally, Little's work of the 1990s led him inevitably into the post-9–11 debate about U.S. policy and the role of the United Nations in addressing transnational terrorism. Little, as noted above, had been one of the voices in the 1990s pressing for explicit attention to the role of religion in world politics. He identified, as the two principle areas of religious impact, nationalism and terrorism.[29] Both were at stake in 9–11, then in Afghanistan and Iraq. In pressing the case for the importance of religious analysis, Little concentrated less on the ethics of war and more on the positive capacities of religious peacebuilding. In a 2005 address at Case Western Reserve University, he proposed, "that there has been a kind of revolution in thinking about violent conflict and the constructive role of religion."[30] He described his own work as an effort to shape the "hermeneutics of peace," seeking consensus among religious, "that the pursuit of justice and peace by peaceful means is a sacred priority,"[31] which should be used as an internal critique by religious traditions regarding texts and practices.

Inevitably, however, the 9–11 attack and the U.S. engagement in two wars in Muslim countries required Little's attention. In an address at Harvard's Weatherhead Center for International Affairs in late 2002, he offered an insight into his basic perspective. Even before the invasion of Iraq in 2003, Little argued that: "[e]ver since the September 11 attacks of last year, I have resolutely believed that the response to terrorism, by the United States and other nations, ought to be undertaken squarely within the confines of what I will call the 'international system.'"[32] The system to which he refers is the UN Charter and supporting texts of human rights and humanitarian law. While Little recognized the response in Afghanistan as corresponding to these restraints, his view, even in 2002, of U.S. policy toward Iraq, was one of defiance of international norms and headed for a "neo-colonial undertaking."[33] This early critique of Iraq policy was joined in varying degrees during the last decade by a substantial body of opinion within the United States and around the world.

A decade after 9–11, however, there remain broad normative issues which go beyond case analysis of both Afghanistan and Iraq. While the phrase "war on terror" has thankfully been dropped from the U.S. policy lexicon, the elements of that strategy leave issues that the Just War ethic must address. The first is relatively straight forward: it is defining the status of nonstate actors and the use of force. Both legal and moral traditions have sought to keep proper authority strictly limited. Little's useful baseline of the international system as the norm for addressing terrorism means that nonstate actors have little chance of being designated as "proper authorities." Second, more complex is the various meanings of intervention; shortly after 9–11, United States officials argued that sixty countries in the world harbored terrorists. Did this mean that the U.S. or any country attacked could follow the logic of terrorism wherever it led? Some commentators argued that those who supported humanitarian intervention in the 1990s had undermined the nonintervention rule in its entirety. But this confuses two kinds of intervention: what I would call Great Power intervention and humanitarian intervention. They differ in purpose, often in motive and in their impact on the international system. The nonintervention rule was designed to moderate Great Power conflict, the kind the "war on terror" involves. One can hold it in stringent fashion and still find room for well-defined, limited humanitarian uses of force.

A world capable of three distinct kinds of war is much in need of normative restraint and direction. Little is still at work and thankfully so.

NOTES

[1] James Gustafson, "Roman Catholic and Protestant Interaction in Ethics: An Interpretation," in *Theological Studies* 50 (March 1989): 44–69.

[2] James T. Johnson, *Just War Tradition and the Restraint of War: A Moral and Historical Inquiry* (Princeton, NJ: Princeton University Press, 1981), 121–171.

[3] Cf. D. B. Robertson, ed., *Love and Justice: Selections from the Shorter Writings of Reinhold Niebuhr* (New York, N.Y.: Meridian Books-The World Publishing Company), 241–260; Richard Wightman Fox, *Reinhold Niebuhr: A Biography* (New York, NY: Pantheon Books, 1985), 224–248.

[4] John C. Ford, S.J., "The Morality of Obliteration Bombing," in *Theological Studies* 5 (1944): 261–309.

[5] John Courtney Murray, S.J., *We Hold These Truths: Catholic Reflections on the American Proposition* (New York, NY: Sheed and Ward, 1960), 265.

[6] A sampling of Niebuhr's analysis and commentary on war and peace is found in D. B. Robertson, ibid.; Murray has four chapters in *We Hold These Truths* on "The Uses of Doctrine"; Ramsey's voluminous writings on the ethics of war are collected (but not entirely) in *The Just War: Force and Political Responsibility* (New York, NY: Charles Scribner's, 1968).

[7] See, for example, "The Atomic Bomb," and "The Hydrogen Bomb," in D. B. Robertson, ibid., 232–237.

⁸ A selective sampling would include: James Douglass, *The Nonviolent Cross: A Theology of Revolution and Peace* (New York, NY: Macmillan, 1966); Stanley Hauerwas, *Vision and Virtue: Essays in Christian Ethical Reflection* (Notre Dame, IN: Fides Publishers, Inc, 1974), 197–221; Paul Peachey, "Minorities with a Mission in the Church," in Paul Peachey, ed., *Peace, Politics, and the People of God* (Philadelphia, PA: Fortress Press, 1986), 25–46.

⁹ The literature on the kinds and causes of war in the last sixty years is enormous. Again, a sampling: Lawrence Freedman, *The Evolution of Nuclear Strategy* (New York, NY: St. Martin's Press, 1983); McGeorge Bundy, *Danger and Survival: Choices About the Bomb in the First Fifty Years* (New York, NY: Random House, 1988); Laura W. Reed and Carl Kaysen, eds., *Emerging Norms of Justified Intervention* (Cambridge, MA: American Academy of Arts and Sciences, 1993), 7–15, 15–36, 91–110; Philip Zelikow, "The Transformation of National Strategy," *National Interest* 71 (Spring 2003): 17–28; Barry Posen, "The Struggle Against Terrorism: Grand Strategy Strategy and Tactics," *International Security* 26 (Winter 2001–2002): 39–55.

¹⁰ Henry A. Kissinger, *Nuclear Weapons and Foreign Policy* (New York, NY: Doubleday Anchor, 1957), 1.

¹¹ David Little, "Religion, Conflict and Peace," in *Case Western Reserve Journal of International Law* 38 (2006): 96.

¹² Again, the literature on humanitarian intervention is enormous; for the normative history of intervention cf. R. J. Vincent, *Nonintervention and International Order* (Princeton, NJ: Princeton University Press, 1974); for a policy perspective cf. Stanley Hoffmann, "The Politics and Ethics of Military Intervention," in *Survival* 37 (1995–1996): 29–51; for a critique cf. Stephen J. Stedman, "The New Interventionists," in *Foreign Affairs* 72 (1993): 1–16.

¹³ Cf. Michael Walzer, "The Politics of Rescue," in *Social Research* 62 (Spring 1995): 53–63; and Michael Ignatieff, "The Seductiveness of Moral Disgust," in *Social Research* 62 (Spring 1995):77–98. The issue [*Social research* 62 (Spring 1995)] is dedicated to the theme: "Rescue: The Paradoxes of Virtue."

¹⁴ Catherine Guicherd, "International Law and the War in Kosovo," in *Survival* 41 (Summer 1999): 19–34.

¹⁵ Kofi Annan, "Annual Report to the General Assembly" (Sept. 20, 1999): "While the genocide in Rwanda will define for our generation the consequences of inaction in the face of mass murder, the more recent conflict in Kosovo has prompted important questions about the consequences of action in the absence of complete unity on the part of the "international community." (http://www.un.org/News/Press/docs/errors/99999999.sgsm7136.html Last accessed: June 3, 2014).

¹⁶ Michael Walzer, "After 9–11: Five Questions About Terrorism," in *Arguing About War* (New Haven, CT: Yale University Press), 130–142; Michael Howard, "Managing in Emergency," in *Foreign Affairs* 81 (Jan–Feb 2002): 8–13.

¹⁷ Murray, ibid., 263.

¹⁸ Daniel Philpott, "The Challenge of September 11 to Secularism in International Relations," in *World Politics* 55 (2002): 66–95; Eva Bellin, "Faith in Politics: New Trends in the Study of Religion and Politics," in *World Politics* 60 (2008): 315–347.

[19] Walzer, ibid., 3–22.

[20] Negative peace—the absence of war—is correlated with the ethics of war; positive peace connotes more than preventing violence.

[21] Vatican II, "Gaudium et Spes" (The Pastoral Constitution on the Church in the Modern World) in Walter M. Abbott, S.J., ed., *The Documents of Vatican II* (New York, NY: Guild Press, 1966), para. 78; 290.

[22] David Little uses the following forms of keeping and building peace: peace enforcement, peacemaking, peacekeeping and peacebuiling. Cf. "Religion, Conflict and Peace," ibid., 102.

[23] David Little, "The Role of the Academic in Times of War," Lecture at St. Olaf's College, Northfield, MI (September 27, 2007).

[24] David Little, "Humanitarian Intervention: A Theoretical Approach," in J.I. Coffey and Charles T. Mathews, eds., *Religion, Law and the Use of Force* (Ardsley, NY: Transnational Publishers, 2002), 117–128.

[25] Guicherd, ibid., 19–25.

[26] David Little, "Humanitarian Intervention," ibid., 117.

[27] Ibid., 126.

[28] J. Bryan Hehir, "Military Intervention and National Sovereignty: Recasting the Relationship," in ed., Jonathan Moore, *Hard Choices: Moral Dilemmas in Humanitarian Intervention* (Lanham, MD: Rowman and Littlefield Publishers, Inc., 1998), 42–46.

[29] David Little, "Religion, Conflict and Peace," ibid., 100.

[30] Ibid., 96.

[31] Ibid., 97.

[32] David Little, "Iraq, The United States and the Future of the International System," in *Centerpiece* 16 (Fall 2002): 2.

[33] Ibid., 10.

10.
War and the Right to Life: Orthodox Christian Perspectives

Marian Gh. Simion

Considering the semantic intricacies of "the right to life," as elicited by Article 3 of the Universal Declaration of Human Rights, this chapter investigates the ultimate convergence between human rights philosophy and Orthodox Christianity on the question of collective violence. As human rights philosophy had been central to David Little's intellectual legacy, I hope this chapter will make a contribution—albeit from an exclusively theological perspective—to the stance on the "right to life," as defined in the ethical tradition of Orthodox Christianity. The general opposition to violence, along with a lack of consensus over the adoption of Just War theory represents one of Orthodox Christianity's foremost structural assets to human rights philosophy. Its dogmatic refusal to accept human sovereignty over the death penalty reinforces the right to life, while humanity's free will is upheld as theodicy.

In general, Orthodox theologians agree that the Orthodox Church does not have a Just War theory in the Western sense. While abhorring war, historical records indicate that the Orthodox Christians have often been involved in brutal military enterprises, cases in which, in the public square, the Orthodox Church failed to remain loyal to the pacifist principles of the Gospel and early Christian martyrdom. Concerned both with preserving its reputation of a martyr church and with the creation of a public image of an anticipatory Samaritan, the Orthodox Church made concessions to the state by occasionally endorsing its authority to use lethal force against internal and external aggression. These concessions were broad in nature and were only made out of a conscious strategic interest of both church and state to protect the defenseless against any form of abuse and also maintain political stability.

In contemporary theological circles, the "just war" paradigm is often perceived as a proxy endorsement of collective violence, by contrast with the "justifiable war" paradigm (sometimes coined as a "lesser evil"), which is more acceptable in a terminological sense. Nevertheless, expressions such as "just" or "justifiable" are treated generally as a sine qua non Trojan horse against the pacifist legacy of Orthodox Christianity. At the same time, the semantic difference between "just" and "justifiable" should not be underestimated, as the expression "justifiable" can often represent the answer to church's occasional complicity to violence. Ironically, this suspicion runs contrary to the original Western intent behind the Just War theory, which, by appealing to reason, strived to set obstacles against the rush to violence.

The lack of consensus that Orthodox Christianity displays over the justifiable use of force emerges from several factors such as (1) comprehensive theological opposition, (2) church-state relations, (3) legislative jurisdiction, (4) influences of the law of *jihād*, (5) the mechanisms of paradox and scapegoat, (6) Slavic cultural influence, (7) nationalism and patriotism, (8) canon law's ambivalence on the use of force, (9) the dilemma of military service, (10) the principle of causality, and (11) a feminine defense paradigm. As a result, in order to investigate how Orthodox Christianity reconciled the pacifist principle of the Gospel with its duty to protect the weak and vulnerable in face of violent abuse, one must start by looking into the nature of church-state relations, Byzantine Canon Law, as well as theological, historical, liturgical, and ecclesiological factors. This is because the Orthodox Church never governed public affairs, and, as a result, was never in control of an army to draft and develop law enforcement policies, as was the case with the Western Church following the fall of Rome under the Visigoths in A.D. 410. These duties simply fell under the jurisdiction of the state, following a specific legislative procedure. Thus, when dealing with the issue of internal or external use of force, the Orthodox Church acted exclusively from an advisory perspective.

Comprehensive Theological Opposition

In its history, the Eastern Church offered a comprehensive theological opposition to war. Highly influential Greek and Latin Church Fathers, who lived and wrote during the formative years of Christianity, strongly criticized military enterprises of the state while trying to maintain the consciousness of guilt and penance for soldiers. Following a detailed literature review of the early Christian references to war, John C. Cadoux concludes that the early Christian writers clearly indicate, "how closely warfare and murder were connected in Christian thought by their possession of a common element—homicide. . . . The strong disapprobation felt by Christians for war was due to its close relationship with the deadly sin that sufficed to keep the man guilty of it permanently outside the Christian community."[1] In terms of the relevance of these writings throughout the development of the early church, Roland Bainton concludes that "the history of the church is viewed by many as a progressive fall from a state of primitive purity, punctuated by reformations which seek a return to a pristine excellence. The first church fathers are thus held to have been the best commentators, and if the early church was pacifist then pacifism is the Christian position."[2] Such an attitude toward the relevance of the early church Fathers is the norm in Eastern Christianity, where any acceptable theological work is expected to be consonant with these early precepts, so as to conform to this "primitive purity."

Another significant aspect was the negative attitude toward the weakness of the human body, which was viewed as a source of spiritual failure. This attitude started during the period of anti-Christian persecutions, and grew within the monastic circles. Thus, the "war" against the human passions had managed to transfer the concept of warfare from a real life situation to an internal human passion. As a result, one no longer had to wage war against the invader, but against one's own passions stirred by the Devil, the true invisible enemy. This not only created disapproving attitudes toward physical war, but led to an increased miscommunication between real life situations and spiritual goals. During the Ottoman period, Orthodox elders known as the *Kollyvades*[3] revived the early tradition of the Desert Fathers by collecting seminal spiritual works on prayer and later incorporating them into a large collection known as *Philokalia*. *Philokalia*, in conjunction with Lorenzo Scupolli's highly influential theological work *The Unseen Warfare*, and the *hesychastic movement*, together served as mechanisms of discouragement against any spirit of revolt against their Muslim oppressors.

Church-State Relations

In the history of church-state relations, the Orthodox Church has been subject to a variety of governing systems that manifested attitudes ranging from persecution to power sharing. In the West, the destruction of Rome in A.D. 410 by the Visigoths left a church immature and vulnerable to embracing claims for political governance, while in the East the church faced this political vacuum only a thousand years later, when the Byzantine Empire fell under the Ottomans in 1453.

In Eastern Christianity, during the first fifteen centuries, the Byzantine model of church-state separation implied that each institution had specific responsibilities toward the public. In theory, according to the principle of *synallilia* (co-mutuality) or *symphonia* coined during the reign of Emperor Justinian (A.D. 527–565), the church was entrusted with the spiritual salvation of the community, and the state with its material well-being, including internal policing and external defense, even though tensions were often present due to mimetic rivalries. According to Georgios Matzaridis, "not everything developed smoothly; tendencies toward overstepping one's bounds, mainly from the side of the state, have been noted. Powerful emperors many times wanted to intervene in matters that were of the competence of the church. Their dispositions, however, met the resistance of ecclesiastical agents, particularly of monks and lay members of the church."[4]

As a result, while the church never made any decision about war, theologians approached this issue from an advisory perspective, ensuring that the state, in its alleged concern with the defense of the community, did not overstate its role. Basically, the church made it un-canonical for its clergy to take government jobs, particularly in the military, as their duty was to proclaim the Gospel. A wide range of canons imposed deposition of clergy involved with "worldly affairs." Three Canonical Collections (*Hippolytean Canons*, *Egyptian Church Order*, and *The Testament of our Lord*) of the mid-fourth century had specific stipulations concerning the involvement of the clergy in the military. According to Cadoux, these canons "mark clearly and distinctly the views which prevailed in wide circles"; however, "they possessed no generally binding power."[5] Additionally, the *Apostolic Cannons* (Canon VI; Canon LXXXI; Canon LXXXIII—forbidding clergy participation in public offices and military), the canons adopted by the *First Ecumenical Council* (Canon XII), *Fourth Ecumenical Council* (Canon III, Canon VII—forbidding married clergy and monks to participate in public offices and military), *Local Council of Sardica*: Canon VIII (forbidding clergy to go before a civil magistrate), and *Local Council of Constantinople* (A.D. 861: Canon XI) appear relevant to clerical non-involvement in military or state affairs.[6]

Legislative Jurisdiction

In Eastern Christianity, the codification of Civil Law and Canon Law took place during the same period of time, and as parallel projects.[7]

Under the Byzantine State, the Canon Law was part of the Civil Law, and it included collections such as *Nomocanons*, *State Codex*-es, *Novelae* (laws regulating dogmatic decisions of the church), *Institutiones*, *Ecloga*, *Prohiron*, *Epanagoga*, *Basilicalae*, and *Hexabiblos*.[8] With bishops acting as public judges,[9] the church ruled over aspects of family law,[10] while the question of public defense was under the sole legislative jurisdiction of the state.[11] Although somewhat overstated, this model of legislative jurisdiction was also implemented by Prince Vladimir in Russia, following his conversion to Orthodox Christianity, as he established two courts: one religious, one secular. Based on this dual court system, a plaintiff or a defendant had the right to choose between a bishop as president of the court, or a lay presiding judge. As Dimitri Pospielovsky writes, "[t]he ecclesial court received jurisdiction over all moral transgressions of the laity: matrimonial and divorce matters, polygamy, blasphemy, foul language, matters related to dowry, kidnapping of brides, rape, property fights within families."[12]

Under the Ottomans, the policy of *millet*[13] reduced the applicability of Canon Law exclusively to the Christian community.[14] The legal jurisdiction over internal and external defense was solely the responsibility of the Ottoman State.[15] The public law of most medieval semi-autonomous states subjected to the Ottoman rule included Canon Law as well, and it replicated the Byzantine model to a large extent.[16] Some of the widely used collections included *Ton aghion Sinodon*, *Nea Sinatroisis* (1761), *Sillogi Panton ton ieron ke tion kanonon* (1787), *Kontakion* (1798), *Pidalion* (1800), *Athenian Syntagm* (1852), *Canonical Regulations*, and others.[17] With the creation of nation states, and with the secularization process of the mid-nineteenth century, public law had eliminated completely the jurisdictional claims of the Canon Law in the public life. Consequently, while Canon Law remained fundamental for the new statutes of national churches, in public life its weight was reduced to mere ethical guidelines.

Mimetic Influence of the *Law of Jihād*

With the Islamic military advances in the East, both the church and the state had to join forces not only in fighting the aggressors, but also in learning the rules of the enemy, particularly when attempting to negotiate peace agreements.[18] In this sense, the interpretation offered by Islam on the meaning of sacrifice was often mirrored by Christianity as a matter of mere pragmatism. As a result, it became mandatory for the church to doctrinally engage its counterpart on the enemy's side, who, in the words of Saint John of Damascus, were nothing but Christian heretics. For the Muslims, such dialogue was acceptable only in the context of truces permissible under the conditions imposed by *dar al sulh* (the house of treaty).[19]

Situated at the Arab-Byzantine frontier (*thughūr*), two eighth-century Arab scholar-ascetics, Abū Ishāq al-Fazārī and Abdallah al-Mubārak, were among the earliest and perhaps the most influential Muslim scholars to debate the laws of war in terms of *siyar* (Islamic international law that implies treaties) and *jihād* (implying confrontation). On the Russian front, during the Tatar/Mongol yoke that lasted from 1238 until 1480, the Russians often had to make war and peace with their Muslim enemies, particularly due to the cruelty of the Tatar tax collectors, *baskaks*.[20]

A first concrete example that displays a possible influence of the law of *jihād* over Russian Orthodox justification of war is the alleged conversation that took place between Constantine–Cyril and Caliph Mutawakkil[21] in A.D. 851 in the context of a Christian diplomatic mission to the Saracenes.[22] A second case of suspected influence of *jihād* was recorded in the mid–960s, in the context of a dispute between Patriarch Polyeukos of Constantinople and Emperor Nikephoros Phokas. To further glorify his heroes, the emperor demanded that his soldiers, who had been killed on the battlefield, be canonized as martyrs and declared saints of the church. The Patriarch successfully opposed him by citing Saint Basil's *Canon 13*, with the interpretation that the soldiers who killed on the battlefield may be guilty of violating the commandment "Thou shall not kill" (Exod. 20:13).[23] While this example of jurisprudence relates more to the relationship between church and state, it nevertheless reveals that this view of martyrdom was understood by the Byzantine emperor as an active path of defending faith through war rather than as a passive act specific to the first three centuries. As a result, the emperor's understanding of martyrdom was highly similar to the concept of martyrdom "in the path of Allah," whereby one sacrifices oneself for missionary purpose in a military sense.[24]

A third example of a possible influence of *jihād* over Eastern Christianity is the service of blessing soldiers and weapons in the Slavo–Byzantine rite, particularly in the context of the final blessing bestowed upon the soldier, which says, "Let the blessing of Triune God, Father, Son, and Holy Spirit, come down on and remain upon these weapons and those who carry them *for the protection of the truth of Christ*, Amen."[25] From a historical perspective, it is possible that this rite displays a Western Christian influence. At the same time, however, the Islamic influence cannot be underestimated. It seems natural to assume that this prayer must have been invoked for the purpose of protecting "the truth of Christ," in the context of Islamic practice of forced conversion of its subjects.

A fourth possible case of mutual influence between *jihād* and Eastern Christianity is the concept of salvation through spiritual war. This is visible in the second millennium's literature of *Philokalia* as well as in the concept of "the greater jihād," manifested as an inner struggle for spiritual ascent. Striking similarities can be noted between the Orthodox hesychasm (quietist asceticism), and the spiritual struggle of the *Murid* (seeker) in Islamic Sufism, as particularly recommended by Hakeem Tirmidhi's spiritual treatise *On Jihād al-Nafs* (Fighting the Ego). Although reserved to secluded monks, Mantzaridis insists that "the significance of hesychasm for the social life of the faithful cannot be underestimated . . . the contribution of hesychasm in the sustenance of peace and the perseverant tolerance of long term subjugation to captors of other religions and beliefs is well known."[26]

The Mechanisms of Paradox and Scapegoat

The paradox mentality, which in many ways is specific to numerous Orthodox subcultures, had infused a sense of comfort with various dissonances within the principle of causality, particularly when this principle faced illogical arguments. Such ambivalence between the involvement in brutal collective hostilities and the clear theological refusal to validate the instrumental use of defensive violence as a public good can be puzzling to Western logic, in its occasional encounter with Orthodox Christianity. This theological attitude can appear as rather counter cultural, bold enough to even contradict humanity's primary instincts for possession and self-defense. Nevertheless, making the case for a successful symbiosis between phenomenological traits of religious instincts and an institutionalization process that remained anchored in non-violence, one can find no dissonance between human rights advocacy and Orthodox Christian commitment to "the right to life."

Often understood as religion's contribution to social stability, the scapegoat[27] mechanism is deeply embedded in Orthodoxy as a consciousness which virtualized the enemy into a spiritual surrogate entity, Satan. At the doctrinal level, the unequivocal teaching that all humans are made in God's image prevented the demonization of the enemies except, of course, in specific cases, where such a theological position never succeeded in becoming the common social conscience. A case in point might be Slavic Orthodoxy, which still displays an elite-driven version of Orthodox culture.[28] This demonization found expression in sacred art through various intrusions in iconography, such as in the depiction of Saint Demetrios sitting on the top of a horse and "killing" emperor Maximian, in a severe violation of history, or in the depiction of Jesus holding a sword in Visoki Dečani Monastery in Kosovo that contradicts history and the essence of the Gospel. In the case of Slavic Christianity, during times of war, the immediate tendency was to return to the surviving pre-Christian folk manifestations of dualistic antagonism.[29] Additionally perhaps, the process of transition from paganism to Christianity (which resurrected and escalated the almost-forgotten Early Christian demonology),[30] posed an easy temptation for a convergence between military foes and malefic spiritual entities whose death was deemed as necessary.

The Slavic Cultural Influence

With the Christianization of the Slavs, a new worldview started penetrating Eastern Christianity. In terms of doctrine of defense, the inherent dualistic culture of the Slavs, deriving perhaps from the *Belobog-Chernobog* antagonism,[31] has unavoidably led to a dualistic Christian worldview, which, in combination with Christian asceticism, saw good and evil as identifiable with spirit and matter, respectively. This dualistic worldview often emerged in heretical movements, which either viewed the human body as evil, such as the Bogomils, Khlystys, and Skoptzys,[32] or simply demonized political establishments, as was the case with the Bogomils and the Raskol anarchists. Due to this inherent dualism, the Slavs seem to have left a hefty influence on the justification of war, which strongly contradicted the pacifistic nature of the Gospel. In a sociological sense, dualism favored not only an us-versus-them attitude but also proceeded to the demonization of adversaries and the justification of violence.

Nationalism and Patriotism

Challenging Christian universalism—whereby humanity is created in the image of God (Gen. 1:26–27), and the fact that "there is neither Jew nor Greek" (Gal. 3:28)—nationalism became a messianic political philosophy claiming that one can be "saved" from the dangers of this world only by belonging to a nation that organized itself into a state. Created in Western Europe and emphasizing the political unit of nation-state, nationalism was soon exported into Eastern Europe where it developed new depths of political dualism, thus dividing the Orthodox Christians by lines of history, language, and ascribed territories. If until then, the Ottomans (under whom a large part of the Orthodox Christians lived), offered an a priori ghetto recognition of a unified Christian community (*Rum millet* or "Roman Nation"), nationalism divided this Christian community between smaller autonomous and autocephalous Orthodox churches. While selected Orthodox theologians expressed discomfort with nationalism for reasons emerging from the traditional Christian universalism, the strongest and yet ineffective opposition came from the Ecumenical Patriarchate, as numerous high-ranking Greek bishops and metropolitans lost significant administrative privileges in churches that became autocephalous. At the Local Synod of Constantinople in 1872—a synod ignited by the unilateral establishment of a separate episcopate by the Bulgarian community in Constantinople[33]—both nationalism and racism were condemned in the strongest terms.

Canon Law's Ambivalence on the Use of Force

In its legal tradition, the Orthodox Church had consistently used a canonical procedure that was based on compassion and adaptability rather than on penitence, and it often raised the question of defensive force directly and indirectly. Yet, the canons used in this procedure served largely as advisory guidelines and not as effective laws. From an institutional perspective, this canonical procedure refers to the *internal* self-defense of the members of a society against lawbreakers, and to the *external* self-defense of a state against a foreign invasion. In terms of *internal* self-defense, the church favors a more penitential perspective, due to the fact that the offender can be identified as an individual endangering the life of the community. As far as *external* self-defense is concerned, the Orthodox Church seems to be more restrictive in endorsing war for the very fact that in a war two allegedly innocent soldiers are confined into a situation that they have no choice but to impose the death penalty on each other, even in the absence of guilt. Never organized as a state, the Orthodox Church made concessions to the state for strategic and pastoral reasons. Acting on moral grounds, the procedure used by local Orthodox Churches, when in limited situations they sanctioned the use of defensive force, was mainly *consultative* with a *concessional* component. The *concessional component* appeared mainly when the state expected (even coerced) the church to offer its endorsement for military action, and not when the church enjoyed full freedom and autonomy, thus acting as a moral factor on the basis of pragmatism and ethics of non-violence. The *consultative* nature of the canonical procedure was designed to maintain the influence of the church within the state, serving as an interventional mechanism which appealed to the consciousness of the soldiers on the battlefield.[34]

The Dilemma of Military Service

Two of the most widely cited canons on the military service, which had been universally adopted by the Orthodox Church, include *First Epistle of Athanasius the Great, addressed to the monk Amun*, which favors the imposition of the death penalty by the soldiers over their combatant enemies, and Saint Basil's *Canon 13*, which forbids communion to soldiers who killed combatant enemies.

On the one hand, the *First Epistle of Athanasius the Great, addressed to the monk Amun* unambiguously states that "it is not permissible to murder anyone (Exod. 20:13), yet in war it is praiseworthy and lawful to slay the adversaries. Thus at any rate those who have distinguished themselves in war are entitled to and are accorded great honors, and columns are erected in memory of them reciting their exploits."[35] This canon represents a clear illustration of an objective concession made by the church in order to impose conformity with orthodoxy, as well as to sustain the morale of the Christians from North Africa, struggling to survive the forced conversion to Islam. Nevertheless, Mantzaridis doubts whether this canon ever represented the position of the church, or it rather represented a mimetic expression describing the political behavior of an entity beyond the realm of the church. As he writes, this text must not be misconstrued and understood as an ecclesiastical sanction of war-time murders. Here Athanasius the Great is simply presenting the position of the state *vis-à-vis* the murders committed during war. He does not assert that they are endorsed or even permitted by the church, but that they are permissible by the law and extolled by the world. This is what the carefully selected terms "praiseworthy and lawful" express. *What is lawful is not necessarily also Christian.* And what is praiseworthy by some is not, ecclesiastically speaking, a wondrous act. The ecclesiastical position in this text is formulated with the verbs "remissible and pardonable."[36]

On the other hand, *Canon 13* of Saint Basil the Great states that "our Fathers did not consider murders committed in the course of wars to be classifiable as murders at all, on the score, it seems to me, of allowing a pardon to men fighting in defense of sobriety and piety. Perhaps, though, it might be advisable to refuse them communion for three years, on the ground that they are not clean-handed."[37] In this canon, Saint Basil challenges an apparent status quo, whereby the church, on the basis of Saint Athanasius's canonical letter, silently sanctioned the state's use of armed defensive violence. To keep the church and the state aware of their moral responsibilities, Saint Basil considered war as a sinful act, even when conducted for defensive purpose. Therefore, the consciousness of sin and guilt remained a necessary process for the purpose of spiritual salvation of soldiers who killed enemy combatants. Patrick Viscuso's "Christian Participation in Warfare," discusses the debate between Saint Athanasius's *First Epistle* and Saint Basil's *Canon 13*, in light of three prominent Byzantine canonists: John Zonaras (twelfth-century), Theodore Balsamon (twelfth-century), and Matthew Blastares (fourteenth-century). Both John Zonaras and Theodore Balsamon counseled against enforcing Saint Basil's opinion to forbid communion by citing Saint Athanasius's canonical letter which approved (even praised) the killing of enemies during times of war.[38] What is interesting about this jurisprudence, analyzed by Viscuso, is its timing, as the Byzantine Empire was struggling to survive Islamic aggression, the Crusades, and Slavic anarchy in the Balkans. Nevertheless, Matthew Blastares, in his encyclopedic canonical work *The Alphabetical Collection*, argued that Saint Basil's counsel for exclusion from communion was correct and should be enforced on the basis of theological, scriptural, and historical rationales.

The Principle of Causality as Reflected in *Ius ad Bellum*

The classical Western understanding of the Just War theory is anchored into the principle of causality; that defensive violence is often necessary when the innocent is harmed (i.e., just cause for humanitarian reasons). Orthodox Christianity, however, applies this logic at a deeper level, seeing the cause of an invasion as the result of humanity's spiritual failure, and as a progression toward self-destruction rooted in the original sin. For instance, the medieval Moldovan ruler Stephen the Great (1457–1504)—also a recently canonized saint in the Romanian Orthodox Church—in the testament stone (*pisania*) placed at the entrance in the church of Neamțu Monastery—directed to be written that Constantinople fell under the Muslims "because of our sins" (*pentru păcatele noastre*); therefore not because of a more mundane reason such as a foreign invasion. The same argument appears also in his letter to Ivan the Third of Moscow, indicating that the Orthodox lands (e.g., contemporary Greece, Bulgaria, Serbia, and Romania), "fell under the pagans because of our sins."[39]

The Feminine Defense Paradigm

The feminine defense paradigm had been a dominant motif in Orthodox Christianity, which deconstructed the masculinity of war and consistently skewed the meaning of violence away from an exclusive physical expression. This paradigm helped to prevent the adoption of a Just War theory due to structural and phenomenological implications. First, it affected the institutional self-perception of the Orthodox Church; second, it redefined human connectedness; and third, it deeply influenced the spiritual life of the Orthodox Christians in terms of feminine protection, as expressed in devotion to the Virgin Mary.

Institutional Self-Perception

In order to implement it in the sacramental life of the church, Orthodox theologians expanded and applied the *theandric* doctrine (the union of the divine and human natures in Christ) to the relationship between Jesus Christ and the church. One of the most remarkable venues is the metaphor of a mystical marriage, where the church becomes a typology for the feminine, such as "the Bride of Christ" (Eph. 5:22–33).[40] Although this metaphorical analogy is often an obscure component of dogmatic theology, it had been enforced in the liturgical life of the Orthodox Church through mnemonic associations with the family structure. Thus, the message expressed in Eph .5:22–33 had been consistently reinforced through the homiletic tradition in the contexts of the sacrament of marriage. An implicit consequence is that this gender motif affected the church's social self-perception in relation to the state. This self-perception stimulated the church toward adopting social responsibilities fitting for maternal instincts. For instance, the church's jurisdiction over family law and inheritance ensured a more compassionate and distributive sense of justice—a definite alternative to an arguably retributive sense of justice implied by a masculine model.

Redefining Human Connectedness

The theandric doctrine also imported the feminine model as a creational and redemptive theme.[41] Here, the authoritative image of the *Theotokos* ("birth-giver of God"), which during the fifth century had received a meteoric rise in popular devotion, art, and homiletics,[42] was implemented in the Orthodox spirituality through various motifs and mnemonic associations that appealed to the immediate social life. A prominent example is the portrayal of the *Theotokos* by Proclus of Constantinople. In order to emphasize the redemptive role of the *Theotokos* in the history of salvation, Proclus uses various metaphors designed to illustrate the life-giving qualities, the maternal instincts, meekness and the celebration of life. Thus, for Proclus, Virgin Mary is "the spiritual garden of Eden in which dwells the second Adam," "the new Eve, whose obedience nullified the disobedience of her primal mother and fulfilled the saying 'Let us make woman as a helper to man.'" The Virgin Mary is a harbor, a sea, a ship, a wall, a bridge, a city, a palace, a throne, a festival, a workshop, a forge, a book, a flower, a bridal chamber, the morning sky, heaven, and the like.[43] One of the most distinctive portrayals of the Virgin's womb is the conventional image of the workshop (εργαστήριον) "in which the unity of the divine and human nature was fashioned."[44] The effect of such imagery and mnemonic analogies over the Orthodox society was to contribute to a sense of social cohesion, which in essence collectively celebrated meekness and life, rather than valor and sacrificial death—thus discouraging any rush to violence. Furthermore, such illustrations simply maintained that violence leads to alienation, destruction, and death and that it ultimately destroys and humiliates God's own creation.

The Virgin Mary as "Defender General"

Apart from doctrinal and cultural elements designed to influence the collective consciousness, the feminine defense paradigm appears more overtly in the context of Orthodox hymnography, specifically in the Akathist Hymn. As one of the most remarkable spiritual narratives, the Akathist Hymn evokes the miraculous intervention of the Virgin Mary as a "defender general" (τῇ ὑπερμάχῳ στρατηγῷ) of the imperial City. Based on accounts provided by the *Synaxarion* (account of the feast days) and the *Triodion* (liturgical collection with services customized for the Great Lent), in the summer of A.D. 626, the city of Constantinople came under a massive attack conducted simultaneously by the Persians and the Scythians (Avars and Slavs), while Emperor Heraclius was away with the army. Thus, on August 7th, following processions led by Patriarch Sergius around the city, and persistent prayers conducted particularly at the great church of the *Theotokos* at Blachernae (a church located by the Golden Horn), a hurricane sank the enemy ships and dispersed the enemy troops stationed on land. As this narrative was quickly absorbed by the large public, it became a model of faith to put one's hope into the protective qualities of the *Theotokos*, even in military contexts. In fact, miraculous interventions were also reported for similar events in A.D. 677, 717–718, and 860, when the *Theotokos* maneuvered the forces of nature in order to defend the imperial City. As the Akathist Hymn introduces the *Theotokos* as "defender general of the winning" (Τῇ ὑπερμάχῳ στρατηγῷ τὰ νικητήρια), the logical implication is that the imperial City is dedicated to her (Ἀναγράφω σοι ἡ πόλις σου Θεοτόκε), and she becomes the City's most powerful protector. The effect of the Virgin Mary's portrayal as a "defender general" over the consciousness of war cannot be underestimated. In a historical sense, the remembrance of the siege of Constantinople of A.D. 626, as well as the miraculous intervention of the Virgin Mary is often depicted on the outer walls of various churches in Moldova.[45] In a spiritual sense, this portrayal had refocused the public's attention on the spiritual dimensions of war, once the "defender general" image made its way into the Divine Liturgy, where it was repeated on a daily basis. Furthermore, while the "defender general" motif remained exclusively associated with the Virgin Mary, the female defense paradigm was transferred to numerous female saints along with their instinctively peaceful qualities.[46]

Thus, within the spirituality of warfare, the feminine motif had been profound and complex enough to have influenced the attitudes toward war more directly. It is clear that such influences generated attitudes that often prevented wars of aggression,[47] while wars of defense increasingly involved non-violent means. Moreover, with the Virgin Mary's patronage over the imperial City and civil society, the Orthodox Church advocates human interaction (including with enemies), based on sharing of humanity, reconciliation, maternal instincts, nurturing, restoration and recreation of relationships, social connectedness, forgiveness, and meekness.

Conclusion

In conclusion, one could argue that the Orthodox Church has a rather ambiguous record in its endorsement of defensive violence. In spite of terminological tensions, in Orthodox spirituality the typical erudition and flair toward the meaning of death has been ambivalent in the sense that it projected a struggle between antique fatalism and Christian hope. At the same time, the most logical way to ensure that death occurs at the will of the Creator is to be passive about it, rather than dying in an active engagement even if in the defense of the weak and vulnerable. The paradox inherent in the meaning of death also alters the meaning of history from linearity (historic time) to circularity (liturgical time), thus undermining both the logic of causality (fundamental to the Just War theory), as well as the mimesis of conflict. At the spiritual level, this sense of ambivalence can only be clarified in light of the practice of spiritual exercise (ασκήσεις), whereby the members of the church fail and then rise again. By remaining loyal to the teachings on non-retaliation inherent to the Gospel (Matt. 5:38-42), the Orthodox Church has made strong efforts to resist temptations for the justifications of violence and adoption of a Just War theory.

NOTES

[1] John Cadoux, *The Early Christian Attitude To War* (London: Headley Bros Publishers, LTD, 1919), 57.

[2] Roland H. Bainton, *Christian Attitudes Toward War and Peace: A Historical Survey and Critical Re-evaluation* (Nashville, TN: Abingdon, 1979), 66.

[3] Timothy Ware, *The Orthodox Church* (London: Penguin Books, 1993), 100.

[4] Georgios I. Mantzaridis, "Orthodox Observations on Peace and War," in *Just Peace: Orthodox Perspectives*, eds. Semegnish Asfaw, Alexios Chehadeh, and Marian Gh. Simion (Geneva: WCC Publications, 2012), 117–26, 121.

[5] Cadoux, *The Early Christian Attitude To War*, 127.

[6] Denver Cummings, tr., *The Rudder* (Chicago: The Orthodox Christian Educational Society, 1957).

[7] Philip Schaff, "Excursus on the History of the Roman Law and its Relation to the Canon Law," in *The Seven Ecumenical Councils* in NPNF Second Series, vol.14 (Peabody: Hendrickson Publishers, 2004), 24–35.

[8] Ioan N. Floca, *Drept Canonic Ortodox, Legislație și Administrație Bisericească*, vol.1 (București: Editura Institutului Biblic și de Misiune al Bisericii Ortodoxe Române, 1990), 70–150.

[9] Ibid., vol.2, 299–300.

[10] Cummings, *The Rudder*, 977–1007.

[11] Patrick Viscuso, "Christian Participation in Warfare: A Byzantine View," in *Peace and War in Byzantium Essays in Honor of George T. Dennis, S.J.*, eds. Timothy S. Miller and John Nesbitt (Washington, D.C.: Catholic University of America Press, 1995), 33–40.

[12] Dimitri V. Pospielovsky, *The Orthodox Church in the History of Russia* (Crestwood, NY: St. Vladimir's Seminary Press, 1998), 25–26.

[13] Ware, *The Orthodox Church*, 89; Richard Clogg, *A Concise History of Greece* (Cambridge: Cambridge University Press, 1992), 10–11.

[14] Andrew Wheatcroft, *The Ottomans: Dissolving Images* (London: Penguin Books, 1995), 72–74; Steven Runcimann, *The Great Church in Captivity: A Study of the Patriarchate of Constantinople from the Eve of the Turkish Conquest to the Greek War of Independence* (Cambridge: Cambridge University Press, 1985); Ware, *The Orthodox Church*, 89.

[15] Ware, *The Orthodox Church*, 88.

¹⁶ Mircea Păcurariu, *Istoria Bisericii Ortodoxe Române* (Cluj–Napoca: Editura Dacia, 2002), 78–189.

¹⁷ Floca, vol.1, 122–50; vol.2, 304–5.

¹⁸ Michael Bonner, "Some Observations Concerning the Early Development of Jihād on the Arab–Byzantine Frontier," in *Studia Islamica* 75 (1992): 5–31.

¹⁹ Majid Khadduri, *War and Peace in the Law of Islam* (Baltimore, MD: The John Hopkins Press, 1969); John L. Esposito, *Unholy War: Terror in the Name of Islam* (Oxford: Oxford University Press, 2002); Joseph Schacht, *An Introduction to Islamic Law* (Oxford: Clarendon Press, 1964), 148.

²⁰ Pospielovsky, *The Orthodox Church in the History of Russia*, 15, 37.

²¹ Robert Browning, "Byzantine Scholarship," in *Past and Present* 28 (July 1964): 8.

²² Francis Dvornik, *Byzantine Missions among the Slavs: Saint Constantine–Cyril and Methodius* (New Brunswick, NJ: Rutgers University Press, 1970), 286–87; David K. Goodin, "Just War Theory and Eastern Orthodox Christianity: A Theological Perspective on the Doctrinal Legacy of Chrysostom and Constanine–Cyril," in *Theandros: An Online Journal of Orthodox Christian Theology and Philosophy* 2.3 (Spring 2005); JBC: Jubilee Bishops' Council of the Russian Orthodox Church, *The Orthodox Church and Society: The Basis of the Social Concept of the Russian Orthodox Church* (Belleville, MI: St. Innocent/Firebird Publishers, 2000).

²³ John H. Erickson, "An Orthodox Peace Witness?" in *The Fragmentation of the Church and Its Unity in Peacemaking*, eds. Jeffrey Gros and John D. Rempel (Grand Rapids, MI: William B. Eerdmans Publishing Company, 2001), 48–58.

²⁴ Khadduri, *War and Peace in the Law of Islam*, 55–82.

²⁵ My emphasis added. For an English translation of the Serbian version of this prayer together with the ritual itself—as published in the *Euhologion/Trebnik* (Kosovo, 1993)—see http://www.incommunion.org/2004/10/18/chapter-7 (Last accessed: July 2, 2014)

²⁶ Mantzarides, "Orthodox Observations on Peace and War," 126.

²⁷ René Girard, *Violence and the Sacred*, tr. Patrick Gregory (Baltimore, MD: John Hopkins University Press, 1979), 1–67.

²⁸ Tomáš Špidlík, "Le difficoltà della democrazia nei Paesi slavi," in *Politica dell'Est. Una lettura critia del ruolo dei cristiani nel sociale e nel politico* (Roma: del Centro Aletti, 1995), 17–24.

²⁹ Thomas Butler, "Blood Feuds and Forms of Peacebuilding in the Old Yugoslavia," in *Overcoming Violence: Religion, Conflict and Peacebuilding*, eds. Rodney L. Petersen and Marian Gh. Simion (Boston, MA: Boston Theological Institute, Newton Centre, 2010), 228–36.

³⁰ Cyril Mango, "Diabolus Byzantinus," in *Dumbarton Oaks Papers* vol. 46 (Papers in Honor of Alexander Kazhdan: Homo Byzantinus, 1992), 215–23.

³¹ Pyotr Simonov, *Essential Russian Mythology: Stories that Change the World* (San Francisco, CA: Thorsons, 1997), 4.

³² Petru I. David, *Călăuză Creștină* (Arad: Editura Episcopiei Ortodoxe, 1987), 64–79.

³³ Hildo Bos and Jim Forest, *For the Peace from Above: An Orthodox Resource Book on War, Peace and Nationalism* (Athens: Syndesmos Press, 1999), 130.

³⁴ Goodin, op.cit.

³⁵ Cummings, *The Rudder*, 759–760.

³⁶ Mantzaridis, "Orthodox Observations on Peace and War," 119.

³⁷ Cummings, *The Rudder*; Bos and Forest, *For the Peace from Above*; Viscuso, "Christian Participation in Warfare," 37–39.

³⁸ Georgios Rhalles and Michael Potles, Σύνταγμα των θείων ιερών κανόνων 4:132–33, as quoted in Viscuso, "Christian Participation in Warfare," 37–39.

³⁹ *Ștefan cel Mare Și Sfânt: Portret în cronică* (Suceava: editura Mușatinii, 2004), 5.

⁴⁰ Dumitru Stăniloae, *Teologia Dogmatică Ortodoxă vol. 2. ediția a III-a* (București: Editura Institutului Biblic și de Misiune al Bisericii Ortodoxe Române, 2003), 214–18. See also Isidor Todoran and Ioan Zăgrean, *Teologia Dogmatică, manual pentru seminariile teologice* (București, Editura Institutului Biblic și de Misiune al Bisericii Ortodoxe Române, 1991), 299–301.

⁴¹ There are various studies which have elaborated on this subject. Yet, without offending the numerous remarkable reference works, one may quickly consult Jaroslav Pelikan, *Mary Through the Centuries: Her Place in the History of Culture* (New Haven, CT: Yale University Press, 1996), 39–65; Kyriaki Karidoyanes FitzGerald, "The Eve-Mary Typology," in *Anglican Theological Review* (LXXXIV 3): 630.

⁴² Brian E. Daley, S.J., "'At the Hour of our Death': Mary's Dormition and Christian Dying in Late Patristic and Early Byzantine Literature," in *Dumbarton Oaks Papers* 55 (2001): 72.

⁴³ Nicholas P. Constas, "Weaving the Body of God: Proclus of Constantinople, the Theotokos, and the Loom of Flesh," in *Journal of Early Christian Studies* 3.2 (Summer 1995): 169, 177–80.

⁴⁴ Constas, "Weaving the Body of God," 182.

⁴⁵ Ene Braniște, *Liturgica Generală* (București: Editura Institutului Biblic și de Misiune al Bisericii Ortodoxe Române, 1993), 555.

⁴⁶ Gerald A. Parsons, "From Nationalism to Internationalism: Civil Religion and the Festival of Saint Catherine of Siena, 1940–2003," in *Journal of Church and State* 46.4 (2004): 861–85.

⁴⁷ Due to these attitudes toward war and enemies, Emperor Leo VI often had difficulties getting the members of the society to share the war expenses, unlike the Arabs (their enemies), who gathered voluntarily, and all members of the society shared the expenses and the rewards of warfare. See G. Dagron, "Byzance et le modèle islamique au Xe siècle, à propos des *Constitutions tactiques* de l'empereur Léon VI," in *Comptes rendues des séances de l'année de l-Académie des inscriptions et belles-lettres* (Paris, 1983), 219–43.

11.
Swords to Ploughshares, Theory to Practice: An Evolution of Religious Peacebuilding at USIP

Susan Hayward

As David Little's former student—who now works in the programmatic descendent of the Religion, Ethics and Human Rights initiative at the United States Institute of Peace (USIP), in which Little was a senior scholar—I seek to bear witness to the contributions he made in his work at USIP, not only to the understanding of the relationship between religion, nationalism, and conflict, but also to the evolution of religious peacebuilding as a practice. Little's work in Washington, D.C., in the 1990s sowed the seeds that we continue to harvest in USIP's Religion and Peacebuilding (R&P) program, which was created following the conclusion of Little's project, and is, in many ways, a response to and an extension of it. The experience of R&P has affirmed much of what Little's project concluded. Primarily, that in a conflict which is driven (in whole or part), by exclusionary religious nationalism, or violations of rights related to fundamental beliefs and religious freedom, efforts undertaken to promote legal and social norms of tolerance can contribute to peace. The aim of this chapter is to trace how recent on-the-ground work of the Religion and Peacebuilding program has borne out, and challenged, some of the theoretical conclusions of Little's work at USIP.

The Seed Sown

Little's work at USIP was established in the early 1990s, in the shadow of the Cold War's demise. This was a pivotal time in the field of conflict analysis and peacebuilding. Conflict theorists and policymakers were seeking to understand the sustenance—if not proliferation—of identity-based internal state conflicts around the world, as well as to discern how the end of the Cold War transformed local and global economic, political, and social dynamics. They had, it seemed, no shortage of options for case studies. In every major region of the world—from East Africa to South Asia to the Middle East—civil war, or major civil strife, was raging. These were not all new conflicts, but rather those that had been overshadowed by the larger battle between the United States and the Soviet Union, or those that had only been interpreted with a Cold War hermeneutic; a local manifestation of the battle between the global super-powers. The fall of the Berlin Wall led to new interpretations and analyses of conflict dynamics, particularly as manifested in internal conflicts. For many of the civil conflicts of this period, the enemy line was marked by ethnic, linguistic, or religious identity. Increased attention to these identity-based fault lines spurred increased attention to social analyses of conflict—for example, the role of group identity formation in stratifying societies in a conflictual manner, creating dysfunctional inter-group relations that justified human rights violations and exclusionary state policies and structure that could, in turn, devolve into situations of war.

This new analytical interest led to new emphases in active work to build peace. After all, how one defines the root causes and drivers of conflict has consequences for how one determines it best to build peace. And so, the increased attention to social processes of group-identity formation in divided societies sparked a new enthusiasm in the peacebuilding field for activities promoting social transformation in places where adversaries must learn to coexist peacefully. These included projects that focused on facilitated inter-group (including interfaith) dialogue, cooperative conflict resolution trainings and workshops, and social activities like sporting events for members of different groups to engage with one another in a safe environment in stratified environments in which inter-group interaction was limited.[1] Key to these sorts of initiatives was a conviction that peace could be bolstered through person-to-person contact across lines of conflict.[2]

These practices, many of their proponents argued, were to accompany but not displace political and economic reforms addressing the conflict's root causes and drivers.

A striking component in many of the conflicts during this time was religion. In the preceding decades the secularization thesis, supported by sociologists from Max Weber to Peter Berger, had predicted the demise of religion as an influential social, political, and economic sector in global affairs. The secularization thesis undoubtedly drew life from the practice of viewing nearly all global conflict through a Cold War optic, and so failed to account for the influence of religion. However, a fresh look at these conflicts in the 1990s challenged the undue influence of this thesis. Not only was religion a factor in many of these conflicts with respect to demarcating the conflict divide and in shaping mutually competing nationalisms, but religious actors and institutions played active roles in both exacerbating conflict and facilitating peace. Indeed, during this time and subsequently, civil wars in which religion was a factor appeared to be on the rise, as did religious influence in politics around the world.[3]

Little's work at USIP explored the persistence of religious dynamics in politics and conflict long before many others in Washington, D.C. were willing to look at religion's influence in earnest. Religion was, and still is, to many in the academic field of international relations and western diplomatic sphere a topic *non-grata*. It was often dismissed as a superficial symptom of economic or political issues—and so ultimately irrelevant—or ignored out of basic fear that to engage religious ideas and spiritual leaders was to risk "opening a can of worms," unleashing complicated emotional furor and irrational claims that could derail the "rational" work of negotiation on which diplomacy depends. However, a small group of analysts and activists in Washington, D.C. in the 1990s challenged the diplomatic sector's willful ignorance of the religious sector. Their challenge proved prescient in 2001 when, with the events of 9–11, it became clear that religion could no longer be ignored as a factor directly impacting international politics.

Little's program contributed to explanations of why it was important to understand the role religion was playing in conflict around the world, and laid the foundation for discerning how diplomats and peacebuilders might respond to and contain religion's destructive contributions to international security. The body of work he produced as a senior scholar in the Religion, Ethics and Human Rights initiative, and as director of the Religion,

Nationalism and Intolerance working group, looked at the relationship between ethno-religious-nationalism, inter-communal intolerance and human rights violations, exclusionary governance and institutions, and violence. In particular, the projects looked at what role the violation of rights related to nondiscrimination and free exercise of religion played in fueling violent conflict, particularly in identity conflicts. These rights, enshrined in documents such as the *UN Declaration on the Elimination of All Forms of Intolerance and Discrimination Based on Religion or Belief*, guarantee people the right not to be discriminated against based on their fundamental beliefs, and protect the free expression and exercise of religious and other fundamental convictions. The project presented conclusions, based on its case studies of Sri Lanka, the former Yugoslavia, Sudan, and Tibet, among others, that conflict was intensified by violations of these rights.[4]

Little's work at USIP focused in particular on the phenomenon of religious nationalism. From Iran to Israel to Ireland and beyond, issues of nation-state structure and governance were (and remain) often (but not always) deeply infused with religion. This is hardly surprising. As Little pointed out, not only are most religions deeply concerned with creating standards for political conduct, justice, and the use of force, but devotion to national cause has a religious color to it, conjuring symbols, rituals, cultural, and linguistic heritage.[5] The marriage of religion and nationalism, however, risks alienating particular groups in pluralistic societies, given that religious nationalism often draws from a single tradition. Moreover, the case studies demonstrated how exclusionary religious nationalism and human rights violations appeared to be related to one another, with the former creating the foundation on which the latter were justified. For example, the case of Sri Lanka showed how Sinhala Buddhist nationalism, as an ideology, grew in the early half of the twentieth century and provided justification to mobilize support for legal measures passed by mid-century that discriminated against the Tamil minority by restricting their access to universities and government positions.[6]

Little's research showed that the violation of the rights of free exercise based on religious identity, and the influence of exclusionary religious nationalism intensified conflicts. These religious elements, over time, fueled the conflicts by raising commitments to the cause, transforming the objectives, justifying the violence, and further entrenching absolutist conflict divides. It is important to note that the project did not argue that religion was the root or the original source of these conflicts, which often erupted due to political and economic factors. However, religion became a driver of the conflicts over time, contributing to their imperviousness to resolution.

Little's work, illuminating the role of religion, was significant in better understanding ongoing conflicts, and revealed implications for peacebuilding. Broadly, religious ideology, and resources used to propagate intolerance, and justify human rights violations, and violence, could not be dismissed as epiphenomenal or insignificant. These drivers, as all political, economic, and social drivers of conflict, would need to be engaged directly in the pursuit of their transformation for sustainable peace to take root. To begin, protection of the rights of nondiscrimination and free exercise, which are largely considered to set the conditions for environments of tolerance, would seem to enhance the prospects for peace. Protections of these rights could also, Little hypothesized, help restrain religious nationalism from teetering into exclusionary tendencies that privilege one group over another in formal or informal ways, such as by officially (constitutionally, legally, or otherwise) restricting a group's access to political or economic arenas, or by social segregation and the propagation of prejudicial attitudes and behaviors. Protection of these rights would require work through formal and informal processes to encourage legal and state processes to protect these rights, as well as activities to bolster social norms in support of pluralism and tolerance.

Offshoot: The Religion and Peacebuilding Program

After Little left the USIP, David Smock launched the Religion and Peacemaking (R&P) program—now called Religion and Peacebuilding—which built on Little's conclusions about the need and the possibility for religion to serve as a positive force in building peace, particularly in divided societies marked by religious strife. In that sense, R&P's operating premise, that religion can and does serve as a *positive* force for peace, was an abrupt shift in focus from where Little's research project began, and on which it had dwelled: religion's role in stoking the flames of structural and overt violence. Yet, R&P's work, in many ways, emerged from Little's analysis about the influential role of religion as a factor in modern conflict and its impact on governance. Thanks to Little's project, USIP had carved out a niche for itself in Washington, D.C., as a resource center for understanding the relationship between religion, conflict, and peace. The Institute also realized the importance of continuing to explore this gap in the wider field of conflict management.

The program launched its analytical work with roundtable discussions on the varied teachings and active on-the-ground work of communities within the three major Abrahamic traditions (Islam, Judaism, and Christianity). These surveys, building on earlier studies done by Little and Smock, while recognizing the deep ambivalence toward conflict within many traditions, and their multiple responses to it, also illuminated the depth and breadth of resources within religious traditions supporting peacebuilding and human rights.[7] These peace-supporting resources included specific teachings that examined the causes for conflict and the means to prevent its eruption, as well as propositions about how best to deal with conflict, and how to foster social, political, and economic values that promote peace with justice. The focus on the active work of religious communities in peacebuilding overseas, meanwhile, raised awareness of the actors and opportunities already available for peacebuilding.[8]

On a practical level, R&P took a particular interest in the role of interfaith dialogue as a tool for building peace. Its initial on-the-ground work supported interfaith dialogue in divided societies, particularly targeting influential religious elites. An example of this was the Alexandria Process in Israel–Palestine, which brought together senior Muslim, Jewish, and Christian religious leaders to build relationships with one another and to discuss various issues at the heart of the conflict. A study led by Smock, which led to the publication of the book *Interfaith Dialogue and Peacebuilding*, examined the peacebuilding capacity of interfaith dialogue, as well as its limits.[9] In Sudan, Macedonia, Nigeria, and elsewhere, R&P supported inter-religious dialogue encounters pursuing similar objectives—broadly, to bridge divides, reduce mutual demonization, and explore avenues for practical collaboration on peacebuilding. Over the years R&P has also supported projects that reach into communities beyond religious elites—engaging women, youth, lay, and educators. Moreover, R&P's interfaith encounters extend beyond dialogue to include training in best practices of conflict resolution and peace organizing. More recently R&P has focused on religious education, supporting the integration of peacebuilding and pluralism to standard curricula in religious schools. In Pakistan and Indonesia, R&P

has worked with organizations to produce material framing concepts and practices of peace, religious tolerance, non-violence, and human rights within the Islamic tradition.

One of R&P's objectives is the promotion of religious pluralism, which in our mind is an environment in which multiple faiths operate openly and relate to each other in constructive ways. This goes beyond mere "tolerance" in which different groups put up with one another while harboring bias, or fail to actively engage with one another. We seek to encourage appreciation for religious diversity and the benefit of multiple perspectives and approaches to fundamental issues. This does not mean we seek for everyone to agree with one another, but rather to understand and appreciate one another. In seeking this goal, we remain fixed on an endpoint Little recognized as necessary for an environment of peace.[10] This positive and rather expansive definition of religious tolerance (or pluralism), depends on more than mere legal protection, however. The legal measures, which are essential, provide the skeletal infrastructure that will offer certain groups recourse if their rights are being violated, and seek to ensure that formal institutions take efforts to ensure non-discrimination in policies and practice. But the environment our program aims to develop depends as well on the maintenance of social norms: on broad public attitudes and behavior in formal *and informal* spaces that reflect and support religious tolerance. It may not break the law for two different religious communities to voluntarily segregate their schools and markets, and in fact prejudicial language that falls short of hate speech may well be legally protected as free speech, but these practices can help fuel misunderstandings and violence that can undermine sustainable and just peace.

In many of the divided societies in which R&P operates, we have found that where there is little space for engagement between communal groups, bias and stereotypes proliferate, misunderstandings and misperceptions abound, and trust erodes across lines of difference. These existential separations allow antagonistic group identities to form, and the "other" group is seen as one with whom there is little common ground, or a community that profits at the expense of one's own community. Social leaders within each community, such as preachers, parents, and teachers, may perpetuate ideas that reinforce these processes of social group construction and individual identity formation. When a particular group is disenfranchised (or perceives itself to be disenfranchised or under attack because of some aspect of its identity), this creates even greater attachment to one's group identity and fuels the sense that other groups are either ignorant of the group's unique dignity or needs, or are actively seeking to destroy it. This not only leads to violent local outbursts, such as we see for example in periodic Christian–Muslim violence that fuel conflict in Kaduna State in Nigeria, but also creates broad public support for policies.

So, whether through seeking to bridge the chasms between religious communities through facilitated dialogue, or by integrating religious peacebuilding curricula into seminaries and *madrassas*, the objective is to fortify positive religious attitudes and narratives, and, in turn, behaviors that promote peace, justice, and religious pluralism. Through inter-religious engagement (or intra-religious, in those cases in which the engagement is with sectarian communities in the same tradition, such as our work with Sunni and Shīʻa Muslims in Pakistan or with Catholic and Protestant women in Colombia), the purpose is to understand the narrative and experience of the other community, to dispel bias and myths that fuel discrimination, and to strengthen religious commitments and effective action to promote peace, human rights, and pluralism. In this, we have sought to operationalize some of the recommendations made by Little about the best means to mitigate the destructive role of religion in modern conflict.

Collecting the Harvest, Plotting the Future

When I was in Sri Lanka several years ago, during the period marking the military conclusion of its civil war, I met with various religious leaders in the Eastern province who were involved in inter-religious peacebuilding and had a council that responded to local and national conflict. They opposed military solutions to the conflict and supported minority rights. There are several similar inter-religious councils around the island, and they have been growing in strength and receiving increased attention, particularly by international donors, as alternative and effective avenues to peacebuilding in Sri Lanka. These leaders in the East told me that a couple weeks earlier, a Colombo-based inter-religious council had come to visit them. This council was accompanied by soldiers and touted the Government's pro-war message. It seemed the Sri Lankan Government had become aware of the power of a multi-religious narrative in support of a particular policy. It recognized the need to employ religious leaders from beyond the majority Sinhala Buddhist community to support the government position and directly challenge the multi-religious narrative opposed to war. And so it had created its own inter-religious council and was sending it around the island to offer multi-religious legitimacy to the Government's military campaign underway at the time; to show it as something that was not merely a reflection of Sinhala Buddhist moral imperative, but a broader religious moral imperative.

This encapsulates the sort of religious narrative warfare that takes place in some conflict zones—here embodied as the battle of the inter-religious peace councils. These two councils were articulating competing interpretations of the conflict and prescribing a different religious response to it, presenting both as a position transcending religious difference, and so representing the best outcome for the multiple communities in Sri Lanka—in other words, a "pluralist" argument. Of course, the government's council was supporting a policy that many have argued epitomizes Sinhala domination, underscored by historical trends shaped by Sinhala Buddhist nationalism.[11] But which narrative would convince ordinary Sri Lankans seeking to determine the proper ethical response to the conflict raging around them?

Meanwhile, in Europe, we find another pertinent example illustrating the complexity of contemporary religious dynamics in conflict. Here the arrival of new immigrants from Africa, the Middle East, and Asia has shifted demographics significantly and created remarkably multi-cultural populations where before there was a dominant Anglo-Christian culture. The attempts by some governments to pursue policies and practices that embrace multiculturalism have not always been easy, consistent, or successful. German Chancellor Angela Merkel, for example, argued that the German government's attempts to promote and embed multiculturalism as a social and institutional value failed.[12] The strains caused by the new immigrant populations on political, economic, and social institutions have led to a resurgence of exclusive, xenophobic nationalisms. A potent example of the violent consequences of this is Anders Behring Breivik in Norway, who killed eight people when he detonated bombs in Oslo, in July 2011, and then assassinated sixty-nine people, mostly teenagers, at a summer camp run by a liberal political party. In his manifesto, Breivik railed against the Norwegian government's embrace of multiculturalism, and he denigrated Islam and Muslim immigrants to Europe.

He called for a militant re-establishment of predominant European Christian culture by violent attacks on immigrant communities and liberal Europeans who accommodate and support these communities.

What is made clear in these examples is that the work of building religious pluralism and tolerance is no easy task that can be achieved through mere rhetorical persuasion, or the existence of legal measures of protection. As we see in the Sri Lankan example, religious leaders who want to amplify a pro-peace religious narrative must think carefully and strategically about how this narrative can prevail. Good intentions and public statements will not be enough, as counter-arguments seek to undermine and challenge their pro-peace messages. Ultimately, the work of religious peacebuilding needs to move from the articulation of social and legal norms and connections promoting environments of pluralism and human rights to transformation of political and economic institutions and ideologies so that they reflect these norms. The example from Europe, meanwhile, demonstrates that even in places where religious freedom is legally protected and pluralism is tolerated and embraced, there can be instances of violent attack not only against another religion, but against the very idea of pluralism and multiculturalism. This, in turn, conjures a point made by K. M. de Silva of Sri Lanka, as recorded by Little in his work. De Silva argued that Sinhala Buddhist nationalism carried much more emotional appeal and attachment than did concepts of multi-ethnic polity, which came off as an abstraction.[13] A question that quickly derives from this observation for those seeking to support peacebuilding in religio-ethnic-nationalist conflicts from the theoretical perspective presented by Little, is the degree to which the passion associated with exclusionary nationalism can ever similarly drive pluralistic and inclusive nationalisms.

Perhaps it is impossible to detach the emotional attachment of a community to one form or another of nationalism from the political, economic, and social interests inherent in those nationalisms. Policy interests can determine the powerful grip of an argument, just as rhetoric can drive political and economic interests. What wins out is determined not just by the strength of the argument, despite what democratic purists will say, but also political, social, and economic calculations of those with power—including religious elites. As such, the "argument" for tolerance or pluralism alone is not enough. And so inter-faith dialogue, or pockets of religious elites touting pluralism and peace, is not enough. What is also needed is institutional transformation to ensure that pluralistic nationalisms are mutually motivated by political, economic, and social institutions. In other words, one needs to work to ensure that politicians, businesspeople, and other actors have a self-interest in a pluralistic society. One needs to ensure the maintenance of the institutions that establish a political, economic, and social systems dependent on pluralism. And so one needs to embed pluralism into the institutions themselves—so that the status quo that elites will seek to maintain is a pluralistic one. This requires creating mutual connections and dependencies between religious communities, both business and political. It means ensuring markets both large and small, political parties, schools, and so on, are integrated as well.

Of course, the work of promoting religious freedom and nondiscrimination is more complex and difficult than it appears at first blush. The religious peacebuilding field has come to recognize this in spades as it has developed. As such there has been a great emphasis in the field about the need to "move beyond dialogue." Yes, interfaith dialogue is important, and is increasingly recognized as such by international bodies and political leaders. But it is not the end-all of religious peacebuilding and the sole avenue to build religious pluralism. It, along with intra-faith dialogue, is rather the starting place. If religious peacebuilding limits itself to interfaith dialogue, dialogue fatigue can set in, not to mention wariness, if all that talk does not turn into collective action to transform the political, economic, and social injustices often persistent in conflict zones. I have witnessed how minority religions—or those who do not hold political or economic power—often become frustrated with dialogue if their unjust reality is not changing despite the emergence of stronger social ties between them and majority communities. Dialogue, then, might be understood more as the means to develop the relationships and commitments, to create and nurture social norms in support of pluralism and tolerance, in order to continue the work of peacebuilding.

Moving beyond dialogue, the field must increasingly focus on ensuring that the entire retinue of religious resources is skillfully employed to influence dynamics in support of peace. These resources, as I understand them, can be identified as 1) preaching and public argument, 2) scripture and tradition, 3) religious education, 3) ritual, 4) leadership (both formal and informal), and 5) religious institutions including faith-based organizations and places of worship. These resources must be effectively employed—

given the level of conflict or violence—in the area in which they are working: conflict prevention where there is relative stability, resolution of active violence, or reconciliation in the aftermath of violent conflict. Finally, it requires the field to integrate more successfully with other streams within the larger field of conflict management. These are all pressing needs.

Let us break this down with a couple illustrations.

First, let us consider the religious resource of ritual, as used in the work of post-conflict reconciliation in Northern Uganda, where Joseph Kony has led his Lord's Resistance Army against the Ugandan government for over twenty years. Many of the ex-combatants—often children who were forced to do atrocious acts of violence—have been returning home in recent years. These combatants were themselves tortured and indoctrinated by Kony's army. Kony and his movement have drawn very heavily on religious language, ritual, and symbolism to justify and motivate his cause. In this context, local communities have been using ritual to guide reconciliation processes between returning combatants and the communities to which they return. Most well known is the ritual of *mato oput*—a process in which the returning combatant sits face to face with the family or individual he has harmed, and with the entire community around them as witness. There is a truth telling, the ex-combatant is encouraged to recognize his responsibilities, and a communal decision is made about what acts of reparation the combatant must do for the individual and community; an indigenous model of restorative justice. At the conclusion the perpetrator and the victim's family share a drink made from a local root that is bitter in taste, to recall and bury the bitterness of their soured relations. This drink is the heart of the *mato oput* ritual. Following the ritual the wider community ensures the promises made are upheld.

There are other rituals used in Northern Uganda, such as the *gomo tong*, which is a bending of spears to symbolize the end of hostilities. There are also cleansing ceremonies for former soldiers. War is said to get inside the psyche of soldiers and feeds on their soul. And so, a cleansing ritual is used to mark the soldier's break from a violent past. In Mozambique, these sorts of rituals are described as a process of "getting the war out," or "getting the violence out" of the individual and social body.[14] And there are rituals conducted for survivors of violence as well, involving meals and healing baths provided by the community and ointments applied that are understood to heal both the body and the spirit. In all of these rituals, the entire community participates. The suffering of individuals in war affects the wider community. And so the community must find healing by helping the individual heal. Personal and social transformation is inter-related and so mutually sought.

These rituals are enacted in an environment where religion has been used to motivate violence and to cause spiritual internal violence for combatants and their soldiers. The use of healing religious/cultural rituals helps undo the damage of dysfunctional religion. It replaces the religious narrative of violence with one of healing within the person and community. It replaces the use of religion that tore people apart with one that brings people together—not in a superficial way that fails to wrestle with what has taken place—but in an honest, authentic, and powerful way.

A second example is the use of religious institutions in conflict prevention when mobilized as an early warning and response system, via mosques, churches, and temples that exist throughout a conflict landscape. Through such mobilization, the actors associated with them open lines of communication with each other to relate what is happening in harder-to-reach rural areas and to mobilize a response when tensions that have the potential to erupt into violence arise. Pastor James Wuye and Imam Mohammed Ashafa, local R&P partners in Nigeria—whose work was illustrated in Little's book *Peacemakers in Action*,[15] have sought to establish such an early warning system. They have trained a network of actors, including religious leaders, to respond to conflict when it erupts, and to manage it through nonviolent mediation and response.

While both of these examples illustrate effective ways of mobilizing a resource to address a situation of conflict, neither are solutions in themselves. The ritual processes described may restore the dignity of some individuals, families, and local communities. Nevertheless, when the larger national or international structure continues to deny justice and to violate human rights, and so continues to offend the dignity of many of its citizens, healing cannot be complete. These rituals can complement but not replace the national and political processes. Similarly, the mobilization of a network of religious institutions to respond to local pockets of tension or isolated acts of violence in the process of containing and preventing violent conflict can contribute to building peace, but must be combined with other programs in order to establish sustainable peace that address root drivers of conflict; unless they risk a simple "band aid" approach.

Mapping and understanding the various roles that different religious resources can play and the ways they can be best leveraged in conflict settings is a first step to more effective religious peacebuilding. It necessitates moving beyond a paradigm of religious peacebuilding that is limited to work promoting pluralism and religious freedom, although this goal may remain clearly at the center of the work. This means thinking more strategically about religious networks, institutions, and their impact on peacebuilding.

Finally, the field of religious peacebuilding cannot afford to act in isolation. Religious peacebuilding needs to better engage with the secular realm of peacebuilding, including not only the sectors of business and media, but also secular-oriented organizations, actors, and governments involved in peacebuilding. Only through such coordination can those actors and organizations—currently engaged in positive and effective work—ensure the impact necessary to create change on a large scale.

NOTES

[1] See, for example, R. J. Fisher, "Reflections on the Practice of Interactive Conflict Resolution Thirty Years Out," Twelfth Annual Lynch Lecture, Institute for Conflict Analysis and Resolution, (George Mason University, Fairfax, VA, April 1999).

[2] David Smock, *Catholic Contributions to International Peace* (U.S. Institute of Peace Special Report. April 9, 2001), 11.

[3] Among the explanations offered for the resurgence of religion in the modern world is post-colonial rejection of Western-influenced secularist governing ideologies in favor of traditional and religious legitimacy and governance, the increased space for religious organizations to mobilize and assert themselves in democratic societies, and a backlash against the disintegration of traditional (and often religious) ways of life, in much of the developing world, as a result of modernization and globalization. See, Jonathan Fox and Shmuel Sandler, *Bringing Religion into International Relations* (New York: Palgrave MacMillan, 2004), 12. See also, Tim Shah, Monica Duffy Toft and Daniel Philpot, *God's Century: Resurgent Religion and Global Politics* (W. W. Norton, 2011).

[4] David Little, "Religion and the Prevention of Genocide and Mass Atrocity." remarks at a symposium (United States Institute of Peace. Washington, D.C., April 2008).

[5] David Little, "Religious Nationalism and Human Rights," in Gerard F. Powers, Drew Christiansen and Richard T. Hennemeyer, eds., *Peacemaking: Moral and Policy Challenges for a New World* (Washington, D.C.: U.S. Catholic Conference, 1994), 2.

[6] David Little, *Sri Lanka: The Invention of Enmity* (Washington, D.C.: United States Institute of Peace Press, 1994).

[7] These earlier studies included: David Smock. *Religious Perspectives on War* (Washington, D.C.: USIP, 1992). David Smock, *Perspectives on Pacifism* (Washington, D.C.: USIP, 1995).

[8] David Smock. *Contributions to International Peace* (Washington, D.C.: USIP Special Report No. 69: 2001); David Smock, *Islamic Perspectives on Peace and Violence* (Washington, D.C.: USIP Special Report No. 82, 2002); David Smock, *Faith–Based NGOs and International Peacebuilding* (Washington, D.C.: USIP Special Report No. 76, 2001). An event was held in November 2000 entitled "Mennonite International Peacemaking."

[9] David Smock, ed., *Interfaith Dialogue and Peacebuilding* (Washington, D.C.: USIP, 2002).

[10] David Little, "Tolerance, Equal Freedom, and Peace," in ed., W. Lawson Taitte, *The Essence of Living in a Free Society*. (Dallas: University of Texas Press, 1997).

[11] David Little. *Invention of Enmity*.

[12] Angela Merkel, "German multiculturalism has 'utterly failed'" in *The Guardian* (17 October 2010): (http://www.guardian.co.uk/world/2010/oct/17/angela-merkel-german-multiculturalism-failed Last accessed: August 2, 2011).

[13] K. M. de Silva, *Religion, Nationalism, and the State*. USF Monographs in Religion and Public Policy, no. 1 (Tampa: University of South Florida, 1986), 31.

[14] Carolyn Nordstrom, *A Different Kind of War Story* (Philadelphia: University of Pennsylvania Press, 1997).

[15] David Little, with Tanenbaum Center for Interreligious Understanding, eds., *Peacemakers in Action: Profiles of Religion in Conflict Resolution* (Cambridge: Cambridge University Press, 2007), 247–277.

12.
Religion and Multi-Track Diplomacy

Rodney L. Petersen

Introduction

The stories of the sixteen peacemakers in *Peacemakers in Action: Profiles of Religion in Conflict Resolution* (2007) provide inspiration and insight into issues of religion and diplomacy at different levels of peacemaking. Drawing upon his studied reflection, David Little's summary to that book reflects on two oversimplifications of religion: a consistent association of religion with violent conflict, and an equally misplaced confidence that religion always brokers peace.[1] Is religion a factor in conflict, a force for peace—or both? As an independent player in political affairs, religion has an important moral and ethical role to play in times of conflict and toward the maintenance of human rights.

As the world appears to be both more religious and more conscious of religion's deep pull upon public policy in the twenty-first century, our question begs for analysis.[2] Many factors from the field of political science bear upon the question of the role played by religious actors in times of conflict. It is one that is important for public policy in a world shaped by political struggle, whether such contention is seen to be derivative of human nature or social structure apart from whatever idealism may be brought to public policy.[3]

The question is important for theological and religious studies as it bears upon the shape of an engaged public theology.[4] Efforts by international and national councils of churches, other religious bodies, regional councils of bishops, religious non-governmental agencies, and associations such as that of Muslim scholars, clerics, and intellectuals issuing *A Common Word Between Us and You* (2007), can have significant implications for reducing civil strife and enhancing prospects for regional stability and peace. Yet they do so within an envelope of perceived relationships among such categories as anthropological assumptions, morality, ethics and global order—in addition to different religious commitments in a world increasingly shaped by interfaith realities.

According to a recent Pew Forum poll, a majority or plurality of every major religious tradition believes that diplomacy, and not military strength, is the best way to ensure peace. Religion is a form of power to be reckoned with along with political, military, and economic strength. Religious beliefs and practices must be seen as tools in a toolbox toward good diplomacy.[5]

Religion and Security

In order to find areas of correlation between public policy and public theology around the question of security, we might first think of the term "religion." Often used interchangeably with faith or a belief system, etymologically it is associated with *religio* or *re-ligare*, the first implying a respect for and the latter a binding to what is sacred. Such reference could imply transcendence or often simply mean what we currently mean by "law" given historical and cultural considerations. David Kennedy identifies the importance of doctrine, ritual, and narrative for the relationship between international law and religion.[6] James A. R. Nafziger takes us further when he asks about religion and its functions. He writes that religion can serve at least five functions in the international legal system. These can be described as creative, aspirational, didactic, custodial, and meditative.[7]

Such functional aspects of religion are derived from the value of religion as lodged precisely in its role to shape how individuals and societies put the world together for purposes of personal and social identity.[8] Religion structures meaning. It provides a narrative framework for life. The nature of religion for personal and social identity was noted by Sigmund Freud at the beginning of the last century, although he rejected its function in favor of the emerging sciences as he knew them. In a defining publication, "The Question of a *Weltanschauung*," he describes a *Weltanschauung*, or worldview, as "an intellectual construction which solves all the problems of our existence uniformly on the basis of one overriding hypothesis, which, accordingly, leaves no question unanswered and in which everything that interests us finds its fixed place."[9] Accordingly, for Freud, the sciences overtake other competitors to defining "worldview" such as philosophy, art, and religion. And he goes on to argue that it is from the scientific worldview alone that we gain access to knowledge about origins, direction in life, and ultimate happiness. Correspondingly, religion offers a sense of identity, direction in life, and ultimate consolation.

As a part of the religious interest and renewal in the twenty-first century, the scientific worldview of Freud has often been called "scientism." In this sense it replaces anything that might be offered by theology, or the "science" of God, in matters of origins, direction, and protection or consolation. One way of reading the works of the popular British essayist and lay theologian C. S. Lewis is to see Lewis's entire literary effort as a way to counter Freudian scientism—in literary and other essays, children's stories, and other monographs. In this sense, Lewis might be understood as one of the first "post-modern" writers of the twentieth century. Of course, in retrospect he represents a larger sea change of interest in religion that begins with humane inquiry and effort and can end in radical politics: "Islam is the Answer" runs a popular political slogan—with the Hindutua, a Mahavamsa Mindset, "Iron Wall" Zionism, and apocalyptic Christian Fundamentalism in close pursuit.[10]

One can understand why it is in the power of religion to stabilize or de-stabilize personal or social relationships derivative of a functional understanding of religion. Religion can make for security or deepen anxiety. Regardless of tradition, creed, or theology these polarities can be found in all of our histories. Religion is so important to the question of security in our time that it has become a topic of political interest after its eclipse among policy makers in the twentieth century. Madeleine Albright, former U.S. Secretary of State and Ambassador to the United Nations, in *The Mighty and the Almighty* reports that religion is playing a fundamental role in ordering the world of the twenty-first century.[11] It is shaping policy in the United States. It is caught up in the deepening divisions of the Middle East. Christianity and Islam are in a "race for souls" across Africa and Central Asia.[12] What to do with religion has become a question of such significance that in the United States it is the focus of work for numerous think-tanks and institutions, including the prestigious Center for Strategic and International Studies (CSIS) and its Post-Conflict Reconciliation (PCR) Project.[13] It is a subject of interest in other policy circles and a growing concern of recent National Security Strategy studies of the United States.[14] The report growing out of this project concludes that "[r]eligion is a multivalent force: it . . . has been mobilized to sanction violence, drawn on to resolve conflicts, and invoked to provide humanitarian and development aid. In all of these capacities, religious leaders, organizations, institutions and communities are especially important in shaping the direction of conflict-prevention or reconstruction efforts in fragile states."[15]

Western governments have had to adopt a new understanding and appreciation of religion.[16] This has challenged an often prevailing political realism with what is perceived to be religious idealism, but may in fact be realism in a new garb.[17] Indications of impending changes in the United States, Europe, and elsewhere can be traced back to the mid-twentieth century. An indication of such shifting ground may be seen as early as the recognition of the Bosniacs as a distinct people based upon their religion (Islam) by Josip Broz Tito in 1969, significant for the autonomy granted Kosovo in 1974. Interest in religion's role in shaping public policy has become an increasing reality since the Iranian Revolution of November 4th, 1979. Albright referred to this revolution as "a true political earthquake, like the revolutions of France or Russia," and American foreign policy has yet to deal fully with this. The spiritual identity of the West, and of its churches, was also raised to new self-consciousness with the outbreak of this Revolution. The significance of religion, and what we mean by it, has became only a more pointed reality in evolving geo-politics since 9–11. The Iranian Revolution grounded politics in the debate over identity, set the stage for the end of the Cold War, and drew us rapidly to events now identified as the "War on Terror."[18] International politics since 1979 has become identity politics—since then often a religious contest. Theology has become public theology in a new way.

Civic Goals and Moral Vision

The correlation of public theology in secular democratic societies with public policy means promoting the common good.[19] It has to do with crafting a moral vision so as to engage a wide and often diverse public. There is a history here reflecting an evolving relationship between religion and the state in both Enlightenment and religious thinking in western societies on which Little's scholarship has thrown much light. Norman Thomas traces the further development of a secular vision for human rights, to emerge in the UN Charter (1945) and the Universal Declaration of Human Rights (1948) in which "the churches and their missionary agencies played a pivotal role" if not in later stages of development, certainly at their inception.[20]

In seeking to craft a vision for an effective public theology with respect to public policy, Duncan Forrester argues out of his Christian tradition that public theology is, first, an effort to engage the secular world in terms of its issues while digging deeply into one's own religious tradition for the resources to do so.[21] Second, doing theology in this way offers a constructive contribution to public debate and to human flourishing. It has the potential and aim to make a positive contribution to the world in which we live, a theology that "heals, reconciles, helps, challenges."[22] Third, public theology is ecclesial theology, that is, it is embodied in the life of a community of people who are seeking to give witness to God's reign over all of life. Fourth, public theology is utopian in the sense that it keeps hope alive for a better world. It is open to the creative process that enables solutions to be found to urgent civic problems.

To these four points defining public theology may be added a fifth, the need to be intentionally interfaith in orientation, inclusive of the whole community while allowing for difference within the bounds of public safety. In the "Just Peacemaking" project outlined by Susan Thistlethwaite in *Interfaith Just Peacemaking* (2012), there is an effort made toward the "development of doctrine" carried out on an interfaith basis.[23] In crafting a moral vision to meet civic goals, public theology has to take into account different localities and different publics. John de Gruchy writes of such different localities by noting that "there is no universal 'public theology', but only theologies that seek to engage the political realm within particular localities." There are, however, commonalities, both confessional and ecumenical, in approach and substance between theologies that do this.[24] David Tracy reminds us of the different "publics" with which a moral vision is concerned: academy, church, and society. In the context of a pluralist society there may be many more publics as well, but this delineation is helpful in that it reminds us that different modes of discourse are applicable in different settings. Tracy observes that every "theologian must face squarely the claims to meaning and truth of all three publics" and address each accordingly.[25] For all theology, whether it be fundamental, systematic, or practical (to use Tracy's categories), is "determined by a relentless drive to genuine publicness to and for all three publics."[26]

In terms of the ways by which public theology seeks to promote human flourishing, embody a community's hope in the future, and foster a better world—three of Forrester's four points—such reflection is frequently engaged in issues of justice and peace, terms frequently combined as "justpeace" with particular resonance in specific locations and for specific publics.[27] In reflecting on violence, often borne out of conflict, psychiatrist James Gilligan writes that, "All violence is an effort to do justice or to undo injustice."[28] The implication of this perspective is to deepen our understanding of the social psychological dynamics inherent in violence in civil society and the necessity of a rule of law in specific local and international affairs. Work toward such ends is especially suitable for religious actors and NGOs who are frequently close to a people and work in a specific locale. The method for this work is through that form of diplomacy referred to as "multi-track" diplomacy.

Gilligan's observation opens up for us an important perspective on the nature of violence, its relation to justice and the role of religious actors and others seeking social justice in society. Gilligan calls us to a view of justice that is "restorative," or restorative justice, and toward the creation of societies characterized by "justpeace." The term "restorative justice," originating in indigenous communities and among sociologists and legal scholars, implies that attention be given to the effects of judicial procedures upon victims, offenders, and the community; that is, that victims' needs are met, that offenders learn responsibility, and that communities find safety through just relationships.[29] Our moral vision shapes how we deal with conflict toward the ends of civil society.

Multi-Track Diplomacy

Where there is a perceived imbalance in the distribution of economic, political, and environmental or social resources (social injustice) that coincides with identity-group boundaries, there is potential for violence and for protracted conflict that will further devastate the communities involved. Given its role in framing the authenticity of different worldviews, religion can either contribute to regional peace or be used as an argument to justify conflict in the context of perceived injustices as happened in regional conflicts in recent years as well as in the so-called War on Terror. The rift between religious ethics and international law finds reasons for engagement in such situations.[30]

Conflict theory outlines several approaches which often devolve into either conflict management or conflict resolution. Whereas the former implies taking action to keep a conflict from escalating further, the latter seeks to resolve incompatibilities and such actions often lead to outcomes described as zero-sum, positive-sum, or negative-sum.[31] Both approaches may necessitate the intervention of a third party. Such mediation may be necessary because of the breakdown of communication, an outbreak of violence, or the intractability of parties in negotiation. Such intervention may be inter-personal or it may happen at the group level. It may represent efforts to mediate among elites, middle-range leaders, or grassroots actors, and be appropriate to the level of interaction.[32]

We frequently think of third party intervention in regional conflicts as coming from nation-states. This is the work of political or military leaders through official visits, policy statements, "coercive measures like sanctions, arbitration, power mediation," or "non-coercive measures like facilitation, negotiation, mediation, fact-finding missions and 'good offices.'"[33] This is Track–one intervention or diplomacy. It involves particular resources, positive as well as negative incentives, and can carry all of the coercive potentiality that a state or international organization can bring to bear upon a conflict.

Track-two diplomacy has developed over the past quarter century, as a part of the growing NGO movement and often in response to the unique regional conflicts that have broken open since the end of the Cold War (1989). American diplomat and public policy scholar Joseph Montville coined the expression "track-two diplomacy" in *Foreign Policy Magazine*.[34] The term was first used in an analysis of the field in John W. McDonald's 1987 book, *Conflict Resolution: Track Two Diplomacy*.[35] Pioneered in concept even earlier among scholars like Herbert Kelman, Edward Azar, John Burton, and John Galtung, it has grown considerably as a concept and a recognized form of diplomacy in building an atmosphere conducive to the work of reconciliation. John Davies and Edward Kaufman argue that track-two diplomacy "promotes an expansion of social capital as needed to move from the logic of mutual hostility and imposed solutions (zero- or negative-sum outcomes) to the integrative logic of peace building as a process of collectively addressing human needs, leading zero- or positive-sum outcomes that encourage buy-in by all parties and development of a self-sustaining democratic culture."[36]

Track-two diplomacy can complement "first track" or official diplomacy in that it can initiate new opportunities for communication where little or none exists, foster cross-cultural understanding and pursue joint efforts at dialogue or action when official dialogue is blocked or absent. It can begin, build, and enlarge upon official track-one diplomacy. Public policy and conflict mediators Davies and Kaufman write about the assets that such "citizens' diplomacy" can bring to conflict in the following way: "Second track, or citizens' diplomacy may be broadly defined as the bringing together of professionals, opinion leaders or other currently or potentially influential individuals from communities in conflict, without official representative status, to work together to understand better the dynamics underlying the conflict and how its transformation for sustainable development might be promoted."[37]

Track-two diplomacy has been wisely used, often with success, in numerous areas around the world. Policy analyst and mediator John W. MacDonald cites examples with respect to the former Soviet Union, the PLO in Israel/Palestine, and Northern Ireland.[38] It has made possible a constructive civil society in South Africa after the end of Apartheid. Many cases are documented by Peter Ackerman and Jack DuVall in their study, *A Force More Powerful* (2000).[39] An enlarged understanding of the role of religion in today's world is playing into a growing awareness of the importance of religion in matters of diplomacy, specifically track-two diplomacy, not only in the United States but also within the European Centre for Conflict Prevention.[40] The CSIS Report, "Engaging with

Religion in Conflict-Prone Settings," finds room for just such additional activity and emerging partnerships in a number of cases cited in the report.

The Evolution of Multi-Track Diplomacy

The need for fostering greater social capital around dealing with issues of violence has not only stimulated the development of track-two diplomacy, but also multi-track diplomacy. Since Montville coined the term "track-two diplomacy" to describe the work done by non-elite actors representing non-governmental organizations, further distinction has been made to identify other avenues of diplomacy which, although always unofficial, endeavor to create a climate of receptivity for track-one activity. Search for Common Ground, an NGO working to resolve conflict internationally, defines track-two diplomacy as essentially "people to people" diplomacy undertaken by individuals or private groups. This type of activity may involve organizing meetings and conferences, generating media exposure and political and legal advocacy. Over the last quarter century, MacDonald and Louise Diamond have developed an additional approach to defining the levels of diplomatic intervention, expanding out from track-one to multi-track diplomacy.

In 1992 McDonald and Diamond co-founded the Institute for Multi-Track Diplomacy (IMTD). They defined nine tracks for research and development: government, professional conflict resolution, business, private citizens, training and education, activism, religious, funding, and public opinion/communication.[41] Beyond tracks one and two lay many opportunities for ordinary citizens to play significant roles in peace-building. Nation-states and armies may be able to establish the truce, but only people can build an enduring peace.

Track-two and multi-track diplomacy have been made increasingly possible through the evolution of additional factors that have played into the development of the field. These include:[42]

• The development of methodologies around Interactive Conflict Resolution workshops;[43]

• The expansion of non-governmental organizations over the past half century;[44]

- The development of insight in the field of Social Psychology and related disciplines;[45]
- An expanded sphere of international law and the importance of the rule of law in a world characterized by migration and globalization;[46] A growing recognition of the importance of restorative justice, particularly in formerly colonial regions;[47]
- A growing recognition of the importance of spiritual perceptivity in the work of peace building, certainly beginning with the Fellowship of Reconciliation (1914) in the last century but finding roots deepened in the contemporary efforts.[48]

Multi-Track Diplomacy for Religious Communities

In an effort toward the correlation of public policy and public theology religious communities can be valuable actors in our contemporary political climate where so much violent conflict is related to issues of identity. This has been amply illustrated by Little in *Peacemakers in Action*.[49] Indeed, such is increasingly the case not only at grassroots and middle-levels of social leadership, but even in the international arena. Recent years have seen the formation of the UN Tripartite Forum on Interfaith Cooperation for Peace, on the Alliance of Civilizations, on the acceptance of numerous religious NGOs into the UN system and the NGO Committee on Freedom of Religion or Belief to name only a few areas of development.[50]

Religious communities are communities of memory and identity. The struggle with the past and with the nature of forgiveness, the problems of "re-membering" after periods of destruction, intermingle with the problem of memory and faithfulness to the past and with forgiving and the problem of guilt and reconciliation with the past.[51] With political as well as issues of deep humanity involved in the very tragedy of violence, theologian Paul Ricoeur writes that "at the heart of selfhood and at the core of imputability, the paradox of forgiveness is laid bare, sharpened by the dialectic of repentance in the great Abrahamic tradition."[52] What is at issue here is nothing less than the power of the spirit of forgiveness to unbind the agent from his act. Writing autobiographically, theologian Miroslav Volf asks, "So from the start, the central question for me was not whether to remember. I most assuredly would remember and most incontestably should remember. Instead, the central question was how to remember rightly. And given my Christian sensibilities, my question from the start was, how should I remember abuse as a person committed to loving the wrongdoer and overcoming evil with good?"[53]

Author and theologian Flora Keshgegian re-scripts Christian narrative in a way reminiscent of Desmond Tutu's *No Future Without Forgiveness*, by musing on the nature of time and narrative in relation to the dynamics of forgiveness by writing:

> As we engage in intentional practices, cultivate new habits, and relearn the contours of hope, what will be the effect on how we tell time? How will time's tale change? Our narratives of time may well change to be less linear and ends-driven, not so relentlessly comedic and more multi-dimensional. We may become better schooled in living with complexity and multiplicity, ambiguity and indeterminacy.[54]

What makes the work of religious actors so powerful is that they can address the deepest needs of a shared public narrative or worldview and offer the possibility or the re-storying of a person or people's experience. Cycles of revenge or anger can be lifted up through forgiveness and repentance into a new narrative that re-humanizes the offender, deepens meaning for victims, and lays out meaningful steps toward enhanced community safety and historical meaning. Legal scholar and Dean of Harvard Law School Martha Minow even argues that forgiveness may even be a "third order" human right, making possible healthy social and economic rights and development which, in turn, promote what are normally thought of as human rights associated with the UDHR agenda.[55]

A Closing Consideration:
The Ambiguous Social Character of Religion

The unfolding of the "Arab Spring" as well as current political debate in the United States reminds us of the ambiguous social character of religion for statecraft arising from its necessary and independent voice in political affairs.[56] Thus far we have argued for the self-conscious role of religious actors in multi-track diplomacy. This is necessary if not always offering a clear path or set of procedures. Still, three points that arise in the Christian tradition with varying degrees of applicability to all religions offer a word of caution. Each draws us back to Freud's observations about religion, its functions, and the worldviews that come into play with religious actors.

First, religion will always be an unstable partner to official (track–one) diplomacy. Religion finds its limitations for public policy from the fact that it locates itself in a larger moral order than that of the state, Freud's sense of direction to be derived from a worldview. This is the prophetic role of religion as documented classically for its social function by theorists such as Max Weber and Ernst Troeltsch. In the Judeo-Christian tradition this is seen in the text which finds the anointing of a king over Israel (Saul) accompanied by the establishment of the office of prophet (1 Sam. 8–10). Among Christians, the New Testament bears a certain ambiguity toward the state as illustrated in contradictory visions raised up in Rom. 13 (authority as established by God) and Rev. 13 (the state as a destructive beast).[57]

Second, Freud reminds us of the priestly role of religion when he writes of religion's function to comfort and provide for our ultimate happiness. Often in tension with the prophetic role of religion, sociologist Peter Berger reminds us of the way in which religion may be employed to legitimate "social institutions by bestowing upon them an ultimately valid ontological status, that is, by *locating* them within a sacred and cosmic frame of reference." Religion has been employed to create taken-for-granted worldviews that often allow "the institutional order [to] be so interpreted as to hide, as much as possible, its *constructed* character."[58] We are well aware of the fact by now that many of the conflicts that employ religion or draw upon religious imagery do so in order to "mask" other political, economic, or socio-ethnic grievances.[59]

Third, beyond the prophetic and priestly functions of religion, there is an additional factor which relates to the complexity of multi-track diplomacy in contemporary political affairs, the question of what "identity" religion represents. Political theorist Jayne Docherty from the Conflict Resolution Program of Eastern Mennonite University writes of the complexity today in strategic negotiations with the active political participation of non-governmental organizations.[60] Such organizations, which can build social capital by building and enlarging upon official track-one diplomacy also bring their own agendas which may be different in greater or lesser ways from official statecraft. In the end, however, this is a reason to keep religion at the table, working and bargaining with others in good faith. The dialogue and mutual understanding that can arise underscores the value of such cross-boundary institutions as the World Council of Churches, the World Jewish Congress, Parliament of World Religions, the Alliance of Civilizations, and that of the Muslim scholars, clerics, and intellectuals issuing, *A Common Word Between Us and You.*

NOTES

[1] David Little, with Tanenbaum Center for Interreligious Understanding, eds., *Peacemakers in Action: Profiles of religion in Conflict Resolution* (Cambridge: Cambridge University Press, 2007), 219–48.

[2] Monica Duffy Toft, Daniel Philpott and Timothy Samuel Shah, *God's Century: Resurgent Religion and Global Politics* (New York: W. W. Norton & Company, 2011).

[3] In distinction from idealism in public policy, the world of political realism is often seen to be framed by a view that finds political contention to be derivative of human nature (Hans Morgenthau, *Politics Among Nations*, New York: Mc-Graw Hill, 1948/2005) or that of structural factors (John J. Mearsheimer, *The Tragedy of Great Power Politics*, New York: W. W. Norton & Company, 2003).

[4] Public theology for public culture was framed by Jacques Maritain, Reinhold Niebuhr, and Abraham Heschel from the middle of the twentieth century. More recently it is the subject of wide ranging scholarship as with James Cone, Barbara Jordan, Don Shriver, Max Stackhouse, Susan Thistlethwaite, and Benjamin Valentin, to name a few, and is the subject of much debate in the popular culture. On public theology with reference to public policy, see Raymond Helmick, S.J., and Rodney Petersen, eds., *Forgiveness and Reconciliation: Religion, Public Policy and Conflict Transformation* (Philadelphia, PA: Templeton Press, 2002).

[5] *U. S. Religious Landscape Survey Religious Beliefs and Practices: Diverse and Politically Relevant* published by The Pew Forum on Religion and Public Life, June 2008; and later updates.

[6] David Kennedy, "Images of Religion in International Legal Theory," in *Religion and International Law*, eds. Mark W. James and Carolyn Evans (Boston: Martinus Nijhoff Publishers, 2004), 151.

[7] James A. R. Nafziger, "The Functions of Religion in the International Legal System," in *Religion and International Law*, eds. Mark W. James and Carolyn Evans (Boston: Martinus Nijhoff Publishers, 2004), 155–76.

[8] Robert K. Merton, *Social Theory and Social Structure* (New York: Macmillan Publishers, 1968), 229.

⁹ Sigmund Freud, *New Introductory Lectures on Psycho-Analysis*, ed. and tr. James Strachey (New York: W. W. Norton & Co, 1965), 195–96.

¹⁰ Tariq Ali, *The Clash of Fundamentalisms: Crusades, Jihads and Modernity* (New York: Verso, 2002).

¹¹ Madeleine Albright, *The Mighty and the Almighty* (New York: HarperCollins Publishers, 2006).

¹² Eliza Griswold, *The Tenth Parallel: Dispatches from the Fault Line Between Christianity and Islam* (New York: Farrar, Straus and Giroux, 2010).

¹³ Liora Danan, *Mixed Blessings: U.S. Government Engagement with Religion in Conflict-Prone Settings. A Report of the Post-Conflict Reconstruction Project* (Washington, D.C.: CSIS, 2007).

¹⁴ ERPCS, *Engaging with Religion in Conflict-Prone Settings*, Report of the Center for Strategic and International Studies Post-Conflict Reconstruction Project, August 2006 (http://www.whitehouse.gov/nsc/nss/2006/ Last accessed: April 1, 2014).

¹⁵ Danan, *Mixed Blessings*.

¹⁶ One place to begin to trace this reassessment is in the work by Douglas Johnson and Cynthia Sampson, *Religion, The Missing Dimension of Statecraft* (New York: Oxford University Press, 1995).

¹⁷ Douglas Johnston, *Faith-Based Diplomacy Trumping Realpolitik* (New York: Oxford University Press, 2008). See also his more recent book, *Religion, Terror, and Error: U.S. Foreign Policy and the Challenge of Spiritual Engagement* (Westport, CT: Praeger, 2011). Johnston argues that the United States needs to rethink old assumptions with respect to religion and expand the scope of its policymaking to include religion.

¹⁸ Felix Wilfred, *The Sling of Utopia: Struggles for a Different Society* (New Delhi: ISPCK, 2005).

¹⁹ John W. de Gruchy, "Public Theology as Christian Witness: Exploring the Genre," in *International Journal of Public Theology* 1 (2007): 26–41.

²⁰ Norman E. Thomas, *Missions and Unity: Lessons from History, 1792–2010* (Eugene, OR: Cascade Books, 2010), 221–40. See the argument by Hilary Charlesworth, "The Challenges of Human Rights Law for Religious Traditions," in *Religion and International Law*, eds. Mark W. James and Carolyn Evans (Boston: Martinus Nijhoff Publishers, 2004), 401–15.

²¹ Duncan B. Forrester, "Working in the Quarry: A Response to the Colloquium," in *Public Theology for the 21st Century*, eds. William Storrar and Andrew R. Morton (Edinburgh: T&T Clark, 2004), 431–38.

²² Ibid., 436.

²³ Susan Thistlethwaite, ed., *Interfaith Just Peacemaking* (New York: Palgrave Macmillan, 2012).

²⁴ John W. de Gruchy, "From Political to Public Theologies: The Role of Theology in Public Life in South Africa," in *Public Theology for the 21st Century*, eds. William F. Storrar and Andrew R. Morton (Edinburgh: T&T Clark, 2004), 45–62.

²⁵ David Tracy, *The Analogical Imagination: Christian Theology and the Culture of Pluralism* (London: SCM Press, 1981), 29.

²⁶ Ibid., 31.

²⁷ See Glen Stassen, *Just Peacemaking: Transforming Initiatives for Justice and Peace* (Louisville, KY: Westminster John Knox Press, 1992); John Paul Lederach, *The Moral Imagination: The Art and Soul of Building Peace* (New York: Oxford University Press, 2005); Kay Pranis, Barry Stuart, and Mark Wedge, *Peacemaking Circles: From Crime to Community* (St. Paul, MN: Living Justice Press, 2003).

²⁸ James Gilligan, *Violence: Reflections on a National Epidemic* (New York: Vintage, 1996).

²⁹ Howard Zehr, *Changing Lenses* (Scottdale, PA: Herald Press, 1990), 181.

³⁰ William P. George, "Looking for a Global Ethic? Try International Law," in *Religion and International Law*, eds. Mark W. James and Carolyn Evans (Boston: Martinus Nijhoff Publishers, 2004), 483–504.

³¹ Sharma Mantha, *Handbook on Conflict Management Skills* (Hyderabad: Centre for Good Governance, 2001).

³² Lisa Schirich, *The Little Book of Strategic Peacebuilding: A Vision and Framework for Peace with Justice* (Intercourse, PA: Good Books, 2004), 71.

³³ Cordula Reimann, "Assessing the State-of-the-Art in Conflict Transformation," in *Berghof Handbook for Conflict Transformation*, eds. Martina Fischer and Beatrix Schmelzle (Berlin: Berghof Research Center for Constructive Management, 2004).

³⁴ William D. Davidson and Joseph V. Montville, "Foreign Policy According to Freud," in *Foreign Policy* 45 (Winter 1981–82): 145–57; Joseph V. Montville, *The Arrow and the Olive Branch: A Case for Track Two Diplomacy: The Psychodynamics of International Relationships* (Lexington, MA.: Lexington Books, 1990); and Joseph V. Montville, "Religion and Peacemaking," in *Forgiveness and Reconciliation: Religion, Public Policy and Conflict Transformation*, eds. Raymond Helmick, S.J. and Rodney Petersen (Philadelphia, PA: Templeton Press, 2001), 97–116.

³⁵ John W. MacDonald and D. B. Bendahmane, eds., *Conflict Resolution: Track Two Diplomacy* (Washington, D.C.: Foreign Service Institute, 1987).

³⁶ John Davies and Edward Kaufman, "Second Track/Citizens' Diplomacy: An Overview," in *Second Track/Citizen's Diplomacy: Concepts and Techniques for Conflict Transformation*, eds. John Davies and Edward Kaufman (New York: Rowman & Littlefield, Inc., 2003), 3.

³⁷ Davies and Kaufman, "Second Track," 2.

³⁸ John W. MacDonald, "Multi–Track Diplomacy," in *Beyond Intractability*, eds. Guy Burgess and Heidi Burgess (Boulder, CO: Conflict Resolution Consortium: University of Colorado, 2003), 52–54.

³⁹ Peter Ackerman and Jack DuVall, *A Force More Powerful: A Century of Nonviolent Conflict* (New York: St. Martin's Press, 2000).

⁴⁰ Paul van Tongeren, Malin Brenk, Marte Hellema and Juliette Verhoeven *People Building Peace: Successful Stories of Civil Society* (Boulder, CO: Lynne Rienner Publishers, 2005).

⁴¹ John W. MacDonald, "The Need for Multi–Track Diplomacy," in *Second Track/Citizen's Diplomacy: Concepts and Techniques for Conflict Transformation*, eds. John Davies and Edward Kaufman (New York: Rowman & Littlefield, Inc., 2003), 49–60.

⁴² Ronald J. Fisher, "Historical Mapping of the Field of Interactive Conflict Resolution," in *Second Track/Citizen's Diplomacy: Concepts and Techniques for Conflict Transformation*, eds. John Davies and Edward Kaufman (New York: Rowman & Littlefield, Inc., 2003), 61–77.

⁴³ Jay Rothman, *Confrontation to Cooperation: Resolving Ethnic and Regional Conflict* (Newbury Park, CA: Sage Publications, 1992).

⁴⁴ Roland Hoksbergen and Lowell M. Ewert, eds., *Local Ownership, Global Change: Will Civil Society Change the World* (Monrovia, CA: MARC Publishing, 2002); Richard Falk, *Religion and Humane Global Governance* (London: Palgrave, 2001).

⁴⁵ Louis Kriesberg, *Constructive Conflicts: From Escalation to Resolution* (New York: Rowan & Littlefield, 1998).

⁴⁶ Brian Z. Tamanaha, *On the Rule of Law: History, Politics, Theory* (Cambridge University Press, 2004); Tarek Mitri, ed., *Religion, Law and Society: A Christian-Muslim Discussion* (Geneva: WCC Publications, 1995).

⁴⁷ Howard Zehr, *Changing Lenses* (Scottdale, PA: Herald Press, 1990); John de Gruchy, "From Political to Public Theologies: The Role of Theology in Public Life in South Africa," in *Public Theology for the 21st Century*, eds. William F. Storrar and Andrew R. Morton (Edinburgh: T&T Clark, 2004), 45–62; Rupert Ross, *Returning to the Teachings* (Toronto: Penguin Group, 1996).

⁴⁸ Emmanuel Clapsis, ed., *Christian Spirituality and Violence* (Geneva: WCC Publications: Geneva, 2007); Walter Wink, ed., *Peace Is the Way: Writings on Nonviolence from the Fellowship of Reconciliation* (Maryknoll, NY: Orbis Books, 2000); Dorothy Friesen, "Social Action and the Need for Prayer," in *Peace Is the Way: Writings on Nonviolence from the Fellowship of Reconciliation*, ed. Walter Wink (Maryknoll, NY: Orbis Books, 2000), 124–28; Elise Boulding, "Envisioning the Peaceable Kingdom" in *Peace Is the Way: Writings on Nonviolence from the Fellowship of Reconciliation*, ed. Walter Wink (Maryknoll, NY: Orbis Books, 2000), 129–34.

⁴⁹ Little, *Peacemakers in Action*; Helmick and Petersen, *Forgiveness and Reconciliation*.

⁵⁰ Abdullahi An-Na'im, "Religion and Global Civil Society: Inherent Incompatibility or Synergy and Interdependency?," in *Global Civil Society Yearbook 2002*, eds. Helmut Anheier, Marlies Glasius, and Mary Kaldor (Oxford University Press, 2002), 55–76.

⁵¹ Paul Ricoeur, *Memory, History, Forgetting* (Chicago: University of Chicago, 2004).

⁵² Ibid., 459.

⁵³ Miroslav Volf, *The End of Memory: Remembering Rightly in a Violent World* (Grand Rapids, MI: Eerdmans Publishing Co., 2007).

⁵⁴ Flora Kesgegian, *Time for Hope* (New York: Continuum, 2006); Desmond Tutu, *No Future Without Forgiveness* (New York: Image, 2000).

⁵⁵ Martha Minow, "What is Forgiveness?" in *BTI Magazine* (Numbers 12:2–13: 1–2/ 2013–2014): 7–11.

⁵⁶ Matthew Ritter, "Universal Rights Talk/Plurality of Voices: A Philosophical-Theological Hearing," in *Religion and International Law*, eds. Mark W. James and Carolyn Evans (Boston: Martinus Nijhoff Publishers, 2004), 417–82.

[57] Walter Wink, "Facing the Myth of Redemptive Violence," in *Christian Peacemaker Teams* (Aug 23, 2006).

[58] Peter Berger, *The Sacred Canopy: Elements of a Sociological Theory of Religion* (Garden City, NY: Anchor Books, 1969), 33.

[59] Scott Appleby, *The Ambivalence of the Sacred* (New York: Rowman and Littlefield, 1999); Raymond Helmick, "Does Religion Fuel or Heal in Conflicts?," in *Forgiveness and Reconciliation: Religion, Public Policy and Conflict Transformation*, eds. Helmick and Petersen (Philadelphia, PA: Templeton Press, 2002), 81–96.

[60] Jayne Seminare Docherty, *The Little Book of Strategic Negotiation: Negotiating During Turbulent Times* (Intercourse, PA: Good Books, 2005).

13.
Developing a Human Rights Lens on Religious Peacebuilding

Scott Appleby

The field of inquiry that explores the relationships among religion, conflict, and peacebuilding—if no longer in its infancy—is now facing what could be a protracted adolescence. To the rescue, as in so many areas, is our distinguished honoree. David Little's writings on religion and human rights contain significant insights to be developed and applied to his and others' work on religion, conflict and peacebuilding.

In general, the scholarship in this latter area is underdeveloped and lacks the kind of analytical rigor that Little will surely contribute in his so-called retirement. The field is stuck for the moment in a descriptive-analytical mode without sufficient theorizing. Well established by this point is the fundamental observation that religions—especially with regard to their attitudes toward violence and practices of resistance to political oppression and structural or social injustice—are both internally diverse and plural. They are also ambivalent, that is, capable of sacralizing both acts of lethal violence *and* heroic nonviolent witness, advocacy, and activism in the face of perceived injustice. The key challenge now, in considering the inconstancy of religious communities and movements regarding the appropriate, ethically sound *means* of pursuing justice and obeying the divine will, is to identify the conditions under which they choose tactics, and the relationship between sets of conditions and particular choices. Under what conditions do religious actors choose to behave toward the religious or secular other in a manner commensurate with a trajectory toward life, healing, and reconciliation found embedded within the religious tradition? Why and when do some faith-inspired actors recognize the enemy's inherent human dignity and rights, and restrict recourse to deadly violence against the enemy?

A step in this direction of getting at "conditions under which" is to study those religious actors who, struggling within the cycle of war or related forms of deadly conflict, have nonetheless attempted to observe the highest standards of human rights. In light of the bellicose attitudes and behaviors adopted by their co-religionists in times of heightened tension, these religious actors—by virtue of their willingness to try to avoid violence, enter into dialogue with the other, and perhaps even move toward forgiveness and reconciliation—are outliers. They qualify as peacebuilders insofar as they develop local or national methods of conflict resolution and transformation derived from the repertoire of symbols and rituals available within the religious tradition. In South Africa and Northern Ireland, for example, daring individuals have turned to scriptures and communal practices to move their aggrieved co-religionists to exhaust the requirements of retributive justice, and head into the realm of mercy, compassion, restorative justice and healing.

To date, Little has contributed to the study of these "daring" religious peacebuilders by focusing on their personal characteristics as individuals. Specifically, he has overseen the profiling of Muslim, Christian, and Jewish women and men identified as peacemakers by the Tanenbaum Center for Interreligious Understanding's Program on Religion and Conflict Resolution. (Tanenbaum identifies peacemakers from non-Abrahamic traditions as well.) In his introduction to the volume he edited for Tanenbaum Center for Interreligious Understanding, *Peacemakers in Action: Profiles of Religion in Conflict Resolution*, Little specifies several characteristics shared by these individuals typical of the religious peacebuilder. The latter's effectiveness derives from the position he holds in the religious communities. She is indigenous to the community, has a reputation as one who has suffered with the community, and is a respected religious practitioner. He possesses the credibility to draw on scriptural, doctrinal, ritual, and other religious sources in the effort to humanize the "other," in cultural and religious terms resonant with the co-religionists. The peacemaker, further, has a reputation for integrity and fairness; this does not preclude him or her from holding strong views and convictions—quite the contrary—but generally these convictions are placed in the service of the common good and the building of sustainable and just relationships across ethnic, religious, or political lines of division. These faith-inspired peacemakers, Little tells us, tend to be people not only of profound religious faith, but of deep emotional intelligence, naturally empathic, so that they embody the doctrine common to the Abrahamic faiths—that all people share a core humanity created in the image of God, and therefore deserve to be treated with unblinking respect and compassion. Beyond this, the peacemakers are "ordinary people," some introverts, others extroverts, drawn from all backgrounds and walks of life. Dramatic conversion stories sometimes figure into their personal narratives.

Yet, the peacemakers share across cultures and religions an experience that separates them from their co-religionists: "[i]n coming to understand our Peacemakers and how their public stature enables them to do their work, we were struck by a sad irony," Little writes. "They are effective because of their religious identity and their membership in the local community. And yet, almost all the Peacemakers experience a profound sense of being isolated, even when they enjoy support from families or religious communities."[1]

To add to this portrait, I reviewed the chapter that Little and I co-authored for a book on *Religious Peacebuilding*.[2] A theme explored in that essay is the centrality of the selective retrieval, from the host religious tradition, of theological and moral warrants for privileging reconciliation over vengeance, and nonviolence over violence. Religious peacebuilders strive to place reconciliation and restoration on the same footing as retribution in the panoply of orthodox responses to injustice. In this regard, the religious peacebuilder's task is similar to that of the religious human rights advocate, namely, that of grounding human rights within the religious tradition, or at least of legitimating their practice in the ethical-juridical norms of the religious tradition.

Beyond that, the religious peacebuilder has two additional tasks, both daunting. The first is to develop and popularize a theological narrative that prioritizes nonviolence, forgiveness, and reconciliation as the fundamental orientation, not just an option, within the tradition. This orientation must then become the hermeneutic lens through which religious scholars, jurists, and leaders interpret the meaning of justice within the tradition. Building on that foundation, the religious peacebuilder attempts a second feat. It is not sufficient to espouse theological principles of peace and justice, reconciliation, and restoration. Within the community, the social *practices* of peacebuilding must be adopted, including the methods of conflict prevention, mediation, capacity-building, interreligious and interethnic dialogue, and institution building for sustainable peace.

This is a farther shore than one might imagine. One cannot expect religious actors, including and perhaps especially religious officials, to be prepared to act in a peacebuilding capacity. Peacebuilding is, after all, a profession, not merely an avocation, and people must be tutored in and disciplined to a profession. This takes time and resources, not least educators and trainers. At a more fundamental level, however, is the need for a career and vocational reorientation. A religious leader is not trained as a mediator, conciliator, expert in transitional justice, or educator for peace. I remember being struck by how eager a classroom of African Catholic bishops was to hear our message of strategic peacebuilding, how receptive many bishops were to the concept—and yet how utterly surprising to them that they were being called to act in that capacity "on the ground," "in the real world."

All of this raises questions about the conditions under which a community shifts its fundamental orientation toward socially engaged peacebuilding, and about the relationship between human rights discourse and practice, on the one hand, and religious peacebuilding, on the other.

On these questions Little's thinking on religion and human rights offers a potentially significant contribution. I refer specifically to the conditions for the possibility of religious peacebuilding established by the state, and the related question of the status of religious majorities and minorities within the state. There is a growing body of literature authored by political scientists such as Al Stepan, Timothy Shah, and Dan Philpott, that argues that the key variable in advancing both democratization and human rights is the autonomy of religious bodies from the state, within a robust enforcement of religious freedom. The touchstone for this discussion is Stepan's notion of twin tolerations as the guide for religion-state relations.

Little's contribution is related to this line of argument but also distinct from it, I believe. With Abdullahi An-Na'im, Abdolkarim Soroush, and Abdulaziz Sachedina, among others, Little wants to assert, on the one hand, the right and indeed the obligation of religious communities to participate in the ongoing pubic debate about the precise meaning and legal instantiation of human rights in a given cultural context, and, on the other hand, he and his colleagues want to lend vigorous support, from within the religious community, to the "secular" notion that external constraints must be placed on religious behavior in the public sphere where there is a conflict between universal human rights norms and interpretations of the religious tradition that would lead to behavior violating these norms. An-Na'im would add that religion loses its character as religion when it seeks to enforce its religious teachings through state power. Little makes the point with his typical force on such questions: "The whole idea (as with the drafters of the Universal Declaration) is that there exists a universal, indubitable and unavoidable standard of moral appraisal of the behavior of authorities of all kinds, including state authorities" (and, of course religious authorities).[3]

What does Little et al's, insistence on these twin constraints—on the state and on religious authorities—have to do with the hoped-for development of the theory and practice of religious peacebuilding?

A clue is found in the aforementioned reference to the isolation of the religious peacebuilder. One of the consequences of being identified in the religious community, as well as in the secular or pluralist political community and the state, is the question of one's role and relationship vis-à-vis these two entities. The religious peacebuilder attempting to address conflicts between a state or political authority and a religious community or communities, or within a state and between religious and ethnic communities competing for resources and political power, must mediate between and among competing and clashing norms and regimes of power and authority. How is she to be guided by twin constraints or twin tolerations? How is she to translate deeply held religious commitments into second order bridge discourse? How is he to get a hearing within the religious community and the larger pluralist community and attempt to bridge these communities of discourse? This has been the challenge for religious figures who would be mediators in this grand sense, from the Dalai Lama to Desmond Tutu to Tariq Ramadan, and yet the challenge has been insufficiently analyzed and theorized.

Little's insistence on developing case-tested rubrics and guidelines indicates a way forward. This question of mediation of competing discourses and power relations is the grist for a mill of comparative case studies in peacebuilding, religion and the state.

The Mennonite Case: Discipleship, Peacebuilding, and the State

On the question of competing conceptualizations of power and the public role of faith communities, consider for example, the case of the evolution of the Mennonite community. Widely recognized as pioneers in faith-based conflict transformation, Mennonites played a constructive peacebuilding role in Nicaragua, Somalia, South Africa, Northern Ireland, and elsewhere beginning in the 1980s. Active in international relief work since First World War, Mennonite leadership in religious peacebuilding is an outgrowth of the church's humanitarian mission, and a result of its internal evolution in the twentieth century from quietism and separatism to positive engagement with the world.

Travails in the twentieth century, occasioned by their unpopular responses to the world wars, led Mennonites to rethink central aspects of their theological heritage: the validity of separatism, the social consequences of their form of pacifism, and the practical meaning of "mission" or evangelization.

From the late seventeenth century, when they first settled in North America, American Mennonites practiced a self-protective withdrawal from the world around them. A stringent dualism, by which the outside world was seen as sinful beyond redemption, and a radical pacifism served as the theological and moral underpinnings of this stance. Traditionalist hard-liners condemned any formulations of nonviolence that legitimated engagement with external political or social concerns. "Gandhi's program [of *satyagraha*] is not one of nonresistance or peace," Guy F. Hershberger wrote. "It is a form of warfare" to be avoided by Mennonites.[4]

For many thoughtful Mennonites, however, the world wars, state-sponsored mass violence, the genocides of the twentieth century, and the growing momentum and salience of the human rights movement eroded this traditionalist theology. During the First World War American Mennonites were denounced as "slackers" for refusing military service and were accused of reaping the benefits of national security without contributing to its cost.

Voices from within the Mennonite community began to question whether passivity in the face of injustice was the appropriate way to imitate Christ, and in 1920 the North American churches created the Mennonite Central Committee (MCC) to address the needs of Russian Mennonites displaced and impoverished by the Bolshevik revolution. During the Second World War Mennonites extended their social concern beyond the traditional "mutual aid" programs for church members suffering spiritual and financial hardship. Mennonite conscientious objectors performed alternative service in Civilian Public Service camps, fought forest fires, served as human subjects in medical research, and worked in mental health hospitals, where they exposed the widespread cruel and inhuman treatment of patients. The creation in 1942 of the Peace Section of the MCC signaled this new willingness to protest against human rights abuses and injustices wherever and to whomever they occurred. After the war, Mennonites began to leave their rural homesteads to seek higher education, enter the professions, and join the mainstream of social life. Reflecting on these experiences Mennonite thinkers John Howard Yoder and C. Norman Kraus developed a theology of active peacemaking that challenged Hershberger's rejection of social engagement.[5]

MCC relief work was enormous in scale, especially considering the size of the church; many North American families contributed one or more members to spend several years in volunteer service. During the 1960s and 1970s, domestic and international outreach expanded dramatically through the Mennonite Disaster Service, another MCC subsidiary. Radicalized by their participation in the civil rights and anti–Vietnam War movements MCC workers began to challenge their fellow Mennonites to address the systemic conditions that created human rights violations. Such stirrings of conscience inspired Mennonites to study professional mediation and conciliation techniques. In 1976 William Kenney circulated a proposal based on the work of Adam Curle, a Quaker conciliator, Gene Sharp, a scholar of nonviolent resistance, and James Laue, a sociologist and the director of Washington University's Crisis Intervention Center in St. Louis. The proposal envisioned a professional class of peacemakers rooted in the local churches and congregations; the result was the Mennonite Conciliation Service (MCS), established in 1978, after church leaders consulted secular organizations such as the American Arbitration Association to determine the best ways to fill the "methodological vacuum" within a church rich in the theology of peacemaking, but now finding itself woefully inadequate in its practice. Mennonite colleges and seminaries began to offer courses and programs in conflict mediation and management.

The practice of MCC relief and development workers, whenever possible and appropriate, involved becoming members of the communities they served. MCS took a similar long-term approach to conflict resolution. In 1983 MCS expanded its operations to meet heightened demand from both Mennonites and non-Mennonites for training in mediation techniques; and in the 1990s, as women and African Americans assumed prominent leadership positions, MCS developed expertise in conflicts stemming from gender inequities, racism, and inner city poverty. Until the mid-eighties, however, the international wing of the MCC remained focused on relief and development work. A new initiative emerged in the summer of 1984, Joseph S. Miller recounts, when thousands of Mennonites gathered in Strasbourg, France, for the 11th Mennonite World Conference and heard keynote speaker Ronald J. Sider's challenge, delivered under the rubric "God's people reconciling," for Mennonites to form groups of Christians who were willing to risk their lives in the cause of peacemaking by entering conflict zones and mediating between hostile peoples. Sider shrewdly reminded his audience of their 450-year history of martyrdom, migration, and missionary proclamation, and he argued that the God of Shalom had been preparing Mennonites for this very moment. "The next 20 years will be the most dangerous—and perhaps the most vicious and violent—in human history," Sider predicted. "If we are ready to embrace the cause, God's reconciling people will profoundly impact the course of world history." The events of the Strasbourg Assembly thereby led to the creation of Christian Peacemaker Teams (CPT)—initially envisioned by Sider as a "nonviolent army of international peacekeepers"—and, eventually, to the establishment of the International Conciliation Service of the MCC. [6]

Having served as a church worker in Spain and a mediator with Spanish-language skills, John Paul Lederach, a Mennonite graduate student studying conflict resolution under Paul Wehr at the University of Colorado, was sought out by refugees from the wars raging throughout Central America; in 1985, the MCC asked Lederach to go to the region as a trainer in conflict resolution. In training Moravian church leaders to mediate the violent conflict between the Sandinista government of Nicaragua and the Miskito Indians, Lederach recognized how important were the trust and good relations built up over years by MCC relief workers in the region. He also found conflict mediation at the international level to be exceedingly complex: one had to negotiate Sandinista interests, internal subdivisions in the Indian groups, external factors such as foreign influence (the CIA and contras, attempting at the time to topple the Sandinistas, did not welcome efforts to make their life easier), and threats to personal safety (including reports of a CIA contract on his life and plans to kidnap his daughter). Thus, while he believed conflict transformation should become an integral part the MCC's overseas work, Lederach was aware that Mennonites needed a significant amount of preparation for the task.

By the end of 1988 Lederach had become the director of MCS, and was spending much of his time in international reconciliation efforts; the International Conciliation Service (ICS) formalized this role and empowered Lederach and his associates to draw on a worldwide network of friendships and contacts that had developed over the seven decades of MCC relief and development work. The ICS devoted its resources to training and education, program development, consulting, and invited intervention in a variety of conflict settings. Lederach proposed that MCC channel a percentage of its relief and humanitarian funding to specific peacemaking initiatives, and he led the way in educating various MCC constituencies about the close connection between the two types of service. Ethnic and religious conflict was a primary cause of endemic poverty and malnutrition in so many settings, he reminded Mennonite congregations and MCC host country partners, and MCC relief work provided the type of long-term, day-to-day presence needed for successful conflict transformation. These relief workers, with their reputation for integrity, disinterested service and long-term commitment, had inadvertently prepared the way for intentional Mennonite efforts at conflict transformation. By 1995 Mennonites were supporting an annual budget of $43 million, more than 900 full-time volunteers or salaried workers were stationed in fifty-seven countries, and thousands of part-time volunteers in the United States devoted countless hours packing containers of food, clothing, and medicines to be shipped overseas.[7]

As trusted outside partners, the Mennonites of the ICS launched peacemaking initiatives in Nicaragua, Colombia, and Somalia. They adopted a comprehensive approach, attempting to address the immediate human suffering, the root problems generating the cycle of violence, and the need for secure space where enemies could meet and where diverse and opposing concerns and interests could converge. Recognizing the foolishness and futility of trying to impose North American models of conflict resolution, Lederach began to devise mediation strategies suggested by cues and patterns elicited from the culture in question. Eventually, MCC mediation trainers ran their students through exercises based on language and culturally resonant images and symbols. The "elicitive method," as it came to be called, was on display in numerous conflict settings as the international Mennonite peacemaking programs mushroomed in the late 1980s.

The emergence of the MCC as a leader in the inchoate field of religious peacebuilding and human rights added a new dimension to the familiar question of the relationship between Mennonite relief and development work and the church's specifically religious mission. It is a question being asked by and about other religious communities and organizations newly involved in track-two diplomacy. From its inception the MCC was concerned less with "making people into Christians" than with providing disaster relief and encouraging economic development—in itself a powerful witness to gospel values. Because the MCC functions as a consortium encompassing the full spectrum of churches, from the most traditional to the most progressive in the Anabaptist family, one would expect a similar range of attitudes regarding the meaning of "mission" and the desirability of proselytism. In fact, few MCC or ICS workers deliver direct, uninvited presentations of the Christian faith; such an approach, most feel, would undermine the profound Mennonite commitment, equally rooted in religious conviction, to the nurturing of relationships of trust and mutual understanding. Such relationships respect and even cherish the particularity of the other even as they seek to identify a common ground.

In light of the Mennonite church's long history of separatism and theological dualism, its turn to active engagement is striking—another instance of religious traditions evolving in promising directions as they become accustomed to their twenty-first-century roles and social locations as crosscultural, transnational, nongovernmental actors. Today's Mennonite peacemakers retain the traditional commitment to separation of church and state, the elimination of coercive power from the religious domain, and the notion of a separate nonviolent realm for "the meek." But the notion of the sacred community has been broadened to include not only those who confess Jesus Christ, but all those who reject coercion and violence.

The distinctive characteristics of Mennonite peacemaking—openness to non-Mennonite cultural values, the ability to elicit fruitful mediation procedures from the communities in conflict, and so on—reflect specific moral values (e.g., Christian humility) and religious characteristics (e.g., an ecclesiology based on group discernment and an exalted view of community). The church's prayers, songs, sermons and rituals proclaim that entering compassionately into the suffering of others is to obey and imitate Christ. The comprehensive relationships Mennonites build extend their role as mediators beyond the merely instrumental, and their identification with the suffering parties means that Mennonite mediators are hardly a "third party" in the usual sense of the term.

Neither are they insiders, however, and the long-term commitment to a place and people required by the elicitive approach is extraordinarily demanding. Shuttle-style mediators and diplomats avoid the isolation that comes with a time-intensive commitment to a conflict; Mennonite peacebuilders, by contrast, avoid or contain loneliness and burn-out by bringing community with them, in one way or another. Rites of commissioning by the home congregation, prayer and ritual calendars shared across oceans and time zones, and other missionary customs reinforce the sense of fellowship; in some settings, the mediator joins a worshipping community of MCC relief workers, however small, already in place.

The courage and human rights commitment of these NGO-based peacemakers is not in question. The methods of the ICS peacemakers, especially the elicitive approach, unfold within a cultural approach to conflict transformation which both complements and challenges more conventional approaches. Grounded in the mediators' expertise in local religion and culture developed over long-term, on-site presence in the community, the cultural approach attempts to avoid the moral and political utilitarianism of crisis-centered diplomacy and its focus on immediate outcomes. (The defenders of the elicitive approach argue that, once established, it also proves effective in crisis management.) Through the agency of intermediaries the MCC/ICS seeks to establish working relationships across cultural lines, especially among mid-level community leaders (mayors and other local officials, teachers, judges, security officers, and so on), and to focus attention on the plight of the poor and the suffering—those citizens and refugees displaced by unjust economic policies, social discrimination or mass violence. The Mennonites believe that these people, and the social conditions from which they suffer, stand at the heart of conflict, and must be involved in a process of social transformation that addresses the root causes of the conflict.

In sum, this is a case of religious actors acting precisely as religious people and contributing in a professionally sophisticated and effective manner to the resolution and transformation of deadly conflict. It illustrates the convergence of human rights activism and faith-based peacebuilding, even as it raises questions about tensions between the two. Moving beyond the celebration of individuals and their personal traits—though this is a central part of the story—this kind of case study, set in comparative context, promises to yield the kind of analytical rigor in the study of faith-based peacebuilding, that characterizes Little's own work in religion and human rights.

NOTES

[1] David Little, with Tanenbaum Center for Interreligious Understanding, eds., *Peacemakers in Action: Profiles of religion in Conflict Resolution* (Cambridge: Cambridge University Press, 2007), 6.

[2] David Little and Scott Appleby, "A Moment of Opportunity? The Promise of Religious Peacebuilding in an Era of Religious and Ethnic Conflict," in eds., Harold Coward, Gordon S. Smith, *Religion and Peacebuilding* (Albany, NY: SUNY Press, 2004), 1–23.

[3] David Little, "Religion, Human Rights, and Secularism: Preliminary Clarifications and Some Islamic, Jewish, and Christian Responses," in eds., William Schweiker, Kevin Jung, Michael A. Johnson, *Humanity Before God: Contemporary Faces of Jewish, Christian, and Islamic Ethics* (Minneapolis: Fortress Press, 2006), 256–283.

[4] As quoted in Joseph S. Miller, "A History of the Mennonite Conciliation Service, International Conciliation Service, and Christian Peacemaker Teams," in eds., Cynthia Sampson and John Paul Lederach, *From the Ground Up: Mennonite Contributions to International Peacebuilding*, (Oxford: Oxford University Press, 2000), 6.

[5] Leo Driedger and Donald B. Kraybill, *Mennonite Peacemaking: From Quietism to Activism* (Scottsdale, Penn.: Herald Press, 1994), 71.

[6] This passage based upon a revised version of Appleby, *The Ambivalence of the Sacred: Religion, Violence and Reconciliation* (Lanham, MD: Rowman & Littlefield, 2000), chapter 4.

[7] Joseph S. Miller, "Who are the Mennonites?" in eds., Sampson and Lederach, *From the Ground Up: Mennonite Contributions to International Peacebuilding*, 275–280.

14.
Toward a Polycentric Approach to Conflict Transformation

Atalia Omer

I argue in this chapter that David Little's theoretical insights concerning the role of religion in conflict and peacebuilding processes can be expanded to accommodate a global outlook on the dynamics of conflict and conflict transformation. By a "global outlook," I mean that the analysis of conflict and the designs and praxis of programs of conflict transformation need to shift toward a polycentric orientation that captures the role of global networks of solidarity, interest groups and diasporas, in influencing the dynamics of conflict and peace. How and why an exploration of diasporas and homeland politics is relevant for processes of peacebuilding is, however, a discussion that demands further pondering in Little's work.

I begin by defining peacebuilding. I concur with Scott Appleby and John Paul Lederach's articulation of the concept of 'peacebuilding' as denoting an essentially multifaceted and multidirectional process that must involve a multidisciplinary and strategic outlook and alliances among local and global actors. They define "peacebuilding" as "a set of complementary practices aimed at transforming a society riddled by violent conflict, inequality, and other systemic forms of injustice into a society oriented toward forging a *justpeace*."[1] "Strategic peacebuilding," the authors continue, "develops around the critical question of 'who' and 'what types of processes' will be needed to initiate, develop, and sustain the desired transformation."[2]

While this approach highlights peacebuilding as a comprehensive process requiring an intentional coordination of analysis and activism on a variety of levels from human rights advocacy to international law, humanitarian aid, international NGOs, peace enforcement practices and local folklore, and cultures and structures, it presupposes the thoroughly local character of conflicts and thus thoroughly external character of global networks and agents involved in one capacity or another in affecting conflict and peace. This underlying local-global dichotomy animates Appleby and Lederach's emphasis on the principle of "indigenous empowerment," which grounds conflict transformation in the cultivation of "the human and cultural resources from within a given setting," so that the setting will not be defined "as the problem and the outside as the answer."[3] Hence, "external agents of change" involved in processes of conflict transformation would need to focus on "the validation of the people and the expansion of resources within the setting."[4]

The study of the increased impact of diasporas on the dynamics of conflict and peace, however, challenges this dichotomization of the local and the external. For instance, in her research of both the Tamil and Sinhalese Sri Lankan diasporas in the West and their relations and involvements with the conflict in Sri Lanka, Camilla Orjuela writes:

> Today's "warriors" in the ongoing conflict in Sri Lanka do not all wear military outfits and linger in the jungles of the war-ravaged South Asian island. Among them are thousands of people with placards outside the UN complex in Geneva advocating Tamil rights to self-determination. There are protestors in down-town Toronto urging the international community to help Sri Lanka fight Tamil terrorism, conference organizers in Oslo and Tokyo, lobbyists in New York and London and enthusiasts in every corner of the world creating yet another website for the benefit of their distant homeland. The war is waged in all parts of the world.[5]

While connected on a variety of ethnic, religious, cultural, and national or symbolic levels to the local population entangled in violent conflict, diasporas often function concretely as "external agents of change" by providing remittances, lobbying, reconciliation and development funds, humanitarian aid, lobbying and consciousness raising efforts, arms, and so forth. The focus on the diasporas, as I further illustrate below, therefore challenges the assumption that the "people" is somehow confined within a prescribed geopolitical space categorized as "local" where violence is waged.

Diasporas can and usually do reinforce and reify definitions of people-hood and narratives of common descent and destiny but also in virtue of their locations challenge the meanings and boundaries of identity, and being at, and fighting for, a "home[land]." Simon Turner suggests that the interrelations between a homeland and diasporas constitute "a single political field that happens to be spread geographically."[6] But with geographical and contextual variations come substantive divergences (born out of a multiplicity of contexts) in defining the boundaries of membership in the community. The diasporas partake in and provide resources for the definition and possible redefinition of the "people" and the terms of the conflict. Thus, neither the "setting" nor the "people" is confined to a local space because what resources the diasporas may provide would depend in large part on a thick analysis of their contexts of domicile. Drawing on Little's view of the "nation" as an interpretative subjective construct aimed at but not confined to political configurations in the form of a "state," I contend that those divergences between "homeland" and "diasporas" could facilitate the proliferation of loci of analysis and foci of peacebuilding efforts which are yet under-explored both in peace studies and specific scholarship on diasporas and conflict. The first part of this chapter elaborates on why Little's approach to the question of nationalism, religion, and peace could accommodate and enrich the study of diasporas and conflict. The second part looks at why a focus on diasporas and other global solidarity movements could open up new venues for peacebuilding.

Nationalism, Religion, and Peace: Nation versus State

In confronting the question of ethno-religious national conflicts, Little insists on two interrelated sets of analytic distinctions—the one between the "nation" and the "state" and the other between the nation-state's modes of liberality or illiberality. These ideal types are located at the heart of his complex approach to the role of religion in conflict and peacebuilding because illiberal and exclusionary conceptions of nationhood are often associated with ethnoreligious-centrist interpretations of identity and violations of minority rights. This suggests that while religion is no more a cause of conflict than power constraints, economic incentives, or other geopolitical considerations, it is just as relevant to peacebuilding as the latter variables. In particular, the religion variable cannot be overlooked because—as Little's comparative work at the U.S. Institute of Peace and subsequent studies highlight[7]—a strong correlation may be identified between levels of tolerance of minorities and respect for religious freedoms, on the one hand, and the resort to violent means of resolving conflicts by invoking religious or chauvinistic warrants, on the other. This is true in the case of the Sudan where state violence is often premised on Islamicized–Arabized conceptions of the nation. It is also certainly applicable to Palestine–Israel where acts of violence against the Palestinians are often legitimated by invoking religious or biblical, or other ethnocentric warrants, and where the commitment to the idea of a "Jewish democracy" in and of itself implies undemocratic acts of violence.[8]

While religion plays different roles in different conflicts, its involvement often relates to legitimizing exclusionary ethos and political objectives, and to recruiting people who are willing to commit the ultimate sacrifice. Therefore, the role of religion and religious people and leaders in peacebuilding, as Little's work suggests, is (among other things) an interpretative one in that it involves the retrieval of resources from within the religious traditions and histories that might enable more liberal or civic interpretations of the "nation."[9] Notably, while often the selective retrieval of religious resources and narratives legitimates chauvinistic tendencies, this does not mean that the "nation" is religious or bent upon implementing a theocracy. Often nationalists, who invoke religious claims to vindicate their political agenda, are self-proclaimed secularists. The case of Israeli secularists exemplifies this point because declaring their view of Judaism as "history," "culture," and "nationality," they reinterpret religious warrants (like the concepts of "return to the land" and the "ingathering of the exiled") to mean historical facts rather than metahistorical aspirations.[10] Likewise, in constructing the ideology of Christo-Slavism, Serb nationalists painted the historical Prince Lazar as a Christ-like figure and his defeat against the Ottomans in the 1389 Battle of Kosovo as a paradigmatic narrative of martyrdom.[11] The reimagining of Serbia as ethnically pure, however, did not entail the establishment of a theocratic Christian state.

In such cases, the interpretative or hermeneutical process of rethinking alternative modes of narrating national histories is what is meant by religious peacebuilding.[12]

While "religion" may be deployed cynically by political leaders to manipulate the masses (a charge often leveled by social scientific accounts that view the role of religion as mostly epiphenomenal),[13] Little argues that the fact that religious and cultural resources captivate the popular imagination points to the deep "elective affinity" between markers of identity such as religion, ethnicity, and nationality—a point he borrows from Max Weber who defined nationalism as essentially a "belief in subjective descent," and as involving a perception of "choseness" and a "providential mission" aspiring for a political manifestation in a "state."[14] The distinction between the nation and the state also suggests multidirectional processes where not only how the "nation" is defined, or perceived vis-à-vis religion, or ethnicity, affects state practices, but also *vice versa*: how state institutions, including their legal frameworks, may affect the definition of the "nation."[15] This multidirectionality suggests creative potentialities for reimagining the "nation," and thus its legitimizing ethos. This re-imagining may have profound effects on questions of peace and justice because more inclusivist interpretation of the "nation" would entail less exclusivist state infrastructures and policies. Amplifying the interaction between the institutions of the "state" and conceptions of the "nation" is the study of nationalism as a theory of political legitimacy reflective of subjective sense of entitlement and fluid boundaries of belonging. The view of nationalism as a theory of political legitimacy is indeed central to any attempt at a productive analysis of ethnoreligious national conflicts and their transformation.

Indeed, the nation-state may be the immediate focus of questions of peace and justice, but the analysis of peacebuilding processes cannot overlook the role of diasporas both in increasingly influencing the course of conflicts and in negotiating the boundaries of the "nation." Little's delinking of the two terms of the nation-state (the "nation" and the "state") is effective in enabling a space for rethinking alternatives to chauvinistic and religio- and ethnocentric interpretations of nationhood. But the study of the roles of diasporas in conflict suggests that this process of rethinking needs to be a polycentric one, and involves more than just reinterpreting how religious, ethnic, and national markers of identity could relate to one another in a way that will be peace-promoting.

Glocal Conflict Transformation

By deploying the notion of a "glocal conflict transformation" in the title of this section, I play on the concept of "glocalization" popularized in the 1990s by theorists of globalization.[16] "Glocalization" means adopting global products to local tastes and preferences. In the context of my analysis, however, "glocalization" means that because local conflicts involve global forces and agents, their transformation would involve a substantive engagement with those forces. Here the focus is not on the UN, the EU, NATO, multinational corporations, and international NGOs, but rather on people and their conceptions of people-hood: those who share cultural, religious, ethnic, national, and symbolic affinity and act on it in a variety of ways that influence the cycles of conflict. In developing the concept of "conflict transformation," Lederach has famously focused on the transformation of underlying relational patterns rather than on exclusively putting out episodic explosions and fires.[17] Therefore, recognizing that relational patterns that affect the dynamics of conflict are not necessarily limited to one geographic locality invites expanding the foci of peacebuilding. Certainly, some conflicts will present more global dimensions and intricacies than others, but the patterns of globalization (including multiplying diasporic communities and fast channels of communication) heighten the potential destructive and constructive character of multiplying the interrelated spaces where conflicts are waged.

Elsewhere, I take Little's point—on the subjective, dynamic, and fluid (but not predetermined or inevitable) character of national identities—as my starting point in developing a thickly contextualized method of peacebuilding that focuses on marginalized or subaltern groups that occupy hybrid locations within political frameworks defined by exclusionary interpretations of belonging. Scrutinizing those hybrid spaces, as I suggest, would involve amplifying a critique of the interrelation between power and religion that is already present in Little's approach and his work with Appleby on the potential role of religion in peacebuilding processes which focus on the creative resourcefulness found in recognizing the internal plurality of a tradition and the irreducibility of religion to nation.[18] But this method which I refer to as the "hermeneutics of citizenship" further examines the possibility of innovation and reimagining that may be located in hybrid identities that challenge, in their very experiences and historicity, purist chauvinistic conceptions of membership and historiography. Hence, an introspection of the relevant religious tradition implicated in ethnoreligious national conflicts—an approach which has become a hallmark of the subgenre of religious peacebuilding—constitutes only one part of imagining the process of conflict transformation. But moving away from a focus on the possibilities of change located in the margins from within geopolitical boundaries, this chapter explores why Little's approach to questions of religion and the transformation of ethnoreligious national conflicts could be expanded also to account for the influence of religious, national, and ethnic diasporas on the dynamics of conflict and peacebuilding. In order to assume this research trajectory, one needs to push Little's framework beyond a methodological nationalism or the theoretical restriction of identity conflicts to state boundaries.

The Nation beyond the State

Little's understanding of the "nation" as irreducible to territory, history, and political configurations and as a subjective and interpretative concept—one that hangs on a "belief in common descent and destiny"—calls for the retrieval and cultivation of alternative conceptions of identity in order to challenge and reform exclusionary and violent conceptions of nation-statehood. This retrieval calls for some fluency in the religious and cultural histories and resources available in every context. In focusing on the transformation of ethnoreligious nationalism, Little highlights alternative interpretations of the traditions which could be more conducive to liberal interpretations of citizenship, and thus drastically reduce the likelihood of violent conflicts. To be sure, what motivates Little's approach to the process of rethinking the interrelation between chauvinistic and unjust state practices, and indices of identity such as religion, ethnicity, and culture, is the recognition that exclusionary or illiberal interpretations of the "nation" reside at the heart or the root of violent conflicts. The obvious focus therefore is the alleviation of those undergirding unjust practices on the level of the "state" in order to mitigate the immediate and local conditions of violence. However, as a focus on diasporas and other global networks of solidarity reveal, the actual process of rethinking and renegotiating conceptions of the "nation" has multiple loci. But, despite resisting the conflation of "nation" and "state," Little still confines the analysis of political, social, and cultural justice within the geopolitical boundaries of the nation-state.

Political theorist Nancy Fraser challenges the confinement of justice discourses to the geopolitical boundaries of states in what she deems a "post-Westphalian era."[19] Looking primarily at issues like the environment and economic justice, Fraser argues that deliberations over policies should involve all those who are affected by certain policies regardless of political borders. Little's approach to nationalism and peace, likewise, highlight that the "who is affected" question is not defined by and reduced to state boundaries and other political and historical circumstances. Little's account therefore suggests that the "who" under consideration is neither an obvious nor a fixed entity and, the move beyond seemingly axiomatic positions on how religion and ethnicity relate to conceptions of national identity may enable the transformation of conflicts involving identity claims.

But, while Little's differentiation between the nation and the state challenges Benedict Anderson's modernist notion of the nation as *imagined community* that is territorially bounded,[20] Little's approach does not explicitly theorize how transnational solidarity movements, diasporas, and homeland and identity politics may be involved in the dynamics of conflict and peacebuilding, precisely on the level of imagining or reimagining the parameters of the "nation." Global processes such as the legacy of colonialism and international agents like UN peacekeepers become a part of the analysis only insofar as they provide an explanatory variable as in the history of colonialism,[21] or an external mediating force as in the case of peace enforcement strategies.[22] Still, I contend that Little's approach could encompass an analysis of the interrelated trans-geo-political sites of conflict, contestation, and rhetoric. In fact, it could enrich the study of diasporas and conflict by centralizing the elastic properties of identity and modes of identification with a group and subsequently illuminate peacebuilding as entailing also a deeply introspective process of rethinking collective narratives and interpretations of cultural and religious resources in construing those narratives (which may prove inconsistent with the demands of *justpeace*).

Thus, even if at the end Little wishes to relate changing conceptions of nationhood to structural reform on the level of state infrastructures, his effective analysis of nationalism, as a theory of legitimacy, may need to be taken to its logical conclusion, and connect the study of specific instances of conflict to a broader exploration of national imaginations (across and beyond political boundaries). The challenge is to conceptualize the global dimensions of conflicts without abrogating and diminishing the significance of their localities and authenticities. Consequently, the question is not whether it still makes sense to use the framework of the nation-state as a locus of analysis, but how to incorporate and perhaps bracket the trans-border characters of the "nation," whether it comes in the form of diaspora politics, powerful lobbies, or solidarity movements.

Therefore, Little's insistence on nationalism as a theory of political legitimacy, and on the "nation" as a subjective space open for reinterpretation (and one that cannot be analyzed as interchangeable with the state), makes his approach conducive for an analysis that centrally integrates the role of the diasporas both in negotiating the boundaries of identity and national entitlements, and in conceiving of strategies of peacebuilding. However, such a turn to the study of the role of diasporas would necessitate an initial scrutiny of the homeland-host-land dichotomy and of the role of solidarity movements that do not necessarily entail ethnic, national, or religious ties of activists, questioning how local identity politics in the so-called host countries affect the diaspora's involvement in conflicts "back at home," and an analysis that situates the diasporas in a broader discussion of interest groups and lobbying practices. Before proceeding, a few definitional comments concerning the meanings of "diaspora," "solidarity network," and "interest groups" are in order as well as an overview of how these entities relate to international conflicts.

Clarifying the Terms

First, the concept of "diaspora" has just recently lost its capital "D" which limited its descriptive application primarily to the "Jews" (as well as occasionally Africans, Armenians, and Greeks), and expanded to include many more ethnic, religious, and other groups.[23] I concur with Bahar Baser and Ashok Swain who underscore that "diaspora" defies a simple dichotomization of homeland versus host-land: "It does not matter whether the diasporas' concept of homeland is an actual homeland or just a symbolic attribution," because, and here the authors cite Steven Vertovec, "'[b]elonging to a diaspora entails a consciousness of, or emotional attachment to, commonly claimed origins and cultural attributes associated with them.'"[24] The view of "diaspora" as "consciousness of" certain common narratives and attributes, and as capturing a definitional experience of displacement and longing for (re)placement, does not necessarily entail a physical experience of displacement, nor a physical "return" to a land, but rather it could denote a reclaiming of a lost past, a "golden age," or an anticipation for the "end time." Diaspora can become a part of the politics of nostalgia. It is, therefore, important to expose the interrelation between the meanings of the far and near "home," and how the symbolic construal of the diaspora-home dynamic enables participation in and critique of the social, cultural, and political landscapes of the diasporas (in which one's family may have dwelt for many generations), as well as actual interventions in violent conflict zones.

Indeed, it makes sense to discuss a concept of "symbolic diaspora." By symbolic diaspora I mean a diasporic consciousness that is not necessarily grounded in a physical experience of displacement from a homeland. Both "home" and "diaspora" are contested concepts and experiences because often they reflect a symbolic construction rather than a descriptive account of uprootedness and displacement. For example, Sayid Qutb—the ideologue of the Muslim Brotherhood in Egypt—declared life in Egypt as life of estrangement from the dominant *jahili* secular culture. While supposedly "at home," a variety of Hasidi communities in Israel, likewise, think of themselves as living in a diaspora because of their theological resistance to the secular Zionist undertaking. Another example of the contested concept of diaspora is the fact that every once in a while, one hears a report about (usually young) Muslim Americans who decided to fly to Afghanistan and take on the fight against the United States or about a British- or French- or Dutch-Muslim citizen who plots terrorist attacks. These decisions may indicate something about the experience of marginalization of Muslim communities in America and Europe, but one not necessarily defined by an actual memory and experience of displacement from a "homeland."

Yossi Shain helpfully distinguishes between "stateless diasporas, irredentist and secessionist groups that reside in the 'near abroad' and wish to reconfigure the boundaries of existing states to include their current places of residence within their desired homelands,"[25] and "far-removed diasporas that are well established and organized in their countries of domicile and who have embraced life outside their ancestral homeland."[26] Hence, the binary of diaspora and homeland may be symbolic as well as actual, signifying experiences of social, political, cultural, and economic displacement or marginalization. The mode in which the liberation of Palestine is articulated in Islamist propaganda constitutes a paradigmatic case of what is meant by the symbolic diasporic orientation. Palestine plays a symbolic role in the popular imaginations and in how it relates to questions of local politics and experiences. The invocation of Palestine as a trope, and the symbolic conflation of the "Zionist entity" and the "U.S." (or "the West" more vaguely)—as done routinely by personalities like Osama bin Laden and the Iranian President Mahmoud Ahmadinejad[27]—indicate an elusive concept of "home" as a symbol of the golden age. Along with rectifying the humiliation born out of the experiences of colonialism and imperialism, the liberation of Palestine signifies redemption and return, echoing and mirroring traditional Jewish conceptualization of return to the land of Zion.

While this symbolic Palestinian diaspora is rhetorically powerful, and resonates strongly in the imagination of Muslims the world over, this rhetorical hold does not translate into concrete actions to alleviate the predicament of the concrete occupied Palestinians and their "near abroad" diaspora. The Palestinian trope is invoked to offer a critique of domestic governments as well as an "empty signifier" of broad historical circumstances and international dominating structures.[28] Frequently, political elites in Arab and Muslim contexts are depicted by their internal opposition as complicit with the Zionists and the "West." In this rhetorical framing, the liberation of Palestine signifies a return to utopia or a golden age. Of course, "utopia" means "no-place." This symbolic Palestinian diaspora therefore de-concretizes the actual physical experience of Palestinian displacement from the actual concrete space that is Palestine. The Palestine trope is of course also invoked by political elites, often to capitalize on the strong emotional and cultural connotations associated with Palestine in order to gloss over or redirect dissatisfactions with domestic issues.

Some researchers of diasporas like Glenn Bowman point to the broadening of the category of diaspora to "encompass all the troubles and tribulations of a diverse, dispersed and heterogeneous population," or as Keith Axel contends, to the fact that "there need not even be a homeland from which the diaspora is dispersed, for there to be a 'diasporic imagining.'"[29] The upshot of this argument, according to Turner, is that "we must take the *emic* notion of diaspora seriously and perceive it more as a process and an aspiration than a sociological fact."[30] This insight can provide an analytic lens to understand why certain youth in the slums of Paris and Algeria, for example, identify so emotionally with the Palestinian predicament to the degree of associating the alleviation of their own misery with the liberation of Palestine.[31] The question is thus not only how and why the Palestine trope is invoked as a rhetorical tool, but also why does it work effectively?

Hence, the notion of a symbolic diaspora blends into the second related concept of "solidarity." Solidarity movements and other global networks of support of a "cause" associated with civil or other wars fight on behalf of a group's rights without necessarily claiming "common origins and cultural attributes" with the group whose flag they carry. Yet, such solidarity movements tend to reify their "cause" and represent a bifurcated account of "rights" and "wrongs," one that may function as "strategic essentialism"[32] but is not necessarily contributing to constructive processes of conflict transformation and change. The case of the global Palestine solidarity movement again exemplifies this argument.

What I call the global Palestine Solidarity Movement is comprised of diverse groups and individuals, from trade unions and churches to politicians and celebrities. This transnational social movement is located primarily in western urban centers like Boston, Toronto, London, Brussels, and New York. This movement takes up the cause of Palestine to the exclusion of any consideration of legitimate Israeli claims, narratives, memories, and fears. The activists in this movement would often accessorize their appearance with the Palestinian Kafiya and are quick to deploy categories like "apartheid" and "Nazi" to describe the Israeli regime (resembling the currency of protest used in Islamist contexts).[33] While the movement's critique of Israeli policies may be legitimate and accurate, it often results in a total de-legitimization of Israel and its perspective. The activists belabor an important distinction between their critique of Israel and any possible association with the label of anti-Semitism. The various groups and organizations subsumed under this global movement tend to feature their (usually prominent) Jewish members on their websites and as occasional spokespersons.

Underscoring this distinction between Judaism, Jewish people, and Zionism/Israel, however, results in overlooking or dismissing where these categories powerfully intersect and why they do. This attitude is embodied in the words that cost Helen Thomas her iconic seat as the dean of the White House Press Core in June of 2010. In her response to the question: "what about Israel?"—a question posed to her by a freelance amateur Journalist who is also a rather hawkish New York rabbi—Thomas replied: "Tell them to get the hell out of Palestine. . . . They can go home to Germany, Poland." The obvious argument here is that rather than occupying other people's home, they [Israelis/Jews] should return to wherever they came from. While Thomas gave voice to the Palestinian counter-narrative and one that is systematically silenced especially in American political and cultural discourses, her statement overlooks nuances of Jewish histories and experiences, and the fact that they are centrally relevant to any attempt to envision processes of conflict transformation.[34]

The operative and ironic word in Thomas's response is of course "home." Indeed, the experiences of the Holocaust and the Nakba, as well as of decades of occupation and cycles of violence, all constitute important variables in transforming the Palestinian-Israeli conflict. Edward Said recognized that as well. In developing his method for thinking about just peace, Said wrote: "[w]e need to think about two histories not simply separated ideologically, but together, contrapuntally. Neither Palestinian nor Israeli history at this point is a thing in itself, without the other. In so doing we will necessarily come up against the basic irreconcilability between the Zionist claim and Palestinian dispossession. The injustice done to the Palestinians is constitutive to these two histories, as is also the crucial effect of Western anti-Semitism and the Holocaust."[35] Yet, the blunt statement by Thomas shows that the global Palestine movement glosses over such complexities while declaring its agency and objective in working toward peaceful outcomes.

This becomes an important focus of analysis because such global solidarity movements could and do exert increased influence on the dynamics of conflict. For example, despite prominently featuring the Turkish flag, the Gaza-bound flotilla of May 2010 was described by the many activists on board as a humanitarian mission intended to alleviate the sufferings of Gazans under a prolonged Israeli siege. The flotilla was stopped and attacked by Israeli commandos on international waters, before reaching the shores of Gaza, and resulted in nine deaths of foreign self-identified unarmed humanitarians. The images that emerged out of this tragic episode worked to delegitimize Israel, and Israeli policies rationalized it as a necessary defense against attacks on southern Israel coordinated by the ruling Hamas party in Gaza. Images of the attack on the humanitarian ships circulated widely, mobilizing a host of interested parties to protest and speak specifically against Israeli policies with regard to Gaza, but also more broadly about the occupation of Palestine. These acts of protest also intended to further exert pressure on policy making in various key locations around the world and increase economic, political, and cultural boycott efforts among other tactics. The immediate result of the growing international pressure was the lessening of the extremity of the blockade on the Gaza Strip as well as a significant blow in the arena of international public opinion.

Hence, the aftermath of the Israeli raid against the Gaza flotilla—and the broad global outrage that images of attacks on more or less unarmed humanitarians invoked—exemplifies that solidarity movements are now formed as global networks of influence, and cannot be excluded from an analysis of the conflict which has become their cause and often raison d'être. The analysis becomes more complicated when humanitarian assistance seems to be entangled with political agenda. Consequently, a study of the influence of the global Palestine Solidarity Movement will have to probe the motivations for choosing the particular cause of Palestine over that of the Kurds in Turkey. In the same way in which the Palestine trope in contexts of Muslim and/or Arab majority necessitated inquiring into the complex historical, religious, cultural, and political circumstances—an examination of the motivation for partaking in the global Palestine Solidarity Movement—will necessitate a thick engagement with local political, social, religious and cultural landscapes, and structures, whether the focus is New York or Paris, London, or Rome.

This point about, on the one hand, the symbolic Palestine diaspora construed in Islamic rhetoric and the global solidarity movement with Palestine, on the other, already pushes the boundaries and loci of conflict transformation. This expansion is both geographic and discursive in the sense that it invites analysis of global systemic issues, cultural imaginations, and concrete engagements with socioeconomic and political contexts. This polycentric approach to conflict analysis—one that includes inquiring into the influences and motivations of symbolic and global diasporas and solidarity movements, on public opinion, and on de-concretizing the actual conflict in the land of Palestine–Israel—may also translate into strategies of conflict transformation. I chose to dwell on this particular case of Palestine because it clarifies that the symbolic and the rhetorical are under-theorized in conflict analysis and therefore provide yet unexplored terrains in conflict transformation processes. The two examples I provide show that external global networks—whether loosely assuming the concept of Palestine as a trope describing a host of ambiguous evils or as a human rights and humanitarian cause (like Darfur)—influence the dynamics of conflict and its representation, and thus, may have something to do with constructive change and peacebuilding efforts.

But more often than not, diasporas intervene in the dynamics of conflict in a variety of other ways. Shain explains that diasporas become passively relevant to international conflicts when they are co-opted onto a national narrative as in Israel's assumption of its position as the spokesperson and representative of the Jews the world over, and when they are implicated in international conflicts merely by virtue of their ethnic, national, and religious affiliation with a certain homeland.[36] Shain continues that diasporas become active players in international affairs affecting a homeland conflict especially when they achieve a certain degree of integration into democratic societies as well as considerable economic, social, cultural, and political capital. Shain writes to this effect: "[w]hen they achieve transnational economic or political clout (or both), diasporas can, and do, directly affect identities and homeland policies."[37] Therefore, "active diasporas" need to be taken into account "as an independent actor in the conflict resolution process" because they "appear to have made peace negotiations into a three-level game for their homelands' leaders, and those leaders have suffered when they have tried to limit the negotiation process to a two-level framework."[38]

Likewise, in their study of diasporas' involvement in peacebuilding, Baser and Swain argue that diaspora communities could potentially play a positive role in third party mediation processes in the homeland. But even with a nascent recognition of the potential agency of diasporas in affecting change of policy and public opinion, most analysts deem diasporas as obstacles inhabiting processes of conflict transformation and peacebuilding. Baser and Swain explain that the common consensus in the study of diasporas and conflict is "that the diaspora members, by sending large remittances as well as challenging huge funds through welfare organizations close to insurgent or terrorist groups, contribute to the conflict escalation rather than support constructive conflict transformation."[39] A widely cited case exemplifying diasporas' involvement in the perpetuation of conflict is that of the Irish diaspora community in the United States and its significant financial support of the IRA during the 1980s and 1990s. But studies show that the diasporas of Sri Lankan Tamils, Sikhs, Kurds, Kosovar, and Eritreans among others in America and Europe are similarly implicated in their respective "homeland" conflicts.[40] In addition to financial support and remittances, diasporas provide fertile grounds for the recruitment of guerrillas for the homeland struggles, a fact that clarifies why "diasporas are seen as part of the problem, not as part of the solution."[41]

Indeed, there is a growing strand in the literature on diasporas that does focus on diasporas' potential role as agents of peacebuilding when they function through the political channels of their countries of domicile (lobbying) and when they participate in international aid efforts.[42] It is in this context that diasporas begin to function as an interest group, which is the third interrelated term deserving clarification in the context of this discussion of diasporas and conflict perpetuation and transformation. The terms and cultures of engagement in the diasporic spaces then become variable in the analysis of conflict and peacebuilding.

Notably, in multicultural contexts, pushing nationalist agenda and causes elsewhere, becomes the entry point of diasporas onto the climate of identity politics—one that celebrates difference within the limits of the liberal multicultural framework and without threatening the charge of "split loyalty." Hence, diasporas' involvement with causes abroad need to be situated in a broader landscape of the multicultural climate in which they partake. At the national meeting of the American Academy of Religion in 2009, Saba Mahmood stressed a connection between taking on the cause of religious liberties and minority rights and underlying Western diplomatic agenda and a host of powerful think tanks and interest groups. Mahmood's presentation echoed Andrew Rich's study of think tanks which highlights the diminishing influence of think tanks upon the terms of public debate.[43]

This conclusion resonates with Michel Foucault's notion of discourse. For Foucault, discourse constructs the topic. It defines and produces the objects of our knowledge. It governs the way that a topic can be meaningfully talked and reasoned about. A discursive formation that includes the circulation of power via a net-like organization encompassing academia, the media, and so forth enables the cultivation of what Foucault called a "regime of truth." The analysis of think tanks suggests that despite their proliferation and ubiquity they in effect sustain a regime of truth.

Indeed, a brief perusal through the relevant section of the website of the Brookings Institution that deals with the "Islamic world" and "terrorism" reveals that the breadth of research is limited by the policy interests of the United States. In fact, it is not clear whether U.S. policy focus is influenced and shaped by the research produced in powerful high-impact public policy research organizations, or whether such think tanks have become an instrument for authorizing policy agenda. This quandary becomes more complex when reflecting on the advocacy role assumed by many think tanks in Washington D.C. The topics covered by the researchers of the Brookings in the areas of "the Islamic world" and "terrorism" correspond with the topics that occupy the headlines in the media more broadly. I highlight the case of the Brookings because it presents itself as a neutral, value-free research center. Still, its research products suggest that the Brookings is beholden to certain normative postulations about political Islam, that—as political theorist Elizabeth Shakman Hurd contends—are rooted in particular assumptions about the relationship between the "religious" and the "secular," assumptions which are interlaced with orientalist attitudes.[44] This constitutes a discursive obstacle in the Foucauldian sense. The implication for conflict transformation and peacebuilding efforts would thus include tackling those discursive formations.

Once again, the boundaries of a "regime of truth" are illuminated when one attempts to study the coverage of the Palestinian-Israeli conflict within the context of interest groups and think tanks that dominate the production and reproduction of knowledge in Washington D.C. and more broadly in American political and cultural imaginations. Here, the controversial *The Israel Lobby and U.S. Foreign Policy* by John Mearsheimer and Stephan Walt (2007) serves as an orienting point of departure. Mearsheimer and Walt explain that what they call "the Israel lobby" comprises of "a loose coalition of individuals and organizations who actively work to steer U.S. foreign policy in a pro-Israel direction."⁴⁵ This would include American Jews, Christian Zionists, neoconservatives, and so forth. The authors argue that the total effect of this strong current is negative as pertains to United States' interests in the region. In other words, the agenda advanced by the lobby works against the geopolitical interests of the United States. Critiques of this argument abound.⁴⁶ Suffice it to mention that such critiques focused on basic flaws in the research, and supposed misrepresentation of facts and quotes and on retrieving dark memories of anti-Semitic conspiracy theories—among other concerns.

It is my view—contra to Mearsheimer and Walt—that the question of U.S. support of Israel goes beyond geopolitical considerations (or miscalculations). But—drawing on Melanie McAllister's thesis in *Epic Encounters: Culture, Media, and U.S. Interests in the Middle East Since 1945* (2001)—U.S. support of Israel reflects a deep cultural and religious affinity and presuppositions concerning the "Western" and "democratic" character of the Israeli state. McAllister writes that while U.S. foreign policy may be grounded in material and military realities, it develops in a cultural context. McAlister highlights the role of popular culture in shaping the ways American define their interests in the Middle East. American perceptions of the Middle East are framed by particular narratives and draw on religious beliefs, news media accounts and popular culture. Echoing Hurd's analysis of the undiminished hold of the discourses of secularism, I contend that the cultivation of innovative research that could affect a transformation of the terms of the discussion rather than the mere supply of "talking-points" would have to confront the "Judeo-Christian" discursive formation so central and defining of the production of policy research. According to Hurd, "[t]he common claim of Judeo-Christian secularism of all varieties . . . is that Western political order is grounded in a set of core values with their origins in (Judeo)–Christian tradition."⁴⁷ Hurd further contends that international relations theory has been beholden to this discursive tradition. This is especially apparent in Samuel Huntington's "Clash of Civilizations" thesis where he argues normatively about the special characteristics of the West: individualism, human rights, separation of church and state, and so forth. A move beyond the "clash of civilizations" frame would, Hurd argues, necessitate deconstructing the secularist discourse and rethinking the relationship between "religion" and the "political." This insight is relevant to the study of the Israeli-Palestinian conflict because a perceived cultural affinity between Israel and the United States is likewise grounded in a presumed civilizational affinity. How diasporas and other advocacy groups engage the lobbying culture and its undergirding assumptions therefore becomes an important context of research for peace and conflict studies.

The American Israel Public Affairs Committee (AIPAC) provides a prominent example of how diaspora nationalisms, especially in the northern American and European contexts, frequently assume the form of an interest group, as they partake in lobbying policy makers and influencing public opinion through research and advocacy for the homeland cause. AIPAC and similarly strong self-proclaimed pro-Israeli interest groups and lobbies are often associated with exacerbating the Israeli–Palestinian conflict. In light of the above discussion of interest groups, the case of AIPAC demonstrates how diaspora nationalism actively influences the dynamics of conflict through its political and cultural influence. This powerful lobby is an important player in a broader landscape that is receptive to the construal of Israel as a Western democracy at the heart of a region that is otherwise depicted using an orientalist brushstrokes. In its lobbying tactics, AIPAC amplifies an interpretation that conflates Zionism with Judaism, and thus renders any critique of Israel as anti–Semitic—an accusation which the global Palestine Solidarity Movement tries to repel by making Judaism entirely irrelevant to the discussion. An analysis of conflict needs to identify this rhetorical clash and imagine concrete ways to re-conceive those attitudes in a way that will be consistent with the non-paternalistic peacebuilding agenda articulated by Appleby and Lederach in their effort to think strategically about conflict transformation. Such a scrutiny will have to take into account not only the rhetorical construal of national identities by various spokespersons, but also how they interact with and are affected by the political and cultural discourses in their contexts of domicile.

But the homeland politics of the Jewish diasporas has, for the most part, defined the scope and modus operandi of diaspora nationalisms.[48] The diasporic experience enables the conflation of religious and national or ethnic signifiers of identity in a way that contributes to reifying those constructions. This symbolic conflation of the religious and national dimensions of their identity needs to be explicated and scrutinized as a way of thinking through their potential role in processes of peacebuilding.

This type of rethinking becomes especially urgent when homeland conflicts are defined through the invocation of ethnoreligious national agenda. But diasporas are not reduced to their most powerful and vocal lobbies and lobbyists, as exemplified in the emergence of J-Street as a counter-voice to AIPAC.[49] Jewish Voice for Peace (JVP) provides another example as well as the prophetic voices of scholars, activists, and religious leaders like Judith Butler and Michael Lerner. Those voices put forward, in varying degrees of intensity, alternative interpretations of the Jewish meanings of Israel, and consequently of questions of peace and justice in Israel–Palestine. While significantly weaker than AIPAC, those voices provide important resources for conflict transformation that include a substantive rethinking of the relationship between Judaism and Israel. Caught in a "regime of truth," AIPAC echoes a particular Zionist ethos and teleology that increasingly does not capture the imagination and sense of identity of non-Israeli Jews.[50]

Likewise, in the already mentioned study of Tamil and Sinhalese diasporas, Orjuela echoes the view that for the most part the diaspora would replicate the polarization at home, in Sri Lanka. Some segments within those diasporas are involved in directly supporting warring parties, canvassing international support, and in development and reconstruction efforts (which also could function to reinforce and even deepen reified differences).[51] The Sri Lankan diaspora of both Tamils and Sinhalese, in this respect, are "passive diasporas" because, as Orjuela contends, it "mainly plays a role in the conflict that is subordinated to and supportive of that of the leaders in the homeland."[52] But, despite replicating the terms of the conflict in diverse locations—as if the diasporas represented tentacles leading back to the homeland—the diaspora condition also provides potential resources and contexts for creative interventions that resist the reigning discourse about the conflict. Orjuela highlights that the cases of the Sri Lankan diasporas show that "there are examples of diaspora groups that challenge the logic of war, for instance by calling for non-violent conflict resolution, condemning atrocities by all sides and engaging in cross-ethnic dialogue."[53] As in the case of JVP and J-Street, even if small in comparison to the divisive tendencies of various lobbies, ethnic media, and activists in the diasporas, those counter-voices, Orjuela contends, "challenge the polarized views of the two sides and the discourses saying that war is the only solution."[54] Further, the analysis of why and how diasporas engage homeland conflicts also needs to take into account other factors like gender and class, which underscore the internal plurality of those groups and the diverse ways in which they could interact with processes of conflict transformation, including the choice of completely disengaging from any involvement in the conflict.

In light of the discussion of the Jewish, Palestinian, and Sri Lankan diasporas—a discussion that sought to question the fixity of categories like "home"—I contend that scholarship that views peace processes as necessarily involving the diasporas as active agents, needs to be expanded to include thickly contextualized analyses of the internal plurality within the diasporic communities, and recognize the patterns that enable the reification of national, religious, and ethnic markers of identity in the diasporic contexts, and thus, more often than not, facilitate a radical and bellicose approach to the "homeland conflict." This analysis that moves beyond the most vocal and or powerful lobbies and spokespersons of various "causes" may open new avenues for peacebuilding processes that further enrich the clearly diminishing conceptual currency of a two-dimensional focus on domestic concerns (contained within the nation-state), and diplomatic efforts. Even if it was not designed to go in this direction, Little's work on religion, ethnonational conflicts, and peacebuilding could provide important insights for this undertaking which would necessitate renegotiating how ethnic and religious identifications relate to the construal of national boundaries.

Toward a Polycentric Approach to Peacebuilding

The view of "diaspora" as amounting to a consciousness of a common history and of shared attributes, despite geographic diversity, is consistent with Little's analysis of nationalism as a form of belief and conviction in a common descent.[55] But, the conception of a unified people is one that exists only in the rhetorical construal of national historiographies. Shain helpfully underscores that "[i]n reality, neither the diaspora nor the homeland community ultimately dominates the process of constituting and communicating national identity."[56] In fact, the geographic distance between diasporas and homelands could enable substantive interpretative variations, born out of contextual factors. The question concerning whether the homeland influences the diasporas or vice versa, Shain continues, "depends on their relative strength, which is determined by, among other factors, monetary flows, cultural productions, community leadership, and transnational political parties."[57]

Thus, while Little's conceptual framework for the study of religion, conflict, and peacebuilding is focused on the nation-state as the most basic locus of analysis, his approach is conducive to an analysis that takes into account the influence on the dynamics of conflict and peace affected by global networks of interest groups, solidarity movements, and diasporas. Expanding Little's approach in this way to include an analysis of such variables would, however, necessitate questioning the premises of political and cultural configurations in the locations and/or epicenters of such movements of solidarity and lobbying efforts. This signals the increased interconnectedness among sites of conflict and could radically expand the vistas and locations of peacebuilding processes and efforts. It could mean that the definition of peacemaking is no longer exclusively embodied in the image of the brave peacemaker who flirts with danger in zones devastated by violent conflict. While the role of the peacemaker as a stranger under fire is still significant, a globalized perspective may redefine conflict as an event with multiple epicenters in which some may be geographically far from the site of the actual fire, but nonetheless important, yet overlooked loci for conflict transformation. By deploying the term "epicenter" here, I allude to Lederach's distinction between the episode and epicenter of conflict. As also evident in his work with Appleby, Lederach views peacebuilding as the process of transforming underlying relational patterns rather than just responding or reacting to explosions. Centrally integrating the diasporas, solidarity movements and the critical influence of interest groups into the analysis of conflict exposes the multiplicity of epicenters, and thus expands the sites where conflict transformation processes can take place. Hence, Appleby and Lederach's comprehensive approach to peacebuilding also needs to move beyond a confining dichotomization of the "local" and the "global," to include a view that takes into account the proliferation of the localities of conflict, and thus of potential sites for constructive change. The global dimensions of conflict cannot only be understood as the diffusion of conflict to other arenas of contestations across geographic terrains, but rather as introducing important variations in how conflicts may be framed and reframed.

To reiterate, recognition of the influence of diasporas and other transnational networks on the trajectories of conflict and peace in zones affected by nationalist struggles and civil wars could carry important practical implications to processes of peacebuilding. The conceptualization of peacebuilding agenda is now not merely focused on the important on-the-ground efforts to mediate among parties locked in seemingly intractable conflicts, undergo educational initiatives and retrieve resources within the background cultures that challenge chauvinistic interpretations of identity and promote more inclusivist political orientation and practices among various other spheres of activities. Imagining peacebuilding as a polycentric process does not only suggest an international outlook that brings to bear humanitarian aid and diplomatic efforts, human rights advocacy and intervention by international bodies like the UN and NATO. In addition to these spheres of activity which are often featured as pivotal to peacebuilding strategies, other foci of research open up when one identifies the influence of global cultural and political networks of solidarity. Despite frequent rhetorical assertions of a unified sense of people-hood, as often echoed in diasporic national politics, activism, and segregated living, diasporas offer many possible divergences from dominant narratives produced and reproduced at home and by powerful spokespersons like AIPAC. As I suggest in developing the method of the hermeneutics of citizenship, a thick exploration of counter-narratives and subaltern identities that do not fit into the dominant national historiography facilitates an internal and micro process of rethinking the boundaries of belonging. Likewise, a thick exploration of diaspora communities and voices may also contribute to conflict transformation. This is also because diasporas' perceptions of identity and identification would also carry significant repercussions in terms of practical aid, whether financial, military, political, and cultural to the "homeland."

Finally, I conclude that a recognition of the role of diasporas in reproducing ethnoreligious rhetorical claims and in fueling conflicts—not only through the power of the purse but also on the level of public relation—clarifies the importance of integrating the analysis of diasporas to envisioning processes of peacebuilding and conflict transformation. The discussion above shows that the underlying disentanglement of the "nation" from the "state" indeed can enable incorporating into the analysis of conflicts variables beyond their geopolitical confines, from a global analysis of hegemonies to the exploration of symbolic diasporas and their relevance to homeland conflicts. I argue that such scrutiny of global frameworks and trans-state perceptions of solidarity or symbolic nationalism can prove critical in conceptualizing strategies for moving toward conflict transformation. Part of what may be needed is de-intensifying the symbolic and extra-territorial variables in order to work constructively toward re-envisioning nationalisms in a mode that exhibits greater consistency with justice. While the peacebuilding process is global and polycentric at the end, the focus of the process is the transformation of a conflict locally. Yet, a local focus cannot bracket the increasingly complex yet creative spaces of global influences.

The focus on the retrieval of religious and cultural resources is especially central to Little's study of the potential role of religion and religious leaders in peacebuilding in a global context. Those peacebuilding efforts, however, need to concentrate more broadly both on the analysis of the influence of diasporas and on what could be done on that level of influence in terms of consciousness-raising, education, advocacy, and critique. Broadening the study of ethnoreligious national struggles to include a sustained study of the diasporas, however, paves the way to the study of political and cultural discourses in the "countries of domicile," as part and parcel of the analysis of conflict and of strategizing peacebuilding schemas.

NOTES

[1] The authors also define the normatively orienting concept of justpeace as "a dynamic state of affairs in which the reduction and management of violence and the achievement of social and economic justice are undertaken as mutual, reinforcing dimensions of constructive change." John Paul Lederach and Scott Appleby, "Strategic Peacebuilding: An Overview," in eds. Daniel Philpott and Gerard F. Powers *Strategies of Peace: Transforming Conflict in a Violent World* (Oxford: Oxford University Press, 2010), 35. [here 23].

[2] Ibid., 36.

[3] Ibid., 28.

[4] Ibid.

[5] Camilla Orjuela, "Distant Warriors, Distant Peace Workers? Multiple Diaspora Roles in Sri Lanka's Violent Conflict," in *Global Networks* 8,4 (2008): 436–452, [here 436].

[6] Simon Turner, "The Waxing and Waning of the Political Field in Burundi and its Diaspora," in *Ethnic and Racial Studies* (31:4): 742–765, 759.

[7] David Little, "Belief, Ethnicity and Nationalism," in *Nationalism and Ethnic Politics*, 1995. See also David Little and Donald Swearer, "Introduction," in eds., David Little and Donald Swearer, *Religion and Nationalism in Iraq: A Comparative Perspective* (Cambridge, MA: Harvard University Press, 2006).

[8] See for example Oren Yiftachel, *Ethnocracy: Land and Identity Politics in Israel–Palestine* (Philadelphia: University of Pennsylvania Press, 2006).

[9] See also David Little and Scott Appleby, "A Moment of Opportunity? The Promise of Religious Peacebuilding in an Era of Religious and Ethnic Conflict," in eds., Harold Coward and Gordon S. Smith, *Religion and Peacebuilding* (Albany: State University of New York Press, 2004), 1–23; and R. Scott Appleby, *Ambivalence of the Sacred: Religion, Violence and Reconciliation* (Lanham, MD: Rowman & Littlefield Publisher, 2000).

[10] See Atalia Omer, "Religion vs. Peace: A False Dichotomy," in *Studies in Ethnicity and Nationalism* 10/2008; 7(3): 109–131.

[11] See Michael Sells, "'Pilgrimage' and 'Ethnic Cleansing' in Herzegovina," in eds., David Little and Donald Swearer *Religion and Nationalism in Iraq* (Cambridge, MA: Harvard University Press, 2006), 145–156.

[12] The designation religious peacebuilding also encompasses the work of religious leaders or other 'religious entrepreneurs' who are inspired by their faith to vocalize opposition to doctrinaire regimes. It also applies to the practice of interfaith dialogues and the involvement of religious symbolisms, rituals and so forth in processes of healing and reconciliation. See for example, Appleby, Ibid.; Coward and Smith, Ibid.; David Little, with Tanenbaum Center for Interreligious Understanding, eds., *Peacemakers in Action: Profiles of Religion in Conflict Resolution* (Cambridge: Cambridge University Press, 2007); Marc Gopin, *Holy War, Holy Peace: How Religion Can Bring Peace to the Middle East* (Oxford: Oxford University Press, 2002); Mohammed Abu-Nimer, Amal I. Khoury and Emily Welty, *Unity in Diversity: Interfaith Dialogue in the Middle East* (Washington D.C.: United States Institute of Peace, 2007); Daniel Philpott, "Religion, Reconciliation, and Transitional Justice: The State of the Field," in *SSRC Working Papers* (October 17, 2007). http://programs.ssrc.org/religion/reconciliation.pdf Last accessed: February 13, 2009); Daniel Philpott, "When Faith Meets History: The Influence of Religion on Transitional Justice," in eds., Thomas Brudholm and Thomas Cushman, *The Religious in Response to Mass Atrocity: Interdisciplinary Perspectives* (Cambridge, UK: Cambridge University Press, 2009), 174–212.

[13] For examples of reductionist analyses of the role of religion in conflict see Paul. Collier, "Economic Causes of Civil Conflict and Their Implications for Policy," in eds., Fen Osler Hampton and Pamella Aall Chester A. Crocker *Turbulent Peace: The Challenges of Managing International Conflict* (Washington D.C.: United States Institute of Peace Press, 2001), 143–62; James D. Fearon and David D. Laitin, "Ethnicity, Insurgency, and Civil War," in *American Political Science Review* 97, 1 (February 2003), 75–90; (Samuel Huntington, "The Clash of Civilizations?" in *Foreign Affairs* 72 (1993): 22–49.

[14] This view of nationalism is also reflected in the work of the theorist of nationalism Anthony Smith. See Anthony D. Smith, *Chosen Peoples: Sacred Sources of National Identity* (Oxford: Oxford University Press), 2003.

[15] See also the work of Anthony Marx for a similar historical analysis of nationalisms in pre–Modern Europe: Anthony Marx, *Faith in Nation: Exclusionary Origins of Nationalism* (Oxford: Oxford University Press, 2003).

[16] See for example Barry Welman, "Little Boxes, Glocalization, and Networked Individualism," in eds., Makoto Tanabe, Peter van den Besselaar, Toru Ishida, *Digital Cities II Computational and Sociological Approaches LNCS 2362* (Berlin, Heilderbeg, New York: Springer-Verlag, 2002), 10–25; Barry Wellman, "Living Networked on and Offline," in *Contemporary Sociology* 28,6 (Nov, 1999): 648–54

[17] John Paul Lederach, *The Little Book of Conflict Transformation* (Intercourse, PA: Good Books, 2003).

[18] David Little, Scott Appleby, Ibid.

[19] Nancy Fraser, *Scales of Justice: Reimagining Political Space in a Globalizing World* (New York: Columbia University Press, 2009).

[20] Benedict Anderson, *Imagined Communities: Reflections on the Origin and Spread of Nationalism*. Verso, 1993).

[21] See David Little and Donald Swearer, "Introduction," in eds., David Little and Donald Swearer, *Religion and Nationalism in Iraq: A Comparative Perspective* (Cambridge: Harvard University Press, 2006), 1–42.

[22] See David Little, "Peace, Justice, and Religion," in eds., Pierre Allan and Alexis Keller, *What is a Just Peace* (Oxford: Oxford University Press, 2006), 149–175.

[23] Bahar Baser and Ashok Swain, "Diasporas as Peacemakers: Third Party Mediation in Homeland Conflicts," in *International Journal on World Peace*, Vol. XXV No. 3 (September 2008): 8.

[24] Ibid.

[25] Yossi Shain, "The Role of Diasporas in Conflict Perpetuation or Resolution," in *SAIS Review* Volume 22, Number 2, (Summer–Fall 2002): 115–144, [here 116].

[26] Ibid., 117.

[27] Mahmoud Ahmadinejad, "Speeches by Iran Supreme Leader Khamenei and President Ahmadinejad at the International Conference in Tehran for Support of Palestine," in *The Middle East Media Research Institute* (March 2009) http://www.memri.org/bin/articles.cgi?Page=archives&Area=sd&ID=SP227409 Last accessed: June 12, 2014;, Osama bin Laden "Speeches" in *The Archives of Global Change in the 21st Century. 2001.* (http://www.september11news.com/OsamaSpeeches.htm Last accessed: June 12, 2014). See also Bruce Lincoln, *Holy Terrors: Thinking about Religion After September 11* (Chicago: Chicago University Press, 2003).

[28] See also Simon Turner, "The Waxing and Waning of the Political Field in Burundi and its Diaspora," in *Ethnic and Racial Studies* 31, 04 (2008): 742–765.

[29] Cited in Simon Turner, Ibid., 746.

[30] Ibid.

[31] See Emmanuel Sivan, "Arab Nationalism in the Age of the Islamic Resurgence," in eds., James Jankowski and Israel Gershoni, *Rethinking Nationalism in the Arab Middle East* (New York: Columbia University Press, 1997).

[32] The concept of 'strategic essentialism' was coined by the post-colonial theorist Gayatri Chakravirty Spivak. It entails a strategy that would enable groups that are clearly

internally diverse to temporarily essentialize their attributes and their sense of 'groupness' for the sake of simplifying 'who they are' in the struggle for gaining political, economic, social and cultural goals.

[33] For a fuller analysis of the Palestine Solidarity Movement, see also Atalia Omer, "'It's Nothing Personal': The Globalization of Justice, the Transferability of Protest, and the Case of the Palestine Solidarity Movement," in *Studies in Ethnicity and Nationalism* (Vol. 9, Issue 3, 2009): 497–518.

[34] See Atalia Omer, "Can a Critic Be a Caretaker too? Religion, Conflict, and Conflict Transformation," in *Journal of the American Academy of Religion* (June 2011 79/2): 459–496.

[35] Edward W. Said, "A Method for Thinking about Just Peace," in eds., Pierre Allan and Alexis Keller, What is a Just Peace (Oxford: Oxford University Press, 2006), 193.

[36] Yossi Shain, "The Role of Diasporas in Conflict Perpetuation or Resolution," in *SAIS Review* (2002): 115–144 [here 119–120].

[37] Ibid., 120

[38] Ibid. See also Jeffrey Knopf's work on developing a framework of 'trans-boundary connections' for analyzing security negotiations. See Jeffrey W. Knopf, "Beyond Two-Level Games: Domestic-International Interaction in the Intermediate-Range Nuclear Forces Negotiations," in *International Organization* 47 (autumn 1993): 599–628.

[39] Bahar Baser and Ashok Swain, "Diasporas as Peacemakers: Third Party Mediation in Homeland Conflicts," in *International Journal on World Peace* (2008), 10.

[40] Ibid., 10–11

[41] Ibid., 11

[42] Jonathan Hall and Ashok Swain, "Capturing Conflicts or Propelling Peace: Diasporas and Civil wars," in eds., Ashok Swain, Amer Rames and Joakim Ojendal, *Globalization and Challenges to Building Peace.* (London: Anthem Press, 2007).

[43] Andrew Rich, *Think Tanks, Public Policy, and the Politics of Expertise* (Cambridge: Cambridge University Press, 2005).

[44] Elizabeth Shakman Hurd, *The Politics of Secularism in International Relations* (Princeton: Princeton University Press, 2008).

[45] John Mearsheimer and Stephan Walt. *The Israel Lobby* (New York: Farrar, Straus and Giroux, 2007), 5

[46] See for example David Gergen, "An Unfair Attack" in *U.S. News & World Report* (April 3, 2006); Alan Dershowitz, "A Reply to Mearsheimer Walt 'Working Paper'" (April, 2006).

[47] Hurd, Ibid., 38.

[48] (see for example Sheffer 2007)

[49] According to its official website, *J–Street* emerged as an organization intended to give "political voice to mainstream American Jews and other supporters of Israel who, informed by their progressive and Jewish values, believe that a two-state solution to the Israeli-Palestinian conflict is essential to Israel's survival as the national home of the Jewish people and as a vibrant democracy." See jstreet.org/about/about-us

[50] For an illustration of this point, see Peter Beinart, "The Failure of the Jewish-American Establishment," in *The New York Review of Books* (June 10, 2010) http://www.nybooks.com/articles/archives/2010/jun/10/failure-american-jewish-establishment/ Last accessed: June 12, 2014)

[51] Orjuela, 438 ff.

[52] Ibid., 449.

[53] Ibid., 437.

[54] Ibid., 444.

[55] Other theorists of nationalism highlighted the subjective and interpretative character of nationalism.

[56] Shain, 118.

[57] Ibid.

15.
Rethinking Islamist Politics: Bringing the State Back In

Scott Hibbard

Introduction

The assassination of Anwar al-Sadat on October 6, 1981 was a defining moment in the rise of Islamist politics. The event is also seen as a paradigm of the Islamist threat, though one that is fundamentally mistaken. Sadat was killed by extremists associated with the organization *Islamic Jihad*, a militant group that had penetrated the Egyptian army and sought to spark an Islamic revolution. As Sadat watched a military parade commemorate his "victory" in the 1973 War with Israel, a truck carrying the young Islamists veered out of the parade line and raced toward his reviewing stand. Stopping abruptly in front of the presidential entourage, four soldiers leapt out, firing automatic weapons and hurling grenades. Sadat was killed almost instantly. As the presidential security scrambled to react, the lead assassin shouted: "I am Khalid Islambouli. I have killed Pharaoh, and I do not fear death."[1]

The traditional understanding of this event is indicative of the conventional wisdom regarding Islamist politics writ large. Sadat is typically seen as a secular leader gunned down by religious fanatics. As such, his assassination is assumed to embody a broader struggle between secular elites and Islamist opposition groups. At issue is not just a competition for power, but a conflict between modernity and tradition, secularism and religion, state and society. This notion of a tectonic struggle between religious activists and modernizing elites—and the corresponding "battle for global values"—was central to the Bush Administration's characterization of the "war on terror."[2] These assumptions similarly inform the neo-conservative understanding of Islamo-fascism,[3] Mark Juergensmeyer's notion of a new "Cold War,"[4] and popular perceptions of the U.S. military's continuing engagement in "overseas contingency operations."[5] In each instance, the defining issue is the ideological competition between enlightenment norms of the West and the exclusive visions of social life embodied in a resurgent religion. As such, the underlying political struggle is viewed as a competition between differing value systems, with Islamist groups and activists emerging autonomously from the realm of civil society to challenge the institutions (and vision) of the modern, liberal/secular state.

At face value, this interpretation of Islamist politics, and particularly Islamist militancy, appears self-evident. Sadat's assassins were inspired by the writings of Sayyid Qutb and were vehemently opposed to Egypt's turn toward the West. Similarly, the al-Qaeda operatives associated with the 9–11 attacks, as well as the militants who continue to fight American forces in Afghanistan, Yemen, and elsewhere, are commonly characterized as "unmodern men" invariably hostile to Western—and modern—values.[6] Scratch the surface, however, and what you find is a much more complex, and far more interesting story. In Egypt, for example, the policies of Sadat were far from secular.[7] On the contrary, his tenure in office was defined by the conscious effort to promote Islamic fundamentalism through the institutions of the modern state.[8] He greatly expanded religious education, increased Islamic programming on state-run television, and built mosques with government funds. The regime also cooperated with—and actively sought to co-opt—Egypt's Islamists, including the Muslim Brotherhood.

Similarly, the rise of Islamist politics—and militancy—throughout South Asia can be directly related to the state support Islamist groups received from pro-Western governments. This support was a central feature of the ideological politics of the Cold War. Successive American Administrations (and their regional allies) saw in the Islamist movement a useful tool for containing Soviet influence and the secular nationalism advocated by the socialists and communists in these regions. From 1979 onwards, Sunni fundamentalism was also used to contain the Shī'a radicalism that emerged from the Iranian Revolution. This strategy of using an extremist—and often militant—version of Sunni Islam as an ideological bulwark against geopolitical rivals came to fruition with the U.S. support for the *mujahedin* fighting the Soviets in Afghanistan during the 1980s. The creation and support of various militant groups—including the Taliban—by the Pakistan intelligence services in the 1990s reflected a similarly instrumental approach to religious politics.

The resurgence of Islamist politics in the post–Cold War era, then, did not occur as precipitously—nor as spontaneously—as many assume. Nor did this movement emerge organically from civil society. On the contrary, state support for Islamist organizations from the 1970s onward is a key, though largely overlooked, variable in explaining the rise (and the potency) of the Islamist movement. While Islamist groups were a marginal force during the 1950s and 1960s, their political fortunes changed dramatically in subsequent decades when state elites in Egypt, Pakistan, Saudi Arabia, and elsewhere sought to use Islamist ideas and activists for their own purposes. In the process, state actors contributed greatly to the popular perception that illiberal renderings of Islam—and the exclusive visions of social life that they inspire—are somehow more authentic than their liberal counterparts. This is not to argue that the social movements associated with the Islamist trend are unimportant, or that the content of the ideas do not have causal force in their own right. Rather, the claim here is that the groups and ideas associated with Islamic fundamentalism benefited enormously from state support, while modernist (or liberal) interpretations of Islamic tradition historically associated with the political left correspondingly suffered.

The following pages examine this trend in Egypt and Pakistan. The primary focus of the two cases is on the orientation of state leaders towards conservative (or illiberal) renderings of religious tradition, and how this attitude changed during the 1970s and 1980s.[9] This chapter will also examine the origins of the international *jihādist* movement, and the support that militant groups received (and continue to receive) from Pakistani and other intelligence services. The latter part of the chapter will then re-examine the conventional interpretation of Islamist politics in light of this history. While many assume that modern states are, by definition, supportive of secular norms and identities, the reality is quite different. On the contrary, fundamentalist Islam has been a central feature of the state-building project in both countries and has benefited enormously from official support over the past four decades. The effort by state actors to co-opt Islamist ideas and activists also helps to explain the dominance of the Muslim Brotherhood in the period following the 2011 Egyptian revolution, and the corresponding marginalization of the secular and liberal alternatives. This re-evaluation of the Islamist movement also sheds light on the continuing tension between the United States and Pakistan over the latter's support for Islamists militants, an issue that was embarrassingly evident with the killing of Osama bin Laden on Pakistan soil in 2011.

State Promotion of Islamist Politics

Egypt

While Egypt's primary Islamist opposition group, the Muslim Brotherhood, was ruthlessly suppressed during the 1950s and 1960s, it was resurrected in the 1970s and 1980s with state support. The key figure in this transition was Anwar al-Sadat, the Egyptian leader who succeeded Gamal Abdel Nasser as president after the latter's death in 1970. Nasser was a charismatic leader whose brand of Arab nationalism embodied a secular (and socialist) vision of national development. In Sadat's first speech as president, he affirmed his commitment to Nasser's legacy and pledged to rule in cooperation with the collective leadership of the Egyptian ruling party, the Arab Socialist Union (ASU). This facade of unity, however, cloaked deep divisions within Egypt's political elite over the future of the country. On the one hand, the Marxists, unreconstructed Nasserists, and pro-Soviet "centrists" all remained committed to Nasser's vision of secular Arab nationalism and the principles of the 1952 revolution. This faction included the then-Vice President Ali Sabri and others who remained in positions of authority. Opposing them were Sadat and his allies, all of whom had become disaffected with Egypt's socialist experiment, and sought to chart a new course for the country. Sadat's effort to consolidate political power, and to redefine Egyptian politics, would thrust him into the heart of Egypt's religious debates.

Sadat's break with the Nasserist left required an alternate base of political support. He found this support among the traditional elites and landowners who had been marginalized under Nasser's rule, as well as key members of the military and the security services. The confrontation between Egypt's competing political forces came to a head in May 1971, when the vice president and ninety of his supporters were accused of conspiring to overthrow the government, and subsequently arrested and removed from office. These events came to be known as the Corrective Revolution, and marked the beginning of the reorientation of both Egypt's domestic and foreign policies.

The defining feature of this new orientation was Sadat's abandonment of the state's previous commitment to a socialist and secular vision of national development. This change was evident in the embrace of market oriented economic polices (the *infitah*, or opening), and the adoption of a program of de-sequestration (reversal of land reform). This new direction was also evident in Sadat's embrace of conservative religion. As noted above, the Sadat regime greatly expanded religious education in government schools, increased Islamic programming on state-run television, and provided funding for the construction of thousands of mosques. The regime also gave favors (land, construction funds, television airtime), to popular sheikhs in return for their support.[10] The creation of an image of personal piety was a central feature of this strategy. Sadat was depicted as "*al-Rais al-Mumen*" (the believing president) and regularly had his participation in Friday prayers aired on state-run television. Sadat also gave greater latitude to the official *ulema* (religious clerics) within Egypt's religious establishment.

The motivations of the regime were, in part, ideological. Sadat sought to develop a new basis of authority rooted in religion and tradition, not secular Arab nationalism. Part of the motivation, however, was instrumental. The Egyptian regime saw in fundamentalist Islam a useful means for stigmatizing their opponents on the political left, while cultivating a more quiescent—and obedient—population. A theologically illiberal (or conservative) interpretation of Islam was, thus, invoked to sanction a new era of conservative politics. State and religion during the Sadat period would be used to support existing patterns of social and political order, not to change them.

A key feature of Sadat's new orientation was the normalization of relations with Saudi Arabia. The Saudi royal family had been a bitter rival of the Nasser regime in the Arab Cold War.[11] Sadat's rapprochement with Saudi Arabia in the 1970s, then, helped to reshape the ideological context of the region, and was central to Egypt's re-alignment with the West. Sadat perceived the financial support that the Saudis could provide as essential to his country's economic development in the aftermath of the 1967 War. For its part, the Saudi leadership was keen to eliminate the influence of Arab nationalism in Egypt, and to avoid the kind of intra-Arab conflict that defined the Nasser period. Saudi Arabia had been deeply troubled by Nasser's populist rhetoric and by his revolutionary policies, both of which challenged the legitimacy of Saudi Arabia's ruling family and their control of the region's oil wealth. The normalization of relations during the Sadat era, then, served the interests of both governments. It also marked the beginning of a period in which the Gulf monarchies used their newfound oil wealth to promote a conservative or *salafist* interpretation of Islam throughout the region, a trend that would greatly influence Egyptian politics and culture.

Government support for Islamic groups and institutions was central to Sadat's new orientation. The regime, for example, involved the official religious establishment in redefining the ideological basis of the Egyptian state. The venerated mosque and university complex of Al-Azhar was greatly expanded, and a new campus was constructed with funds from the Saudi government. State funding for religious education through the Azhar system (which was controlled by state-appointed officials) was also increased, as was funding for religious publications produced by Al-Azhar and other state supported religious institution. One such institution, the Supreme Council of Islamic Affairs, defined and articulated the official interpretation of Islam for both state and society. The Sadat regime also initiated an anti-Leftist campaign, which involved the official *ulema* issuing a series of *fatwas* (religious edicts) that equated Communism with impiety, and charged communists with "hav[ing] no faith."[12] These efforts were intended to stigmatize the socialist holdovers from the Nasser era, and to use the population's intrinsic support for Islam as a means of strengthening their allegiance to state authority. The accusation of impiety explicit in such *fatwas* served as a dangerous precedent in the stigmatization of alternative ideas, a trend which would take an ominous turn in the Mubarak era when Islamists targeted secular thinkers on similar grounds.

The Sadat regime's effort to cooperate with—and actively co-opt—Egypt's Muslim Brotherhood was another part of this strategy. Sadat's alliance with the Brotherhood was intended to provide a grassroots basis to his rule, and to blunt opposition to Sadat's reversal of policies that

Nasser had implemented to help the poor. The rapprochement between Sadat and the Brotherhood was mediated in 1971 by King Faisal of Saudi Arabia, Fouad Allam (the head of Egypt's State Security), and an Egyptian businessman and Sadat confidant named Osman Ahmed Osman. As part of a negotiated agreement, the Brotherhood agreed to renounce the use of violence and promised not to engage in anti-regime activities. In exchange, the Brotherhood was given greater freedom of action and the right to continue a peaceful advocacy of Islam.[13] The Sadat regime released thousands of Islamist political prisoners over the course of the next four years (1971–75), and allowed other members of the Brotherhood to return from exile. Sadat's domestic intelligence services also supported an array of Islamist student groups on Egypt's university campuses throughout the 1970s. The universities were a primary arena of political activism, and remained dominated by the Marxist groups that had developed under Nasser. Hence, constraining their influence was essential, and support for Islamist student groups was seen as a useful means toward this end.

Finally, the adoption of a new Constitution in 1971 provided a greater role for Islam in Egyptian politics. Article 2 of the Constitution designated Islam as the official state religion, and the Shari`a as "*a* principle source of legislation." Although the provision was vague, the fact that the Shari`a was mentioned so prominently in the constitution was itself significant, and represented a victory of sorts for the Islamists. This provision was further amended in 1980, to make Islamic law "*the* principal (or primary) source of legislation" (*al-masdar al-ra'isi*). The reintegration of Islam into Egypt's legal codes was further promoted by the National Assembly in the late 1970s. This was done in order to "bring Egyptian statutory law into total agreement with Shari`a provisions,"[14] and was adopted largely under pressure from the Muslim Brotherhood. In conceding these issues, Sadat completed the project of dis-embedding secular norms in Egyptian public life. By 1980, Islam was the official state religion, and both the political institutions of the country and the legal codes provided a means for the continued Islamization of the public sphere.

The underlying problem with this strategy, however, was that the Islamists—whether in the official religious establishment, the universities, or in the Muslim Brotherhood—proved to be unreliable allies. More to the point, the regime's ability to control the forces it unleashed was limited. After Sadat's historic trip to Jerusalem in 1977, many of these former supporters turned on the "believing President." Some of the younger activists would later form the militant organizations of the 1980s and 1990s, which included *al-Gama'a al-Islamiyya* (The Islamic Group) and *Islamic Jihad* (Holy War).[15] Others would find alternative avenues of opposition, including the professional syndicates that became dominated by the Muslim Brotherhood in the 1990s. What radicalized the Islamists was, on the one hand, the discontent over the regime's failing economic policies, and the lack of progress on such fundamental issues as education, housing, and transportation. On the other hand, Egypt's rapprochement with Israel and the West was enormously problematic. While the left felt Sadat was betraying Nasser's legacy, the Islamists saw him as betraying Islam. The end result was that the Islamist groups which had long benefited from the government's protection now "rebelled against the role [which] the regime had assigned them—that of counterbalancing the various forces of the left—and political Islam changed from being a functional supporter of the regime to posing the main threat to it."[16]

By the end of the Sadat era, religious politics in Egypt had taken on a life of its own. Islamist groups had emerged as the dominant opposition to the state, a movement ironically facilitated by the regime's own policies. While Sadat had successfully marginalized the political left, he "had let the genie out of the bottle."[17] And with his assassination in 1981 by members of *al–Jihād*, "the genie had struck him down."[18] More to the point, this shift in policy set the stage for the Mubarak era. While Hosni Mubarak, Sadat's successor, characterized his government as a bulwark against Islamic fundamentalism—and a defender of the secular vision of modernity—the reality was otherwise. As in previous years, the Egyptian government continued to promote a close association of religion and state, and used public education, the media and other state controlled institutions to promote a more obedient (if illiberal) vision of Islam. The government also relied upon the security services to monitor and repress anti-regime activists (both religious and secular), which included alternately tolerating and constraining the Muslim Brotherhood. Throughout the Mubarak era, however, the regime sought to portray itself as the authentic defender of religious tradition (not the Islamists), and empowered the official religious establishment to serve this end.

In attempting to co-opt Islam for its own purposes, however, Mubarak ceded the long-standing ideological debate over whether Egypt ought to have a secular or a religious state. This was a recurring question that had defined the ideological politics of the country for much of the twentieth century.[19] At issue was not just the proper role of religion in public life—and whether the state ought to enforce Islamic orthodoxy in society—but was also linked to fundamental questions of identity. Was Egyptian nationalism intrinsically Islamic, or could it accommodate Egypt's large Christian population in a non-discriminatory manner? While Nasser had firmly endorsed a secular state—and a religiously inclusive Egyptian national identity—Sadat had opened the door for a re-negotiation of this matter. The ideological ambivalence of the Mubarak regime, and its support for the conservative *ulema*—who joined the government in opposing the militants of the 1990s—further entrenched Islamist attitudes in Egypt's public institutions. The Mubarak regime thus helped to normalize a political (and religious) discourse that was antithetical to secular norms and identities, even while stigmatizing the militants who advocated the violent overthrow of the regime. The implications for minority rights, secular norms, and freedom of thought were far reaching.

The abandonment of the secular project in Egypt, then, provides the context for understanding not only Sadat's assassination, but also the rise of the Islamist movement in Egypt more generally. The effort of successive regimes to co-opt religion into the service of the Egyptian state had validated Islamist ideas about politics, religion, and national life. It also facilitated the Islamization of Egypt's public sphere. This history also sheds light on the subsequent dominance of the Muslim Brotherhood as a political force in the aftermath of the 2011 revolution. Thirty years of active efforts to marginalize the political left—and the liberal visions of secular modernity associated with it—produced an ideological milieu that benefited the various elements of the Islamist movement at the expense of the secular left. There was, consequently, little debate during the 2011 and 2012 elections over the proper role of religion in public life, the treatment of minorities, or whether or not the state ought to enforce religious law, because the state had long since ceded these debates to the Islamist trend.

Pakistan

Perhaps the most interesting feature of the Egyptian narrative is its applicability to countries other than Egypt. Sadat's policies were not anomalous, nor limited to the Middle East. On the contrary, the conscious manipulation of conservative (or illiberal) religion by state elites was widespread throughout the 1970s and 1980s. In countries as diverse as Malaysia, Pakistan,[20] Turkey,[21] Sudan,[22] Morocco, and Algeria, ostensibly secular state actors sought to co-opt the ideas and activists associated with Islamic fundamentalism. In each of these cases, illiberal or exclusive interpretations of religion were used to provide a "priestly" affirmation for existing patterns of social and political power, and a popular basis for politically conservative governments. In this context, theologically conservative interpretations of religion were a central feature of the ideological debates of the period, and were used to challenge liberal (and secular) visions of social order.[23] As in Egypt, state actors invoked Islamic fundamentalism to sanction a new era of conservative politics.

This trend was especially pronounced in Pakistan, where the Islamization of the public sphere was a project led not by the Islamist opposition, but by the state. Created in 1947 by the partition of British-ruled India, the early constitutional debates in Pakistan hinged on whether the state would have a Muslim identity—though remain largely secular—or whether the state would be committed to creating the kind of Islamic order envisioned by Islamists such as Mawlana Maududi, the founder of the *Jamaat-i-Islami* (Pakistan's pre-eminent Islamist political party). In other words, would Pakistan be a homeland for South Asia's Muslims, or would it be a religious state? Pakistan's founder and first Governor General, Muhammad Ali Jinnah, was a Western educated lawyer who had little interest in creating the kind of Islamist order advocated by Maududi or others. Moreover, the diversity of the Pakistani population—which included secular Muslims, a large Shīʻa minority, and numerous ethnic and linguistic groups—made the question of imposing a particular interpretation of Islam upon society a sensitive matter. There was even a lack of consensus over such basic issues as "what is Islam" and "who is a Muslim?"[24] What dominated the constitutional debates of the 1950s and 1960s, then, was a relatively modernist vision of Islam that was consistent with basic norms of non-discrimination. It was this understanding of Islamic tradition that informed Pakistan's early state-building project, even if the military actively used religious parties—and the Islamist ideology—to justify its interventions in domestic politics.

Debates between modernists and fundamentalists over religious interpretation—and over the proper relationship between religion and the state—became more pronounced in the 1970s. In 1971, the country's civil war led to its division and the subsequent creation of Bangladesh. The war also ushered in a brief period of democratic rule. Zulfikar Ali Bhutto, the leader of a leftist political party, the Pakistan Peoples Party (PPP), attracted support from both the lower classes and the large Shī'a population with his calls for a secular and socialist state. Bhutto's government, however, increasingly endorsed conservative interpretations of Islam as part of an effort to cultivate ties with, and secure financial aid from, the oil-rich Gulf monarchies. Bhutto subsequently conceded a number of contentious political issues to the Islamists in Pakistan—declaring the Ahmadiyya sect as non–Muslim, for example, and prohibiting alcohol and gambling—though the PPP did retain its commitment to a progressive vision of socio-economic reform. In the 1977 national elections, the PPP was opposed by a coalition of religious parties that included the *Jamaat-i-Islami*, with each side invoking Islam to justify their competing political agendas. The latter drew significant support from a variety of societal forces—including members of the military and Pakistan's large landowners—that opposed the PPP's economic policies.

Despite Bhutto's victory in the 1977 elections, his tenure in office was short lived. Three months after the elections, in July 1977, the military removed Bhutto from power and installed General Muhammad Zia-ul-Haq as president. The new government subsequently put Bhutto on trial in 1979, convicted him of assassinating a political rival, and had him put to death by hanging. These events marked the beginning of a new period of military rule and state-led Islamization.

The defining feature of General Zia-ul-Haq's tenure in office was his effort to create a system of government that closely tied Islam to the state. In doing so, Zia-ul-Haq abandoned the inclusive nationalism of his predecessors, and embraced the *Jamaat-i-Islami* and their vision of an Islamist order. This program entailed the active promotion of a conservative (or fundamentalist) interpretation of Sunni Islam that was both intolerant and anti-Shī'a. The goal of Zia-ul-Haq's policies was two-fold. First, the invocation of Islam was meant to delegitimize Bhutto's socialist policies and to provide a religious sanction for military rule. Second, the top down program of Islamization was meant to create a religiously uniform public sphere and, hence, a more quiescent—and politically unified—population. The Zia-ul-Haq regime subsequently promoted a range of polices affecting law, education, economics, and religious practice. These changes included new laws requiring the observance of fasting during Ramadan, the introduction of *Hudood Ordinance*'s punishments in the Penal Code,[25] and the establishment of new *Shari'a* Courts to determine whether or not existing law was consistent with Islamic mandate. There was also an effort to create an Islamic taxation system, and other changes to the economic system to make it more consistent with Islamic prohibitions on interest. Another feature of this program was the adoption of a blasphemy law, which made the denigration of the Prophet or the teachings of Islam punishable by death or imprisonment. Although Zia-ul-Haq was killed in a mysterious plane crash in 1989, the close association of Sunni fundamentalism and the state remained.

While much of Pakistan's Islamization program was domestic in orientation, the role of Islam—and Islamic militancy—in Pakistan's foreign policies was enormously influential. In this context, Islamist (or fundamentalist) conceptions of Islam were a central part of the Cold War effort to contain both Soviet and Iranian (i.e., Shī'a) influence in the region. This was clearly evident during the 1980s, when the Pakistani intelligence services, the so-called Inter-Service Intelligence (ISI), served as the main conduit for money and arms provided by the United States and Saudi Arabia to the *mujahedin* fighters in Afghanistan. Pakistani support for Islamic militants in Afghanistan, however, continued well after the Soviet withdrawal in 1989. Throughout the 1990s, the ISI provided military, financial, and political support for a variety of militant groups, and used them as "proxies" to further Pakistani foreign policy goals throughout the region. The ISI helped to create and fund groups such as *Lashkar-e-Taiba*, *Jaish-e-Mohammed*, and other militants active in the Kashmir region of India. Similarly, the Pakistan Interior Ministry was instrumental in the creation of the Afghan Taliban, providing it with arms and military advisors, and facilitating the Taliban's rise to power in the early 1990s.[26]

Pakistani support for the Afghan Taliban throughout this period was linked to the country's regional interests. Given the existence of a hostile India to its east, Pakistan tried to ensure the existence of a friendly regime to its West. This entailed a policy of supporting the Pashtun ethnic population at the expense of the Hazara population (which is Shī'a and has ties to Iran) and the Tajiks (which have ties to Turkish Central Asia). The Northwest Territories of Pakistan are predominantly Pashtun, and it is from these tribes that the Afghan Taliban were formed. Interestingly, the most effective fighting force during the 1980s Afghan War were the Tajiks in the north, headed by Ahmad Shah Massoud, though this latter group received the least amount of aid from the United States and Saudi Arabia. Because the funding and military supplies for the *mujahedin* were coordinated through the Pakistani ISI, most of the resources were directed to Pashtun groups, such as those led by Gulbuddin Hekmatyar and Jalaluddin Haqqani.[27] These leaders were vehemently anti-Western, and would later become closely allied with both the Taliban and al-Qaeda, but were favored by the ISI. They were also seen as useful allies by Western security services during the height of the Cold War.

It was out of this milieu that the international jihādist movement emerged. American assistance to the mujahedin is estimated to have been between six and eight billion dollars over the course of ten years, a figure that was matched dollar for dollar by Saudi Arabia. There were also 30,000 to 40,000 foreign-born Muslims—the so-called "Afghan Arabs"—who came from a variety of countries to fight in Afghanistan. Among these recruits were fighters as well as organizational personnel that raised money, set up training camps, and coordinated the effort on the ground in Afghanistan. One of these young men was Osama bin Laden, whose office of special services (*mektab al-khedamat*) provided the organizational basis to what would later come to be known as al-Qaeda. A central feature of the Afghan war was the establishment of an infrastructure of training camps in Pakistan, Islamic schools (or *modaris* pl. *madrassah*) throughout the region, and an international fundraising network. The unintended consequence of these policies was the creation of an international movement that would live on after the war.[28] Once the Soviets withdrew from Afghanistan, many of the Afghan Arabs left for other conflict regions such as Kashmir, Chechnya and Bosnia, or returned to their home countries. This set the stage for the spread of Islamic militancy throughout the Middle East and

North Africa during the 1990s, the creation of *al–Qaeda*, and, ultimately, to the events of 9–11.

The effect of these policies upon popular understandings of Islam was far reaching. Traditional interpreters of Islam were marginalized, and supplanted by the more intolerant—and militant—ideology that was born of the Afghan war. This was particularly true in Afghanistan, where the civil war that followed the Soviet withdrawal destroyed "age-old Afghan tolerance and consensus" and "divided Islamic sects and ethnic groups in a way that before was unimaginable to ordinary Afghans."[29] Much of this was due to the fact that those who received most of the funding during the war with the Soviets were the most ideological and extreme. The nature of this religious ideology was also thoroughly modern, insofar as it saw the capture of state power as key to the transformation of civil society. The subsequent effort to promote political unity through a coercive uniformity is more akin to the collectivist ideologies of the early twentieth century (fascism or communism) than a return to traditional religion.[30] In any event, the Islamist ideology that emerged from the cauldron of the Afghan war provided little room for dissent—either in religion or politics—which would be apparent when the Taliban government came to power in the early 1990s.

The impact upon the region's politics was similarly transformative. The spread of Islamist militants and ideas to Chechnya, Kashmir, and to the various countries from which the so-called Afghan Arabs originated had a profound impact upon these societies throughout the 1990s. The unintended consequences—or "blowback"—of these policies also included the creation in the al-Qaeda, and the attacks carried out against American targets both at home and abroad. While the nineteen hijackers who carried out the 9–11 plot were either Egyptian and Saudi, the events of that day brought uncomfortable scrutiny to the Pakistani military and security services. Pakistan's longstanding ties to the Taliban in Afghanistan (where al-Qaeda was then based) now became a significant liability. Although Pakistan's president, Pervez Musharraff, acquiesced to U.S. demands and joined the "war on terror," this was never a whole-hearted commitment. On the contrary, support from Pakistan's military for combating Islamist militancy in the region was ambivalent at best, and duplicitous at worst.

Pakistani support for Islamist militants continues to be a challenge for the United States and other countries, particularly India and Afghanistan.

The 2008 attacks in Mumbai which killed 101 civilians, for example, were carried out by *Lashkar-e-Taiba*, a Pakistan based militant group with long-standing ties to the ISI.[31] Similarly, the Afghan government of Hamid Karzai long complained of Pakistani support for the Taliban insurgency that continued to threaten the post–2001 Afghan government. Continuing Pakistani complicity with Islamist militants was laid bare with the 2011 killing of Osama bin Laden in Abbottabad, Pakistan, a small town 30 miles from the capital, Islamabad. While it is not clear that Bin Laden was sheltered by Pakistan officials, it is hard to imagine otherwise. The town itself is home to Pakistan's military academy and the house reportedly was a former ISI safe house.[32] This has been just one of many instances that have strained U.S.–Pakistani relations, and raised questions about the Pakistani government's commitment to opposing militant extremism.

Such revelations should not be surprising given the fact that the close connection between the Pakistani government and Islamic militancy goes back over four decades. Moreover, from the perspective of the Pakistani intelligence services, Islamist militants remain a useful ally in their regional competition with India. U.S. government officials had long suspected Pakistani government officials of duplicity on this front, and assumed Pakistani intelligence knew the whereabouts of senior al-Qaeda and Taliban leaders. The U.S. official documents that were leaked in 2010 highlight these tensions. Of the numerous revelations that the so-called "Wikileaks" documents revealed, none was more damning than the allegation that the Pakistani intelligence services continued to support the Taliban in its war against the United States and the Afghan government. Specific allegations include the "collusion" between ISI agents and Taliban operatives to assassinate Afghan leaders and to organize militant networks fighting American forces in Afghanistan. Such actions were seen as particularly egregious given the fact that Pakistan had received billions of dollars in aid since 9–11 to fight these same groups.[33] While it is difficult to verify the information, the leaked documents "confirm a picture of Pakistani double-dealing that has been building for years."[34]

The ramifications of these policies on Pakistani society have also been dire. While leaders such as Zia-ul-Haq may have seen Sunni fundamentalism as a useful means of building popular support among the majority population, the country has paid a steep price for these policies. The anti-Shī'a bias of militant Sunni fundamentalism has fueled sectarian division, violence and instability throughout the country. Moreover, it is not clear to whom the Islamist militant groups ultimately answer. Like the Islamists in Egypt, the militant movement in Pakistan has taken on a life of its own that now threatens its former patron. What is clear, however, is that both the ideology and the network associated with the international *jihādī* movement emerged with the aid and funding of state actors. While this network may have served an ostensible purpose during the Cold War, the unintended consequences continue to shape the region. Far from being a struggle for freedom, the so-called war on terror may be better characterized as an effort to contain the damage of earlier policies, and to put the "genie back in the bottle."

Rethinking Islamist Politics

What, then, do these cases and events tell us about Islamist politics, and particularly about the relationship between religion and the modern state? To begin with, it is clear that Islamist politics did not emerge in a vacuum, or autonomously from within the realm of civil society. While the early Islamists enjoyed some degree of grassroots support, the organizations and ideas associated with Islamic fundamentalism were politically marginal well into the second half of the twentieth century. Their political fortunes changed, however, in the 1970s and 1980s when state actors chose to support Islamist ideas and activists instead of working to repress them (as was evident in Egypt, Syria, and elsewhere). The Islamist movement also received an enormous boost from the rise in prominence of Saudi Arabia, and from the oil wealth that flowed into the Gulf monarchies from 1970 onward. The "resurgence of Islamist politics" that has defined the post–Cold War era, then, is not, as is commonly assumed, a battle between religious actors and secular states over enlightenment values. The reality is that, at least from the 1970s onward, state elites throughout the Middle East and South Asia more commonly chose to "ride the tiger" of an exclusive religious politics instead of confronting it.[35]

Second, the cases highlight the deep divisions within Islam over both interpretation and application. Particularly during the Cold War, differing interpretations of religion informed the political fault lines of the region. Modernist (and liberal) interpretations of Islam were associated with socialist programs of national development, and provided a foundation for the relatively inclusive forms of secular nationalism. By tolerating a degree of religious and ethnic diversity, these inclusive forms of national identity provided the basis for the kind of fundamental compromise essential to multi-ethnic, multi-religious societies.[36] Islamist or fundamentalist Islam, on the other hand, provided the basis for more exclusive versions of the nation and identity. These more illiberal (or *salafist*) interpretations of Islam were associated with politically conservative groups and found support among those who sought to maintain existing patterns of social hierarchy. The competition between modernist and fundamentalist Islam, then, informed the ideological divisions both within countries as well as between them. These religious differences were evident in the political divide between the U.S.-backed Gulf monarchies and the socialist republics supported by the Soviet Union. It ought not be surprising then, that with the end of the Cold War, and the collapse of the political left, a strong Islamist movement would be left in its wake.

These competing visions of both religion and society are an important part of the ideological context that gave rise to Islamist extremism. As the cases above illustrate, the competition between liberal (or modernist) interpretations of tradition and illiberal interpretations reflect the continuing tension between competing interpretations of a given religious tradition and the pattern of social life that each envisions.[37] The liberal or "modernist" interpretation of religion, for example, is premised upon the uncertain nature of belief, and the fallibility of humans to accurately interpret either scripture or God's will. Liberal religious interpreters also tend to read their tradition as metaphorical, not literal truth. They, consequently, tend toward accommodation on matters of conscience and free thought. This tolerant outlook provides the basis for secular political governance insofar as we mean non-discrimination in matters of belief. In this context, each individual (and community) forsakes its right to religious and ethnic preference in exchange for others relinquishing similar claims.

Illiberal or exclusive interpretations of religion, on the other hand, commonly inform ethnic nationalisms and other exclusive forms of social life. This understanding of religion tends to take a more literal reading of their particular tradition, emphasize revelation over reason, and believe that religion is defined by an unchanging moral framework. Advocates of an illiberal approach to religion tend to claim that their understanding of tradition (and *only* their understanding) is true and right and reflective of God's Will. Such religious certitude diminishes the proclivity for religious tolerance because differing perspectives are seen as either heresy (incorrect belief) or apostasy (lack of belief).[38] Hence, the realm of individual conscience is, from this view, legitimately circumscribed, and conformity in matters of belief is seen as an important basis of social unity. The intolerance of alternative belief is commonly extended to political dissent, and those who oppose the will of the community (or its self-proclaimed spokesmen), are commonly characterized as unpatriotic, treasonous, or self-hating members of the group.

The internal debates over whether to create a secular or an "Islamic" state, then, reflect both religious and political differences over how to interpret a shared tradition for a modern context. David Little's work on religion, nationalism, and human rights sheds light on these tensions. Although the broader dispute is commonly seen as simply a question of politics, debates over religious interpretation, national identity, and the moral basis of social life are also involved. So, too, are debates over the proper relationship of religion to political authority, and whether or not alternative understandings of religion or fundamental belief ought be accorded equal treatment. Those who argue for a close association of Islam and the state believe that collective self-actualization requires a public sphere defined by the ethnic and religious motifs of the majority community. This raises basic questions about religious tolerance, and whether the institutions of the modern state ought to be non-discriminatory in matters of religion and belief. In this context, those who support an inclusive vision of religion and social life are invariably at odds with those who advocate a more explicit Islamic order.

What is most surprising about the cases discussed above is the changing role of the state on precisely these issues. While state leaders tended to defend pluralist conceptions of social order in the mid-twentieth century—and the liberal or modernist Islam that informed inclusive national identities—this orientation changed in subsequent decades. From the 1970s onward, state actors abandoned earlier commitments to an inclusive public sphere and promoted a more illiberal rendering of Islamic tradition as a basis of state authority. Liberal and secular norms were subsequently delegitimized, and an exclusive vision of society (and the nation) became embedded in state institutions. This was particularly evident in Egypt, where Sadat's religious turn greatly influenced long-standing debates over the compatibility of secularism and Islam. In Pakistan, religion was always central to national identity, but the exclusive vision of Sunni fundamentalism only became predominant with Zia-ul-Haq, as "the political commitment to an ideological state gradually evolved into a strategic commitment to *jihādi* ideology."[39] In both cases, fundamentalist religion was central to a new era of conservative politics that used religious tradition to sanction state authority.

These cases also bring into question many of the assumptions commonly made about tradition and modernity. On the one hand, it is clear that modernity is *not*, by definition, secular, liberal, and progressive, nor does the Islamist project represent a retreat into tradition. On the contrary, modernity manifests in diverse ways, alternately liberal and illiberal. The Islamist ideology is just such a modern construct. The theoretical basis of Islamism was created in early twentieth century by activists who were very much influenced by ethnic conceptions of national identity, and who modeled their political organization on the European fascists. While the appeal of the ideology may be rooted in popular faith commitments, the Islamic order envisioned by the Muslim Brotherhood or the *Jamaat* are thoroughly modern, and do not represent a return to some traditional pattern to social life. Moreover, the aims of the Islamist movement have always been defined by the quintessentially modern project of using the state to reshape civil society.

Similarly, the cases discussed above undermine the widespread belief that state actors are, in fact, willing to defend enlightenment—and secular—norms. This ought not be surprising. As Little has ably demonstrated, nationalist (or ethnic) visions of social life regularly draw upon religious symbols and motifs to reinforce social solidarity and to mobilize populations along national or communal lines.[40] By linking human existence to a transcendent realm, religion helps to legitimize—and sacralize—political authority or claims to such authority, and this generates a corresponding obligation to obey.[41] This understanding of modern religious politics helps to explain the continued saliency of religion to the modern (or post-modern) politics, and, particularly, to the state. The real question, then, is whether the type of religion that is being invoked in the state project is consistent with an inclusive vision of social life—one tolerant of minority populations, religious difference and political dissent—or whether it is informed an exclusive one.

This last point highlights the diverse ways in which religion is invoked within a contemporary political context. At times religion can be inclusive—and supportive of values—and other times it can be exclusive and inform the worst forms of chauvinism. Similarly, religion is frequently used to critique existing patterns of social order—the so-called "prophetic" function of religion—while at other times it is used to sanction an existing set of power relations. This latter, or "priestly," function of religion is used to sanctify political power and to imbue relationships of dominance with the aura of legitimate authority. While the first is intended to mobilize popular participation in politics, the goal of the latter is more often to constrain such involvement. In either instance—whether prophetic or priestly—the ultimate aim is to link the narrow political interests of a particular group to that of national, moral, and religious purpose.

These issues highlight the limitations of the conventional narrative of Islamist politics, which, above all, assumes two things: first, that Islamic fundamentalism is invariably prophetic—that is opposed to an existing pattern of social order—and, second, that states are consistently secular, or at least supportive of a progressive (and inclusive) vision of social life. As the case studies indicate, however, neither of these assumptions holds true. Rather, different interpretations of Islam were mobilized at different points in time and for very different ends. The Nasserists and early Pakistani political leaders, for example, supported a modernist interpretation of Islam as part of their vision of nationalist development. Modernist Islam in this context served a "priestly function" in the 1950s and 1960s and provided a religious basis for an inclusive nationalism. Moreover, the state at that time sought to repress (or at least marginalize) the Islamist vision, particularly in Egypt. It is from this earlier period that the Islamist ideology emerged in a "prophetic" manner to challenge Arab and secular nationalists. It is this dynamic that gave rise to the assumption that states are invariably secular and opposed to Islamist opposition groups.

As the cases illustrate, however, state leaders long ago abandoned the secular (and liberal) project, opting instead to co-opt exclusive interpretations of Islam as a basis of authoritarian rule. While competition between state elites and Islamist opposition groups has remained, in today's world this competition has little to do with ideology. In other words, the "war of values" between enlightenment norms and an exclusive "Islamo-fascism" has little bearing on reality. The competition in recent years has not been between secular norms and fundamentalist religion, but, rather, between opposing political interests that vie with one another for both political power and the mantle of cultural legitimacy. A more nuanced typology of this dynamic is as follows:

POLITICAL USE OF RELIGION		
Interpretation of Religion	Functions of Religion	
	PRIESTLY	PROPHETIC
LIBERAL or "Modernist"	Consistent with Enlightenment Norms[42] (and used to support an inclusive social order)	Non-Violent and Progressive Social Movements[43] (largely tolerant)
THEOLOGICALLY CONSERVATIVE or "Illiberal" religion	Exclusive visions of both religion and society[44] (and largely intolerant of either religious or political dissent)	Opposition "Fundamentalist Movements"[45] (and largely intolerant)

Figure 1

This typology helps to clarify the different renderings of Islamic tradition, and delineates the different ways in which these various interpretations are used politically. The typology (along with the case studies) also sheds light upon the changing fortunes of these competing interpretations of Islam. By promoting one interpretation of religion at the expense of others, state actors greatly influenced internal religious debates and helped to shape popular perceptions about which understanding of religious tradition—modernist or fundamentalist, inclusive or exclusive—was the more legitimate. Under Nasser, Jinnah, and other post-Colonial leaders, for example, modernist religion thrived, while a more conservative rendering of Islamic tradition flourished under Sadat, Mubarak, and Zia-ul-Haq.

State support of Islamic fundamentalism, in short, helps to explain why an exclusive interpretation of both Islam and society emerged so forcefully in the post–1973 era, and is now seen as more culturally authentic.

The case studies also illustrate the limited utility of co-opting conservative religion. The fundamental error that Sadat (and others) made was in assuming that an illiberal rendering of Islamic tradition would necessarily be supportive of the status quo, that is, a theologically conservative interpretation of Islam would *invariably* be politically conservative and not revolutionary. As the cases illustrate, however, this was not the result. In Egypt, Sadat's effort to co-opt the Islamists did not result in a compliant population, but, rather, empowered activists who were willing to oppose the regime when Sadat's policies no longer accorded with the Islamists' interests and vision. Sadat, in short, did not understand that a theologically conservative (or illiberal) Islam could be both revolutionary (or prophetic) and priestly.[46] Islamist groups that have been supported by the Pakistani authorities (as well as by Saudi Arabia) have proven to be similarly unreliable. In both instances, many of those aided by state institutions for instrumental reasons turned on their former patrons when state leaders waivered on issues central to the Islamist cause.

This more nuanced understanding of the Islamist politics (and militancy) demonstrates how misleading was the Bush Administration's characterization of the "war on terror." Far from a struggle between freedom and tyranny—or between open and closed visions of society—the war on terror was, in essence, a competition for political control in a region where all sides invoked illiberal renderings of religious tradition to sanction their competing ends. This is not to say that divisions between competing conceptions of religion and society do not exist. Clearly, they do. Particularly in the aftermath of the Arab uprisings of 2011, there is a vibrant debate between the progressive forces of tolerance, liberalism, and democratic reform, on the one hand, and the regressive forces of intolerance and repression on the other hand. However, states such as Saudi Arabia, Pakistan, and Egypt—America's key allies in the war on terror—have consistently opposed the kinds of freedom for which America ostensibly stands (political freedom, religious freedom, and the rights of women). Moreover, these states have long supported the Islamist ideas and militant groups that America has been fighting for well over a decade. What we see today, then, is not a competition between freedom and tyranny, but rather a struggle for power and interest clothed in a rhetoric that hides more than it reveals.

Conclusion

The close association of an illiberal rendering of Islamic tradition and state authority remains a central feature of contemporary politics in the Middle East and South Asia. Particularly in the aftermath of the 2011 revolution, the Muslim Brotherhood sought to promote a more central role for conservative Islam in public life. In pursuing such policies, during its brief time in power, the Brotherhood continued the trend initiated over forty years ago by the Sadat regime, which has undermined the intellectual basis for a liberal modernist Islam and an inclusive social order. Similarly, in Pakistan, state institutions remain a primary supporter of both Islamist ideas and militant organizations. While the intention of Zia-ul-Haq and others may have been to create a more culturally homogenous—and politically unified—society, the result was quite the opposite. Contemporary Pakistan is rife with sectarian division and the central government has largely lost control of its Northwest provinces. It is this highly militarized region of Pakistan that is home to the Pashtun tribes that comprise the Taliban and which shelter members of al-Qaeda.

The second issue that emerges from this analysis is how disconnected the popular understanding of Islamist politics is from the reality on the ground. The conventional narrative of Islamist militants opposing progressive state elites has shaped American popular perceptions of the wars in Iraq, Afghanistan, and the Horn of Africa. And, yet, this narrative is wildly off the mark. The Islamization of society—and the promotion of Islamist ideologies—has always been a top down affair in Pakistan, and increasingly so in Egypt as well. Moreover, this trend was abetted by these countries' superpower patron over the course of several decades. Hence, the so-called war on terror was never about competing visions of society, or between individual freedom and religious tyranny. As appealing or simplistic as this view may be, it masks a deeper reality. Saudi Arabia and Pakistan, in particular, have long been the source of Islamist militancy and ideology, and this has worked at cross-purposes to American foreign policy goals, particularly since the mid–1990s. Nonetheless, American policymakers and conservative commentators continue to promote a mistaken view of Islamic activism, and to explain American policies as the defense of individual freedom and enlightenment norms, even if their closest allies work against such ends.

The continued vibrancy of the Islamist movement, then, needs a more comprehensive explanation. It is not simply the result of a failed modernity project, nor is it due solely to the efforts of religious revivalists. These are important factors, but on their own do not explain the continuing strength of the Islamist movement. The role of governments and state actors in actively promoting an illiberal rendering of Islamic tradition is a third, and largely overlooked variable that also needs to be accounted for. As the cases demonstrate, the resurgence of Islamic fundamentalism was greatly influenced by the conscious support by state actors over the past several decades, the influx of Saudi oil money, and the association of modernist Islam with Arab socialist republics. The effort to use a theologically conservative Islam to eradicate the political left has had an enduring influence upon the societies in question, and upon popular perceptions of religious and cultural authenticity. Efforts to use religion by state elites have also helped to normalize Islamist ideas and organizations. While this trend may be the legacy of past government policy, the implications for the future are clear: as long as state actors remain wedded to an exclusive discourse of Islamist ideas, they will remain part of the problem, not the solution.

NOTES

[1] Cited in Gilles Kepel, *Muslim Extremism in Egypt: The Prophet and the Pharoah* (Berkeley: University of California Press, 1993), 192. For more on the material covered in this chapter, see Scott W. Hibbard, *Religious Politics and Secular States: Egypt, India and the United States* (Baltimore: Johns Hopkins University Press, 2010).

[2] See for example, President George W. Bush, "Address to the National Endowment of Democracy," (October 6, 2005). See also Tony Blair, "A Battle for Global Values," in *Foreign Affairs* (January/February 2007).

[3] Norman Podhoretz, *World War IV: The Long Struggle Against Islamofascism* (New York: Doubleday Press, 2006).

[4] Mark Juergensmeyer, *Global Rebellion: Religious Challenges to the Secular State, from Christian Militias to al-Qaeda* (Berkeley: University of California Press, 2008).

⁵ The expression "overseas contingency operations" supplanted the "war on terror" as an official description of American military operations after the election of President Barak Obama. See Scott Wilson and Al Kamen, "'Global War on Terror' is Given a New Name," in *Washington Post* (March 25, 2009).

⁶ Michael Mazarr, *Unmodern Men in the Modern World: Radical Islam, Terrorism and the War on Modernity* (New York: Cambridge University Press, 2007).

⁷ For more on these events and the argument in this chapter, see Scott W. Hibbard, *Religious Politics and Secular States: Egypt, India and the United States* (Baltimore: Johns Hopkins University Press, 2010).

⁸ By fundamentalisms I am referring to the religiously inspired political movements that are defined by a commitment to certain fundamental (or foundational) beliefs and the corresponding effort to transform society in light of these principles. The key feature of fundamentalisms is the combination of religious and political motivations. See Gabriel Almond, Scott Appleby and Emmanuel Sivan, *Strong Religion: The Rise of Fundamentalisms Around the World* (Chicago: University of Chicago Press, 2003).

⁹ I am indebted to Zoya Hasan for her terminology and thoughts on a similar transformation in India. See Zoya Hasan, "Changing Orientation of the State and the Emergence of Majoritarianism in the 1980s," in K. N. Panikkar, *Communalism in India: History, Politics and Culture* (Delhi: Manohar, 1991).

¹⁰ The total number of mosques in Egypt grew from roughly 15,000 in the mid–1960s to 27,000 in 1980. These statistics are from Egypt's Central Agency for Public Mobilization and Statistics, and cited in Anwar Alam, *Religion and State: Egypt, Iran and Saudi Arabia* (Delhi: Gyan Sagar Publications, 1998), 96.

¹¹ See Malcolm H. Kerr, *The Arab Cold War: Gamal Abd Al-Nasir and His Rivals, 1958-1970* (New York: Oxford University Press, 1971).

¹² Malika Zeghal, "Religion and Politics in Egypt: The Ulama of al-Azhar, Radical Islam, and the State (1952–94)," in *International Journal of Middle East Studies* 31, No. 3 (August 1999): 381.

¹³ More on this rapprochement, including the contents of the six-point agreement between Sadat and the Muslim Brotherhood, can be found in Nemat Guenena and Saad Eddin Ibrahim, *The Changing Face of Egypt's Islamic Activism* (unpublished manuscript submitted to the US Institute of Peace, September 1997).

¹⁴ Francis Cabrini Mullaney, *The Role of Islam in the Hegemonic Strategy of Egypt's Military Rulers (1952–1990)*, unpublished dissertation (Harvard University, 1992), 169.

¹⁵ Mary Anne Weaver quotes Hosni Mubarak as saying that Sadat was "responsible for the formation of *al-Gama'a [al-Islamiyya]*" the primary militant group of the 1990s. Mary Anne Weaver, *A Portrait of Egypt: A Journey Through the World of Militant Islam* (New York: Farrar, Straus and Giroux, 1999), 165.

¹⁶ Nabil Abdel-Fattah, *Veiled Violence: Islamic Fundamentalism in Egyptian Politics in the 1990s* (Cairo: Khattab Press, 1994), 49.

¹⁷ Farag Foda, a secular writer assassinated in 1992, cited in Fouad Ajami, *The Dream Palaces of the Arabs: A Generation's Odyssey* (New York: Pantheon Books, 1998), 206.

¹⁸ Ibid., 206.

[19] See Alexander Flores, "Secularism, Integralism, and Political Islam: The Egyptian Debate," in eds., Joel Beinin and Joe Stork, *Political Islam: Essays from Middle East Report* (Berkeley: University of California Press, 1997). See also Hibbard, *Religious Politics and Secular States*, chapters 2 and 3.

[20] For a discussion of these trends in Malaysia and Pakistan, see Seyyed Vali Reza Nasr, *Islamic Leviathan: Islam and the Making of State Power* (Oxford University Press, 2001).

[21] See M. Hakan Yavuz, *Islamic Political Identity in Turkey* (New York: Oxford University Press, 2003).

[22] See Francis M. Deng, *War of Visions: Conflicts of Identities in Sudan* (Washington: Brookings Institution Press, 1995).

[23] Liberal in this context is used narrowly to identify patterns of society that place a premium on individual liberty, and are otherwise consistent with enlightenment norms.

[24] John Esposito, *Islam and Politics* (Syracuse: Syracuse University Press, 1984), 115.

[25] The so-called "*hudood* punishments" derive from the Quran and prescribe severe corporal punishment for offenses such as adultery, drinking of alcohol, theft and bearing false witness. These include flogging (whipping), the severing of hands and stoning.

[26] See Stephen Coll, *Ghost Wars: The Secret History of the CIA, Afghanistan and Bin Laden, from the Soviet Invasion to September 10, 2001* (New York: The Penguin Press, 2004). See also, Martin Ewans, *Afghanistan: A Short History of Its People and Politics* (New York: Perennial Press, 2002). Saudi Arabia was another key supporter of the Taliban movement.

[27] See Ahmed Rashid, *Taliban: Militant Islam, Oil and Fundamentalism in Central Asia, Second Edition* (New Haven: Yale University Press, 2010), and Mahmood Mamdani, *Good Muslim, Bad Muslim: America, The Cold War, and the Roots of Terror* (New York: Doubleday Press, 2005), chapter 3.

[28] Mary Anne Weaver, "Blowback," in *Atlantic Monthly* (May 1996).

[29] Rashid, *Taliban*, 83.

[30] John Gray, *Al-Qaeda and What it Means to be Modern* (New York: The New Press, 2003).

[31] Eric Schmitt, Somini Sengupta and Jane Perlez, "US and India See Militant Links to Pakistan," in *New York Times* (December 2, 2008).

[32] Ashfaq Ahmed, "Bin Laden Compound in Pakistan Was Once and ISI Safehouse," in *Gulf News* (May 3, 2011). Gulfnews.com

[33] Mark Mazzetti, Jane Perlez, Eric Schmitt, and Andrew Lehren, "Pakistan Aids Insurgency in Afghanistan, Reports Assert," in *New York Times* (July 25, 2010).

[34] "Pakistan's Double Game," editorial in *New York Times* (July 26, 2010).

[35] The reference is to Nasr's characterization of Zia-ul-Haq's efforts to co-opt Sunni fundamentalism in the 1980s. See Seyyed Vali Reza Nasr, *Islamic Leviathan: Islam and the Making of State Power* (Oxford: Oxford University Press, 2001).

[36] The reference is to Clifford Geertz, "The Integrative Revolution," in Clifford Geertz, ed., *Old Societies and New States: The Quest for Modernity in Asia and Africa* (Glencoe: The Free Press, 1963).

[37] R. Scott Appleby, *The Ambivalence of the Sacred: Religion, Violence and Reconciliation* (New York; Rowman and Littlefield Publishers, Inc., 2000), 27.

[38] These distinctions are not uniform, however. For example, Calvinist beliefs are theologically conservative, but tend to eschew a close link between religion and state.

[39] Hussain Haqqani, *Pakistan: Between Mosque and Military* (Washington, D.C.: Carnegie Endowment for International Peace, 2005), 3.

[40] See for example David Little, "Belief, Ethnicity and Nationalism," in *Nationalism and Ethnic Politics* Vol 1, No. 2, Summer 1995 (London: Frank Cass, 1995), or David Little and Donald Swearer, eds., *Religion and Nationalism in Iraq: A Comparative Perspective* (Cambridge, MA: Harvard Center for the Study of World Religions, 2006).

[41] David Little, *Religion, Order and Law: A Study in Pre-Revolutionary England* (Chicago: University of Chicago Press, 1984).

[42] This would include Nasser's use of Islam or the notion of 'civil religion' in the American tradition.

[43] An example of this would be the Indian independence movement, or at least the vision of it supported by Mahatma Gandhi, Rabindranath Tagore, and the *Jamia Millia Islamia*.

[44] This would include the regimes of Zia-ul-Haq (Pakistan), Saudi Arabia, Sudan under the National Islamic Front, revolutionary Iran, and post–1970 Egypt.

[45] This would include the Islamist opposition movements throughout the Middle East and North Africa.

[46] As Kepel has noted, the devout middle class see Islamist ideology was an affirmation of their identity and position, while, for the young urban poor, the Islamist vision is a demand for social revolution. Cf. Gilles Kepel, *Jihad: On the Trail of Political Islam* (Cambridge, MA: Harvard University Press, 2001).

16.
Religion and Politics: Seeking a Reconciliation

Natalie Sherman & David Gergen

Time and again, in recent years, we have witnessed religious forces roiling the political landscape. In one of the closest elections in American history, those who went to church regularly provided an edge to Republican George W. Bush, outscoring secular voters who cast a large majority of their ballots for Democrat Al Gore. More recently, a fight over abortion nearly derailed the passage of national health care reform. Religious objections prompted the National Portrait Gallery to remove part of an exhibit, causing an uproar at the Smithsonian Institution. A proposal to build a mosque near the site of the World Trade Center sparked a heated national debate. In the aftermath, a fundamentalist preacher burned a Koran and, as General David Petraeus warned, set off murderous rampages in Afghanistan. The list goes on and on.

What are we to make of the potentially explosive mix of religion and politics in America? How disruptive is religion to constitutional democracy? Does religion contribute to factionalism and polarization? What should the role of religion be in the public square? What is the best way to secure peace in a democratic society with its many diverse and often opposing views?

In this chapter, we will first examine the argument that religion's ever-increasing divisiveness necessitates a strict secularity of the state. Then, we will make the case for religion's importance to democracy as a force for good. Finally, we will work to answer the questions posed in the previous paragraph. Where many have called for clear-cut rules or "consistently applied principles" to settle the church-state questions once and for all, this chapter puts forward an alternative view. We argue that our belief in a separation of church and state has always posed questions without easy answers and attempts to find clear-cut rules are unlikely to succeed. Instead, in the tradition of American pragmatism, it seems far better to settle our differences as we reaffirm democratic principles favoring competitive debate and openness to change. Policymakers should not dictate a policy based on a particular faith—or, in the vernacular, cram it down people's throats—rather, in determining the common good, we should welcome constructive arguments rooted in faith.

A Deepening of Divisions

To be sure, the Supreme Court, in *Lemon v. Kurtzman* (1971), came down firmly on the side of codifying a strict separation of church and state. That decision barred states from reimbursing religious schools for the salaries of secular teachers but the majority opinion had wider implications. Writing on behalf of an eight–person majority, Chief Justice Warren Burger argued that religious differences challenge the bounds of political debate, and are less effectively mediated by the normal democratic process than other disagreements. "Ordinarily, political debate and division, however vigorous or even partisan, are normal and healthy manifestations of our democratic system of government," Burger wrote. "But political division along religious lines was one of the principal evils against which the First Amendment was intended to protect. . . . The potential divisiveness of such conflict is a threat to the normal political process."[1] For Burger, religion stood out among other forces, as particularly crippling within a democracy; indeed, he saw it as a threat to democratic political life. The fear that religious differences could tear apart a society was translated into a demand that the state be not just unaffiliated but secular, creating what Richard John Neuhaus has called "the naked public square."[2]

Was Burger right about the dangers of religion? Americans remain among the most devout people in the Western, developed world, even as our internal divisions are growing. According to one survey, religiosity, measured as formal religious adherence, has grown from 17% in 1776 to 62% in 1980.[3] A 2008 Pew Forum survey found that 92% of the population believes in God or a universal spirit, and a majority say religion is important to them, attend religious services regularly and pray daily.[4] But Protestantism no longer dominates. That same Pew survey found that affiliation with Protestant religions had fallen to 51%, while 16% reported they were unaffiliated.[5] These changes are even more dramatic when examined generationally: 25% of those between the ages of 18 to 29 described themselves as unaffiliated, compared to just 8% of those over the age of 70. With such dramatic pluralism—and an ever-growing number of atheists—the endorsement of one particular religious tradition over another becomes increasingly controversial. That seems a recipe for continued friction.

Indeed, there is evidence that religion correlates to stark divisions within the American people. Religious groups tend to cluster geographically, with Catholics disproportionately represented in the northeast and evangelicals in the south.[6] Religious differences also translate directly into our public debates. Of the 39% of the population that attends church at least once a week, 50% identify as political conservatives, more than twice as many as those who attend seldom or never.[7] Outbreaks of religiously motivated violence—attacks on gynecologists, religious jihād—amplify fears that religion will tear the country apart.

As our diversity has grown, so too has the prominence of religion in public debate. One explanation comes from Princeton scholar Robert Wuthnow, who has argued that government's expansion since the 1960s into areas such as medicine and other social programs that were once the province of religious groups has created increased points of contact between religion and government, and in return, increased debates about the relationship between the two.[8] Religious groups, particularly those on the right, have also vigorously re-entered politics, flushed out of their quietude by the conviction that their beliefs were being stripped from them by the government. Crucial turning points came with Supreme Court decisions opening doors to abortions and closing school house doors to student prayer. Those decisions, *Lemon v. Kurtzman* included, convinced the evangelicals that instead of staying on the sidelines, they needed to get into the arena and fight, and we have been off to the races ever since. Evangelicals helped to elect Jimmy Carter in 1976, but they soured on him during his presidency and bolted for Ronald Reagan in 1980. Nonetheless, they have remained a significant part of the conservative, Republican base ever since, even as every White House has worked hard to attract followers of organized religions as well as secular voters. Roman Catholics, once a firm part of the Democratic base, have now become swing voters, eagerly pursued by both parties. In the midst of these struggles for votes, religion holds an increasingly prominent role in public policy discussion.

Nowhere was that more evident than in the protracted debates over President Barack Obama's health care initiative. Despite much partisan wrestling, it was not the Democratic-Republican divide that nearly doomed the bill. It was internecine Democratic warfare about abortion that swung crucial votes away from the bill, making it much more difficult to pass. Only after the insertion of the Stupak Amendment, which barred insurance plans offered in the public exchanges from covering abortion, could the bill get through. In this instance, Stupak may have held the pen, but by all appearances, Catholic bishops were guiding his hand.

When Fears Ran the Other Way

Modern day concerns that religion should be kept out of politics because it is a source of disunity represent an important and less understood shift in our conception of the separation of church and state. In the early days of the republic, citizens were no stranger to religious diversity, but they blamed an intrusive state for making those divisions dangerous. Their views on the subject were forged in the torment of the Thirty Years War and the rise of absolutist governments in England and France, and they hoped to create a society in which the state did not increase its power by interfering in personal religious practice. The subject was of such importance that a new code for dealing with the problem was articulated in the Constitution's First Amendment, which stated: "Congress shall make no law respecting an establishment of religion, or prohibiting the free exercise thereof." Their goal in creating this amendment was to secure religious freedom. The best way to do so, they believed, was to make sure it did not become a tool for the state, an instrument of political proxy.

In trying to sort out issues of separation today, it is worth paying attention to these early fears—as well as the early views of the role religion should play. For the bar was only raised in one direction. The Founders expected, and indeed encouraged, the idea that religious belief should guide public life. "Of all the dispositions and habits which lead to political prosperity . . . religion and morality are indispensable supports," wrote George Washington in his farewell address, echoing a widely held view.[9] In the centuries since, people of religious faith have been behind many of the most significant movements for social reform in our history. They championed the abolition movement; they guided Progressives into inner city slums at the turn of the century. During the Civil Rights movement, leaders such as Martin Luther King, Jr., emerged from the pulpit. They spoke of civil disobedience and dissent, and were driven by belief in a better world. As Washington predicted, religion has proven essential to the democratic project, prompting citizens to pursue virtue as a goal. At a time when many on the Left worry about the influence of religious forces on the Right, it is especially important to remember how much religious faith has been intertwined with progressive political traditions.

Religious organizations continue to represent a tremendous force for good in American life. In his definitive work on American social capital, *Bowling Alone*, Robert Putnam called "faith communities . . . arguably the single most important repository of social capital in America."[10] He found that half of all volunteering and philanthropy occurs within a religious context, and those groups spend roughly 15 to 20 billion dollars annually on social services.[11] In *Dreams from My Father: A Story of Race and Inheritance* President Obama describes the role of churches in the community as that of "a great pumping heart" and muses to a minister about his efforts to combat decay in Chicago's South Side, "[i]f we could bring just fifty churches together, we might be able to reverse some of the trends you've been talking about."[12] For many, religion supplies the moral underpinnings for our society.

Thus, there are powerful arguments that trying to keep people of faith out of the political arena should not be the focus. Instead, we should recognize that religious values and morality are not only relevant, but critical to a healthy democracy. People who embrace this alternative view have been identified by Noah Feldman as "values evangelicals."[13] They believe—and we are among them—that the goal of the state is to create a more just world, and that faith can help define what that world might look like.

The Argument in Favor of Competitive Debate

What role should the government then play in balancing religion's divisiveness with its great capacity for good? If not a strict separation, and the secular vision articulated in *Lemon v. Kurtzman*, then what? The Supreme Court, the standard authority when it comes to governmental boundaries, fails to offer clear guidance. Even in the Lemon ruling, Burger noted, "[c]andor compels acknowledgment . . . that we can only dimly perceive the lines of demarcation in this extraordinarily sensitive area of constitutional law. . . . The language of the Religion Clauses of the First Amendment is, at best, opaque."[14] For many, the Supreme Court's seeming inability to decide what the separation of church and state means is a source of great frustration. Linda Greenhouse, the longtime Supreme Court reporter for the New York Times, described the back-and-forth with impatience: "[t]he court has spent years making a nearly complete hash out of the public display of religious symbols."[15]

And criticism is not restricted to those outside of the process. Justice Antonin Scalia—in his scathing 2005 dissent disapproving the Supreme Court's decision to order the removal of the Ten Commandments from the state courthouses in Kentucky—lambasted his colleagues for failing to decide the case based on a "consistently applied principle."[16] "What distinguishes the rule of law from the dictatorship of a shifting Supreme Court majority is the absolutely indispensable requirement that judicial opinions be grounded in consistently applied principle," he declared. "That is what prevents judges from ruling now this way, now that—thumbs up or thumbs down—as their personal preferences dictate."[17] But he concluded, the Court's practice is far more arbitrary: "Sometimes the Court chooses to decide cases on the principle that government cannot favor religion, and sometimes it does not."[18]

Is the dance Scalia describes such a bad thing? James Madison recognized early on the dangers of "faction" to the nascent republic, but argued that America's democratic institutions had found a way of peaceably mediating disputes. In his famous Federalist Number 10 he wrote, "[a] religious sect may degenerate into a political faction in a part of the Confederacy; but the variety of sects dispersed over the entire face of it must secure the national councils against any danger from that source."[19] Madison intended to keep the state out of people's private practice of religion, but he did not expect that it would prevent people from exercising their religious values in the public arena. If the view was endorsed by a minority, there was no cause for worry—they would be prevented from coercion at the ballot box. If the view was endorsed by a majority, he saw two hopes for mitigating its danger. First, he expressed hope in good leadership. When that failed, he argued in favor of a large, inclusive republic, one that would mediate the dangers of a faction through a large competition of ideas.

Madison's explanation of the separation of church and state relies on the competition of ideas and the ability to battle out problems via the ballot box. Contemporary thinkers follow his reasoning. Feldman, for instance, has proposed a near-absolute financial separation between church and state, while pushing for the allowance of more religious symbolism and speech in politics.[20] The barring of federal funds addresses the fears of what he calls "legal secularists" about religion fostering political division. Meanwhile, on the subject of religious speech, Feldman argues that his proposal is grounded in the principle of "liberty of conscience," writing, "[s]o long as all citizens have the same right to speak and act free of coercion, no adult should feel threatened or excluded by the symbolic or political speech of others, however much he may disagree with it."[21]

Feldman echoes Madison's vision of the relationship between church and state in two important ways. First, he believes that religious arguments are and should be subject to scrutiny under the competition of ideas, and looks to voters to decide who wins the debate. Second, he also looks to a more pluralistic society to prevent against the dangers of religious speech or symbols becoming oppressive, writing, "[i]n this latest demographic version of a religiously diverse environment, where Protestants may soon cease to be a majority in the United States, the danger that Christmas crèches or prayer at high-school graduations will marginalize non-Christians is substantially decreased."[22] Feldman's prescription surely does not answer the question of how religion will guide public life. Instead, his vision relies on this being constantly debated.

A vision that relies on debate presupposes certain ground rules. As John Rawls has written, "[j]ustification in matters of political justice is addressed to others who disagree with us, and therefore it proceeds from some consensus: from premises that we and others recognize as true, or as reasonable for the purpose of reaching a working agreement on the fundamentals of political justice."[23] America's status as a "creedal" nation, in Sam Huntington's classic characterization—one more defined by ideas than nation—means that this consensus is more easily recognized and defined. Rawls writes of "society's main institutions, together with the accepted forms of their interpretation," as the "fund of implicitly shared fundamental ideas and principles."[24]

Religion here has an important role in public life, so long as it is willing to debate within the confines that American society has dictated. As then-Senator Obama said in 2006, "Democracy demands that the religiously motivated translate their concerns into universal, rather than religion-specific, values. It requires that their proposals be subject to argument and amenable to reason. . . . Politics depends on our ability to persuade each other of common aims based on a common reality."[25] Thus, although Scalia speaks scornfully of judgments that take into account "the antiquity of the practice" as the "'good reason' for ignoring the neutrality principle," it is precisely that history that creates the grounds of the debate.

Responding to Counterarguments

Others have advanced a series of arguments against this approach. Some, for example, have found such a laissez–faire attitude toward religion disastrous for the morals of the Republic. Patrick Henry gave early, forceful voice to this concern, worrying that virtue—so important to the success of the Republic—would languish without support of religion by the state. Henry called for the establishment of a civil religion.[26] But while the state of American virtue might be up for debate, its fate was certainly not decided by a dearth of religious life. Religion has flourished in America far more than it has in most other developed nations.

Others argue that encouraging an ongoing debate is an inherently secular answer, one that replaces religious values with its own. This is a seductive argument, but one that is ultimately disingenuous and reductive. As one could argue, religion requires belief in a transcendent God, and while reconciling two sources of authority—as this chapter attests—is difficult; that is not because they are at base the same. History proves that it is possible to both believe in God and coexist with government.

As Kathleen Sullivan wrote, "[e]ven if the culture of liberal democracy is a belief system comparable to a religious faith in the way it structures knowledge, it simply does not follow that it is the equivalent of a religion for political and constitutional purposes."[27]

A more complicated critique comes from those who argue that the Founders' faith in process of debate dodges the important questions. Former dean of Harvard Divinity School Ronald Thiemann raised the concern that the Founders' faith in process "is conceptually incomplete and thus politically flawed, since they fail to provide an account of those virtues that will enable free persons to make equality a political reality."[28]

A commitment to democratic process—a belief in debate and competition as the best way to achieve the best possible outcome for society—does in some way fail on this score. This is because it represents what Rawls has called a "political conception of justice," one that, unlike other philosophies—like religious ones—is not comprehensive. Rawls argues that separating political justice from a broader account is necessary in a pluralistic society, but he does not believe this requires a sacrifice of values. He argues that the institutions of democracy foster the values best able to uphold this system, citing a sense of fairness, a spirit of compromise, and the virtue of reasonableness. These are not, he readily admits, comprehensive. They do not address the full social and moral implications of the good life, but they can answer it politically.

Finally, a fourth critique comes in the form of arguing that there are some questions about which peaceful agreement is simply not possible. So be it. Some things, as they say, are worth fighting for. But how to identify those things? It is rare that they come solely from religion. As Abraham Lincoln noted in his Second Inaugural Address, both sides, "read the same Bible and pray to the same God, and each invokes His aid against the other."[29] It is when people begin to espouse views incompatible with democracy—incompatible with the boundaries of the debate—that violence happens. Achieving peaceful debate, then, must rely on strengthening democratic institutions and ensuring that citizens are committed to the ideals those institutions represent.

Summing Up

Religion, then, will influence our politics in chancy, unpredictable ways that change along with the society. It is a peculiarly bumbling path toward justice, but one that perhaps fits best with a democratic mode of governance, one that also takes unsure half steps in its quest for perfection. It is also consistent with religious traditions that remind us of how little we can truly understand God, that it is our effort to do so that redeems us. As Lincoln wrote, "[i]t is quite possible that God's purpose is something different from the purpose of either party—and yet the human instrumentalities, working just as they do, are of the best adaptation to effect His purpose."[30]

NOTES

[1] *Lemon v. Kurtzman*, 403 U.S. 602 (1971).

[2] Robert John Neuhaus, *The Naked Public Square: Religion and Democracy in America* (Grand Rapids, MI: Wm. B Eerdmans Publishing Company. 1984).

[3] Robert Putnam, *Bowling Alone: The Collapse and Revival of American Community* (New York: Simon & Schuster Paperbacks, 2000), 65.

[4] "U.S. Religious Landscape Survey. Religious Beliefs and Practices: Diverse and Politically Relevant." (Washington, D.C.: Pew Forum of Religion & Public Life, June 2008), 3, 5. http://religions.pewforum.org/pdf/report2-religious-landscape-study-full.pdf

[5] "U.S. Religious Landscape Survey. Religious Affiliation: Diverse and Dynamic." (Wasington, D.C.: The Pew Forum on Religion & Public Life, February 2008), 5. http://religions.pewforum.org/pdf/report-religious-landscape-study-full.pdf

[6] Ibid, 69.

[7] "U.S. Religious Landscape Survey. Religious Beliefs and Practices: Diverse and Politically Relevant." (Washington, D.C.: Pew Forum of Religion & Public Life, June 2008),7. http://religions.pewforum.org/pdf/report2-religious-landscape-study-full.pdf

[8] In Frank Lambert, *Religion in American Politics* (Princeton, N.J.: Princeton University Press, 2008), 4.

[9] George Washington, "Farewell Address." 1796. (http://avalon.law.yale.edu/18th_century/washing.asp Last accessed: June 11, 2014).

[10] Robert Putnam, *Bowling Alone* (New York: Simon & Schuster Paperbacks, 2000), 66.

[11] Ibid, 67–8.

[12] Barack Obama, *Dreams from My Father* (New York: Three Rivers Press, 2005), 273–74.

[13] Noah Feldman, "The Church–State Solution," in *New York Times* (July 3 2005). (http://www.nytimes.com/2005/07/03/magazine/03CHURCH.html Last accessed: June 11, 2014).

[14] *Lemon v. Kurtzman*, 403 U.S. 602 (1971).

[15] Linda Greenhouse, "Opinionator: Nine Justices and 10 Commandments," in *New York Times* (August 26, 2010).(http://opinionator.blogs.nytimes.com/2010/08/26/nine-justices-and-ten-commandments/ Last accessed: June 11, 2014).

[16] *McCreary County v. ACLU.* 545 U.S. 844 2005. (dissenting opinion).

[17] Ibid.

[18] Ibid.

[19] James Madison, Federalist No. 10: "The Same Subject Continued: The Union as a Safeguard Against Domestic Faction and Insurrection." in *New York Daily Advertiser* (November 22, 1787). (http://www.ourdocuments.gov/doc.php?flash=true&doc=10 Last accessed: June 11, 2014).

[20] Noah Feldman, "The Church-State Solution," in *New York Times* (July 3, 2005).

[21] Ibid.

[22] Ibid.

[23] John Rawls, "The Idea of an Overlapping Consensus," in *Oxford Journal of Legal Studies* Vol. 7 No. 1 (Spring, 1987): 6. http://www.jstor.org/stable/764257 Last accessed: June 11, 2014).

[24] Ibid.

[25] Barack Obama, "Call to Renewal Keynote Address." (June 28, 2006).

[26] In Frank Lambert, *Religion in American Politics* (Princeton, New Jersey: Princeton University Press, 2008), 9.

[27] Kathleen M. Sullivan, "Religion and Liberal Democracy," in *University of Chicago Law Review* Vol. 59 No. 1 (Winter 1992): 195–223.

[28] Ronald F. Thiemann, *Religion in Public Life: A Dilemma for Democracy* (Washington, D.C.: Georgetown University Press, 1996), 26.

[29] Abraham Lincoln "Second Inaugural Address." (March 4, 1865). (http://www.theatlantic.com/past/docs/issues/99sep/9909lincaddress.htm Last accessed: June 11, 2014).

[30] Abraham Lincoln. "Meditation on the Divine Will." September, 1862. (http://showcase.netins.net/web/creative/lincoln/speeches/meditat.htm Last accessed: June 11, 2014).

17.
The Core of Public Reason: Freedom from Arbitrary Pain and Death

Christian Rice

Those of us who value our interactions with David Little know well his steady argument that the drafters of the international human rights documents were making a radical philosophical point, and not just a practical one: certain rights inhere in the condition of personhood and their existence is knowable to and authorized by "the conscience of mankind," as the preamble to the Universal Declaration of Human Rights (UDHR) states. A logical consequence of these claims is that the rights articulated in the Declaration are universal entitlements and their authority does not depend on any specific comprehensive doctrine or thick conception of the good, religious or otherwise.[1] Little has often reiterated these points because he holds that so much is at stake if these fundamental premises are undermined. But in an age when it is fashionable to speak of normativity as the construct of particular discursive practices, an argument that suggests that rights are indeed universal moral entitlements is sure to invite questions.

In this chapter, I will suggest that one should think of many of the rights enumerated in the international human rights corpus as the content of a doctrine of public reason.[2] Using John Rawls's understanding of public reason as a guide, I invite us to think about the international human rights corpus as the global specification of a form of public reason. Following Rawls, I understand public reason to be a commitment to a shareable set of values understood to be a free-standing political conception of justice; that is, a conception of justice introduced for political purposes that is intentionally absent of metaphysical ideas that might be controversial. I hope to demonstrate that the moral logic of the international human rights documents has a strong kinship with Rawls's thoughts on public reason. Finally, moving beyond Rawls, I attempt to advance our understanding of public reason by suggesting that, at its core, public reason should be understood as a set of fundamental moral entitlements that protect all human beings from arbitrary pain and death. When it comes to the administration of pain and death, public reason will demand that governments always conduct such business transparently.

Rawls and Public Reason

The fact that basic individual rights continually need to be defended from the threat of arbitrary incursions is certainly unsettling. It begs the practical question, "What needs to be in place to guarantee that one's rights do not fall victim to arbitrary infringement?" One response to this challenge is the design of a conception of public reason. To act in accordance with the ideal of public reason would be to act on the basis of a shareable set of values that appear reasonable to all citizens. On matters that affect the basic entitlements of citizens, it is hoped that public reason becomes the *lingua franca* of the society. To argue on the grounds of public reason implies that certain reasons will fail to qualify as justifiable reasons to one's fellow citizens on matters pertaining to basic moral entitlements.

Scholars promote several different manifestations of public reason doctrines. Rawls argues that if reasonable people can agree to specific principles of justice, then it seems that they could also agree on certain guidelines to ensure the application of these norms. These guidelines are the features of public reason, which he takes to be a logical extension of his original position. He writes:

> In justice as fairness, and I think in many other liberal views, the guidelines of inquiry of public reason . . . have the same basis as the substantive principles of justice. This means in justice as fairness that the parties in the original position, in adopting principles of justice for the basic structure, must also adopt guidelines and criteria for applying these norms. . . . In securing the interests of the persons

they represent, the parties insist that the application of substantive principles be guided by judgment and inference, reasons and evidence that the persons they represent can reasonably be expected to endorse.[3]

Rawls accommodates multiple forms of public reason, so long "as the limiting feature of these forms is the criterion of reciprocity, viewed as applied between free and equal citizens, themselves seen as reasonable and rational."[4] He states that his theory of justice is just one acceptable form of public reason and he invites others to propose alternative, more reasonable forms that conform to his limiting features. The limiting features of all acceptable forms of public reason are a focus on individual liberties and their moral priority over comprehensive conceptions of the good.

Simply put, fairness dictates that all citizens articulate their reasons for public policy in translatable terms; this is the obligation of reciprocity. He writes:

> There is no reason why any citizen, or association of citizens, should have the right to use state power to decide constitutional essentials as that person's, or association's, comprehensive doctrine directs. When equally represented, no citizen could grant to another person or association that political authority.[5]

Presuming that citizens will embrace a multiplicity of comprehensive doctrines, reasonable people could not be expected to endorse policies that would affect the basic constitutional consensus, unless the rationale for such policies was accessible to all persons. Rawls argues that we should call upon the values latent in our Western political culture to construct a "freestanding" political conception of justice. While such political values are logically detachable from comprehensive moral doctrines, Rawls encourages citizens to draw upon their comprehensive worldviews to support them. He hopes that an overlapping consensus will emerge, which will undergird his free-standing political conception. In fact, so long as one supports the free-standing consensus, one can be motivated by any reasons whatsoever to support it.[6] Rawls quotes approvingly the Sudanese Muslim scholar Abdullahi An-Na'im's claim that "as long as all are agreed on the principle and specific rules of constitutionalism, including complete equality and non-discrimination on grounds of gender or religion, each may have his or her own reasons for coming to that agreement."⁷ Importantly, this is not to say that Rawls is arguing that norms emerge simply because of agreement by consensus. To the contrary, Rawls believes that his political theory, justice as fairness, generates a set of norms which then happen to find agreement in many, but, of course, not all comprehensive worldviews.

Public reason is not treated simply as a suggested ideal with respect to society as a whole, but as the necessary frame of discourse for elected officials and those who act on behalf of the government. Rawls writes that public reason applies as a civil duty to the following: the decisions of judges (especially the justices of the U.S. Supreme Court), the decisions of government officials (especially chief executives and legislators), and to "the discourse of candidates for public office and their campaign managers, especially in their public oratory, party platforms, and political statements."⁸ It applies most strictly to the courts. Rawls writes:

> This is because the justices have to explain and justify their decisions as based on their understanding of the constitution and relevant statutes and precedents. Since acts of the legislative and the executive need not be justified in this way, the court's special role makes it the exemplar of public reason.⁹

It should be noted that public reason is not a legally enforceable standard with respect to the views of private citizens or private organizations. Such entities comprise the background culture, and here it is appropriate for there to be robust discussions and debates emanating directly from comprehensive moral doctrines.¹⁰ Nonetheless, insofar as citizens are deciding directly on matters of basic justice via referenda or voting, they should act *as if* they are public officials, and, as such, should abide by the ideal of public reason. Rawls writes that "when firm and widespread, the disposition of citizens to view themselves as ideal legislators, and to repudiate government officials and candidates for political office who violate public reason, is one of the political and social roots of democracy, and is vital to its enduring strength and vigor."¹¹

Rawls's articulation of public reason is a clear embodiment of a core commitment of the liberal tradition—that respect for one's fellow citizens demands that laws be translated into terms understandable to all.

Thomas Nagel speaks to this point sympathetically, "This liberal restraint comes from our special moral relation to fellow members of our society—a collectivity that can coerce each of its members, but only if it claims to act in the name of all of them."[12] Rawls, standing in this tradition, unequivocally prioritizes the basic welfare of the individual by demanding that, when it comes to matters of basic justice and constitutional essentials, it is the state's responsibility to protect its citizens from laws that are not publicly justifiable to all of its citizens.

Public Reason's Kinship with the Human Rights Documents

Here I wish to note the similarity between Rawls's doctrine of public reason and the intentions of the drafters of the UDHR. Indeed, very similar to Rawls's theory penned in response to utilitarian theories of justice, the human rights revolution sought to remove basic human rights forever from the winds of political calculus. Drafted after the barbarous atrocities of Nazism, the UDHR drafters sought to guarantee that no political regime could ever again disturb those rights. To quote the Belgian delegate, Henry Carton de Wiart, "The essential merit of the Declaration was to emphasize the high dignity of the human person after the outrages to which men and women had been exposed during the recent war."[13] The moral logic of the documents follows from this commitment to human dignity. The legitimacy of all governments will be measured by their adherence to these rights, which are, by definition, equal and common rights. Moreover, limitations on certain fundamental rights can never be imposed, and, when they are necessary, limitations must be publicly justified, and tailored narrowly to meet the compelling state interest at stake with the least burdensome infringement necessary.[14]

While there are differences with Rawls, they do not diminish the fact that important aspects of Rawls's understanding of public reason can be superimposed onto the international human rights documents with little difficulty.[15] It is certainly plausible to claim that the human rights documents represent an effort to outline an understanding of public reason.[16] Of particular note is the prevalent assumption that such rights are not tied to any one particular comprehensive worldview for their justification. Johannes Morsink, in his detailed history of the drafting process, notes that the document is secular, or, one could say in Rawlsian language, public,[17] by intent. Morsink endeavors to show that the drafters rejected the notion that human rights were somehow dependent upon a particular comprehensive worldview. He writes:

> It is clear from this segment of drafting history that the Universal Declaration is a secular document by intent. This outright secularism is a more honest stance than the ambiguous trickledown theory of the classical period. And for that very reason certain fundamentalist or evangelical groups are uncomfortable with or even antagonistic toward the document. As these critics see it, human rights can only live in the house of religion. But that is precisely what the majority of the drafters rejected when they refused to be drawn into the theological disputes raised by . . . [certain] amendments.[18]

Morsink goes on to note his agreement with the 1948 assessment of René Cassin, one of the chief architects of the documents. Cassin noted that one of the reasons that the documents received nearly universal global acceptance was precisely because the document intentionally avoided metaphysics and was a thoroughly secular document.[19] Here it is also worth quoting the Thomist Jacques Maritain, who makes known his strong sympathy with the founding documents in *Man and the State* (1951). He writes powerfully:

> But the all-important point to be noted here is that this faith and inspiration, and the concept of itself which democracy needs—all these do not belong to the order of religious creed and eternal life, but the temporal or secular order of earthly life, of culture or civilization. The *faith* in question is a *civic or secular* faith, not a religious one. . . . A genuine democracy cannot impose on its citizens or demand from them, as a condition for their belonging to the city, any philosophic or religious creed. This conception of the city was possible during the "sacral" period of our civilization, when communion in the Christian faith was a prerequisite for the body politic. In our own day it has been able to produce only the inhuman counterfeit, whether hypocritical or violent, offered by the totalitarian States which lay claim to the faith, the obedience, and the love of the religious man for his God; it has produced only their effort to impose their creed

upon the mind of the masses by the power of propaganda, lies, and the police.[20]

This is not to say, however, that the human rights paradigm is meant to discourage theological reflection regarding human rights or other matters. Indeed, quite the opposite could be argued. The documents strive to protect a great diversity of comprehensive viewpoints, and seek to ensure that all persons are free in the realm of conscientious belief and practice (Article 18 of the UDHR),[21] so long as that practice does not violate the limitations mentioned in Article 29, which include the public order and the equal rights of others. Yet, the logic of the human rights documents demands that one's comprehensive worldview, religious or otherwise, must, in fact, bow to a non-negotiable set of fundamental entitlements. Of course, we should not forget that the documents were forged in response to the atrocities of Nazism, and the drafters were aware that Hitler's vision rested on an untranslatable and entirely self-regarding comprehensive doctrine, whose expression resulted in the deaths of countless individuals, over which any "morally healthy human being" would be horrified.[22]

The drafters firmly believed that human rights are to be justified independently of comprehensive worldviews. As such, restrictions to rights are expected to be in terms that are publicly translatable. That is, should a situation arise in which a state might seek to lift the presumption in favor of extending such rights, reasons must be given that are logically independent of a comprehensive worldview. Indeed, the Human Rights Committee has been quite explicit on this point. Echoing Rawls, with respect to limiting rights on the grounds of public morals, the Committee has noted that the definitions of threat to public morals cannot rely exclusively on one comprehensive moral doctrine. It notes, "The Committee observes that the concept of morals derives from many social, philosophical, and religious traditions. [Thus] limitations on the freedom to manifest a religion or belief for the purpose of protecting morals must be based on principles not deriving exclusively from a single tradition."[23]

A Modified Doctrine of Public Reason

The value of bringing Rawls's thoughts into conversation with the international human rights documents is that Rawls helps to explicate the moral logic enshrined in the documents. However, while Rawls's insights on public reason are quite valuable, the way he determines the specific content of public reason is much less compelling. Rawls's theory of justice is quite famously a contract theory through which the basic liberties are specified by agreement of the parties in the original position. The reason for agreement on Rawls's two principles of justice and the liberties which the principles specify is that the parties would conclude that it is to their mutual advantage to agree to these liberties behind the veil of ignorance. For example, not knowing your particular economic status, you would agree to Rawls's difference principle, where wealth inequality is only tolerated if such inequality actually benefits the least well-off.

While many of the liberties that Rawls's theory yields are quite desirable, reaching agreement on basic entitlements through this process seems to have the unwelcomed effect of excluding certain recipients. In her book *Frontiers of Justice*, Martha Nussbaum does a masterful job at pointing to the limitations of grounding basic entitlements in a commitment to reciprocity. She writes persuasively about Rawls:

> In terms of the citizens of the Well-Ordered Society and their knowledge, there are limits to the commitment to reciprocity that is demanded of citizens. They are asked to accept, on grounds of justice, a situation that may be less advantageous to them than one that they might find in a nonegalitarian society. But they accept these "strains of commitment" secure in the knowledge that their fellow citizens are all "fully cooperating members of society over a complete life." They do not accept the additional strain of extending their commitment to citizens who are not similarly productive, and who might therefore be dominated (although other ethical virtues may suggest that they should not be).[24]

As Nussbaum emphasizes, Rawls can offer no rationale for extending basic entitlements to those, such as the mentally or physically handicapped, (or non-human animals)[25], who do not appear roughly equal and could be dominated. Only those citizens who are "similarly productive" are the parties to the contract, because, in order to have incentive to stick to the contract, persons must have the same capacity with respect to their potential for domination. Rawls simply cannot explain why the parties should extend justice to those less productive. Rawls does suggest that accommodations for those who are not roughly equal should be handled during a later stage, after the basic principles of justice have been chosen, but justice for these individuals then ceases to be an unqualified right and is a secondary consideration.[26] It seems clear that Rawls's theory limits justice for some as basic entitlements only attach to a certain type of persons.

Nussbaum's well-known alternative is her capabilities approach, which instead of grounding basic entitlements in reciprocal advantage, grounds such entitlements upon an account of what human beings actually need to flourish, given the type of beings we are. Importantly, she agrees with Rawls on the critical point that her list of basic entitlements should take moral priority over competing values that emerge from comprehensive conceptions of the good life. She writes that we can view her list of capabilities as a "module" that can be endorsed by people who otherwise have very different conceptions of the ultimate meaning and purpose of life.[27] Thus, while making certain minimal metaphysical claims about the nature of human beings, she nonetheless believes that these assumptions can be the content of an overlapping consensus of values. Nussbaum is comfortable referring to her capabilities approach as a form of public reason. There is much to commend in Nussbaum's theory. She presents us with an exhaustive list of basic entitlements and makes a compelling case that a life denied access to such entitlements falls below an acceptable moral threshold. Moreover, because she does not share Rawls's starting point, basic justice can be extended to all whose dignity seems to require it, including animals.

Yet, I wonder whether her capabilities approach, which relies on moral intuitions about what is owed human beings given what they need to flourish, could also be augmented. Her theory is open to the criticism whether an account of what is required to provide a life consistent with human dignity provides sufficient justificatory force to undergird entitlement claims. Nussbaum herself seems to acknowledge that it may not, and, for this reason, suggests that rights language should still serve as an accompaniment to her approach. She writes:

> There is no doubt that one might recognize the basic capabilities of people and yet still deny that this entails that they have rights in the sense of justified claims to certain types of treatment. We know that this inference has not been made through a great deal of the world's history. So appealing to rights communicates more than does the bare appeal to basic capabilities, without any further ethical argument of the sort I have supplied. Rights language indicates that we do have such an argument and that we draw strong normative conclusions from the fact of basic capabilities.[28]

For Nussbaum, rights language, despite her quarrels with it, is still valuable because "it reminds us that people have justified and urgent claims to certain types of treatment . . . to say, 'Here's a list of things that people ought to be able to do and to be' has only vague normative resonance. To say, 'Here is a list of fundamental rights' is more rhetorically direct.'"[29]

While there is much to commend about Nussbaum's capabilities approach (and I heartily welcome it as an accompaniment to the human rights approach), I think she may miss the reason why rights language tends to strike us with more urgency and normative force. I argue that certain entitlements appear to be self-evidently justified, as they are tied to certain moral facts that are manifestly knowable to normal, rationally competent beings. These entitlements are derived from what some philosophers have referred to as necessary moral truths. And, unlike Nussbaum's approach, which needs to presuppose a fairly rich metaphysic prior to staking normative claims, in this approach, the normative force of certain entitlement claims is immediately apparent to reason, requiring no deep metaphysical exploration— an exploration which can be controversial. While the scope of such entitlements is smaller than Nussbaum's capabilities, I think their justification is on less controversial philosophical ground, and, as such, can even more satisfactorily serve as a minimal moral floor which all comprehensive doctrines need to respect. I argue that such entitlements should function as the core content of a public reason doctrine.

I argue that a certain class of actions always and everywhere seems to lack sufficient rational justification because they are tied to facts that seem to necessarily generate moral disapproval. To quote A. C. Grayling:

> There are certain facts about sentient creatures, and most obviously human beings, that are value-soaked right through, and whose truth is what makes certain moral assertions true. For example, the capacity of sentient beings for suffering and pleasure, and their preference in general for the latter over the former, place an immediate constraint on the choices of an agent aware of this fact and conscious of the conformity of his own preferences with it. To charge someone with cruelty, malice, sadism, and the like, if he harms other sentient creatures despite knowing that, like himself, they would prefer not to be harmed, rests squarely on appeal to these very facts.[30]

To use an example borrowed from Judith Jarvis Thomson's marvelous work *The Realm of Rights*, if one chooses to torture a baby just for fun (or one could add here for one's private material gain), there seems to be something necessarily morally wrong with this action, since, given what we know about pain, one cannot even imagine a plausible explanation how such an action for such a purpose could be acceptable. If one would attempt to justify one's action by appealing to the gratification one receives by torturing a baby, society might refer to such a person as a psychopath, precisely because this person appears to offer "profoundly incomprehensible" reasons for morally abhorrent behavior.[31] Little writes quite perceptively:

> [Psychopaths] appear to assume that by referring to the fact that their own interests are satisfied or advanced, they have somehow given a "reason" to their victim for inflicting pain, or for failing to relieve it. But when causing pain or being indifferent to it is the issue, *it simply makes no sense* to refer to one's own satisfaction, and the psychopath does not appear to *know* that.[32]

Thus, when it comes to the matter of causing pain, it seems that reasons are only potentially justifiable when they can be said to be comprehensible literally to everyone and anyone—that is, when such reasons are trans-subjective. This, I believe, establishes the fact that each and every human being has an inherent right always and everywhere against the arbitrary infliction of pain.

As such, there simply appears to be no good reason for a person, group, or government to inflict pain upon another for its private pleasure;

since, all things being equal, pain is an undesirable state, reasons for its infliction need to be transparent, carefully scrutinized and comprehensible to all. This is a commitment to public reason at its most basic level. Indeed, the international human rights paradigm appears to accept the fact that certain actions seem *necessarily* to lack credible justification. Nonderogable rights are those rights which can never be abridged, presumably because there is never a conceivably good reason for doing so. One has a nonderogable right, for example, against arbitrary killing. Importantly, if a person is to be legitimately subjected to pain or death, such an action can only be justified if reasons can be given which are trans-subjective in nature. Little has noted that such "special reasons" might fall into three categories: punishment for a previous offense, restraint or deterrence against committing a future offense, and the notion that such an action seeks the good of the person (a therapeutic justification).[33] These three reasons —the punitive, deterrent, and the therapeutic—all have the similarity of being justifiable from a trans-subjective, impartial or objective point of view.

It should not come as a surprise, then, that many societies invest a great deal in seeking to ensure a clear distinction between licensed killing, which has the character of being rationally justifiable, and arbitrary killing. Little notes along these lines that:

> It is interesting that, whatever culture human beings inhabit, they set up stringent *certification procedures* and *testing standards* according to which they invest certain "officials" with the right to deal in coercion, pain, and death. In fact, such certification procedures and standards are a consuming subject of ritualization in any society (including our own). Insofar as this is true, it shows two things: First, wherever there is a question of putting or leaving someone in pain, or of coercively restraining or injuring someone, those concerned must meet stringent "eligibility requirements" of a technical and/or ritual sort. Second, these officials must perform or execute their punitive or therapeutic tasks according to solemnized standards and techniques. That is all a way of saying that such people must stand *publicly accountable* for engaging in acts that inflict or permit pain, coercion, killing, and so on.[34]

Of course, the utter absence of public accountability is typical of many totalitarian regimes. One thinks of the clandestine measures, like secret torture prisons, routinely employed by such regimes (and by many non-totalitarian regimes, as well!) with the specific purpose of avoiding public scrutiny. The point I wish to make here, however, is that liberal states often do have mechanisms in place to demonstrate to their citizens the distinction between licensed and arbitrary killing. Reasons must be presented for such actions that are clearly "public" in nature. Public accountability is critical, one might say, precisely because the state must bear the burden of proof in demonstrating the rational credibility of engaging in acts that, other things being equal, are considered to be morally wrong. This requires a transparent and open process of political and legal deliberation.

The United States Justice Department's now infamous 2004 "torture memo," which argued for a dramatic redefinition of what counts as torture, was seen by many as troubling because of the attempt by the government to restrict the transparency of this practice. Notwithstanding the very legitimate discussion over whether torture is *ever* morally permissible, another morally troubling aspect of this memo was the attempt to justify the practice of torture outside the reach of public review. The central points of this memo are worth recalling, as summarized by David Luban, who writes that this memo

> concluded that inflicting physical pain does not count as torture unless the interrogator specifically intends the pain to reach the level associated with organ failure or death; that inflicting mental suffering is lawful unless the interrogator intends it to last months or years beyond the interrogation; that enforcing criminal laws against presidentially authorized torturers would be unconstitutional; that lawful self-defense can include torturing helpless detainees under the name of self defense; and that interrogating detainees under torture may be justifiable as a lesser evil, through the legal defense of necessity.[35]

The memo is particularly worrisome because it reflects a concerted effort on the part of some in the United States Justice Department to exempt torturers from the traditional standards of American jurisprudence, in the name of national security and necessity. It has the effect of attenuating the demand that government present the public with rationally credible reasons for torture. If the president can presumably authorize the torture of anyone, and is not subject to the oversight of Congress, what mechanisms remain in place to protect against the unjustified use of torture—torture conducted for reasons that strain rational credibility? Such behavior, if it is to be morally justifiable, simply must be conducted transparently, since when it comes to the infliction of pain, death, and imprisonment on a person, only certain reasons suffice as good reasons for the conducting of such actions.

Of course, there will likely be disagreement as to whether such a reason is finally a good reason for the infliction of harm on another. Take the death penalty, for example. As a society, we may conclude that the death penalty may not, at the end of the day, be morally justified. But it is, at least, credible to think that the death penalty *could* be morally justified, either as a legitimate form of retributive punishment or as a possible deterrent. In other words, it is possible to conceive a legitimate rationale for the death penalty, since, under carefully proscribed circumstances, reasons for the death penalty can present themselves as rationally comprehensible to all persons, even if, as a society, we might conclude that the harm of the death penalty might outweigh any significant benefit. In other words, there *might* be an acceptable reason for the state putting someone to death, provided that this penalty is conducted in a publicly accountable way.[36] Conversely, it appears that there is *no possible good reason* for the unwanted infliction of harm by a person on another for that person's purely private amusement. Because this reason can under no circumstances claim to be trans-subjective, it ceases to be an acceptable reason at all. It is thus necessarily immoral, given our basic awareness of the obvious unpleasantness of pain.

Conclusion

While this might be considered to be the outlines of a fairly minimal perspective on public reason, it is no small requirement to insist on the necessity that the state offers rationally credible, trans-subjective reasons to its citizens and to the world, when the state engages in the infliction of pain, death, and imprisonment. Dictators and democratic governments alike must be held accountable to such a requirement. Refreshingly, at least a basic notion of moral equality seems built into the structure of the moral universe, since *all* of us, *ex hypothese*, are equally entitled to reasons for actions that put us in pain[37]—reasons that are rationally credible, trans-subjective, and impartial. Indeed, Little contends that this "structure of permissible reasons" demonstrates the natural moral equality of human beings. He writes that psychopaths

> fail to grasp what the rest of us, when we reflect on it, seem incapable of doubting: that all human beings are equal as soon as they start giving reasons for inflicting pain or for failing to relieve it, for killing, imprisoning, et cetera. No one individual's pleasure is so special as to justify putting or leaving another in pain, or for destroying, maiming or harming another.[38]

To understand public reason in this way might also help us sharpen our thoughts about comprehensive doctrines and the reasons for which they must be sidelined. Whatever the outer boundaries set by a commitment to public reason may be, I think it can also be said that public reason has a core. With respect to a certain type of actions—I have focused here on actions that cause pain—the state needs to conduct its business in a transparent manner, as the state must bear the burden of proof for engaging in behavior that, all things being equal, is manifestly immoral. With respect to these actions, the presence of a religious justification sanctioning pain cannot make the morally outrageous now acceptable.

NOTES

[1] It should be noted that the logical independence of a set of outside moral constraints does not suggest antagonism or indifference on the part of the human rights documents to religion. Little notes that, quite to the contrary, "human rights law is in fact *deferent* to such [religious] concerns." Little writes that "part of that deference is guaranteeing free, equal and open expression and practice consistent with . . . authorized limits. . . . The authorized limits would decidedly not exclude religious or philosophical commentary on public affairs, including the domain of the secular. . . . The only proviso is that when it comes to passing laws or rendering judicial decisions in the public arena, the actions must rest on 'public reason' rather than particular religions or beliefs" Little, "Religion, Human Rights, and Secularism: Preliminary Clarifications and Some Islamic, Jewish, and Christian Responses," in *2003 Sharpe Lectures* (October 21–23, 2003), University of Chicago Divinity School, 29–30.

[2] Since the publication of John Rawls's *Political Liberalism* (New York: Columbia University Press, 1996), the notion of public reason has garnered considerable attention among political theorists.

³ John Rawls, *Political Liberalism*, 225.

⁴ John Rawls, *The Law of Peoples* (Cambridge, MA: Harvard University Press), 141.

⁵ Rawls, *Political Liberalism*, 226.

⁶ Rawls differs here from the view of public reason advocated by Robert Audi. Audi suggests that public reason requires that all citizens abide by the principle of secular motivation. Audi writes that "one has a (prima facie) obligation to abstain from advocacy or support of a law or public policy that restricts human conduct, unless one is sufficiently motivated by adequate secular reason" [Robert Audi and Nicholas Wolterstorff, *Religion in the Public Square: The Place of Religious Convictions in Political Debate* (Lanham, MD: Rowman and Littlefield, 1997), 28–29.]

⁷ Rawls, *The Law of Peoples*, 151.

⁸ Ibid., 133–4. Rawls notes that public reason applies in its most strict sense to the judiciary.

⁹ Rawls, *Political Liberalism*, 216.

¹⁰ Ibid., 215. Rawls is very clear that the idea of public reason does not apply to the background culture, which consists of "churches and associations of all kinds, and institutions of learning at all levels, especially universities and professional schools, scientific and other societies" (Rawls, *The Law of Peoples*, 134). He writes, "Sometimes those who appear to reject the idea of public reason actually mean to assert the need for full and open discussion in the background culture. With this political liberalism fully agrees" (Rawls, *The Law of Peoples*, 134).

¹¹ Ibid., 136.

¹² Thomas Nagel, "Progressive, but not Liberal," *The New York Review of Books* 53, no. 9 (May 25, 2006): 46.

¹³ Johannes Morsink, *The Universal Declaration of Human Rights: Origins, Drafting, and Intent* (Philadelphia: University of Pennsylvania Press, 1999), 37.

¹⁴ According to a statement issued in 2006 by the Group of Experts of the International Religious Liberty Association in Siquenza, Spain, "limitations [on religious freedom] must be 'directly related and proportionate to the specific needs on which they are predicated' [HRC commentary]. That is, even if a concern for public order or the rights of third parties is raised, . . . such concerns are sufficient to override the religious freedom rights only if they represent pressing or compelling social needs that cannot be furthered in a less burdensome manner."

¹⁵ While Rawls famously grounds primary goods through reciprocal acceptance among the parties in the original position, to the contrary, the drafters use language that implies that human rights inhere naturally in the human being. Johannes Morsink contends:

> Linguistic similarities create the presumption that the drafters of the Universal Declaration had an Enlightenment view of human or natural rights as somehow located in human beings simply by virtue of their own humanity and for no other extraneous reason, such as social conventions, acts of governments, or decisions of parliaments or courts. (*The Universal Declaration of Human Rights*, 281).

[16] Little has also suggested that one can, with some revision, superimpose the Rawlsian conception of public reason onto the international human rights paradigm. Rawls's contention—that constitutional essentials be "presented independently of any wider comprehensive religious or philosophical doctrine" (Rawls, *Political Liberalism*, 223)—is also a centerpiece of the human rights paradigm. (David Little, "Human Rights, Public Reason, and the International Protection of Religion or Belief: A Way Forward," 2007.)

[17] Rawls goes to great lengths to distinguish the terms "secular" and "public." He writes: "We must distinguish public reason from what is sometimes referred to as secular reason and secular values. For I define secular reason as reasoning in terms of comprehensive nonreligious doctrines. Such doctrines and values are much too broad to serve the purposes of public reason. Political values are not moral doctrines, however available of accessible these may be to our reason and common sense reflection. Moral doctrines are on a level with religion and first philosophy. By contrast, liberal political principles and values, although intrinsically moral values, are specified by liberal conceptions of justice and fall under the category of the political." (Rawls, *The Law of Peoples*, 143)

[18] Morsink, *The Universal Declaration of Human Rights*, 289.

[19] Ibid., 290.

[20] Jacques Maritain, *Man and the State* (Washington, D.C.: The Catholic University of America Press, 1951), 110.

[21] Article 18 of the Universal Declaration of Human Rights states: "Everyone has the right to freedom of thought, conscience, and religion; this right includes freedom to change his religion or belief, and freedom, either alone or in community with others and in public or private, to manifest his religion or belief in teaching, practice, worship and observance."

[22] David Little, "Human Rights, Public Reason," 2008, 12–13.

[23] General Comment Adopted by the Human Rights Committee under Article 40, Paragraph 4, of the International Covenant on Civil and Political Rights, UN Doc. CCPR/c/21/Rev.1/Add.4, September 27, 1993, paragraph 8, 3.

[24] Martha Nussbaum, *Frontiers of Justice: Disability, Nationality, and Species Membership* (Cambridge, MA: Harvard University Press, 2006), 62.

[25] I think one can probably say that higher animals are owed a certain degree of justice (since we intuitively feel that it is wrong to hurt them unnecessarily), and, therefore, if one follows the line of argument I advance in this chapter, they also have rights. Of course, as animals, they cannot claim their own rights, but, like infants and severely disabled persons, they need an advocate to claim them on their behalf.

[26] John Rawls, "Kantian Constructivism in Moral Theory," in *Journal of Philosophy* 77 (1980): 546.

[27] Martha Nussbaum, "Capabilities as Fundamental Entitlements: Sen and Social Justice" in *Feminist Economics* Vol. IX, No. VII (2003): 42–43.

[28] Martha Nussbaum, *Women and Human Development* (Cambridge, UK: Cambridge University Press, 2000), 100.

[29] Ibid., 100.

[30] A. C. Grayling, "The Birth of a Classic" in *The New York Review of Books* 58, no. 7 (April 28, 2011): 60.

[31] David Little, "Natural Rights and Human Rights" in *Natural Rights and Natural Law: The Legacy of George Mason*, ed. Robert P. Davidow. (Lanham, MD: The George Mason University Press, 1986), 97.

[32] Ibid.

[33] Ibid., 98. Of course, the listing of these categories of "special reasons" is not meant to suggest that these reasons *necessarily* constitute acceptable justification for the state to act in ways that would, as I say, generally be considered to be wrongful.

[34] Ibid., 99 (my italics).

[35] David Luban, "The Defense of Torture" in *The New York Review of Books* 54, no. 4 (March 15, 2007): 37.

[36] While arguments over the death penalty typically do involve (conflicting) appeals to "public interest" (each side claiming that its position best reduces arbitrary killing), opponents of the death penalty regularly stress that the death penalty violates the provision against "cruel and unusual punishment" (Art. 8 of the U.S. Constitution and Art. 7 of the International Covenant on Civil and Political Rights). Opponents make the case that it constitutes arbitrary killing, precisely because such killing can be regarded as excessive when less drastic measures could be taken with respect to punishment.

[37] There are many types of pain, some of which may be more clearly identified as pain. Certainly, physical pain is indisputably pain. Mental anguish may be less easy to identify, but would still qualify as pain.

[38] Little, "Natural Rights and Human Rights," 98.

Afterword

David Little

The most important thing I can say in responding to the esteemed authors represented in this volume is, above all, to thank them for investing the time and labor required for producing their contributions, most of them first as talks at the conference in November 2009 at Harvard Divinity School, and now in expanded form. I was deeply honored by the presentations and lively discussion at the conference, and I am doubly honored now by the supererogatory efforts of all the authors in agreeing to provide finished essays. I also wish to express special thanks to the three editors, Sumner Twiss, Rodney Petersen, and Marian Simion, for their extraordinary work in bringing this volume to completion.

A second point to emphasize is that these chapters are "themselves original contributions," as Twiss says in his Introduction. Blessedly, none of them is simply a gloss on my work, but they are all examples of substantial, independent reflection on subjects of common interest.

If there is a unifying theme tying all these chapters together, it is the *regulation of force*. Understanding a "use of force," at a minimum, as the deliberate infliction of death, impairment, severe pain/suffering, material destruction, or involuntary confinement, it would be hard to deny that a central and urgent preoccupation of all human civilizations is controlling and directing force in keeping with some set of authoritative reasons. It would also be hard to deny that at all times and places practitioners of religion, along with moral and political philosophers, have devoted an enormous amount of attention to providing and justifying one or another set of authoritative reasons for regulating force.

As to Part One, "Normative Prospects: Human Rights Ideas and Religious Ethics," human rights language is all about the legitimate or authoritative use of force; that is, it is about standards for determining when and by whom force may and may not be used. While, as such, human rights language imposes obligations on individuals, it also imposes them upon governments, laying out the limits of punishment and other forcible treatment, as well as the requirements of "due process of law" according to which force may licitly be applied. And when coupled with "international humanitarian law," as codified in the Geneva Conventions and the Rome Statute of the International Criminal Court, the result, in theory at least, is a supervenient body of law encompassing both the national and international regulation of force.

The subjects addressed in Part Two, "Functional Prospects: Religion, Public Policy, and Conflict," are no less focused on the regulation of force, this time in regard to the broader conditions of controlling force in the name of peace and justice, and of understanding the role of religion in that process as well as determining its proper contribution.

Needless to say, in the brief space allotted me, I cannot do justice to all the stimulating questions, challenges, and alternative lines of thinking posed in both parts. Let me simply tip my hat in passing to the most sensitive issues and intriguing suggestions raised in the various chapters.

Part One

Based on what they say, all the authors in Part One (and, likely, in Part Two, as well), appear to agree on three assumptions. 1) That force (as defined) requires justification, implying that "arbitrary force" (the use of force without carefully defended good reasons) is a grave wrong, however differently it might be understood and defended. 2) Human rights law (including humanitarian law) represents, in general at least, a compelling attempt to curtail the practice of arbitrary force, both nationally and internationally. 3) In considering how human rights law shall be justified, a meaningful distinction can be drawn between "religious" and "nonreligious" or "secular" justifications.

However, when it comes to my approach to the justification of human rights, including the place of "religious" and "secular" warrants, differences of opinion and some serious questions and challenges arise.

John Reeder is the most persistent in probing critically the adequacy of my efforts to ground human rights in the "moral incomprehensibility"—"the blatant incongruity, and, hence, patent unjustifiability" (to quote myself)—of giving purely self-serving or knowingly unfounded reasons for using force. He concedes three things: that the inviolability of that prohibition "can be defended without theological grounds" (as I argue), that "an explanation, of course, is not a justification," and that "all of us [presumably] agree with Little that we should not hurt or fail to help for 'obviously mistaken reasons'," though he is doubtful I have shown that the prohibition can reach beyond the in-group.

Moreover, he wonders about the status of the prohibition as a "basic right," including whether it is "absolute" or "prima facie," and whether it might lose its status in places where it is not enforced, since, by definition, a right is an enforceable entitlement to a certain performance or forbearance. Finally, apparently unsatisfied that I have made my case, Reeder suggests that a neopragmatist position, holding that "there are no deliverances of moral reason, no self-evident bottom truths," will, nevertheless, give us as much as we need, and can have, in supporting a prohibition against arbitrary force.

In a nutshell, my argument is that the right against inflicting force for purely self-serving or knowingly unfounded reasons rests on what I think are self-evident claims concerning three things about human beings and the way they work: 1) the natural (i.e., universal) aversion to death, severe pain/suffering, and the other effects of force; 2) the demand for (very) "good reasons" in justifying the infliction of force wherever human beings are in control; and 3) giving reasons presupposes a fixed gap between "justification" and "explanation." It is because the effects of force are so very unwanted that the reasons for using it must be so very good, and "reasons" for using force such as "because I like to," "because I benefit," or "because I can," are no doubt explanations, but *never* justifications; they are simply no reasons at all in the required sense. Similarly, prevarication or misrepresentation is necessarily a much graver offense in regard to giving reasons for the use of force than in matters that do not directly affect others so adversely.

It follows that if arbitrary force (as defined) is a *summum malum* (as Judith Shklar has put it), and if counterforce, taken to be necessary, proportional and effective (nonarbitrary), can curtail it, such counterforce is justified. It is this line of thinking that establishes, I believe, the prohibition against arbitrary force as a basic, universal, and absolute right, meaning that every individual everywhere has an enforceable title to resist arbitrary force in self-defense. The right is absolute, not prima facie, for the same reason that recreational torture is absolutely (always and everywhere) ruled out. (Whether the right is *per se nota*, something undeniable, but only so on reflection, I have no time to go into.) Moreover, if such a right is, in given instances, not enforced, that by no means invalidates the right, but, rather, calls to account those capable of and responsible for enforcing rights. It is, I believe, this rationale—basically, a reconstructed natural rights rationale—that best makes sense of human rights language, and since I do not think neopragmatism yields such a rationale, I do not follow Reeder in considering its adoption.

It is figuring out the correct relation between religious and secular justifications for human rights that brings us to the essays of Gene Outka, John Witte, and Abdulaziz Sachedina. Outka challenges me to explain the connection between my earlier work in John Calvin and natural law and my more recent work in human rights, suggesting that I appear to have forsaken the priority I once gave to theological reasons in Calvin's doctrine of natural law and the relation of reason and revelation. He also worries that I have lost track of the importance of the church as an independent source of moral and spiritual authority, by perhaps embracing what he believes was Roger Williams's growing suspicion of organized religion as an obstacle to an inclusive, religiously impartial civil and political society. He also questions whether my reliance on John Locke overlooks Locke's essentially theocentric philosophy of state, as described by Jeremy Waldron.

While I still consider myself a liberal Calvinist, I have come to reframe my understanding of Calvin, giving much more room than I once did to the place of natural rights as a relatively free-standing point of reference for organizing and directing civil life, and as something based on explicit appeals to "manifest reason" and to those "persons who, guided by nature, have striven toward virtue throughout life." I also discovered that early in his life Calvin favored restricting the jurisdiction of the state to the second table of the Decalogue, implying that the civil government should direct its affairs by a kind of "public reason," grounded in natural rights. Elsewhere, of course, Calvin takes a much more theocentric, if not theocratic, line in regard to the conduct of civil affairs, and even in his more "liberal" frame of mind, he holds that natural reason and natural rights are all ultimately dependent on God.

Still, the "liberal" Calvin, in contrast to his more conservative alter ego, gives weight to a theoretical distinction between the "inward forum" of conscience and the "outward forum" of civil authority that opens the door to a "two-tiered" theory of justification that is implied, I believe, in a human rights approach to the relation of conscience and the state. "First-tier" justifications rest on the sort of appeal to natural reason I outlined above, and are, accordingly, accessible to and incumbent upon everyone "by nature," regardless of religious belief or identity. "Second-tier" justifications involve what John Rawls calls "comprehensive doctrines," things that provide "ultimate" justifications for human rights and, of course, for much else concerning the conduct and organization of human life. In human rights terms, second-tier justifications are matters of conscience, and, as such, are protected by the state against coercive interference, so long as first-tier provisions are not violated.

It is this framework of "split-level appeals" that Williams avowedly derived from the liberal Calvinist tradition, and went on to develop in some important ways. Williams did endorse a form of "public reason" in respect to civil governance, based on a belief in natural rights and entailing equal citizenship regardless of religious belief or identity, as Twiss's chapter compellingly demonstrates. Indeed, more than any study I know, Twiss substantiates Williams's distinctive contribution as a natural rights thinker committed to grounding civil authority in natural reason and common humanity, while simultaneously working to protect the equal right of all to express and manifest religious and other comprehensive beliefs. Twiss leaves no doubt that Williams's "two-tiered" perspective fits comfortably with an ultimate allegiance to a divine authority possessing supernatural rights and privileges. Thanks to Twiss, the study of Williams will hereafter not be the same.

Accordingly, Williams made ample room for religious institutions and practices, despite his own personal millenarian views about the endemic corruption of the Christian church until Christ's second coming. He understood (as I do) the free exercise of a wide variety of communities of conscience, including those with a Calvinist bent, as indispensable to the proper functioning of the civil and political order. Contrary to Waldron, Locke, on my interpretation, also supports this framework of split-level appeals, though he was by no means as liberal in applying it as Williams.

While there is ever so much I agree with and appreciate in the chapters by Witte and Sachedina, I have differences with both of them over this matter of split-level appeals. Neither one addresses the differences between us head-on. Witte represents my view in a way that is not as clear about the relation of religion and human rights as I would like to be, and Sachedina, without acknowledging it, proposes a view of the justification of human rights that is to a degree at odds with mine.

I wish to draw a sharp distinction between a historical connection of religion and human rights and a theoretical one. I agree with Witte's historical account concerning the influence of certain segments of the Christian tradition, including Calvinism, on natural rights, and, eventually, human rights thinking, and I also agree that early Calvinists "insisted that human rights are ultimately dependent on religious norms and narratives." However, Witte fails to bring out sufficiently that the early Calvin, and his liberal followers, like Williams, introduced an independent, "free-standing" appeal to natural reason as the basis for equal citizenship, and thereby left "ultimate" religious commitments as subject to the free exercise of conscience. Calvin certainly believed in the ultimate sovereignty of God over nature, but, at least in his younger years, he did not think such beliefs should be civilly enforced. That is the key *theoretical* tie to modern human rights thinking.

Sachedina starts out making a strong case for the validity of human rights independent of religious warrants as one important basis for universal equality and inclusivity. However, he then goes back on the idea by supposing that there must be some ultimate common religious foundation—a liberal form of Islam, in his view, lest human rights wind up encouraging the privatization and thus marginalization of religion he associates with Western secularism. In my view, he overlooks the idea of split-level appeals by which all human beings, regardless of religion or other fundamental beliefs, are naturally obligated to observe rights protections against arbitrary force on one level, but, on a second level, are free to follow conscience regarding the ultimate justification of rights as part of a comprehensive way of life. This proposal is not equivalent to the privatization and thus marginalization of religion, since protection of and provision for freedom of conscience serves as a critical limit on state control of public life, as in conscientious exemptions from military conscription or Sunday closing laws.

By raising the subject of animal rights, Grace Kao incisively poses a different, and very important, challenge to my position. She is correct that this subject is of growing urgency, and that my emphasis on human rights prohibitions against arbitrary force applies at least up to a point to animals. Inflicting pain on animals for sport, or tolerating cruel conditions in circuses, zoos, and factory farms are the most obvious examples. The fact that animals cannot themselves claim their rights against torture or "cruel, inhuman or degrading treatment or punishment," is, Kao correctly observes, no different from the case of infants or incompetent human beings. Moreover, whether killing animals and consuming their flesh violates the prohibition against arbitrary force is, on my account, deeply perplexing and I am obligated to face up to it and related questions.

However, I doubt that, as Kao suggests, "human rights are not human after all," but are better described as "rights of all sentient beings," or some such. There is, I think, a fundamental reason that human rights are distinctively human. They presuppose responsibility for the self-conscious design and organization of human social life, including the impact on the natural environment. "Having responsibility" requires understanding and accountability, two uniquely human attributes presupposed by (nonderogable) provisions for due process of law and freedom of conscience, religion or belief, along, of course, with a whole range of other civil, political, economic, and cultural rights that do not apply to animals. Human beings hold one another, not animals, accountable for compliance or noncompliance with human rights standards, and though incompetent human beings are exempted from accountability, their incompetence, unlike that of animals, is regarded as a "deficiency" to be overcome to the extent possible. Furthermore, however much human responsibility may extend to applying a limited range of rights protections to animals, Kao herself admits that such solicitude does not include the obligation to enforce rights against arbitrary killing, or "cruel, inhuman or degrading treatment" that animals inflict on one another. I conclude that this distinction is extremely important, and though exactly how far it goes in limiting the applicability of human rights to animals may be unclear, I am bound, thanks to Kao, to think through much further than I have.

The two essays by Donald Swearer and John Kelsay on the comparative study of religious ethics are well-placed since they represent a transition from the narrower focus on religion and the justification of rights to broader questions of the national and international regulation of force in accord with justice and peace, and of religion's role in the process.

In different ways, Swearer and Kelsay both criticize the approach to comparative ethics developed by Twiss and myself in our 1978 book for being too abstract and schematic, and thus ignoring the historical context in which religious practical reasoning takes place. In fact, in an earlier iteration of his chapter, Kelsay considered it curious that with all the interest in Weber as background to our book, Twiss and I paid so little attention to what Weber cared most about: the relation of ethical reasoning to political, legal, economic, and other forms of institutional life. Swearer makes a similar point. He judges my treatment of Theravada Buddhism in Sri Lanka—part of a broader comparative study of ethnoreligious nationalism begun at the U.S. Institute of Peace in the 1990s—as superior to the account contained in our book precisely because it examines the subject in a historical and political context.

I agree with Kelsay and Swearer, and have begun to recast my approach accordingly. Ethics is best studied comparatively, I now believe, in relation to one or another common global theme, such as human rights, war and peace, nationalism, the environment, or economic development. Kelsay is right that if we are to study ethics, we do need certain definitions and categories of analysis, and here the 1978 book may still be of use. But for all that, there is no ignoring the global institutional setting.

Part Two

The study of religion, nationalism, and peace, the focus of much of my work at USIP and later at Harvard, is picked up in various ways in the chapters by Scott Hibbard, Atalia Omer, and Susan Hayward, and it is touched on, at least tangentially, by Scott Appleby. Though they do not mention it explicitly, all four authors respond to a major concern of mine, namely defending something called "the Liberal Peace." That is the thesis, widely held in political science circles, that the orderly and properly sequenced development of robust liberal political and economic institutions, including protection of the rule of law and human rights, is a critical condition of national and international peace, while illiberal or ethnically exclusivist institutions increase the probability of violence. The thesis holds that, along with cultivating domestic peace, robust liberal democracies do not go to war with each other, even though they sometimes engage in violent conflict with illiberal democracies and authoritarian regimes.

None of the four authors challenges the thesis directly; in fact, Hibbard's illuminating examination of the role of the Egyptian and Pakistani governments in encouraging illiberal forms of religious nationalism provides negative confirmation of the thesis. My only quibble with Hibbard is over his understanding of "liberal" beliefs that serve to support inclusive, tolerant, less violent societies. His claim that liberal societies rest on religious and moral beliefs that are altogether "uncertain" and subject to revision, and are rooted in the Enlightenment, does not accord with my understanding of the natural rights tradition. That tradition predates the Enlightenment by a long shot, and holds certain standards, such as the prohibition against arbitrary force and the freedom of conscience, to be inviolate.

Omer, Hayward, and Appleby all take positions that align with a standard criticism of the Liberal Peace I accept: that its proponents do not satisfactorily take religion into account. In her chapter and elsewhere, Omer convincingly shows that "secularist" assumptions underlying nationalist discourse often conceal unexamined religious ideas that cause prejudice against "subalterns" or repressed minorities who do not fit in with the regnant "liberal" narrative. She rightly presses students of nationalism to reconsider radically the meaning of "nation," both domestically by attending to forgotten peoples, and transnationally by considering expatriates in diaspora who frequently exert enormous influence on the home country. Until these groups, many of them religious, are duly accounted for and their interests and ambitions fully assessed, the chances for a just peace are greatly diminished.

Hayward and Appleby concede the importance of instantiating the rule of law, human rights, and especially freedom of conscience in building peace, but they both urge supplementing such activities by engaging religious communities with more down-to-earth practices. I fully endorse Hayward's account of the inventive direction the USIP Religion and Peacebuilding program has taken since my time by developing the use of ritual and local customs and networks in the pursuit of peace. Similarly, I applaud, with Appleby, the mobilization of the Mennonite community in the cause of effective and "full service" peace action. The Mennonites have deservedly become a leading example of the creative role religion can play in peacemaking.

Petersen's chapter connects with Appleby's by also invoking the Mennonites as exemplars of creative peacemaking, and he supplements Hayward's chapter by expanding instructively on multitrack diplomacy and other practical techniques that have been fruitfully employed and developed by religious peacebuilders. The proposals of Omer, Appleby, Hayward, and Petersen are all significant advances on the preliminary work in religion and peacebuilding I undertook beginning in the 1990s.

The chapters by Bryan Hehir and Simion address the just war tradition, sympathetically as viewed from the Western Christian perspective by Hehir, and more skeptically as viewed from the Eastern Orthodox perspective by Simion. My own sympathies lie with the Western tradition, and I fully endorse Hehir's discussion of the new thinking on the subject regarding provisions for "ius post bellum," along with the standard requirements for determining the just use of force before and during a conflict. Taking responsibility for peacebuilding after an armed conflict also provides an important opportunity for religious peacemaking, as does the broadening of our understanding of "last resort" to include the new range of conflict resolution tools so much emphasized of late by religious actors. Contrary to what I may have written earlier, I also heartily endorse Hehir's proposal that the moral principles of just war thinking be employed as a guide to revising the UN Charter in the direction of permitting humanitarian intervention, much along the lines, I would suggest, of the recent "Responsibility To Protect" (R2P) doctrine.

Simion's examination of Eastern Orthodox attitudes toward war adds an utterly new dimension to my understanding of Christian responses to the use of force. Speaking as a distinct outsider, I am prompted to raise a question for further consideration: Given the wide swings of opinion within the tradition between quietistic pacifism, on the one side, and demonization and all-out annihilation of the enemy, on the other, would it not be advisable to make room for a middle way between the two extremes, such as has been represented by the just war tradition in Western Christianity? Whether they are pacifists or not, ought not Christians to strongly favor restrictions on arbitrary force imposed by existing laws that codify just war standards, namely international humanitarian law and the law of armed conflict?

The last two chapters in the volume by Natalie Sherman and David Gergen and by Christian Rice, address the critical point of encounter between public life and religion, or, in terms of my approach, between the two levels of appeal—the first to commonly-held, natural and secular beliefs; the second to predictably diverse comprehensive religious or other fundamental beliefs. I agree with Sherman and Gergen that a healthy constitutional democracy makes as much room as possible for the free exercise of religion and for the open discussion of religion in the public square. But it is the words they quote favorably from President Obama that signal the heart of the matter: In a democracy religious people must translate their proposals "into universal, rather than religion-specific values" because religious proposals intended for public adoption must "be subject to argument and amenable to reason." Obama is appealing here to Rawls's notion of "public reason," which up to a point matches our first level of appeal. That notion is based on the idea that no citizen should be able to use state coercion to enforce the dictates of a comprehensive doctrine, and that therefore the justification of laws and policies that have the force of law in a constitutional democracy must rest on common (natural, secular) beliefs.

This view seems to me basically correct, though Rawls's ideas need to be revised along the lines worked out by Rice in his chapter. Rice improves things by basing the idea of public reason on a human rights foundation, something that, as is by now fully predictable, I find very appealing.

Index of Names

Ackerman, Peter 229, 236 n. 39
Ahmadinejad, Mahmoud 262, 277 n. 27
Albright, Madeleine xxii, xxvii, 224–225, 235 n. 11
Allam, Fouad 286
al-Ash`ari, Abu'l Hasan 160, 164 n. 22
al-Fazārī, Abū Ishāq 193
al-Mubārak, Abdallah 193
An-Na'im, Abdullahi 6, 93 n. 4, 237 n. 50, 242–243, 320
Annan, Kofi 175, 183, 186 n. 15
Appleby, Scott xxxvi–xxxvii, 238 n. 59, 239–250, 252–253, 257, 270, 273, 275 n. 1, 276 n. 9, 276 n. 12, 277 n. 18, 304 n. 8, 306 n. 37, 344–346
Aquinas, Thomas 4, 103, 104, 115 n. 53, 163 n. 11
Asad, Talal 161, 164 n. 23
Ashafa, Imam Mohammed 219
Athanasius the Great xxxv, 198–199
Atta, Mohammed xxiii
Audi, Robert 111 n. 17, 112 n. 19, 119 n. 85, 333 n. 6

Augustine, Saint xxxiv, 4, 40 n. 2, 163 n. 11, 170, 177,
Axel, Keith 263
Azar, Edward 299

Bainton, Roland 190, 204 n. 2
Balsamon, Theodore 199
Bandaranike, S. W. R. D. 144
Bayle, Pierre 7
Basil the Great, Saint xxxv, 194, 198–199
Bennett, John 170
Berger, Peter 209, 233, 238 n. 58
Bhutto, Zulfikar Ali 290–291
Bin Laden, Osama 277 n. 27, 283, 292, 294, 305 n. 26, 305 n. 32
Blastares, Matthew 199
Bowman, Glenn 262
Brandom, Robert 162, 164 n. 20
Breivik, Anders Behring 215
Browne, Robert 23 n. 52, 31
Burger, Chief Justice Warren 308, 312
Burton, John 229
Bush, George W. 281, 301, 303 n. 2, 307

Butler, Judith 271
Cadoux, John C. 190, 192, 204 n. 1, 204 n. 5
Calvin, John xxx, 4, 41 n. 9, 172, 340
Carter, Jimmy 309
Cassin, René 323
Childress, James 40 n. 2, 119 n. 87, 171
Cotton, John 23 n. 52, 31, 46
Curle, Adam 245

Dalai Lama 243
Danforth, John xxv
Davies, John 229, 236 n. 36–37, 236 n. 41, 237 n. 42
Davis, G. Scott 32, 39 n. 2, 43 n. 29, 154–159, 163 n. 12, 163 n. 14, 164 n. 18
de Gruchy, John 226, 235 n. 19, 235 n. 24, 237 n. 47
de Wiart, Henry Carton 322
DeSilva, K. M. 144, 216
Diamond, Louise 230
Docherty, Jayne 233, 238 n. 60
Douglas, Mary 154, 158
Douglass, Jim 172, 186 n. 8
DuVall, Jack 229, 236 n. 39

Eliade, Mircea 157, 164 n. 19

Faisal of Saudi Arabia, King 286
Feldman, Noah 311, 313, 317 n. 13, 317 n. 20
Fingarette, Herbert 154, 158
Ford, S.J., John 170
Forrester, Duncan 226–227, 235 n. 21
Foucault, Michel 34, 268
Francione, Gary 129, 136 n. 27
Fraser, Nancy 259, 277 n. 19
Freud, Sigmund 223–224, 233, 235 n. 9, 236 n. 34

Galtung, John 229
Gass, William 126–127, 135 n. 17

Gellner, Ernst 148–149, 162 n. 2
Gergen, David xxxviii–xxxix, 278 n. 46, 307–317, 347
Geuss, Raymond 107, 111 n. 10, 116 n. 62–63, 117 n. 65–66, 117 n. 72
Gore, Al(bert) 307
Grayling, A. C. 327, 335 n. 30
Green, Ronald M. 117 n. 68, 141, 147 n. 15, 151, 163 n. 5–6, 163 n. 17
Greenhouse, Linda 312, 317 n. 15
Grelle, Bruce 153, 163 n. 11, 165
Grotius, Hugo 7, 170
Guicherd, Catherine 182–183, 186 n. 14, 187 n. 25
Guistozzi, Antonio 157, 164 n. 19

Haqqani, Jalaluddin 292, 306 n. 39
Hauerwas, Stanley 4, 38, 172, 186 n. 8
Hayward, Susan xxxvi, 207–221, 344–346
Hehir, Bryan xxii, xxxiv–xxxv, 169–187, 346
Hekmatyar, Gulbuddin 292
Henry, Patrick 314
Hershberger, Guy F. 244–245
Heyd, David 29, 41 n. 18
Hibbard, Scott xxxviii, 280–306, 344–345
Hitler, Adolf 35–36, 324
Hobbes, Thomas 8, 34, 43 n. 40, 103
Hollenbach, David 171
Hume, David 7, 127, 153
Huntington, Samuel 269, 276 n. 13, 314
Hurd, Elizabeth Shakman 268–269, 278 n. 44, 278 n. 47

Islambouli, Khalid 280
Ivan the Third of Moscow 200

Jaish-e-Mohammed 291
Jefferson, Thomas 4, 7, 10, 21 n. 25, 22 n. 49

Jesus 41, 196, 201, 249
Jinnah, Muhammad Ali 289, 300
John of Damascus, Saint 193
John Paul II, Pope xxiv
Johnson, James Turner 153, 156, 163 n. 11, 170–171, 185 n. 2
Juergensmeyer, Mark xxvii n. 5, 281, 303 n. 4
Justinian, Emperor 191

Kao, Grace Y. xxxii, 120–137, 343–344
Kaufman, Edward 229, 236 n. 36–37, 236 n. 41, 237 n. 42
Kelman, Herbert 229
Kelsay, John 4, 20 n. 3, 20 n. 7, 21 n. 19, 22 n. 28, 23 n. 60, 93 n. 1, 148–165, 344
Kennedy, David 223, 234 n. 6
Kenney, William 245
Keshgegian, Flora 232
Khomeini, Ayatollah xxvi
Kierkegaard, Søren 35, 116 n. 57
King, Jr., Martin Luther 41 n. 9, 311
Kissinger, Henry 173, 186 n. 10
Kluckhohn, Clyde 28–29, 37
Knox, John 23 n. 52, 31
Kony, Joseph 218
Korsgaard, Christine 98, 105–107, 111 n. 10, 113 n. 22, 114 n. 37, 115 n. 48, 116 n. 60–67, 117 n. 71, 117 n. 73, 129, 134 n. 1, 136 n. 26
Kraus, C. Norman 245
Kuhn, Thomas 153

Lafleur, William 154, 156, 163 n. 13, 163 n. 17
Lashkar-e-Taiba 291, 294
Laue, James 245
Lazar, Prince 255
Lederach, John Paul 236 n. 27, 246–248, 250 n. 4, 251 n. 7, 252–253, 257, 270, 273, 275 n. 1, 277 n. 17

Leibniz, Gottfried Wilhelm 97
Lenin, Vladimir xxvi
Lerner, Michael 271
Lewis, C. S. 224
Lincoln, Abraham 315–316, 317 n. 29–30
Linzey, Andrew 131, 137 n. 32
Locke, John xxx, 4, 7–8, 10, 21 n. 25, 32–36, 38, 43 n. 40–41, 43 n. 43, 45–46, 74 n. 1, 97, 103, 112 n. 19, 114 n. 32, 114 n. 37, 114 n. 41, 118 n. 74–75, 340, 342
Lovin, Robin 146 n. 5, 153, 163 n. 10
Luban, David 330, 335 n. 35
Luther, Martin 4, 28, 48

MacIntyre, Alasdair 4, 38, 40 n. 2, 103, 115 n. 43, 115 n. 46, 116 n. 59, 117 n. 64
Madison, James 7, 312–313, 317 n. 19
Mahmood, Saba 267
Mantzaridis, Georgios 195, 198, 204 n. 4, 206 n. 36
Maritain, Jacques 234 n. 4, 323, 334 n. 20
Marx, Karl 34, 283, 286
Mason, George 20 n. 5, 33, 40 n. 5, 110 n. 1, 335 n. 31
Massoud, Ahmad Shah 292
Masuzawa, Tomoko 161, 164 n. 23
Maududi, Mawlana 289
McAllister, Melanie 269
McCutcheon, Russell 161, 164 n. 23
McDonald, John M. 229–230
Mearsheimer, John 234 n. 3, 268–269, 278 n. 45–46
Merkel, Angela 215, 221 n. 12
Miller, Joseph S. 246, 250 n. 4, 251 n. 5
Minow, Martha 232, 237 n. 55
Muhammad, Prophet 77, 291, 303 n. 1
Montesquieu 7
Montville, Joseph 228, 230, 236 n. 34
Moore, G. E. 126

Morsink, Johannes 76 n. 22, 126, 135 n. 14, 322–323, 333 n. 13, 333 n. 15, 334 n. 48
Mubarak, Hosni xxxviii, 285, 287–288, 300, 304 n. 15
Murray, S.J., John Courtney 171, 185 n. 5–6, 186 n. 17

Nafziger, James A. R. 223, 234 n. 7
Nagel, Thomas 99, 111 n. 10, 113 n. 26, 117 n. 65–66, 117 n. 70, 322, 333 n. 12
Nasser, Gamal Abdel 283–288, 299–300, 306 n. 42
Neuhaus, Richard John 308, 316 n. 2
Niebuhr, Reinhold 170–171, 177, 185 n. 3, 185 n. 6, 234 n. 4
Nietzsche, Friedrich xxxii, 34, 103, 111 n. 9, 116 n. 57–58, 117 n. 64, 118
Nussbaum, Martha 102, 114 n. 35, 116 n. 57–58, 325–327, 334 n. 24, 334 n. 27–28

O'Donovan, Oliver 39
Obama, President/Senator Barak 304 n. 5, 310–311, 314, 316 n. 12, 317 n. 25, 347
Olafson, Frederick 107, 117 n. 69
Omer, Atalia xxxvii–xxxviii, 252–279, 344–346
Orjuela, Camilla 253, 271, 275 n. 5, 279 n. 51
Outka, Gene xxx, 20 n. 6, 24–44, 110 n. 4, 111 n. 14, 115 n. 54, 119 n. 87, 119 n. 88, 134 n. 11, 163 n. 3, 340

Pann, Matthew Hisal 123
Peachey, Paul 172, 186 n. 8
Penn, William 45
Petersen, Rodney L. xxxvi, 205 n. 29, 222–238, 337, 346
Petraeus, General David 307

Philpott, Daniel xxvii n. 4, 186 n. 18, 234 n. 2, 242, 275 n. 1, 276 n. 12
Porter, Jean 38–39, 44 n. 49–50, 103–105, 111 n. 6, 114 n. 42, 115 n. 43–44, 115 n. 47, 115 n. 50, 115 n. 52–55
Pospielovsky, Dimitri 192, 204 n. 12, 205 n. 20
Proclus of Constantinople 201, 206 n. 43
Pufendorf, Samuel von 7
Putnam, Hilary 5, 21 n. 15

Qutb, Sayyid 261, 281

Ramadan, Tariq 243
Ramsey, Paul 40 n. 4, 115 n. 54, 150, 162 n. 3, 171, 182, 185 n. 6
Rawls, John xxxix, 100, 126, 135 n. 12, 160, 164 n. 21, 313–315, 317 n. 23, 318–326, 332 n. 2, 333 n. 3–11, 333 n. 15–17, 334 n. 26, 341, 347
Reagan, Ronald 309
Reeder, Jr., John xxxii, 20 n. 6, 40 n. 3, 40 n. 5, 42 n. 22, 43 n. 38, 96–119, 134 n. 11, 163 n. 3, 339–340
Reynolds, Frank E. 138, 141–143, 146 n. 5, 153, 163 n. 10–11
Rice, Christian xxxix, 318–335, 347
Rich, Andrew 267, 278 n. 43
Ricoeur, Paul 6, 231, 237 n. 51
Rorty, Richard 4, 33, 43 n. 37, 97, 110, 111 n. 9
Rousseau, Jean-Jacques 7

Sabine, George H. 30–31, 37, 42 n. 20–21
Sabri, Ali 283
Sachedina, Abdulaziz xxxi, 20 n. 7, 21 n. 19, 22 n. 28, 23 n. 60, 77–95, 242, 340, 342
Sadat, Anwar xxxviii, 280–289, 298, 300–302, 304 n. 13, 304 n. 15

Said, Edward 264, 278 n. 35
Scalia, Justice Antonin 312, 314
Schopenhauer, Arthur 110 n. 3, 112
Schweiker, William 153, 163 n. 11, 250 n. 3
Scupolli, Lorenzo 191
Servetus, Michael 12
Shah, Timothy xxvii n. 4, 220 n. 3, 242
Shain, Yossi 261, 266, 272, 277 n. 25, 278 n. 36, 279 n. 56
Sherman, Natalie xxxviii–xxxix, 307–317, 347
Sider, Ronald J. 246
Simion, Marian Gh. xxxiv–xxxv, 188–206, 337, 346
Singer, Peter 121, 136 n. 19, 137 n. 33
Smith, J. Z. 7, 156, 163 n. 16, 165
Smith, Wilfred Cantwell 141
Soroush, Abdolkarim 242
Stalnaker, Aaron 153, 163 n. 11, 165
Stepan, Alfred 242
Stephen the Great, Saint/ Prince 200
Stout, Jeffrey 40 n. 2, 97, 111 n. 14, 111 n. 16–17, 113 n. 23, 118 n. 80–81, 143, 145, 147 n. 21, 147 n. 28, 151–152, 159–164
Straus, Leo 8–9, 22 n. 33
Suárez, Francisco 170
Sullivan, Kathleen 315, 317 n. 27
Swearer, Donald xxxiii, 20 n. 2, 138–147, 151, 163 n. 5, 276 n. 7, 276 n. 11, 277 n. 21, 306 n. 40, 344

Thiemann, Ronald 315, 317 n. 28
Thistlethwaite, Susan 226, 234 n. 4, 235 n. 23
Thomas, Helen 264
Thomas, Norman 226
Thomson, Judith Jarvis 113 n. 25, 117 n. 73, 328
Tierney, Brian 39, 45–47, 64, 70, 74 n. 1, 74 n. 3–4, 75 n. 16, 113 n. 28

Tito, Josip Broz 225
Toft, Monica Duffy xxi–xxvii, 220 n. 3, 234 n. 2
Tracy, David 163 n. 11, 227, 235 n. 25
Troeltsch, Ernst 151, 233
Tuck, Richard 45, 74 n. 1
Turner, Simon 254, 263, 275 n. 6, 277 n. 28–29
Tutu, Desmond 232, 237 n. 54, 243
Twiss, Sumner B. xxviii–xl, 4, 20 n. 3, 25, 40 n. 3, 45–76, 118 n. 76, 138–142, 145, 146 n. 1, 146 n. 7, 148, 150–153, 156, 158–159, 161–162, 162 n. 3, 163 n. 11, 164 n. 25, 165, 337, 341, 344

Vasak, Karel 16, 23 n. 57–58
Virgin Mary (Theotokos/ "Birth-Giver of God") 200–203, 206 n. 43
Vitoria, Francisco de 170
Vladimir, Prince 192
Volf, Miroslav 231, 237 n. 53

Waal, Frans de 98, 112 n. 20
Waldron, Jeremy 38, 44 n. 43, 45, 74 n. 1, 107, 118 n. 74–75, 340, 342
Walt, Stephan 268–269, 278 n. 45
Walters, Le Roy B. 171
Walzer, Michael 179–181, 186 n. 13, 196 n. 16, 187 n. 19
Weber, Max 3, 138, 144–147, 150–151, 162, 163 n. 4–5, 209, 233, 256, 344
Wehr, Paul 246
White, Morton 45, 74 n. 1
Williams, Roger xxx–xxxi, 4, 11, 21 n. 10, 21 n. 16, 21 n. 19, 21 n. 25, 22 n. 31, 22 n. 38, 22 n. 40–41, 23 n. 55, 31–32, 37, 42 n. 27, 43 n. 28, 45–76, 340–342
Winters, Frank 171
Witte, Jr., John xxix–xxx, 3–23, 45, 74 n. 1, 74 n. 3, 340, 342

Wolterstorff, Nicholas 38, 107, 112 n. 19,
    114 n. 37, 114 n. 41, 118 n. 74, 119 n.
    84, 134 n. 9, 333 n. 6
Wuthnow, Robert 309
Wuye, Pastor James 219

Yearley, Lee 153, 163 n. 11
Yoder, John Howard 172, 245

Zahn, Gordon 172
Zia-ul-Haq, Muhammad 290–291, 294,
    298, 300, 302, 305 n. 35, 306 n. 44
Zonaras, John 199

Index of Subjects

A Common Word Between Us and You (2007) 223, 234
Abrahamic tradition 89, 212, 231, 240
absolutes 102, 108, 118
actors, religious xxiv–xxvii, 209, 222, 227, 232–233, 239–240, 250, 295, 346
Acts and Ordinances of 1647 (Rhode Island) 69
adiaphora 12
Afghanistan xxii, 157, 164 n. 19, 174, 176, 184, 261, 281–282, 291–294, 302, 305 n. 26, 305 n. 33, 307
Africa, (-n) 21 n. 21, 178, 198, 208, 215, 224, 229, 235 n. 24, 237 n. 47, 240, 242, 244, 260, 293, 306 n. 36, 306 n. 45
- African Americans 246
- Horn of 302
agreements, contractual 83
Akathist Hymn 202
al-Ash`ari 160, 164 n. 22
al-Azhar 285, 304 n. 12
Alexandria Process in Israel/Palestine 212
Algeria 94, 263, 289
Alliance of Civilizations 231, 234

American Academy of Religion 155, 163 n. 17, 267
American Arbitration Association 245
American Israel Public Affairs Committee (AIPAC) 270–271, 274
Anabaptist(s) 8, 248
animal(s) xxxii–xxxiii, 104–105, 112 n. 20, 116 n. 59, 116 n. 63, 117 n. 64, 120–137, 325–326, 334 n. 25, 343–344
- advocacy 124, 127
- cross-species equality 125–126
- ethics 121, 124, 134 n. 2
anthropology 149, 155
Apartheid 229, 263
Arab(s) 193, 205 n. 18, 206 n. 47, 255, 262, 265, 277 n. 31, 303, 304 n. 17
- Afghan 292–293
- Arab Socialist Union 283
- Arab Spring xxvi, 232, 301
- nationalism 176, 277 n. 31, 283–285, 299
- world xxii
argument(s) xxx–xxxiii, xxxvi, xxxix, 7–8, 10, 14, 16–17, 19, 24, 34, 46–76,

80–81, 86–87, 105–107, 116 n. 63, 121, 125–128, 132–133, 135 n. 11, 137 n. 31, 148, 151, 156–158, 161–162, 164 n. 25, 170–175, 179–183, 195, 200, 215–217, 228, 235 n. 20, 242, 263–264, 269, 304 n. 7, 307–308, 311–314, 318, 327, 334 n. 25, 335 n. 36, 339, 347
- *Argument from Marginal Cases (AMC)* 125
- normative 24, 180

Armenians 260

arms control 173–174

atheist (-ical) xxiv, 61, 73, 309

attachment 102, 142, 214, 216, 261

authority xxx, xxxiii–xxxiv, 8, 13, 15, 17, 31, 66–67, 75 n. 17, 75 n. 17, 81, 84, 94 n. 8, 111 n. 17, 145, 185, 243, 283, 298, 312, 314, 318
- charismatic 150
- Christ's 41, 26, 29
- civil 23 n. 52, 31, 52, 341
- federalist layers of 13
- legitimate 62, 299
- normative 61, 98
- political 72–73, 88, 243, 297–298, 320
- religious/sacred/spiritual 17, 90, 139–141, 143, 233, 284, 340, 341
- state xxxviii, 188, 285, 297–298, 302

Avars 202

Baathist regimes xxv

base-line, normative 98–99

belief(s) xxxi, xxxviii, 4–5, 16, 22 n. 27, 31, 37, 62–63, 97–98, 100, 102, 105, 107, 110–119, 125–126, 131, 296
- biblical 18
- communal 82
- conscientious 62, 72, 324
- fundamental 16, 140, 210, 297, 304 n. 8, 342, 347
- in God 38, 90, 119 n. 84, 314
- liberty of 63

- moral 97, 103, 345
- religious 14, 31–32, 59, 62–63, 68–69, 71–73, 86, 140, 144–145, 147 n. 15, 147 n. 22, 195, 223, 231, 234 n. 5, 269, 297, 310, 316 n. 4, 316 n. 7, 324, 334 n. 16, 334 n. 21, 341–342
- secular 18, 145, 146 n. 3, 256, 258, 272, 276 n. 7, 306 n. 40, 308, 315, 332 n. 1, 341, 347
- theological xxx–xxxi, 72–73, 306 n. 37
- web of 97, 100, 102, 107, 109
- Western 6

benevolence 19, 26–27, 41, 112 n. 20
- active 29

Berlin Wall 208

Bill of Rights (U.S.) 208

bishop(s) 192, 197, 205 n. 22, 223, 242, 310

blasphemy (-ous) 31, 47, 192
- law 291

Bosnia xxv, xxxv, 175, 225, 292

Brookings Institution 21 n. 21, 146 n. 3, 147 n. 22, 268, 305 n. 22

Buddhism (-t) xxv, xxxiii, 4, 7, 15, 135 n. 16, 138–147, 152, 154, 163 n. 12, 210, 215–216
- Sangha (monastic order) 145
- Sinhala xxxiii, 138–147, 210, 215–216
- Theravada xxxiii, 138–146, 151–152, 344

Byzantine Empire 191, 199

Calvinist(s) xxix–xxx, 3–23, 32, 41 n. 13, 46, 306 n. 38
- American 340–342
- European 13
- liberal 340–342
- modern xxix, 3–23

Canon Law xxix, 204 n. 7
- Byzantine 189, 192
- Orthodox xxxv, 189, 192–193, 197

Cartoons Controversy xxi, xxvii n. 1

Catholic (-ism) xxii, xxiv–xxv, 8–11, 15, 39, 43 n. 41, 94, 164 n. 20, 169–170, 172, 185 n. 1
Central America 174, 246
chauvinism (-t, -tic) 15, 144–145, 255–256, 258, 274, 299
Chechnya 292–293
checks and balances 13
Chicago xxiii, 8, 138, 311
Christ xx, 26, 29, 41 n. 9, 42 n. 28, 44 n. 43, 47, 51–54, 63, 74 n. 8, 194, 201, 245, 249, 255, 214, 220 n. 2, 242, 309–310
- Bride of 201
- office of prophet 14
Christianity
- Catholic xxiii
- Christian Reformed Tradition 25
- Orthodox 188–189, 192, 195, 200, 205 n. 22
- Reformed 23 n. 52, 24–44
- Western 347
Christology (-ical) 28, 50–52, 72–73
Church
- Catholic xxiii, xxiv
- Church Fathers xxxv, 8, 190
- Orthodox xxxv, 188–189, 191, 197–198, 200–201, 203–205
- Reformed 11–12
Church Order 192
- deacons 11–12
- elders 11–12, 101, 190
- pastors 11
- teachers xxiv, 11–12, 213
Church–State separation xxxv, 21 n. 8, 22 n. 49, 30, 189, 191–192, 302, 317 n. 13, 317 n. 20
citizen(s) xxiv–xxvii, xxviii–xxxix, 16, 32, 42 n. 24, 67–68, 79–81, 86–87, 93 n. 4, 94 n. 6, 106, 175, 219, 229–230, 236 n. 36, 236 n. 41, 237 n. 44, 250, 261, 310–311, 313, 315, 319–323, 325–326, 330–331, 333 n. 4, 347

- entitlements of 319
citizenship 30, 93 n. 4, 258, 274, 341–342
civil
- disobedience 41 n. 9, 311
- organization 46, 69
- Rights 10, 13–14, 32, 41 n. 9, 55, 65, 69–70, 245, 311
- society xxxvi, xxxviii, 62, 65, 68, 71, 174, 175, 203, 227, 229, 236 n. 40, 237 n. 44, 237 n. 50, 281–282, 283, 295, 298
Civilian Public Service 245
Code of 1647 (Rhode Island) 46
Cold War xxvii, xxxiv–xxxv, xxxvii, 171, 173–176, 178, 181, 208–209, 225, 228, 281–282, 291–292, 295–296, 305 n. 27
- Arab Cold War 284, 304 n. 11
Colombia 214, 247
colony (-ial, -ism) 35, 69, 76, 79, 81, 94, 144–145, 176, 231, 259, 262
- Massachusetts Bay Colony 46
- neo-colonialism 184
- post-colonial(ism) 79, 145, 230, 277, 300
- Western 176
colonizer–colonized relationship 84
Commandments 13, 26, 40
- first table 14, 27
- second table xxx, 14, 27–28, 55, 65, 67, 70, 340
- Ten (Decalogue) xxx, 14, 27–29, 55, 67, 70, 171, 312, 317 n. 15, 340
- two love 26
common good 18–19, 29, 65, 67–68, 71, 226, 241, 308
commonwealth 31, 65–66
Communism (-t) xxiv–xxv, 19, 281, 285, 293
- states xxv
Community of Saint' Egidio xxv
community, sacred 249

compulsion, religious 46–47, 52, 55–56, 58–61, 66, 75
Concentrated Animal Feeding Operation (CAFO) 133
conflict(s) xxi, xxv, xxvii–xxix, xxxiii–xl, 18, 24, 47, 69, 77, 87, 93 n. 1, 108, 133, 144, 154, 170, 173–181, 184–185, 186 n. 11, 186 n. 15, 187 n. 22, 187 n. 29, 203, 205 n. 29, 207–212, 214–220, 221 n. 15, 222, 225, 227–231, 233–234, 234 n. 4, 235 n. 13–14, 236 n. 31, 236 n. 33–35, 236 n. 38–39, 236 n. 41, 237 n. 42, 238 n. 59, 239–240, 242–244, 246–250, 252–280, 285, 292, 305 n. 22, 308, 345–347
- analysis 208, 220 n. 1, 266
- Balkan xxxv
- ethnic 250 n. 2, 276 n. 9
- prevention xxxvii, 234 n. 4, 236 n. 33–34, 336 n. 36, 236 n. 41, 237 n. 42, 238 n. 59, 244, 247, 249, 252–279
- Sinhala–Tamil xxxiii, 144
- transformation xxxvii, 234 n. 4, 236 n. 33–34, 336 n. 236 n. 41, 237 n. 42, 238 n. 59, 244, 247, 249, 252–279
Congregationalism 23 n. 53
- separatist 31
conscience xxix–xxxii, xxxix, 4–6, 10–11, 13–14, 17, 21 n. 25, 22 n. 27, 23 n. 52, 31–32, 42 n. 24, 45–76, 85–86, 88, 92, 171, 195, 245, 296, 297, 313, 318, 334 n. 21, 341–343, 345
 - inviolability of xxx, 48, 56–64, 70, 72–73
 - normative inviolability of 56, 59–60, 63, 72–73
consensualist egalitarian themes 25
consequentialist 47, 56, 63–64, 72, 75 n. 15
Constantinople 192, 194, 197, 200–203, 204 n. 14, 206 n. 43
Constitutional Experiment 8, 11

consumption 121, 123, 129
- ethics of 121
- human 123
- of animal protein 129
contractarianism 18
Cold War (see War, Cold) xxvii n. 5, xxxiv–xxxv, xxxviii, 171, 173–176, 178, 181–182, 208–209, 225, 228, 281–282, 284, 291–292, 295–296, 304 n. 11, 305 n. 27
Crusades 176, 199, 235 n. 10

dar al sulh 193
Darfur 266
death, meaning of 203
Decalogue (see Commandments, Ten)
Declaration of the Rights of Man and Citizen (France) 16
Declaration of the United Nations Conference on the Human Environment 123
Declaration on the Elimination of All Forms of Intolerance and Discrimination Based on Religion and Belief 71, 210
democracy xxx, xxxix, 7, 11, 20, 40 n. 2, 40 n. 5, 42 n. 24, 70, 79, 94 n. 9, 110 n. 2, 111 n. 16–17, 118 n. 80, 135, 163 n. 8, 255, 270, 278 n. 49, 303 n. 2, 307–308, 311, 314–316, 317 n. 27–28, 321, 323, 347
democratic (-ization) xxiv, xxxviii, 3, 8–9, 11–13, 40 n. 2, 64, 67, 70–71, 74 n. 4, 82, 85–86, 88, 94 n. 6–7, 94 n. 8, 108 n. 76, 216, 220 n. 3, 226, 229, 242, 255, 266, 269, 290, 301, 307–308, 310–312, 315–316, 331
- process 11–13, 308, 315
- theory of society and government 67
deontological 56, 158, 160–161
Desert Fathers 190
determination, (self-) 5, 20 n. 2, 101–102, 107–108
Devil 190

dhamma 138–147
dialogue xxxvi–xxxvii, 81, 85–87, 92, 94 n. 8, 143, 153, 163 n. 11, 176, 182, 193, 208, 212, 214, 216–217, 221 n. 9, 229, 234, 237 n. 55, 240, 242, 271, 276 n. 12
- interethnic xxxvii, 242
- interreligious 153, 163 n. 11, 176, 182, 212
Diaspora(s) xxxvii, 252
- symbolic 261, 263, 274
dignity xxiv, xxxi, xxxiii, 5, 44 n. 47, 48, 72, 78–79, 86–88, 122, 124, 130, 214, 219, 240, 322, 326
- human xxxiii, 72, 79, 86, 240, 322, 326
- of creature xxxiii
diplomacy xxxvi, 174, 178, 181, 209, 222–238, 248–249, 346
- citizens' 229, 236 n. 36
- multi-track xxxvi, 222–238
- track-one (Track I) xxxvi, 228–230, 234
- track-two (Track II) xxxvi, 228–230, 248
- track-three (Track III) xxxvi
Discipleship 244–250
discourse 9, 18, 43 n. 41, 73, 75 n. 12, 78, 82, 82, 84–85, 94 n. 8, 144–145, 152, 155, 158, 160, 163 n. 11, 172, 175, 177, 180, 227, 242–244, 259, 264, 268–275, 288, 303, 321, 345
- authoritarian 80
- citizen xxxviii–xxxix
- fundamentalist 92
- Islamic 84
- normative 148–149, 152, 156, 159–162
- political xxix, 17, 171
divine xxx–xxxi, 15, 18, 38, 42 n. 24, 44 n. 49, 48, 50–51, 66, 70, 78, 89–90, 92, 124, 150, 153, 160, 164 n. 22, 180, 201–203, 239, 317 n. 30, 341
- commands 90, 150

- Liturgy 203
- Will 70, 239, 317 n. 30
dominion 124
Dualism 1, 244
- political 196–197
- theological 248
duties xxix, 5, 8, 11, 13–15, 35, 51, 65, 71, 83–84, 86, 100–101, 107–108, 113 n. 28, 115 n. 52, 136 n. 26, 189
- natural 9
- moral 21 n. 19, 27–28
- public 75 n. 17

Eastern Mennonite University 233
- Conflict Resolution Program of 233
ecclesial (-stical, -ology) xxix, xxxv, 11–14, 25, 30–31, 37, 43 n. 28, 189, 191–192, 194, 226, 249
Ecumenical Patriarchate 197
Egypt xxi–xxii, xxxviii, 93 n. 3, 192, 261, 280–289, 293, 295, 298–299, 301–302, 303 n. 1, 304 n. 7, 304 n. 10, 304 n. 12–16, 305 n. 19, 306 n. 44. 345
elicitive method 248–249
England 3, 13, 20 n. 1, 23 n. 52, 31–32, 306 n. 41, 310
Enlightenment xxix, 3, 7–11, 15–16, 19, 42 n. 24, 139, 226, 281, 295, 298, 300, 303, 305 n. 23, 333 n. 15, 345
enslavement xxxii, 5, 36, 75 n. 12, 130, 137 n. 31
environmental degradation 123
epistemology xxxii, 109, 111 n. 15, 112 n. 17
essentialism, strategic 263, 277 n. 32
Establishmentarians 31
ethic(s)
- Buddhist xxxiii, 138, 145
- Christian xxx, 25, 28, 38–39, 40 n. 2, 40 n. 4, 44 n. 49, 115 n. 53–54, 119 n. 87, 121, 124, 135 n. 11, 153, 171, 186 n. 8

- comparative xxviii, 77, 146 n. 5, 153, 154–158, 162, 163 n. 7, 163 n. 10, 163 n. 12, 164 n. 25, 344
- comparative religious xxxii–xxxiii, 4, 40 n. 3, 76 n. 21, 138–141, 143, 145, 146 n. 1, 146 n. 4, 146 n. 7, 149–153, 155–156, 159–161, 162 n. 3, 163 n. 5, 163 n. 11, 164 n. 25
- divine command theory of 153
- ecumenical 169–187
- of war xxxii, xxxiv, 169–172, 174, 176, 179, 181–182, 184, 185 n. 6, 187 n. 20
- Puritan economic 143
- relational 82
- religious xxviii, xix–xxxiii, 36, 121, 138–141, 143, 145, 148–165, 175, 228, 238, 344
- Theravada 138, 141, 145
ethnocentric (-ism) 120, 255–256
ethnography 148–149, 155, 157, 165
- history and 157
European Court of Human Rights 123
evangelical(s) 11, 309, 311, 323
evil xxxi, 5, 19, 41 n. 9, 42 n. 24, 65, 82, 89, 103, 108–109, 118 n. 82, 163 n. 11, 189–190, 196, 232, 266, 308, 330
extremism 294
- Islamist 296
- Muslim 303 n. 1

factory farm 133, 136 n. 19, 343
faith(s) xxiii, xxvi, xxix, xxxvi, 4, 10–12, 15–16, 18, 79, 84–85, 92, 94 n. 7, 119 n. 84, 186 n. 18, 194, 202, 213, 216–217, 221 n. 8–9, 223, 234, 235 n. 17, 240–241, 250, 276 n. 12, 277 n. 15, 285, 298, 308, 311, 315, 323
- civic 16
- communities 84–87, 91, 244, 311
- Founder's 315
- plurality of 10

- Reformed 22 n. 47, 22 n. 49, 23 n. 52, 30, 40 n. 4, 42 n. 23–25, 43 n. 28
- universal 18
Fascism (-t) 19, 35, 44 n. 48, 126, 293, 298
- Islamo- 281, 300, 303 n. 3
fatwa 285
fitra 89
folklore 253
forgiveness 203, 231–232, 234 n. 4, 236 n. 34, 237 n. 49, 237 n. 54, 238 n. 59, 240–241
foundational (-ism, -ist) xxxii, 5, 7, 10, 39, 43 n. 38, 44 n. 43, 45, 51, 65, 74, 75 n. 13, 83, 87–93, 98, 104, 112 n. 17–19, 114 n. 36, 115 n. 46, 116 n. 59, 118 n. 74, 120, 134 n. 7, 134 n. 11, 141–142, 172, 179, 209, 220, 241, 296, 304 n. 8, 342, 347
- epistemic 104
France xxi, 13, 20 n. 3, 23 n. 53, 42 n. 24, 225, 246, 310
freedom(s)
- hermeneutic of religious 6
- individual 80, 82, 302–303
- of conscience xxix–xxxii, 4, 22 n. 27, 23 n. 53, 45–76, 85–86, 88, 343, 345
- of conscience and religion xxix–xxxii, 45–76, 85, 88
- of religion xxx, 77–78, 85, 88, 231
- religious xxviii–xxix, 4–7, 20 n. 3, 21 n. 8, 21 n. 10, 21 n. 12, 22 n. 41, 22 n. 43, 22 n. 49, 23 n. 54, 45, 207, 216–217, 220, 242, 255, 301, 310, 333 n. 14
- soul-freedom 50–53
fundamentalism 235 n. 9, 304 n. 8, 305 n. 27
- Christian 224
- Islamic 281–282, 287, 289, 295, 299–301, 303, 304 n. 16
- Sunni 281, 291, 294, 298, 305 n. 35

Index of Subjects

Gaudium et Spes 180, 187 n. 21
Gaza(n) 264
- Gaza–bound flotilla 264
gender motif 201
Geneva 5, 31, 253, 338
genocide xxxv, 5, 36, 126, 175, 186 n. 15, 220 n. 244
global livestock sector 123
global meat production 124
global warming 123
God xxiii, xxvii n. 3–4, xxx–xxxii, 5, 9, 14, 21 n. 24, 23 n. 53, 23 n. 56, 26–31, 35, 38, 41 n. 9, 44 n. 43, 45, 47–48, 50–56, 60, 62–66, 69, 74 n. 1, 77–79, 83, 86, 89, 91, 94 n. 8, 100, 103–104, 107, 110, 114 n. 32, 114 n. 37, 118 n. 74–75, 119 n. 84, 131, 134 n. 9, 159–160, 186 n. 8, 201–202, 206 n. 43–44, 220 n. 3, 224, 226, 233, 234 n. 2, 246, 250 n. 3, 296–297, 309, 314–316, 323, 341–342
- Image of 5, 94 n. 6, 124, 196, 241
- image bearers of 14, 124, 196
- the Father 14, 194
- the Holy Spirit 14, 194
- the Son 14, 51, 194
Golden rule xxx, 5, 55
good
- collective 100, 107
- common 18–19, 29, 65, 67–68, 71, 226, 241, 308
- human xxxii, 102, 116 n. 59
Gospel according to Matthew 152, 158
Government(s)
- Civil xxxi, 64–65, 67, 70, 340
- consensual xxxi, 48, 56, 64–72
- republican xxix, 13
- two 31
Greek(s) 8, 26, 41 n. 9, 190, 196–197, 204 n. 14, 260
Ground to Stand On 96, 113 n. 24, 113 n. 27, 114 n. 32, 114 n. 36, 115 n. 53, 117 n. 73, 127, 135 n. 11, 135 n. 13, 135 n. 18, 136 n. 20, 136 n. 29, 136 n. 31, 137 n. 36
group
- evangelical 323
- identity formation 208, 214

Haiti 174
Hamas 265
handicapped 127, 325
Hazara 292
hegemony 8, 95 n. 5
hesychasm 195
- Hesychastic Movement 191
Hindu (-ism) xxv, 15, 135 n. 16
Hindutua 224
history
- hermeneutic of 6
- meaning of 203
- religious 169
- secular 169, 177
holism 48, 97, 143–146, 151–152, 163 n. 7
Holocaust 170 n. 70, 126–127, 136 n. 19, 264
Hudood Ordinance 291, 305 n. 25
human
- being xxxix, 6, 27–28, 32, 38–39, 50, 53, 60, 63, 72, 77–78, 83, 86, 89–90, 94 n. 8, 109, 111 n. 7, 112 n. 19, 114 n. 37, 115 n. 48, 116 n. 59, 117 n. 63, 118 n. 75, 118 n. 84, 121, 125–127, 130, 132, 135 n. 16, 137 n. 35, 148, 159, 165, 319, 324, 326, 328–329, 332, 333 n. 15, 339, 342–343
- duties xxix
- nature xxxii, 6, 27, 29, 38–39, 72–73, 89–90, 97, 100, 104, 114 n. 37, 115 n. 53, 135 n. 12, 163 n. 11, 201–202, 222, 234 n. 3
Human Rights
- Committee 324, 334 n. 23

- documents 33, 86, 318–319, 322, 324–325, 332 n. 1
- foundationless model of 87–88
- foundations for 93 n. 3
- movement 16, 32, 244
- natural xxx, 24–44
- norms 15–19, 73, 243
- universal xxxi, 81, 83, 85–86, 128, 243

humanists, secular 107
humanitarian intervention xxxiv, xxxix, 174–175, 182, 183, 185, 186 n. 12, 187 n. 24, 187 n. 26–28, 346
humility, Christian 249

identity xxiv, xxx, 32, 37, 58–63, 69, 71–73, 81, 106, 116 n. 62–64, 116 n. 72, 134 n. 1, 154, 208, 210, 213–214, 223–225, 228, 231, 233, 241, 254–260, 267, 270–272, 274, 276 n. 8, 276 n. 14, 288–289, 296–298, 305 n. 21, 306 n. 46, 341
idolatrous (-y) 23 n. 53, 31
immigrants 215–216
incest 28
Independents 31
Indians, Miskito 246
individualism 18, 21 n. 13, 21 n. 17–18, 22 n. 36, 22 n. 42, 43 n. 40, 269, 277 n. 16
Indonesia 213
injustice 66, 87, 130, 217, 228, 239, 241, 245, 264
- social 217, 228, 239, 252
- structural 264, 239
instincts, maternal 201, 203
institution building 242
institutions, ethical and religious 30
interests, normative 148
International Conciliation Service 246–247, 250 n. 4

International Covenant on Civil and Political Rights (ICCPR) 71, 128, 334 n. 23, 335 n. 36
International Covenant on Economic, Social, and Cultural Rights (ICESCR) 124
international law 59, 75 n. 13, 125, 176, 182, 186 n. 14, 193, 228, 231, 236 n. 30, 253
- and religion 223
international legal system 223, 234 n. 7
Inter–Service Intelligence (ISI) 291–292, 294, 305 n. 32
intuitionist 126–128, 131
inviolability xxx, 48, 56, 68, 70, 100, 102, 107, 339
- of conscience xxx, 48, 56–64, 70, 72–73
Iranian Revolution, 1979 xxiv–xxv, 225, 281
Iraq 4, 20 n. 1, 146 n. 6, 147 n. 26, 176–177, 184, 187 n. 32, 276 n. 7, 276 n. 10, 277 n. 21, 302, 306 n. 40
Ireland 210
- Northern xxv, 229, 240, 244
Islam (-ic) xxii–xxiv, xxxi–xxxii, xxxviii, 4, 7, 15, 20 n. 7, 21 n. 19, 22 n. 28, 23 n. 60, 77–95, 153, 163 n. 9, 164 n. 23, 176, 179, 193–195, 198–199, 205 n. 19, 212–213, 216, 224–225, 250 n. 3, 255, 262–263, 265, 268, 280–306, 332, 342
- forced conversion to 198
- fundamentalist 282, 284, 296
- *Islam is the Answer* 224
- liberal interpretations of 282, 295
- modernist 297, 299, 302–303
- Peoples of the Book xxxii, 90
Islamic
- Group, The 287
- Jihad 280, 287
- legal–ethical sources 83
- Republic xxiv

- sources, normative 85
- world 92, 93 n. 3, 268

Israel xxi, 210, 212, 229, 233, 255, 261, 263–264, 268–271, 278 n. 49, 280, 287

Israel Lobby, The 268–269, 278 n. 45

ius ad bellum xxxiv, 200

ius gentium xxix, 16–18

ius in bello xxxiv

ius post bellum xxxix, 346

Jaish-e-Mohammed 291

Jamaat 298

Jamaat-i-Islami 289–290

Jew(s) -ish xxxii, 7, 66, 135 n. 16, 136 n. 19, 159, 170, 196, 212, 234, 240, 250 n. 3, 255, 260, 262, 264, 266, 269–272, 278 n. 49, 279 n. 50, 332 n. 1
- Jewish Voice for Peace (JVP) 271

Jihād, (-ist) 163 n. 11, 189, 193–195, 205 n. 18, 235 n. 10, 282, 287, 292, 295, 298, 306 n. 46, 309
- al-Nafs 195
- greater 195

J–Street 271, 278 n. 49

Judaism, (-ic) 15, 159, 212, 255, 264, 270–271

jurisdiction xxxv, 86, 101
- church 192, 201
- civil 52
- domestic 175
- legislative 189, 192–193
- state 209, 340
- universal 75 n. 3

Just War xxxv, xxxix, 4, 163 n. 11, 171–172, 177, 179–184, 185 n. 2, 185 n. 6, 188–189, 200, 203–204, 205 n. 22, 346–347

justice
- as fairness 135 n. 12, 319, 321
- basic 321–322, 326
- Chief Justice 308
- civil 65
- common 47, 54
- conception of 135 n. 12, 315, 318, 320, 334 n. 17
- cultural 259
- distributive 143
- economic 259, 275 n. 1
- God's 21 n. 24, 89
- greater 180
- meaning of 241
- Natural xxx, 48, 53–56, 61, 64, 70, 72
- principles of 319, 325–326
- restorative 218, 227, 231, 240
- retributive 240
- social xxix, 72, 178, 180, 227, 354 n. 27
- theory of 320, 325
- transnational 242, 276 n. 12
- United States Justice Department 330

justifiability, universal 108

justpeace xxxvi, 227, 252, 259, 275 n. 1

just peacemaking 181, 226, 235 n. 23, 236 n. 27

Kantian 104–105, 107, 117 n. 64, 124, 134 n. 1, 136 n. 26, 334 n. 26

Kashmir 291–293

Kingdom of Ends 106, 116 n. 60, 116 n. 62

Kollyvades 190

Kosovo (-ar) xxv, xxxv, 175, 183, 186 n. 14–15, 196, 205 n. 25, 225, 255, 267
Eritrean 267

Kurds 265, 267

language, rights 113 n. 24, 135 n. 11, 326–327, 338, 340

law
- animal 127
- Canon xxix, xxxv, 189, 192–193, 197–200, 204 n. 7
- Catholic natural 9
- Church 11, 113 n. 28

- Civil 17–18, 31, 61, 192
- common (ius gentium) xxix, 17, 19, 75 n. 17
- common law of nations 16
- Golden Rule xxx, 5, 55
- international 59, 125, 176, 182, 186 n. 14, 193, 223, 228, 231, 236 n. 30, 253
- moral natural 55
- natural (jus naturale) xxx–xxxi, 9, 14, 17, 27, 29, 32, 34–35, 37–42, 49, 53, 55–56, 64, 70–71, 75 n. 16, 76 n. 20, 83, 89–90, 110 n. 1, 111 n. 6–7, 113 n. 28, 115 n. 53, 135 n. 54, 150, 171–172, 335 n. 31, 340
- of love xxx
- of nature 64, 114 n. 37
- of Supererogation 29, 40 n. 4, 42 n. 19
- of war xxxiv
- political xxxix, 157
- religious 79, 86
- Roman 4, 204 n. 7
- rule of 3, 11–13, 20, 71, 227, 231, 237 n. 46, 312, 345

leadership xxxix, 79, 86–87, 157, 171, 217, 231, 244, 246, 273, 283, 285, 313
- secular 87

legitimacy
- cultural 78, 84, 300
- moral 182
- political 179, 256, 260
- religious 220 n. 3, 215
- theory of political 256, 260
- universal 120

Lemon v. Kurtzman 308–309, 312, 316 n. 1, 317 n. 14

liberal (-ism) xxx, xxxviii, 4, 9–10, 16, 38, 81, 301
- Enlightenment 7, 15–16
- modern 10
- peace xxxix, 344, 345
- political 4, 20 n. 4, 135 n. 12, 332 n. 2, 333 n. 3, 333 n. 5, 333 n. 9–10, 334 n. 16

- secular 16
- society xxxviii, 79
- Western 7

liberty (-ies) xxix, xxxi, xxxix, 9–13, 16, 30, 35, 46, 50, 54, 69–70, 77, 80, 91
- Calvinist theory of 10
- fundamental 63
- religious 20 n. 7, 21 n. 19, 22 n. 28, 22 n. 40, 22 n. 47, 23 n. 60, 30, 40 n. 4, 42 n. 20, 42 n. 23–25, 43 n. 28, 46, 74 n. 2, 74 n. 7, 75 n. 17, 77, 93 n. 1, 333 n. 14
- of conscience xxxix, 10, 46, 52, 313
- individual 12–13, 131, 305 n. 23

lobby (-ing, -ist) 253, 260, 267–271, 273
- Israel Lobby 268, 278 n. 45

Lord's Resistance Army 218

love 5–6, 25–30, 35, 37, 40 n. 2, 40 n. 4, 41 n. 9, 41 n. 13, 42 n. 28, 47, 57, 108, 103–104, 155 n. 52, 124, 185 n. 3, 323
- of neighbor 103, 115 n. 52
- self- 35, 110 n. 4

lying 28

Macedonia 212
magistrates 13, 65–66, 68
- civil 31, 65, 68
Magna Charta 16
Mahavamsa Mindset 224
Malaysia 289, 305 n. 20
martyrdom 194, 246, 255
- Christian 188, 194
Massachusetts 31
- Bay Colony 5, 46
mediation xxxvi–xxxviii, 219, 228, 242–243, 245–249, 266, 277 n. 23, 278 n. 39
memory 198, 231, 237 n. 51 237 n. 53, 261
Mennonite xxxvii, 221, 244–250
- American 244

- community 244–245, 346
- Eastern Mennonite University 233
- Mennonite Central Committee (MCC) 245–249
- Mennonite Conciliation Service (MCS) 250 n. 4, 245–247
- Mennonite Disaster Service 245
- Mennonite World Conference 246
- peacebuilders xxxvii, 249
- peacemakers 248–249, 250 n. 5
- Russian 245

metaphysics 83, 164 n. 24, 323

Middle East xxi, xxv, 176, 208, 215, 224, 269, 276 n. 12, 277 n. 27, 277 n. 31, 289, 292, 295, 302, 304 n. 12, 305 n. 19, 306 n. 45

ministers 5, 12–13

mission, humanitarian 244, 264

mnemonic analogies 201–202

modernization xxii, xxvii n. 2, 220 n. 3

Moldova 200, 203

moral (-ity) 20 n. 6, 40 n. 3, 40 n. 5, 42 n. 22, 43 n. 38, 48, 75, 81, 83, 89–90, 94 n. 7, 96, 110 n. 4, 111 n. 14, 111 n. 16–17, 112 n. 18, 112 n. 20, 113 n. 23, 114 n. 36, 115 n. 53, 116 n. 58–59, 116 n. 62, 117 n. 63–64, 139–142, 145, 150, 152, 172, 175, 185 n. 4, 223, 311
- absolutes 102
- agents 130
- intuitional xxxii
- intuitionism xxxii

Moravian Church 246

Morocco 289

Movement(s) xxxii–xxxiii, 10, 16–17, 22 n. 49, 131, 136 n. 24, 191, 196, 218, 228, 239, 263–264, 281–283, 287–288, 292, 295–296, 298, 311
- environmental xxxiii
- heretical 196
- solidarity 254, 259–260, 263–266, 270, 273, 278 n. 33

Mozambique 218, xxv

mujahedin 282, 291–292

multiculturalism 44 n. 47, 215–216, 221 n. 12

Muslim(s) xxv, xxxv, 73, 78–95, 135 n. 16, 153, 160, 164 n. 21, 184, 191, 193–194, 200, 212, 214, 216, 223, 234, 240, 261–262, 265, 281, 283, 285–290, 292, 298, 303 n. 1, 305 n. 27, 320
- Bosnian xxxv
- Brotherhood 261, 281, 283, 285–288, 298, 302, 304 n. 13
- jurists 78
- traditionalist 78

Nakba 264

narrative framework 223

National Islamic Front 306 n. 44

National Portrait Gallery 307

nationalism xxv–xxvi, xxvii n. 5, xxxii, 20 n. 2, 138, 143–147, 153, 156, 174, 176, 182, 184, 189, 196–197, 206 n. 33, 206 n. 46, 207, 209–211, 215–217, 221 n. 13, 254, 256, 258–260, 270, 272, 275, 276 n. 7, 276 n. 14, 277 n. 15, 277 n. 21, 275 n. 55, 288, 290, 296, 297, 299, 306 n. 40, 344–345
- Arab 176, 277 n. 31, 283–285
- religious xxvii n. 5, 207, 210–211, 220 n. 5, 258, 344–345
- secular 281, 296
- Sinhala 144–145
- Sinhala Buddhist 210, 215–216

Navajo 19, 36, 136 n. 19, 163, 322, 324

Nazi (-sm) 19, 36, 136 n. 19, 163, 322, 324

networks, global xxxvii, 252–253, 259, 263, 265–266, 273

New Testament 16, 46–47, 233

New York Times 312

NGO Committee on Freedom of Religion or Belief 231

Nibbana/Nirvana 138–147, 163 n. 5
Nicaragua 244, 247
- Sandinista Government of 246
Nigeria xxxvi, 212, 214, 219
non-governmental organizations (NGO) 230, 233
normative (-ity) 106, 111 n. 10, 113 n. 22, 114 n. 37, 115 n. 46, 116 n. 61, 116 n. 63, 117 n. 64, 318
- prospects regarding human rights 28
norms, moral 62, 68–69, 84
Norway xxxvi, 215

objectors, conscientious 245
obligations, human 85
oppression 8, 57, 68, 80
- political 239
- religious 80
- soul 57, 68
order, international 81, 84, 175
Orthodox(y)
- blessing of weapons 194
  - Christianity 188–189, 192, 195, 200, 205 n. 22
  - Church xxxv, 188–189, 191, 197–198, 200–201, 203, 204 n. 3, 204 n. 12–15, 205 n. 20
- Eastern 34, 205 n. 22, 346
- Romanian Orthodox Church 200
- Russian Orthodox Church 205 n. 22
- Serbian Orthodox Church xxxv
- Slavic 195
Oslo 215, 253
Ottoman(s) 190–191, 193, 197, 204 n. 14, 255
Ottoman Empire 176

Pacifism 172, 190, 244
- quietist 346
- radical 244
Pagans 66, 73, 200
pain, logic of 5, 128–130, 132, 137

Pakistan xxxviii, 213–214, 282–283, 289–295, 298–299, 301–302, 305 n. 20, 305 n. 31, 345
Pakistan Peoples Party (PPP) 290
Palestine (-ian) 212, 229, 255, 262–267, 270–271
- Palestine Liberation Organization (PLO) 229
- Palestine Solidarity Movement 263, 265, 270, 278 n. 53
- Palestinian Kafiya 263
Pali Canon 151, 159
Papists 66
parentalist 109
Parliament of World Religions 234
Pashtun 292
passions, human 190
patriotism 189, 196–197
peace
- -making (see peacemaking)
- building (see peacebuilding)
- negative 180, 187 n. 20
- positive 180, 187 n. 20
- sustainable 211, 242
peacebuilder, religious xxxvi, 240–243, 246
peacebuilding xxxiv, xxxvi, 181, 184, 205 n. 29, 207–208, 211–217, 220, 230, 239–251, 252–260, 266–270, 272–275, 276 n. 9, 346
- faith–based 250
Peacekeepers, UN 259
Peacemakers in Action 219, 221 n. 15, 222, 231, 234, 237 n. 49, 240, 250 n. 1, 276 n. 12
peacemaking xxviii, xxxiv, xxxvi, xxxix, 174–175, 181, 187 n. 23, 207–222, 245–249, 273, 346
- Just 226, 235 n. 23, 236 n. 27, 181
Penal Code 42 n. 24, 291
Peoples of the Book xxxii, 90
perceptivity, spiritual 231

Persians 66, 302
person (-hood) 60, 318
- egoistic 34
- non-egoistic 34
perspectival studies 152, 154, 156, 164 n. 25
Philokalia 191, 194
philosophy, Stoic 4, 116 n. 58
piety xxxv, 31, 54, 199, 284–285
piracy xxxi, 59–61, 72–73
polarization, Western–Islamic 87
policy
- foreign xxii, 4, 225, 239, 268–269, 291, 302
- public xxi–xxii, xxvii–xxviii, xxxiv–xl, 122, 156, 221 n. 13, 222–223, 225–226, 228–229, 231, 233, 234 n. 3–4, 268, 310, 320, 333 n. 6, 338
politics
- identity 225, 259–260, 267
- Islamist xxxviii, 280–306
polity, ecclesiastic (-al) 14
polycentric
- approach xxxvii, 252–279
- orientation 252
power
- Great Powers 173
- separation of 13
practical reasoning 139, 143, 150, 159–160, 344
pragmatism (-t) xxxii, xxxix, 80, 193, 198, 308
- neo-pragmatism 96–97, 102–105, 108–109, 113 n. 21, 118 n. 83, 339–340
Presbyterian 5, 11, 22 n. 41, 23 n. 52
President, The Believing (Anwar al–Sadat) 284, 287
products, animal-based 129
proselytism 248
Protestant (-ism) 309
- American 20 n. 3, 23 n. 55
- conservative 9

Psychology, social 231
public
- narrative 232
- square xxii, xxxviii, 78–79, 91, 188, 307–308, 347
Puritans 3, 11, 23 n. 52, 42 n. 24

Quakers 10, 61
Qur'an (-ic) 77, 83, 85, 89, 90, 93 n. 3, 94 n. 7

racism 145, 197, 246
radicalism, Shī'a 281
rape 5, 36, 58–61, 66, 75 n. 12, 192
- soul- xxxi, 60–61, 66, 68, 72–73
rational agency 97, 117 n. 64
rationalism, (-ity) 16, 18, 33–34, 38–39, 52, 72, 78, 83, 88, 90, 91, 96–99, 105, 111 n. 7, 114 n. 37, 115 n. 46, 115 n. 53, 120, 124–125, 127, 130, 132, 152, 162, 177, 180, 200, 209, 265, 320, 325, 327, 329–330, 331, 340
realm
- political 28
reason
- human 54, 88–89
- practical 115 n. 53, 139, 143, 150–152, 159–160, 344
- public xxxix–xl, 160, 318–335, 341, 347
- secularization of 39
regime, autocratic xxiv, 86
relationship
- human-animal 129
- normative 102
relativism, cultural 81
religion
- and Peacebuilding (R&P) 207, 212–213, 219, 346
- and peacemaking xxxiv, 236 n. 34
- and politics xxvii–xxviii, xxxviii–xxxix, 178, 307–317

- exclusive interpretation of 301
- free exercise of 4, 69, 210, 347
- fundamentalist 298, 300
- priestly function of 233, 239
- priestly role 233
- prophetic function of 299
- rise of xxiii, 178–179

religious
- freedom xxviii–xxxix, 4–7, 45, 207, 216–217, 220, 242, 255, 301, 310, 333 n. 14
- militancy 79

Republicans, Civic 11

Responsibility to Protect 68, 175, 180, 322, 346

resurrection 14

revelation xxxii, 9, 27, 37, 84, 88–91, 114 n. 37, 296, 340

revenge, cycles of 232

Revolution xxiv–xxvi, 3, 7, 9, 13, 16, 19–20, 30, 33, 74 n. 1, 183–184, 186 n. 8, 225, 245, 280–281, 283–285, 288, 301–302, 306 n. 36, 306 n. 41, 306 n. 44, 322
- American 33, 74 n. 1
- Bolshevik 245, 225
- Corrective 284
- (in) England 13
- (in) France/French 16, 13, 225
- (in) Holland 13
- Iranian xxiv–xxvi, 225, 281, 306 n. 44

revolutionaries 7
- American 7
- French 7

Rhode Island 11, 31, 46, 69, 76 n. 18
- disestablishment of religion in 11

right(s)
- animal 120–137
- basic 79, 86, 97, 101–102, 108, 114 n. 32, 339
- Civil 10, 13–14, 32, 41 n. 9, 55, 65, 69–70, 245, 311
- Human (see Human Rights)

- inalienable 79–80
- inviolability argument 64, 68, 72
- minority 80, 214, 255, 267, 288
- moral 101
- natural 5, 8, 9, 20 n. 5, 21 n. 9, 21 n. 20, 21 n. 23, 32–34, 40 n. 2, 40 n. 5, 43 n. 31, 43 n. 33, 43 n. 39, 43 n. 41–42, 44 n. 43–44, 45–47, 49, 51, 55–56, 59, 64, 67–73, 74 n. 1, 74 n. 4, 75 n. 16, 76 n. 20, 88, 97, 110 n. 1, 110 n. 4, 111 n. 8–11, 113 n. 26, 113 n. 28, 114 n. 32, 333 n. 15, 340 n. 342, 345
- negative 35, 101
- nonderogable 36, 127, 130–131, 343
- objective 8, 49, 55
- of the individual 13, 80
- positive 97, 101, 114 n. 32, 132
- religious 13–14, 45, 64, 74 n. 3
- subjective 8, 39, 49–50, 55, 74 n. 9, 113 n. 28
- subjective natural 56, 62
- to assemble 12–13
- to educate 13
- to evangelize 3
- to life 107, 113 n. 29, 188–206
- to parent 13, 49, 109, 127
- to speak 13–14, 313
- to travel 13
- tradition 32–34, 345
- women 85, 93 n. 4
- worship 13–14, 301

Rite, Slavo–Byzantine 194, 249, 205 n. 25

ritual xxxvi, 141, 154–155, 205, 210, 217–219, 223, 240, 245, 249, 276 n. 12, 329, 340, 346
- cleansing xxxv, 36, 218
- "getting the violence out" 218
- "getting the war out" 218
- *gomo tong* 218

rum millet 197

Russian(s) 193–194
- Orthodox 194, 205 n. 22, 245

- Raskol anarchists 196
Rwanda 174–175, 180, 186 n. 15

sacrifice xxiii, 19, 66, 100, 141–142, 193–194, 255, 315
salafist 285, 296
Saracenes 194
Satan 195
Saudi Arabia 282, 284–286, 291–292, 295, 301–302, 304 n. 10, 305 n. 25, 306 n. 44
- Royal Family 284
scapegoat 189, 195–196
scholastics, Spanish 170
Scotland 23 n. 53, 31
Scythians 202
Secular (-ism, -ization) xxi–xxii, xxiv–xxv, xxvii n. 2–3, xxxi, xxxviii, 4, 6, 9, 15–16, 18, 23 n. 53, 77–95, 107, 154, 169, 177–178, 180–181, 192–193, 209, 220, 226, 243, 245, 255, 261, 268–269, 280–290, 295–300, 303, 307–308, 310, 312–314, 323, 332, 333 n. 6, 334 n. 17, 338–340, 342, 345, 347
- Judeo–Christian 269
- liberal thesis 91
Semitism, anti- 263–264
September 11, 2001 (9–11) xxiii, 79, 95 n. 9, 172–179, 184–186, 209, 225, 281, 293–294
Serbia(n) xxxv, 200, 255
Shari`a 84, 86, 90, 286
Shari`a Courts 291
Sierra Leone 174–175
Sikhs 267
sinfulness, human xxix, 13
skepticism, Nietzschean xxxii
Slav (-ic) 89, 194–196, 199, 202, 205 n. 21, 255
Slavic cultural influence 89
social
- capital 229–230

- construction 69, 98
- contract 34, 88, 125
- contract theory 34
- National Socialism 36
- nature 106
- order 26, 289, 297, 299, 302
- structure 222
society (-ies)
- liberal xxxviii, 79
- multicultural 92, 215, 267
- pluralist 227
- secular democratic 226
sociology of rationality 150, 162
Somalia 244, 247
South Africa 178, 229, 240, 244
sovereignty
- human 188
- state xxxiv
Soviet Union 174–175, 183
spiritual xxx, xxxii, 14, 28, 30–31, 52, 54, 57–58, 66, 77, 84, 86, 88–92, 139, 153, 190–191, 194–196, 199–204, 209, 219, 225, 231, 245, 340
Sri Lanka xxxv, xxxvi, 4, 138, 143–146, 156, 174, 210, 214–216, 253, 267, 271–272, 275, 275, 344
Standards for Confining Farm Animals 122, 134 n. 3
state
- Islamic 297
- liberal 81, 330
- neutrality of the 80
status, civil 31
Stupak Amendment 310
Sudan xxv, 210, 212, 255, 289, 320
Sunni–Ash`ari xxxi, 89
Sunni–Mu`tazilite xxxi, 89
Supreme Council of Islamic Affairs 285
Supreme Court xxxviii, 308–309, 312, 321
symphonia 191
synallilia (co-mutuality) 191

Syria 295
Tajik 292
Taliban xxii, 282, 291–294, 302
- Afghan 291–292
Tanenbaum Center for Interreligious Understanding 221 n. 15, 234 n. 1, 240, 250 n. 1, 276 n. 12
Tatar/Mongol yoke 193–194
taxonomies and classification xxxiii
teachings, religious xxiii, 20, 80, 83, 243
teleological 8, 83, 140, 142–143, 158, 160–161
Ten Commandments 27, 171, 312
theodicy 188
terrorism xxv, xxxiv, 4, 176, 184–185, 228, 253, 268
- transnational xxxiv, 176, 184
The Cairo Declaration xxxi
theandric doctrine 201
theocentric xxx, 50, 52, 340–341
theocracy 255
theological reflection 324
theology xxiii, xxix–xxx, 3, 14, 38–39, 83, 85, 90, 92, 155, 165 n. 25, 169–171, 181, 201, 222–227, 231, 234 n. 4, 244–246
- Calvinist 3
- public 222–223, 225–227, 231, 234 n. 4
- scholastic xxix
theory (-ies)
- conflict 208, 228
- conspiracy 269
- interest 53
- will 53
Theotokos ("Birth–Giver of God") 201–202, 206 n. 43
Theravada xxxiii, 138–148, 151–152, 344
- Nibbanized 146
think tanks 225, 267–268
thought, Reformed 48

Tibet 4, 210
Tokyo 253
toleration, religious 45
tradition(s) (-al)
- Abrahamic 89, 212, 231, 240
- Christian xxxiv, 5, 7, 30, 170, 177, 226, 233, 269, 342
- communities 15
- liberal 321
- Western Christian 7
Trinity 14, 16
Tripex munus Christi (prophets, priests, kings of Christ) 14
truth(s) 5, 24, 34, 47, 56, 69, 80, 83, 88–90, 97, 100, 102–104, 109, 111 n. 7, 113 n. 25, 116 n. 63, 117 n. 73, 119 n. 85, 126–127, 152, 218, 227, 296, 328, 339
- moral 88–90, 102, 109, 126–127, 327
- natural 56
- necessary 5, 113 n. 25, 117 n. 73
- normative 142
- of Christ 194
- regime of 268, 271
Tunisia xxii
Turkey xxi, 94, 265, 289
Turks 66

U.S. Bill of Rights 33
U.S. Constitution 76 n. 18, 76 n. 20, 310, 335 n. 36
- First Amendment xxxviii, 4, 21 n. 8, 308, 310, 312
U.S. Institute of Peace (USIP) xxxvi, 35, 143, 156, 182, 207–221, 255, 344, 346
  USIP Program on Religion and Peacekeeping xxxvi
Uganda, Northern xxxvi, 218
Ukraine 4, 156
ulema 79, 284–285, 288
UN Charter 182–184, 226, 346

UN Declaration on the Elimination of All Forms of Intolerance and Discrimination Based on Religion or Belief 210
UN Draft Declaration of Principles on Human Rights and the Environment 123
UN Millennium Summit 175, 179
UN Tripartite Forum on Interfaith Cooperation for Peace 231
United Nations (UN) 32–36, 123, 174–176, 180, 184, 224
United Nations Declaration 32–36
United Nations Food and Agriculture Organization (UNFAO) 143
United States Justice Department 330
Universal Declaration of Human Rights xxx, 16, 33, 77, 94, 126, 188, 226, 338
universalism(s) 26–27, 82, 84, 196–197
- dichotomous 83–84
universals, ethical 27–29
utilitarianism 107, 249

Vatican Council, Second xxiv, 170, 180
Vatican II (see Vatican, Second Council)
Vietnam 4, 174, 182, 245
violence xxiv–xxvi, xxxiii, xxxv, xxxvii, 4, 35, 57, 61, 80, 85–86, 172, 174, 181, 188–189, 195–196, 198–200, 202–204, 210–213, 218–219, 225–231, 239–241, 244, 247, 249–250, 254–255, 259, 264, 275, 286, 295, 309, 315, 345
- lethal 239
Virginia Declaration of Rights 33
virtue xxxiv, 20, 24, 26, 28, 31–32, 34, 54–55, 60–62, 72–73, 100, 110, 116 n. 59, 120, 139, 142, 153–154, 165, 240, 254, 266, 311, 314–315, 325, 333, 340
- civic 31–32
- moral 24, 32, 54, 56
Visigoths 189, 191
voluntarism 26, 114 n. 37

war
- Cold (see Cold War)
- interstate 172
- intrastate 172, 182–183
- justifiable 189
- of values 300
- on Terror(ism) 184–185, 225, 228, 281, 293, 295, 301–302
- spiritual 194
- transnational 172, 176
- Vietnam 245
warfare 172–173, 178, 181, 190, 199, 215, 244, 310
- internal 182
- intrastate 182
- modern 171
- religious 18
- spirituality of 203
- typology xxxv
- unseen 191
Washington, D.C. 175, 207, 209, 212, 245, 268, 311
Washington University's Crisis Intervention Center 245
weapons 7, 173, 194
- automatic 280
- nuclear 173, 182
welfare, animal 122
Westminster 5
Westphalian tradition 182
White House 310
- White House Press Core 264
whoredom, spiritual 57
Wikileaks 294
women 57–58, 85, 93 n. 4, 142, 212, 214, 240, 246, 301, 322
- Catholic 214
- Christian 240
- Jewish 240
- Muslim 240
- Protestant 214

World Council of Churches (WCC) 234
    World Jewish Congress 234
World War I (First World War) 244, 173
World War II (Second World War) xxxiv,
    35, 170–173, 183, 245
worldview xxxix, 32, 73, 151, 196, 224, 228,
    232–233, 320–324
 - Christian 196
 - dualistic 196

Yugoslavia 174, 205 n. 29, 210

Zion (-ism, -ist) 224, 261–262, 264,
    269–271
Zionism, Iron Wall 224

CPSIA information can be obtained at www.ICGtesting.com
Printed in the USA
BVOW06*1249130715

408200BV00004B/35/P